the Herbalist's KITCHEN

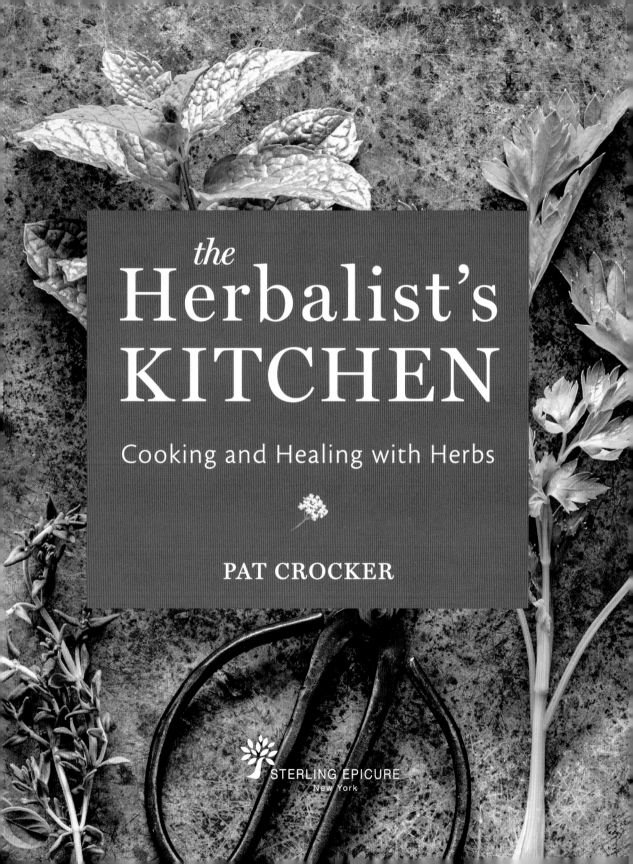

the
Herbalist's
KITCHEN

Cooking and Healing with Herbs

❀

PAT CROCKER

STERLING EPICURE
New York

STERLING EPICURE
New York

An Imprint of Sterling Publishing Co., Inc.
1166 Avenue of the Americas
New York, NY 10036

ISBN 978-1-4549-2627-6

Distributed in Canada by Sterling Publishing Co., Inc.
c/o Canadian Manda Group, 664 Annette Street
Toronto, Ontario M6S 2C8, Canada
Distributed in the United Kingdom by GMC Distribution Services
Castle Place, 166 High Street, Lewes, East Sussex BN7 1XU, England
Distributed in Australia by NewSouth Books
45 Beach Street, Coogee, NSW 2034, Australia

For information about custom editions, special sales, and premium and corporate purchases,
please contact Sterling Special Sales at 800-805-5489 or specialsales@sterlingpublishing.com.

Manufactured in China

2 4 6 8 10 9 7 5 3 1

sterlingpublishing.com

Interior design by Shannon Nicole Plunkett
Cover design by David Ter-Avanesyan

For additional photography and illustration credits, see page 424

To my dear friends, the humble plants that offer comfort, pleasure and health and to the gentle, caring souls who raise them, harvest, share, and enjoy their gifts.

CONTENTS

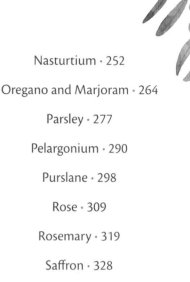

INTRODUCTION

My life has been blessed in ways that I cannot begin to fully understand or explain. The interesting twists and sidesteps along the way have come about not least because of an exquisite dance with humble, helping plants, which enrich our lives in myriad ways yet grow almost without our intervention.

Knowing so many gentle gardeners, people with the earth at their fingertips, I am so often reminded of a line from biblical text, "But the meek shall inherit the earth; and shall delight themselves in the abundance of peace" (Psalm 37:11). I've come to appreciate and understand the earthly and spiritual sanctuaries that are gardens. I've also glimpsed the serenity and peace that plants can bring, and I see that knowledge and use of these unassuming plants is and will continue to be a contributing factor to a healthy, sustainable existence.

I began my lifelong pirouette with herbs with an introductory course at Black Creek Pioneer Village (an 1800s village with period gardens, buildings, and artifacts) in Toronto and at Montgomery's Inn and Community Museum. From that time forward, I've lived, learned, and witnessed the magic of rosemary and comfrey and sage and thyme (to name just a few) on my family's and my own health and well-being. My herb gardens continue to flower and fade and reappear in harmony with the eternal seasonal symphony.

CULINARY HERBALIST

To the best of my knowledge I am the first person to call myself a *culinary herbalist*. Once I began to speak about herbs, I needed a moniker, a slot into which people could easily slide my work, my qualifications, and me.

My perspective is different from that of a medical herbalist. Whereas a traditional herbalist has studied for several years under a recognized master or at an accredited institution, I have learned the basics of herbal medicine so that I can use their healing attributes in food.

I am a *foodie*, a home economist (BAA) by training, with a passion for and an insatiable interest in healthy food, herbs, and nourishing plants. It is known that from the earliest times in human history, people gathered more than one hundred different plant species for consumption over the course of a year. As a culinary herbalist, I use healing herbs in the way the ancients did: by eating them raw and cooking with them in daily meals. I believe that if we can bring our diet closer to that of our ancient ancestors, our bodies will throw off the modern diseases that have come with processing, refining, and adulteration and the systematic decline of fresh fruits, vegetables, and herbs from our diet.

In *The Herbalist's Kitchen*, I approach the tremendous body of herbal information with profound respect, realizing that with every tiny bit of knowledge gained, there is so much more to discover. My profound thanks go out again to my guides and teachers along the garden path.

HOW TO USE THIS BOOK

The Herbalist's Kitchen is actually two books in one. First and foremost, it is a cookbook, so the recipe index lists the recipes as they would be used in a meal. If you are looking for an herbal appetizer or dessert, or any recipe for a course in between, you can see it all at a glance.

It's also an herbal. An herbal (from the medieval Latin *liber herbalis*) is a book of herbs, *herbs* being the common word for plants. Historically, herbals illustrated and recorded the popular medicinal uses of plants. Like those early, handwritten parchment scrolls, this contemporary herbal offers a comprehensive guide to the traditional culinary, medicinal, and cosmetic use of herbs backed up by science. This means that for gardeners and herb practitioners, the book is organized around the individual plants. As any herb grower can attest, when the herbs are ready for harvesting, recipes for using those specific plants had better be at hand. And so the herbs take pride of place—in fact, they direct the structure of the book—and they are profiled in alphabetical order, commanding their own table of contents by herb.

THE DIRT ON HERBS

What Is an Herb?

Every herb writer or blogger, botanist, herb gardener, cook, natural-health practitioner, aromatherapist, landscape architect, herbal cosmetician, wildcrafter, and tea drinker may have a slightly different definition of the word *herb*, and all would be correct. In fact, as the Herb Society of America (see Bibliography) points out, the term *herbs* may mean fleshy (as opposed to woody) seed-bearing plants, from whence comes the term *herbaceous*, but it also includes "trees, shrubs, annuals, vines, and more primitive plants, such as ferns, mosses, algae, lichens and fungi."

I define herbs not by their botanical makeup, but by their ability to offer a specific use to humans. In my definition, a plant (or its parts) may be considered an *herb* if it is used in its fresh or dried form for one or more of the following:

* As a flavoring, ingredient, or garnish in food or beverages

* In a medicinal or personal care preparation

* For fragrance in perfumes, cosmetics, food, or drinks

* As a preservative or a pest deterrent

* As a dye for food or fabrics

* As an edible ornamental or landscaping plant

* In crafts or household cleaners

What Is a Spice?

According to my broad definition, all spices are herbs, but not all herbs are spices. There is a lingering perception that spices are mysterious, expensive, and come from exotic lands. For that reason spices are usually perceived to be more valuable than herbs, which anyone can grow. I do consider spices to be herbs because they meet my earlier criteria; however, I use the term *spice* primarily to refer to tropical plants whose dried or woody parts are highly aromatic. Some examples include cardamom (a pod), cumin (a seed), nutmeg (a fruit), allspice (a berry), cloves (a flower), ginger (a root), and cinnamon (a bark).

HISTORICAL PERSPECTIVE

Herbs, with their timeless scents, uplifting spirits, calming sensibilities, and genuine healing qualities, offer their humble powers in deference to no one. They surrender their gifts of pleasure, health, beauty, and taste to all who would kneel and plant them. Unassuming and demanding no special treatment, herbs are easy to grow, drawing their remarkable qualities from the soil and sun. In most cases, preserving them takes no more effort than simply hanging them upside down to dry. And using them in simple medicinal and cosmetic preparations and in the recipes in this book is nearly as effortless.

From earliest human history, plant knowledge was passed on verbally to one or two disciples who had trained for years in the techniques of identifying, gathering, preserving, and using herbs. Even when written communication began, herbal knowledge continued to be transmitted orally to keep it accessible.

Sometime between 3000 and 2000 BCE, the earliest surviving written herbal medicinal information was inscribed on Babylonian clay tablets. According to *The Complete Medicinal Herbal* by Penelope Ody, "Surviving Egyptian papyri dating back to about 1700 BCE record that many common herbs, such as garlic and juniper [were] used medicinally."

Over the next thousand years China composed its Canon of Herbs, India the Ayurveda, and Assyria and Egypt developed their own written records. But once plant knowledge was written and codified, it passed out of the realm of the illiterate masses.

As Rome's influence extended in the first two centuries of the Common Era, from Great Britain to all of the countries bordering the Mediterranean Sea, the Romans made significant contributions to European and near-Eastern cultures. They excelled in engineering, bath/sanitary innovations, economics, politics, medicine, and, not least, the use of herbs.

Following the decline of the Roman Empire, Europe entered the Middle Ages or medieval times (beginning with the Dark Ages, around the fifth to tenth century, and extending to the end of the 1400s), a period about which little is known due to the lack of written records. At first, it may have been monks tending small monastery gardens that kept the cultivation and use of herbs alive. Gradually, more and more households came to rely on the family plot of "potherbs" and "simples," so that by the end of the fourteenth century, after the devastating Black Death, the women of the household were emerging as the family's lifeline to health through the stillroom and kitchen herb garden. Daughters learned at their mothers' knees about simple medicinal remedies, and these remedies survived in common use again, transmitted mostly through the oral tradition.

As Europe struggled through the Middle Ages, the Arab world adopted the medical theories and herbal remedies of Galen (*ca.* 130–210 CE), a Greek physician and surgeon who lived and practiced in Rome. Thus, explains Ody, the "center of Classical learning shifted east" to Constantinople (now Istanbul) and Persia (now Iran). The botanical and medicinal knowledge gained in the East spread to European and Western cultures during the Muslim conquests, from mid-600 into the Byzantine-Ottoman Wars (1300 to the mid-1400s) and through the beginning of the seventeenth century,

Considered to be a miracle herb at the time, rue is shown in this Austrian illustration from the Middle Ages.

which saw the decline and collapse of the Byzantine or Eastern Roman Empire. During the period of their influence, Muslims incorporated Arabian, Persian, Egyptian, and European herbal and medicinal techniques into a medical canon and at the same time advanced science, mathematics, art and literature, architecture, and astronomy.

By the sixteenth century, when many of the great herbals were written and ornately illustrated, the advancement of plant and medical knowledge went forward only among the few (mostly men) who could read and afford to own these priceless treasures. When ordinary folk (mostly women) gained possession of and applied this potent medicinal plant knowledge, many were persecuted as witches, as happened throughout the fifteenth, sixteenth, and seventeenth centuries. Most wise women were familiar with mandrake, monk's hood, henbane, digitalis, and nightshade, all of which have powerful curative properties, but can be hallucinogenic and ultimately fatal in large doses. The organized, brutal execution of women healers, herbalists, and midwives caused the decline of herbal knowledge and consequently the death of many more people during that time.

Sometime during the 1600s, the term *pharmacopoeia* appeared and was used independently by various medical scholars and physicians in cities across Europe. Pharmacopoeias were compilations of standardized herbal and medical information regarding plants and drugs, their use, and preparation. Right up to the early 1900s, plants were still highly valued as key ingredients for most, if not all, medical preparations.

As early as 1884, cocaine was isolated in the laboratory as a derivative of Andean coca leaves, which had been used for centuries by South American shamans. After that, it became possible to isolate narcotic drugs from plants. By the late 1800s, active plant components or drugs were being synthesized or re-created in the laboratory and from then, the practice of using herbs in tinctures, pills, salves, and other medications began to decline as the use of synthesized drugs gained popularity with doctors and pharmacists.

Despite these developments, throughout most of the nineteenth century when many rural North Americans received a potentially fatal cut, wound, fall, or

Coca leaves prepared as a tea are offered in Peru as a gentle relief from altitude sickness.

burn they continued to rely on the family stillroom or "root and herb" doctors who employed both traditional, native medicinal herbs as well as European healing herbs. At the same time, Shaker collective farm communities in the eastern United States filled the need for dried herbs, herb extracts, oils, distilled waters, ointments, and patent medicines, making herbal remedies available and affordable to all living in Upper Canada and the eastern United States.

Within one century, however, many North Americans and western Europeans have lost that shared knowledge of the power of plants and their direct links to most common drugs. Today most people would be surprised to learn that some 30 to 50 percent of drugs are still derived from plants.

PLANTING AND COOKING WITH HERBS

Herbs are as satisfying to grow and handle as they are to use. Even if you think you don't have the space for an herb garden, one or two pots in a sunny window or on a balcony will green up your living space and your food. Freestanding pots or containers are ideal for herbs because they keep these wandering (some would say invasive) plants in check and make them accessible. Indeed, you can harvest them mere minutes before

adding them to dishes. The best way to take the mystery out of cooking with herbs is to raise a few culinary herbs from seed to seedling to mature plant to flowering plant and from cooking pot to table.

When planting herbs, the most important consideration is that almost all of them require between six and eight hours of direct sunlight every day. Some gardeners recommend amending the soil by digging in bone meal (for phosphorus) or adjusting the soil pH (adding lime to raise alkalinity or sulfur to lower the soil pH), but I simply top up my beds with well-rotted compost. If sowing directly from seed, choose a sunny spot and sow after the threat of frost has passed.

If purchasing fresh herbs from a market, look for organic, bright green sprigs with no sign of wilting, slime, or yellowing. Whether you grow or buy fresh herbs, keep them on the stem until just before you add them to the pot and always wait until right before the end of the cooking time, if possible, before adding all but the most robust of herbs. Cut herbs will keep for at least a week if rolled in a dampened cotton or linen towel in the crisper drawer of the refrigerator.

Herbs add spirit to cooking. They awaken and stimulate the palate, adding an extra dimension of liveliness in return for very little effort. With assertive herbs in the pot, there is less need for salt, butter, and cream. You can add the unexpected with a hint of licorice from tarragon, basil, or fennel. The unmistakable snap of mint in dessert or tea will gently invigorate, and a nip of rosemary or thyme subtly infuses dishes with welcome warmth, especially in winter soup.

To start cooking with herbs, use only one new herb each time you try a dish and be generous. Fresh herbs have a richer, smoother, more complex flavor than dried herbs, which tend to be sharp or bitter. For that reason, fresh herbs can be measured by the handful or sprig instead of the pinch.

Whether you plant and grow herbs, purchase them fresh from a farmers market, or dried from an herb farm or supermarket, you will find that herbs are humble plants with a powerful effect on your well-being. This cookbook (and herbal) is meant to remind you of their magic, power, and mystery. It places that wisdom directly into the hands of people for whom it was meant—the everyday cook, gardener, and health-conscious individual. Knowledge of the power of food goes back to the Greek physician Hippocrates, considered the "father of medicine," who is credited with the quote: "Let food be thy medicine and medicine be thy food." I urge you to dive into whatever intrigues you about herbs: history, science, botany, medicine, or simply their fragrance and flavor. However you have found your way to this book, my hope is that it will spark a lifelong love of the plants that have become my passion. Your life, like mine, will be enriched in so many ways.

the
Healing
HERBS

Angelica

Angelica archangelica

The whole plante, both leafe, roote, and seede,
is of an excellent comfortable sent, savour and taste.

—John Parkinson, *Theatre of Plants*, 1640

With its distinctly anise and slightly muscatel flavor, its pagan tradition and reputation as a magical herb, and its ability to calm stomach disorders, angelica earned a place in the monastic gardens of medieval times. According to Rob Talbot and Robin Whiteman in *Brother Cadfael's Herb Garden*, angelica water was used in the infirmary at Shrewsbury Abbey in England, perhaps as a tonic or a digestive or for coughs and colds. Nicholas Culpeper recommended a double angelica preparation as protection against poison and the plague. His advice was to first make angelica water by steeping the aerial parts in water and then add powdered angelica root. Indeed, during the Great Plague of London in 1665, people were grasping at roots for protection and angelica was the go-to "bite and chaw" herb of the time. In fact, legend holds that the powerful healing action of angelica in preventing contagion was revealed in a monk's dream by an angel during those black days.

FLAVOR

All parts of angelica are sweetly anise with spikes of celery and juniper.

PARTS TO USE

Use all parts of the angelica plant: seeds, stems or stalks, leaves, and flowers.

CULINARY USES

Use young, fresh angelica leaves in teas and to flavor sugar, syrups, and salt; mature fresh leaves make a great wrap for steamed or grilled foods. Fresh chopped angelica leaf teams well with rhubarb for relish and other preserves, softening the tartness of the fruit. The leaves and stems or stalks add a touch of anise to poaching liquids, stuffing, marinades, sauces, and dips. Eat young stalks as a vegetable, or candy them for use in baking and cake decorating. Use the seeds and roots in flavorings for liqueur and teas and you can steam or boil the roots like you would a vegetable.

Angelica is part of the Tudor Physic Garden border at Sudeley Castle, Winchcombe, Gloucestershire, Great Britain.

♥ HEALTH BENEFITS

Angelica root contains antibacterial, antifungal, antispasmodic, and carminative constituents that have an effect on the lungs, stomach, intestines, and blood. The roots and sometimes the seeds are used medicinally in tinctures. Because it is a warming, diaphoretic, diuretic herb, angelica may be used to aid rheumatic complaints, stomach cramps, digestion, coughs, and colds. In India, it is used to treat anorexia nervosa and flatulent dyspepsia.

CAUTION: Large doses can act as calcium-channel blockers that lower blood pressure and widen blood vessels. Take medical doses only on the advice of a medical practitioner and do not exceed the recommended dose. Angelica is not recommended during pregnancy.

GROWING ANGELICA

A tall (over 6 foot), stately biennial, angelica prefers cooler climates and fairly wet conditions but adapts if you plant it in partial shade and rich soil. It flowers in June the second year and self-seeds. If cut back almost to the root, and thus not allowed to set seed, it may live one or more years.

VARIETIES

Angelica joins parsley, chervil, fennel, and caraway in the *Umbelliferae* family but stands out as the tallest and most aromatic. There are between forty and sixty varieties of angelica, with *Angelica archangelica* or "garden" angelica being the most common in Europe and North America.

ALEXANDERS (*A. atropurpurea*) Commonly called Alexanders, this smaller, purple-tinged variety is native to North America, Europe, and other subarctic regions. It was once highly regarded as a medicinal plant.

Angelica gigas

GIGAS (*A. gigas*) This dark purple ornamental originates from China, Japan, and Korea and grows wild in the same conditions as *A. sylvestris*. Use this plant as a unique, bee-attracting plant in the garden, but do not eat it and note that some people are sensitive to its sap.

WILD ANGELICA (*A. sylvestris*) Found growing wild in parts of northeastern North America, this species inhabits woodlands, fields, stream banks, and marshy areas. Due to its prolific nature (one plant produces thousands of seeds), some regions have labeled it an invasive weed.

🌿 ANISE HERBS

Anise is the licorice flavor that is predominant in licorice root (*Glycyrrhiza glabra*) but also detected in other herbs such as angelica. The organic compound that provides the licorice flavor in plants is called *anethole*, and we associate all plants that are high in it with the anise taste of pure licorice. Anethole is soluble in water, which is what causes absinthe to form a milky-white or pale-green cloud (called *louche*) when water is added to the drink. Here are a few other herbs with varying degrees of anise flavor.

BASIL Anise is a subtle undertone to the nutmeg, mint, spice, and menthol tones of the leaves. All basil varieties are widely used in pesto or other sauces and are especially good with tomatoes.

CHERVIL Leaves are delicately sweet and subtly anise. Chervil is essential in the French fines herbes blend and goes well with leeks, beans, and potatoes.

DILL Leaves taste of anise with lemon. Dill is a key ingredient in tartar sauce and is essential for pickles.

FENNEL All parts have an anise aroma and taste that is less pungent than dill. Fennel is excellent with fish, cream sauces, and soups, especially chowders.

FRENCH TARRAGON Leaves have a hot and peppery anise flavor. French tarragon complements soft cheeses, puddings, and fish dishes.

LICORICE (*Glycyrrhiza glabra*) Fresh and dried roots have a clear, sweet anise flavor with slightly salty, earthy undertones. Licorice can be finely grated into baked goods, puddings, creams, and other dishes; decoctions are used to flavor drinks, sauces, or syrups.

SWEET CICELY Leaves are sweet, with licorice and lemon notes. Sweet cicely is good with almonds and is used in sweet or savory dishes and beverages.

WORMWOOD (*Artemisia absinthium*) Leaves are bitter anise. Sugar and water balance the bitterness of wormwood in the alcoholic drink known as absinthe.

Candied Angelica or Ginger

Using honey or sugar to preserve herbs is an ancient method for medicinal and culinary herbalists. The tender young stems of angelica are hollow and sweetly scented with anise, and for centuries they have been preserved using honey or sugar or sugar syrup. The syrup was taken to treat stomach cramps and the candied stems were used to decorate cakes or eaten as treats.

Cut and use the thicker central angelica plant stalks in May and select bright green, smooth stems that are no more than 2 inches in diameter. Cut the stalks into 3- to 4-inch pieces and rinse to clean them. Use a stainless steel or enameled cast iron pot for boiling the stalks. Double or halve the recipe depending on the amount of angelica you have on hand.

This recipe is adapted from a version by Mrs. Raffald, housekeeper to Lady Elizabeth Warburton of Arley Hall in Cheshire, England. Originally published around 1825, it was reproduced in 1952 by Mrs. C. F. Leyel in her book, *Green Medicine*.

Makes about 3 pounds

2 pounds young angelica stems
   or gingerroot cut into strips
   (½ inch wide × 2 inches long)
6 cups sugar, divided

NOTE: Angelica stems will deteriorate if not completely dry. If uncertain, store in an airtight container in the refrigerator for up to 1 month or freeze for up to five months.

1. In a large stainless steel pan or enameled cast iron pot, cover the stems with water, to 1 inch over them. Bring to a boil over high heat. Boil for 8 minutes (boil ginger for 1 hour or just until tender). Using tongs or a slotted spoon, lift stems out to a colander to drain and cool. Discard water or save and use as soup stock.

2. Arrange stems in a single layer on two or more parchment paper–lined baking sheets. Sprinkle evenly with 3 cups sugar, turning stems to coat. Cover loosely with parchment paper and set aside in a cool place (not the refrigerator) for 24 to 48 hours.

3. Transfer the stems, the syrup that has formed, and any loose sugar on the parchment paper to a large pot and add ¼ cup water. Bring to a boil over medium-high heat and continue to

boil for 6 to 12 minutes or until the syrup reaches the soft-ball stage (235°F on a candy thermometer). The syrup will be thick and the angelica or ginger will be transparent. Remove from heat.

4. Line two or more baking sheets with parchment paper. Pour 1 cup sugar into a shallow dish. Using tongs, lift stems, one at a time, out of the pot and roll in the sugar to coat. Transfer to prepared baking sheet and repeat for remaining stems, adding more sugar to the dish as needed. Sprinkle any remaining sugar in the dish evenly over stems.

5. Transfer syrup to a sterilized jar (page 243). Cap, label, and reserve for another use such as an herbal cough syrup, in desserts, or as an ingredient in cordials and other drinks. Store syrup in the refrigerator for up to 6 weeks.

6. Preheat oven to 350°F and turn it off. Set baking sheets in the oven for 48 hours or until the stems are completely dry. Store in an airtight container for 3 months or longer.

ANGELICA FIG GLAZE

Makes 1½ cups

1 cup water
¼ cup white wine vinegar
½ cup sugar
½ cup coarsely chopped fresh or candied angelica stems
½ cup coarsely chopped fresh figs

1. In a medium saucepan, bring water and vinegar to a boil. Stir in sugar, reduce heat, and simmer, stirring frequently, for 2 minutes or until sugar is dissolved. Add angelica stems and simmer for 10 minutes. Using a slotted spoon, lift and discard angelica.

2. Stir in figs and simmer for 10 to 15 minutes or until figs soften. Use immediately or store in an airtight container in the refrigerator for up to 3 weeks.

Roasted Vegetables with Angelica Fig Glaze

Makes 4 to 6 servings

1 small butternut squash, cut into
    2-inch pieces
2 carrots, cut into 2-inch pieces
2 beets, cut into wedges
2 onions, quartered
2 cups mini or fingerling potatoes
    or potato wedges
3 tablespoons melted extra-virgin
    coconut oil or avocado oil
Sea salt
1 red pepper, halved and seeded
3 tablespoons chopped fresh
    rosemary
6 cloves garlic
⅓ cup Angelica Fig Glaze (page 7)
¼ cup chopped fresh angelica
    leaves, optional

1. Preheat oven to 400°F. Line two rimmed baking sheets with parchment paper.

2. In a large bowl, combine squash, carrots, beets, onions, and potatoes. Toss to coat with oil and salt to taste. Spread the vegetables in a single layer on the prepared baking sheets. Place the two pepper halves, cut side down, on one of the baking sheets.

3. Roast in the preheated oven for 10 minutes. Stir the vegetables and turn the peppers over. Roast for another 10 minutes. Stir rosemary and garlic into one sheet of vegetables and stir the vegetables on the other sheet. Roast for another 20 to 30 minutes or until vegetables are browned and tender.

4. Peel and cut the roasted peppers into strips and combine with the mixed vegetables in a large bowl. Add Angelica Fig Glaze and toss to mix. Transfer to a serving dish and garnish with angelica if using.

Pork Chops with Angelica-Spiked Dried Cherry Sauce

4 boneless pork chops
   (3 to 4 ounces each)
2 tablespoons extra-virgin
   avocado or coconut oil
1 small onion, finely chopped
1 cup red wine
1 cup chicken or vegetable broth
1 tablespoon grated orange zest
Juice of 1 orange
2 stems (2 inches long) candied
   or fresh angelica (see note)
⅓ cup dried tart cherries
1 tablespoon honey
1 tablespoon cornstarch,
   dissolved in ¼ cup water

NOTE: If you have fresh or candied angelica, it is lovely in this cherry sauce. Candied angelica has an intensified anise flavor and is softer in texture than fresh. You can also substitute 3 tablespoons coarsely crushed dried leaves of any anise herb: French tarragon, chervil, basil, anise hyssop, dill, or sweet cicely in place of the candied angelica.

1. Preheat oven to 300°F.

2. Place each pork chop between two sheets of plastic wrap. Using a meat mallet or rolling pin, pound to flatten the meat to about ½ inch thick.

3. In a heavy-bottomed skillet, heat oil over medium-high heat. Sauté onion for 3 minutes. Add pork chops and cook for 3 or 4 minutes, turning once to brown on each side. Add wine and bring to a boil. Stir in broth, orange zest, orange juice, angelica, and cherries.

4. Cover, reduce heat to medium-low, and simmer for 8 to 12 minutes, or until pork reaches 160°F on a meat thermometer. Remove chops to a heated plate, cover, and keep warm in the preheated oven.

5. Remove and discard angelica stems from the skillet. Stir in the honey and heat, stirring constantly until incorporated. Stir water and cornstarch into the sauce. Increase heat to medium-high and bring to a boil, stirring constantly. Cook and stir for 3 or 4 minutes or until sauce is thickened. Pour sauce over chops or pour into a small, heatproof jug and pass separately.

Basil

Ocimum species

It's hard to imagine summer without fresh basil, for its spicy, vibrant scent captures the season. Sweet basil is the bestseller on the Herbfarm's plant list and would come in at the top on any herb popularity contest.

—Jerry Traunfeld, former executive chef of the Herbfarm Restaurant
and author of *The Herbfarm Cookbook*, 2000

About three hundred and forty years BCE, basil made the long trek from its native India to Greece with Alexander the Great, who discovered it on a plant-hunting trip. From there, the plant, named basil from the Greek word for king, *basilikos*, spread around the Mediterranean, taking root in the culture and recipes of European countries, especially Italy, where it truly rules the kitchen.

Holy Basil (*O. tenuiflorum*), known as sacred basil and at one time identified as *O. sanctum* (now an outdated botanical name), is still revered in India. Herbalists affectionately refer to holy basil as Tulsi or *the incomparable one* due to its elevated status as an herb for mind-body-spirit along with its reputation for relieving stress.

With more than one hundred varieties, basil is often grouped according to leaf size, shape, or color; method of growth (such as compact); color of stems and/or flowers; or by aroma and taste. My favorite basil for cooking, Genovese basil (*O. basilicum* 'Genovese') has plump, large leaves with a sweet nutmeg flavor, which I find perfect for pesto and for other green sauces, soups, and salads, in egg and pasta dishes, and to flavor fish and chicken.

FLAVOR

Classic basil varieties are warm, spicy-sweet, and peppery with nutmeg overtones and hints of anise and mint.

PARTS TO USE

Use the leaves, tender stems, and flowers.

CULINARY USES

Fresh sweet basil is generally used in savory dishes as well as drinks and beverages, but it can be used in desserts to add a spicy zip. It brightens green salsas as well as tomato sauces, and the spicy fla-

Genovese basil thrives in a kitchen garden in southwestern Ontario, Canada.

vor tones complement egg and custard dishes, garlic, strawberries, and soft cheeses. It is used raw in salads and soups or as a garnish. It is a tender herb, so use it generously with poultry, fish, noodles, or other dishes at the very end of cooking. The leaves turn black easily if bruised, so they should be torn or chopped with a super-sharp knife. Basil does not dry or freeze well, so it is usually made into pesto and then frozen.

♥ HEALTH BENEFITS

Basil aids digestion, promotes normal blood pressure, and reduces gas, stomach cramps, and headaches. The essential oil can be used in a bath or massage to ease nervous exhaustion, mental fatigue, melancholy, or uneasiness.

GROWING BASIL

Basil is a tender annual when grown outside of the tropics. Plant seeds early indoors and transplant seedlings after spring temperatures stabilize over 50°F. Basil needs full sun, average soil, and about 1 inch of water at the roots every week, but it does poorly in wet conditions. It grows well in containers on a sunny deck, balcony, or patio. Pinching the tips will encourage bushy growth.

VARIETIES

In addition to Genovese, interesting sweet basil varieties include the following:

GREEK (*O. ×citriodorum* 'Pesto Perpetuo') This ornamental type is a very compact, column-growing variety and has a variegated leaf with citrus scent.

HOLY BASIL (*O. tenuiflorum*) In North America, it is usually sold as Tulsi. Whatever the name, it adds a bright, bold flavor with loads of anise, mint, and spice, so it asserts itself in creamy dips and big-flavored curries, casseroles, and meat combinations.

LIME (*O. americanum*) According to Rexford Talbert, herb researcher, the narrow, pointed leaves of this variety may have a tangy, citrus-lime flavor and it may be called lime basil, but it is still technically a lemon basil. Use it in teas, or with fish or poultry dishes.

MAMMOTH (*O. basilicum* 'Mammoth') Called "mammoth" because its large leaves grow to lettuce-size proportions, this variety is great for salads and chiffonade.

PURPLE RUFFLES (*O. basilicum* 'Purple Ruffles') The large, frilled, burgundy leaves make it great for salads and garnishing plates.

RED RUBIN (*O. basilicum* 'Red Rubin') A descendant of 'Dark Opal', Red Rubin has beautiful purple-bronze leaves and pink flower spikes.

THAI (*Ocimum* sp.) There are several varieties in this group and all display narrow, pointed, dark-green leaves, deep-purple, rounded flower spikes, and strong anise flavor. This variety is often teamed with seafood in Southeast Asia.

Basil and Walnut Pesto

Pesto (Italian) and *pistou* (French) are names derived from the word for *pestle*, the tool used to grind herbs and spices in a mortar. Both pesto and pistou describe the finely chopped or pounded green sauce made from fresh garlic, herbs, hard cheese, oil, and nuts (though pistou doesn't usually contain nuts). While many people think that only basil is used for making pesto, in fact any green herb (such as cilantro, flat-leaf parsley, rosemary, thyme, sage, French tarragon, and even some flower petals) may be used in combination with or without basil.

My recipe adds a sophisticated twist to the usual basil pesto. It boasts a more mellow and sweeter garlic flavor due to the roasted garlic, and the toasted walnuts add a nuttier dimension than the more mellow pine nuts, often the default choice for pesto. Because the oil is a major component of pesto and pistou, and it is used raw, always use the finest quality extra-virgin olive oil or other polyunsaturated oil such as avocado, walnut, sunflower, or hemp oil.

Strip tender stems and leaves from the coarser basil stalks. Rinse and pat dry using a towel before lightly packing into a dry measuring cup. You can make pesto in a 4-cup mortar or using a food processor. The handmade technique produces a chunkier, more rustic sauce than the one made by machine.

Makes 2 cups

½ cup toasted walnut pieces
1 head Roasted Garlic (page 155)
2 cups fresh basil leaves and
    tender stems
½ cup fresh parsley
¼ cup fresh oregano
½ teaspoon sea salt
About 1 cup extra-virgin oil
    (see headnote)

Using a Food Processor

1. In the bowl of a food processor, pulse walnuts one or two times or until coarsely chopped. Squeeze roasted garlic into the bowl and pulse two or three times to mix with the nuts. Add basil, parsley, oregano, and salt and pulse three or four times to combine.

(continued on following page)

2. With the machine running, add the oil through the opening in the lid in a slow, steady stream, stopping once to scrape down the sides of the bowl. Continue to process and add oil until the pesto reaches the desired consistency. The more oil you add, the more the pesto will progress from a chopped, slightly dry sauce to a smooth, creamy one.

Using a Mortar and Pestle

1. In a medium bowl, combine basil, parsley, and oregano. Toss to combine.

2. Smash the walnuts in a mortar using the pestle until they are the size of peas. Add the mixed herbs, one cup at a time, and grind until the mixture is coarse. Add the roasted garlic and salt and drizzle some of the oil over. Grind, adding more oil as needed, until the pesto is the desired consistency.

● TOOLS: MORTAR AND PESTLE

Pestle (from the Latin *pistillum, pist* meaning "pounded," from the verb *pinsere*) describes the heavy, rounded wood, iron, stone, or porcelain tool used to pound, crush, or grind herbs, spices, or grains. All of this pounding and grinding is done in an equally heavy, deep-sided bowl called a mortar.

Using a mortar and pestle to make pesto, salsa verde, and other herb sauces is a slow but pleasant way to draw out the essential oils and flavors in herbs and spices. Using a mortar in place of a blender or food processor produces a pastier, more rustic sauce that allows the individual ingredients to keep their personality.

My personal herb/spice equipment, clockwise from top right: porcelain mortar and pestle for grinding spices and herbs and making green sauces; small cast iron mortar and pestle for grinding small amounts of woody spices and popping seed pods; spice wok for toasting spices.

Layered Tomato Salad with Basil Vinaigrette

Makes 4 servings

3 avocados, sliced
Juice of 1 lemon
6 assorted heirloom tomatoes, sliced
1 red onion, thinly sliced
1 cup crumbled feta cheese
¼ cup fresh basil chiffonade shreds (see page 16)
½ cup Basil Vinaigrette (below)

1. In a medium bowl, combine avocado slices and lemon juice; toss to coat.

2. On a serving platter, arrange half the tomatoes in one layer. Spread half the onion over and top with half the avocado slices. Repeat the layers using the remaining tomatoes, onion, and avocado.

3. Sprinkle cheese and basil shreds over top. Drizzle vinaigrette over or pass separately.

BASIL VINAIGRETTE

Makes ½ cup

¼ cup Basil and Walnut Pesto (page 13)
¼ cup extra-virgin olive oil or avocado oil
2 tablespoons freshly squeezed lemon juice
½ teaspoon sea salt

In a jar with tight-fitting lid, combine pesto, oil, lemon juice, and salt. Cap with lid and shake to combine.

● HERBALIST TECHNIQUES: CHIFFONADE

Chiffonade is a method of cutting large-leaf herbs into long shreds or ribbons for use in sauces, poaching liquids, and custards and as a garnish. When chiffonade strips of lettuce and sorrel are cooked in butter, the dish is called chiffonade and it is used as a garnish for soups or other dishes. To chiffonade basil, use a large-leaf variety such as Genovese or Mammoth:

1. Stack 3 or 4 leaves.

2. Roll the stack into a cigar-shaped log.

3. Cut thin strips crosswise across the rolled leaves.

4. Separate the strips and use immediately.

Basil Baked Trout

Makes 4 to 6 servings

1 cup shredded carrots
1 cup ½-inch diced parsnips
1 cup ½-inch diced potatoes
1 cup ½-inch diced rutabaga
¼ cup Basil and Walnut Pesto
    (page 13)
Extra-virgin olive oil
2 pounds trout fillets
    (or firm-fleshed fish such as
    whitefish, perch, or halibut)
½ lemon
6 whole fresh basil leaves
Sea salt and pepper

1. Preheat oven to 375°F. In a baking dish, combine carrots, parsnips, potatoes, and rutabaga. Toss with pesto, adding more olive oil if necessary to coat. Roast in preheated oven for 15 minutes.

2. Remove vegetables from the oven and stir well. Arrange fish over top of vegetables in the pan. Squeeze lemon juice over fish and arrange basil leaves over the top. Season with salt and pepper. Drizzle fish with 2 tablespoons oil and bake for 10 to 15 minutes or until fish is opaque and flakes easily with a fork.

Bay

Laurus nobilis

Entre los árboles todos
Se señorea el laurel
Entre las mujeres Ana
Entre flores el clavel.

—Spanish song praising laurel (bay) of all trees, adoring Ana,
and elevating the carnation above all other flowers

Ancient Greek and Roman athletes, heroes, poets, and statesmen are often shown on coins, as sculptures, or in illustrations wearing a headband of bay. But why, you might ask, was bay used to crown such achievers and how did it bestow the highest of esteem? As the Greek myth goes, the beautiful and unsuspecting minor goddess-nymph Daphne was so overwhelmed by the love of Apollo that she pleaded with (and this is where the story gets complicated) either her father, the river god Ladon, or the earth-mother, Gaia, for help. Either way, her prayers were answered and she morphed into the slender and gorgeous  bay laurel tree. Who can blame Apollo? He poured his adoration into the fragrant tree and proclaimed it as a symbol of honor, wisdom (*baccalaureate*, from the Latin for "laurel berries"), and prophetic knowledge.

Many supermarkets now sell fresh bay leaves in the produce section, so seek out fresh whenever possible. Besides being sweeter and more flavorful, the fresh leaves will usually be larger and less expensive than dried bay in a spice jar. Fresh leaves store best if wrapped in a moistened tea towel and placed in a sealed plastic bag on a shelf on the refrigerator door.

Fresh leaves need to be rubbed or bruised to release their aromatic compounds. Rarely are bay leaves crushed before using (except when used in a tea blend) because small bits are too difficult to remove from the cooked dish. Although ground bay is combined in seafood seasoning, it is not widely available as a ground spice because the whole leaves conveniently flavor dishes.

Dried bay leaves should be kept whole in an airtight container in a cool dark place. They should only be stored for one year and then replaced because the essential oils dissipate and the aroma lessens over time.

Two or three dried or one to two fresh whole leaves are enough to spice up a dish that serves four to six people. One leaf in a cupful of boiled water makes a pleasant tea.

A trimmed bay tree, underplanted with sage, flanks the entrance to the tiny herb garden at Ledew Topiary Gardens, in Monkton, Maryland.

FLAVOR

Fresh bay leaves are slightly pungent with a balsamic-nutmeg taste layered with camphor, citrus, vanilla, and pine.

PARTS TO USE

Only the leaves are used in cooking.

CULINARY USES

Fresh or dried bay leaves are robust and release their flavor slowly, making bay an essential herb for slow, long-cooking techniques. Stock (notably court bouillon), soups, stews, sauces, marinades, stuffing, and pickles benefit from fresh or dried bay. It is used as a garnish for hot or cold fish, terrines, and paté, infusing them with its spicy essence. Bay combines well with fennel to flavor fish and poultry and complements allspice, oregano, cardamom, parsley, garlic, sage, lovage, savory, marjoram, and thyme. A key flavoring in béchamel sauces and tomato sauces, bay also helps spike milk and eggs for sweet puddings, custard desserts, and beverages, as well as wines, and baked-bean and lentil dishes. The fresh leaves can be crushed to release the flavor, but dried leaves are usually tossed whole into dishes and removed after cooking.

CAUTION: Remove whole or pieces of bay from food before serving. The sharp edges of the leaves may cause choking or perforate the intestines.

❤ HEALTH BENEFITS

Fresh bay leaves are high in vitamins A and C and folic acid. In *The Green Pharmacy*, Jim Duke credits bay (along with cinnamon, cloves, and turmeric) with facilitating insulin use, thus helping to control diabetes. Bay is an antioxidant and helps loosen mucus when boiled in water and the steam is inhaled. Use bay essential oil in massage oil or bath water for sore muscles and joints due to flu.

GROWING BAY

With its glossy, broad, and deep green leaves, *Laurus nobilis*—also known as bay or sweet bay—is a slow-growing, tender evergreen tree that thrives in warmer climates (Zone 8 or above) in fertile, moist soil. It roots easily from cuttings. Bay can be neatly clipped to create topiary forms, standards, hedges, and other formal shapes that enclose garden beds or make a stunning arched entrance to a patio or garden oasis. Because it is an evergreen shrub, trimming encourages it to bush out to form a dense, green, living wall.

In cooler climates, bay survives northern winters in containers, which should be brought indoors once temperatures drop. A greenhouse is best for overwintering, but a room with full, natural light or grow lights will work. Mist often if the leaves begin to drop. Bay seems to prefer to be slightly pot-cramped but needs to have the roots trimmed to refresh it and keep the tree from growing out of hand.

Bouquet Garni

Cooks from France, Italy, Germany, and many other places around the world use several traditional herb combinations, but somehow the French terms are the ones that have made an enduring impression. And so it is with the seasoning bundle of herbs known as *bouquet garni*, a term that translates to "garnished bouquet."

While there are several herbs that may be used in the little garni package, generally it is comprised of aromatic, woody herbs that can hold up to long-simmering dishes: bay, thyme, sage, savory, and rosemary. Sometimes more perishable herbs such as parsley, chervil, lovage, marjoram or oregano, basil, or salad burnet are added to the bundle, but because those herbs dissipate quickly, garnis made with them are recommended to be added to the dish within the last 30 minutes of cooking time.

I have found that it is easiest to make several bouquets garnis at a time, hang them to dry, and store them for use in winter dishes. If stored in a cool, dry place, they will keep for one season. They also make great decorations for gifts for cooks.

Here's how I make bouquet garni for winter soups and stews or other long-simmering dishes.

For every bundle, you will need the following fresh herbs:

2 large bay leaves, fresh or dried
4 to 6 sprigs thyme, each 3 inches long
3 to 4 sprigs savory, each 3 inches long
2 to 3 sprigs rosemary, each 3 inches long
2 to 3 sprigs sage, each 3 inches long
24-inch piece of twine
Fresh green onion leaves or leek leaves, optional

1. Lay one bay leaf flat on a work surface. Pile the other herb sprigs on top. Cover with the remaining bay leaf. Bind tightly with twine, making a slip knot that can be tightened as the herbs dry and shrink. Leave enough extra twine to hang the bundles.

(continued on following page)

2. Hang bundles in a cool, airy, dark place to dry. Check after one or two days and tighten the loop so that the herbs do not slip out of the twine.

3. When the bundles are fully dried, remove the twine if you wish and replace it with green onion or leek leaves. Tie and knot one leaf around the dried bundle and set aside for the leaves to dry.

4. Store dried bouquet garni bundles in an airtight container in a cool, dry, dark place. Discard after 6 to 8 months.

● BOUQUET GARNI COMBINATIONS

Other bouquets garnis may be designed for specific soups or stews. Here are just a few suggestions for different combinations of herbs that may be bundled into a bouquet garni:

BEEF: bay, thyme, savory, and an outer leek leaf

PORK: celery stalk with leaves, sage, parsley, and thyme

LAMB: rosemary, savory, and garlic wrapped in bay leaves

POULTRY: bay, sage, and marjoram; or lovage, lemon thyme, and marjoram

FISH AND SEAFOOD: bay, lemon balm, and chervil; or bay, dill, and chervil

VEGETABLES: oregano, thyme, and bay for tomatoes; bay, chervil, savory, and parsley for boiled vegetables; bay, lovage, French tarragon, and thyme for root vegetables

Crab and Sorrel Bisque

Makes 6 servings

1 leek, halved lengthwise and
 cut into 3-inch pieces
1 carrot, halved lengthwise and
 cut into 3-inch pieces
1 Bouquet Garni (page 21)
2 pounds fresh or frozen crab
 legs in the shell, cut into
 3-inch pieces
2 tablespoons extra-virgin
 coconut oil or avocado oil
1 small onion, chopped
1 clove garlic, finely chopped
½ cup dry white wine
Juice from 1 lemon
2 cups lightly packed fresh sorrel
 or spinach
1 teaspoon sea salt or to taste
2 cups heavy whipping cream
 (36% butterfat)
6 bay leaves, fresh or dried

1. In a large, heavy stockpot or saucepan, combine 5 cups water, the leek pieces, carrot pieces, and bouquet garni. Bring to a boil over high heat. Add crab legs and cook just until they turn bright pink. Using tongs, lift out and transfer legs to a colander and rinse under cold water to stop the cooking.

2. Remove the meat from the shells and set aside. Return the shells to the stockpot. Reduce heat and simmer the stock for 45 minutes or until reduced to about 4 cups. Strain stock into a large liquid measuring cup or jug. Discard vegetables, shells, and bouquet garni.

3. Meanwhile, coarsely chop the crabmeat. Place in a bowl, cover tightly, and set aside in the refrigerator. The stock may be prepared up to this point, cooled, covered, and refrigerated overnight. Bring to room temperature and continue with step 4.

4. In a large, heavy saucepan, heat oil over medium-high heat. Sauté onion and garlic for 5 minutes or until soft and transparent, reducing heat if necessary to keep from browning. Add wine, lemon juice, and stock and bring to a boil. Reduce heat and simmer for 5 minutes. Add sorrel and salt. Cook, stirring occasionally, for 3 to 4 minutes or until sorrel is wilted.

(continued on following page)

5. Working in batches, purée vegetables and stock using a blender until smooth. Return to the pan and bring to a simmer over medium heat. Stir in cream and cooked crabmeat and heat through. Ladle into bowls and garnish with a bay leaf.

● TECHNIQUES: BRUISING LEAVES

Chefs and cooks bruise fresh herb leaves and sprigs just before adding them to a cooking pot because this technique releases the aromatic essential oils in the cells of the herbs. Due to its brittleness, dried bay will crumble if we try to bruise or crush the leaves, so using kitchen scissors, I make slits in the leaves from each side toward the center rib so that the leaf looks like a feather. More of the leaf is exposed, but the leaf is still intact.

Because the leaf pieces may tear off, I only use this technique in broths or soups in which the liquid is simmering and the leaves are not mashed or crushed by other ingredients.

Bergamot

Monarda didyma

We had Oswego tea in my grandmother's garden in 1860 and my mother
always used to have some branches or leaves of monarda on her table.

—Henry Correvon, *Rock Garden and Alpine Plants*, 1930

Named after Spanish botanist Nicholas Monardez (1512–1588), *Monarda*, or bergamot (also known as bee balm), is a native, eastern North American herb. It became popular in North America when American botanist John Bartram (1699–1777) rediscovered it. *Monarda* was subsequently traded to the English grower and merchant Peter Collinson, and it quickly became a popular plant in eighteenth-century European gardens, thanks to its brilliant and showy pink, purple, or scarlet flower cones that last for several weeks from midsummer onward.

But almost a century before Bartram first sent the seeds of *M. didyma* to England, John Tradescant, the son of the famous English plant hunter by the same name, had discovered a wild bergamot (*M. fistulosa*) in Virginia. He returned with seeds, which, when grown in England, were known as a "wild mint of the Americas" but misclassified as an oregano (*Origanum fistulosum*).

Wild bergamot became known as Oswego Tea, the name originating from the Oswego River in New York where First Peoples of the Oswego Nation harvested it and shared it with explorers and English settlers. After the Boston Tea Party in 1773, American colonists turned to this pleasant, citrus-tasting plant as a substitute for

Showy bergamot blooms in my herb garden for weeks in August.

British imports of Indian and Chinese tea, which, because of their high tax, were used as a rallying point for rebellion.

Interestingly, an essential oil from the rind of the Bergamot Orange (*Citrus bergamia*), a bitter orange—absolutely no relation to the herb *M. didyma*—is added to Earl Grey tea for flavor. Did the bitter orange known as bergamot come into use first, prompting discoverers of the orange-spiked herb to name it bergamot after the secret ingredient in perhaps the most recognized and popular commercial tea? It might just be so.

FLAVOR

Bergamot has a fresh, lemon-lime taste with warm, spicy notes and a hint of mint.

PARTS TO USE

Both the leaves and flowers of bergamot are used.

CULINARY USES

Fresh bergamot leaves and flowers lend their distinctively citrus taste to green salads and fresh fruit cups, light, brothy soups and vinaigrette dressings, salsas, and other sauces, teas and iced beverages. It complements fish, chicken, and pork as well as egg and pudding desserts, yogurt, and soft cheeses. Pop a flower into each individual compartment of an ice cube tray, cover with water, and freeze. Use as flashy ice cubes in punch or summer drinks. When the ice melts, the flowers garnish the beverage. Dried leaves and flowers give a delicate, bright citrus spike to tea blends.

♥ HEALTH BENEFITS

Native Americans used wild bergamot (*M. fistulosa*) in a tea to induce sweating. Medical herbalists use bergamot as a digestive and to relieve or help prevent gas and for fever, spasms, headaches, nausea, and fluid retention. It makes a sleep-inducing tea on its own or when blended with chamomile or linden (*Tilia*).

GROWING BERGAMOT

A showy border and ornamental plant, bergamot is a hardy herbaceous perennial that prefers clay-like or moisture-retaining soil. It should be thinned to keep it from invading and taking over garden beds. Thinning also gives it air to prevent mildew. Bergamot tolerates partial shade. Flowers are harvested when they are fully opened. Pinch back and snip sprigs all season. A very good pollinator plant, bergamot attracts hummingbirds, butterflies, and pollinating insects such as bumblebees and honeybees.

VARIETIES

PETITE DELIGHT (*M.* 'Petite Delight') Unusual with its pink flowers (most bergamot flowers are red), Petite Delight also has some pink markings at the base of its leaves. Beautiful in summer drinks, its aerial parts also make a delicious tea.

WILD BERGAMOT (*M. fistulosa*) Native to northeastern North America, the wild bergamot shows its mint family connection (*Lamiaceae*) with its square stem and small, pink-purple flowers that are crowded together in a terminal spike. Use the leaves and petals (not the green flower head) for tea and to flavor sauces and puddings and other desserts.

Spiced Bergamot Tea Blend

Bergamot is a natural for herbal beverages and tea blends. It complements mint, other lemon herbs, and sweet spices like the ones in this delicious mix. The spices are crushed but not ground—use a small, heavy mortar (cast iron is ideal) and pestle to pound the spices to about the size of short-grain rice.

Herb teas should be enjoyed immediately after brewing because the volatile oils from the herbs evaporate and the taste and medicinal effect are lost.

Makes 2¾ cups tea blend

1 cup dried bergamot leaves
  and flowers
½ cup dried lemon balm
½ cup dried mint
½ cup dried sweet cicely
3 tablespoons dried chopped
  citrus peel
2 tablespoons allspice berries,
  crushed
1 teaspoon cloves, crushed
1 piece (2 inches) cinnamon,
  crushed

1. In a bowl, combine bergamot, lemon balm, mint, sweet cicely, citrus peel, allspice, cloves, and cinnamon. Toss to mix well. Transfer to an airtight container, label, and store in a cool, dry, dark place.

2. Just before making tea, crush a small amount of the blend and use 1 tablespoon for each cup of boiled water.

Fruit in Spiced Bergamot Tea Syrup

Makes 6 servings

2 teaspoons Spiced Bergamot
  Tea Blend (previous page)
¼ cup sugar
Grated zest of 1 lime
Juice of 1 lime
3 mangoes, chopped
3 kiwis, peeled and sliced
1 cantaloupe melon, diced
1 cup halved seedless green
  grapes
Sprigs of fresh mint, for garnish

1. In a saucepan, combine tea blend and ¼ cup water. Bring to a light boil over high heat. Remove from heat, cover, and set aside for 5 minutes to steep. Strain into another pan, pressing the blend to extract as much liquid as possible. Discard blend.

2. Add sugar and lime zest to the tea in the pan. Heat over medium-high heat, stirring frequently for 2 to 3 minutes or until the sugar dissolves and the liquid simmers. Cook, stirring occasionally, for 2 minutes. Syrup should be slightly thickened. Remove from heat and stir in the lime juice. Set aside to cool completely.

3. Meanwhile, combine mangoes, kiwis, cantaloupe pieces, and grapes in a serving bowl. Pour cooled syrup over. Cover and marinate in the refrigerator for at least 2 hours or overnight. Remove from refrigerator and bring to room temperature before serving. Toss gently and garnish with mint.

Moroccan Fattoush with Bergamot Salsa Verde

Makes 4 to 6 servings

¼ cup extra-virgin olive oil

2 tablespoons freshly squeezed
   lemon juice

1 tablespoon cumin seeds, crushed

1 tablespoon sea salt

3 pita bread rounds (10-inch size),
   torn into bite-size pieces

4 tomatoes, seeded and chopped

1 English cucumber, quartered
   lengthwise, thinly sliced crosswise

4 green onions, thinly sliced

1 cup chopped fresh bergamot or mint

1 head romaine lettuce, trimmed,
   cut crosswise into ¾-inch strips

1 cup crumbled feta cheese

1 cup Bergamot Salsa Verde (below)

¼ cup bergamot flowers, fresh or
   dried, for garnish, optional

1. Preheat oven to 350°F.

2. In a bowl, combine oil, lemon juice, cumin, and salt. Whisk to mix well. Add pita pieces and toss to coat. Spread on a rimmed baking sheet, scraping the bowl to drizzle the oil mixture over pita. Toast in preheated oven, stirring once, for 3 to 5 minutes or until golden brown.

3. In a large bowl, combine tomatoes, cucumber, onions, and bergamot. Add the toasted pita pieces, scraping the baking sheet to include the seasoned oil.

4. On a serving platter, pile romaine lettuce. Spoon tomato-pita mixture over lettuce and top with feta cheese. Drizzle Bergamot Salsa Verde over salad. Garnish with bergamot flowers if using.

BERGAMOT SALSA VERDE

Makes 1 cup

¼ cup pistachio nuts

1 piece (1 inch) candied ginger

2 cups lightly packed fresh bergamot

½ cup lightly packed fresh mint

1 teaspoon sea salt

½ cup extra-virgin olive oil, plus
   additional as needed

1 tablespoon freshly squeezed
   lemon juice

In the bowl of a food processor, coarsely chop the pistachios and ginger. Add bergamot, mint, and salt and pulse for 3 or 4 seconds to mix with the nuts. With the motor running, slowly add oil through the opening in the lid. Stop and check the consistency before using all the oil—it should be fairly thin to use as a dressing. Add lemon juice, pulse, and add more oil if needed.

Iced Bergamot Punch

This recipe is an adaptation of a refreshing drink prepared by Chip Abernethy, a volunteer for a garden party at the Minnesota Landscape Arboretum. Chip makes the blueberry vinegar every year when blueberries are in season and her opal basil is abundant. You can make the vinegar one week or one year before you make the Iced Punch drink because vinegar is a natural preservative. When making the vinegar, for every quart (4-cup) glass preserving jar, you will need a 2-piece metal lid.

Makes 1 quart (4 cups)

Blueberry and Honey-Lemon
Herbed Vinegar

2 cups blueberries, crushed
1 handful dark opal basil leaves,
    bruised
3 lemons, scrubbed and quartered
3 tablespoons honey
3 to 4 cups warmed wine vinegar

Ice Block

1 cup fresh bergamot leaves and
    flowers
1 cup fresh opal basil leaves
1 cup fresh rose or clove pink petals

Punch

1 quart Blueberry and Honey-
    Lemon Herbed Vinegar (above)
6 cups sparkling or soda water
6 cups ginger ale

TO MAKE THE VINEGAR: Into each quart (4-cup) wide-mouth preserving jar, add blueberries, basil, lemons, and honey. Pour warmed vinegar over the mixture to within 1 inch of the top. Cap, label, and set aside in a cool, dark place for up to 2 weeks or in the refrigerator for up to 12 months.

TO MAKE THE ICE BLOCK: Wash an empty quart (4-cup) cardboard milk container. Add bergamot, basil, and rose petals. Fill with cool water to within 1 inch of the top. Staple the container closed and stand it upright in the freezer until frozen. At serving time, cut away the container and add the frozen ice block to the punch.

TO MAKE THE PUNCH: In a punch bowl or gallon drink dispenser, combine blueberry vinegar, sparkling water, and ginger ale. Add the ice block to the bowl.

Borage

Borago officinalis

Ego Borago (I, Borage)
Gaudia semper ago. (Bring alwaies [always] courage.)
—John Gerard's translation of an ancient Latin verse accredited to Pliny

Borage has been a familiar "salat" and "potage" herb for centuries. Usually the flowers were dried and sugared or candied, but borage-laced wine was the pre-battle drink of choice for Celtic and Roman warriors and, later, for crusading knights. If it was good enough for soldiers going into war, young women considered it appropriate to serve to their suitors in the hope that it would bolster courage for them to pop the question.

In medieval times, the ethereal buds and flowers of borage inspired tapestry designs, and John Parkinson (1567–1650) in his *Paradisi in Sole* refers to the blue borage flowers as being favorites for "women's needlework."

Jean-Baptiste de La Quintinye (1626–1688), author of *The Compleat Gard'ner* (translated by John Evelyn), grew borage in the potager garden of Louis XIV of France. Borage is one of the plants that sixteenth-century New World historian Peter Martyr d'Anghiera mentioned was planted at the settlement of Isabella on Hispaniola Island by Columbus's companions—likely during his second visit to the island in 1493.

FLAVOR
Borage leaves (see Caution, page 33) and flowers have a clear, cool cucumber taste.

PARTS TO USE

The seeds and blue (or white) flowers are used. *Borago officinalis* 'Alba' produces a white flower that is edible and may be used in the same way as the blue or purple-flowered varieties.

CULINARY USES

Of all the *Borago* species, only *Borago officinalis* is edible. The tender, fresh leaves were once used in soups, pasta dishes, and salads, and to flavor poultry and fish. They were also steamed as a leafy green vegetable or added to mild cheese, yogurt, sour cream, and egg dishes, but they are not widely used in recipes now. The flowers are used in beverages or salads—fresh, dried, candied, or frozen.

Borage is part of an herbaceous border on the outside of the vegetable garden of Master Gardeners Lori and Dave Schaeffer in Douglassville, Pennsylvania.

❤ HEALTH BENEFITS

In anecdotal lore, borage was thought to "lighten the heart." Science is now proving ancient herbalists' belief that borage lifts the spirits and encourages bravery—it has been shown to have mild antidepressant and sedative effects and to stimulate the adrenal glands. Topically, borage leaf poultices are used to treat dry skin and external inflammation, bruises, and swelling. Borage-infused water is used to soothe sore eyes. Borage seed oil is high in GLA (gamma-linolenic acid), a fatty acid that boosts immunity and fights inflammation, one of the first precursors to disease. The oil helps to treat rheumatism, skin conditions, and hormonal complaints and may be substituted for evening primrose oil.

CAUTION: It is now believed that due to small amounts of alkaloids that are known to cause liver damage as well as liver cancer, internal use of borage leaves is not advised, although borage seed oil and very small amounts of the flowers are safe to ingest.

GROWING BORAGE

A self-seeding, hardy annual with remark-able, bright hyacinth-blue, star-shaped flowers, borage prefers sunny, well-drained spots. The gray-green leaves and stems are covered in coarse hairs. Its long taproot discourages replanting, so choose the site carefully.

 DRYING BORAGE FLOWERS

The brilliant blue, star-shaped borage flowers hold their color and add a cool, slightly cucumber essence to drinks, salads, soups, teas, cookies, and baked goods. To dry edible herb flowers, harvest after the dew has dried (midmorning) when flowers are just open, not full-blown. Remove green parts, lightly rinse, and pat dry. Arrange in one layer on a drying rack and set aside in a warm, dark, and airy place. The time it takes to dry leaves and flowers depends on the dryness of the air, but they should be crisp to the touch after a few days.

Store in an airtight container—glass or porcelain—with a tight-fitting lid. Keep for one season only. See Edible Flower Primer, page 261 for a list of edible flowers.

Borage Flower Lemonade

With its fresh cucumber flavor, borage is exceptional in chilled summer drinks. And it has proved to be both refreshing and to have restorative properties. According to seventeenth-century botanist John Gerard, "A syrup concocted of the flowers quieteth the lunatick person, and the leaves eaten raw do engender a good blood." John Evelyn claims, "Sprigs of borage are of known virtue to revive the hypochondriac and cheer the hard student." And according to Lord (Francis) Bacon (1561–1626), "If in the must of wine or wort of beer, while it worketh, before it be tunned, the borage stay a short time, and is changed with fresh, it will make a sovereign drink for melancholy passion."

Makes 6 servings

3 tablespoons grated lemon zest
Juice of 4 lemons
Juice of 2 limes
5 cups water
½ cup, plus 6 tablespoons sugar, divided
½ cup fresh salad burnet leaves or chopped cucumber
24 fresh borage flowers for muddling
6 fresh borage flowers for garnish, optional

1. In a saucepan, combine lemon zest, lemon juice, lime juice, water, and ½ cup sugar. Bring to a boil over high heat. Reduce heat to medium-low and simmer for 5 minutes. Remove the pan from the heat, stir in salad burnet leaves, and set aside to cool. Transfer to a jug and refrigerate for at least 30 minutes or up to 48 hours. If using cucumber, strain it off after steeping. Lemonade may be made ahead to this point.

2. In each of 6 tall glasses, using a wooden spoon or muddler, muddle (press and beat) 1 tablespoon sugar with 4 borage flowers. Add ice cubes and pour chilled lemonade through a strainer into glasses. Garnish with a borage flower if desired and serve with a long-handled spoon for stirring the muddled flower-sugar.

Calendula

Calendula officinalis

The Sun was lord of the Marigold,
Basil and Rocket belonged to Mars.

—Rudyard Kipling, in the poem "Our Fathers of Old" from *Rewards and Fairies*, 1910

alendula is also known as pot marigold. The Latin word, *calendae*, meaning the first day of the month, was likely the inspiration for the name of this plant that flowers almost monthly in its native Mediterranean habitat.

But what's in a name? Herbalists consider calendula to be a medicinal ally, and from antiquity to today it has been a powerful symbol of heat, passion, and protection. Indeed, in an article in *Calendula, Herb of the Year 2008*, herbalist Gert Coleman tells us that "Calendula's sun-loving nature, healing properties, and cheerful presence manifest its magic as an herb versatile enough to be included in healing gardens, kitchen gardens, dye gardens, women's gardens, children's gardens, Shakespeare gardens, saints gardens, and green witch gardens."

And speaking of names, they can get mighty confusing in the botanical world. The common African or French marigolds, those beautiful annual plants that are often found in autumn planters, are actually members of the *Tagetes* botanical family. And while they may resemble calendula, they are inedible and have no known medicinal properties, which is a reminder to always use the Latin name to identify plants.

FLAVOR

Fresh calendula petals are sweetly citrus but earthy. Once dried, the petals are highly floral and perfumed with undertones of vanilla.

PARTS TO USE

The petals and fresh young leaves are used.

CULINARY USE

Fresh and dried calendula petals are used in salads, soups, and one-pot dishes and casseroles. Dried petals perfume sugar and are used in baked goods or puddings. The young tender leaves add zip to salads or are used as a garnish.

At the peak of summer, calendula, nasturtium, and lamb's ears make a showy display in this Boston garden.

❤ HEALTH BENEFITS

Calendula petals hold anti-inflammatory properties and a simple calendula salve soothes and promotes the healing of bruises and other skin irritations (boils, rashes, and shingles) and burns. It is especially effective for poorly healing wounds. Internally, calendula tea or tincture helps to break a fever, relieve ulcer pain, and reduce menstrual cramps. Calendula essential oil is used to treat earaches.

GROWING CALENDULA

A self-seeding, sun-loving, annual border and ornamental plant, calendula is invasive and hardy. The flowers are yellow or orange or reddish orange and either single, with a single row of petals around the center, or double. If the flowers are harvested, the plant blooms from May until first frost.

🌿 A PRIMER OF KEY MEDICINAL HERBS AND SPICES

Growing and enjoying organic vegetables, fruits, and herbs within a whole-food diet is one of the best ways to become and stay healthy. Plants are rich in antioxidants in addition to providing significant vitamins, minerals, and other phytonutrients that help maintain wellness at the cellular level.

Most medicinal teas, tinctures, and other preparations call for dried herbs, so if you wish to substitute fresh for dried herbs in a recipe, you will need to use twice the amount of fresh as dried. Here is a short list of some medicinal herbs to grow and enjoy in meals.

HERBS

ASTRAGALUS (*Astragalus membranaceus*) Effective, safe (even for the very old and the very young), and easy to use in foods, astragalus is an important immune booster. It significantly reduces the negative effects of chemotherapy and steroids on the immune system. Add whole, sliced, or powdered dried roots to soups, stews, and sauces.

CALENDULA Astringent, antiseptic, antifungal, and anti-inflammatory, calendula is used topically to ease skin rashes, blemishes, and sunburn. It also soothes ulcers and digestive problems.

CHAMOMILE German chamomile soothes indigestion and colic in babies (it is mildly sedative); it eases stress and tension; and it relaxes and helps with sleep. It is used topically to soothe rashes, cuts, and swollen skin because of its anti-inflammatory properties.

ECHINACEA (*E. purpurea* or *E. angustifolia*) Echinacea boosts the immune system and is effective against colds and flu because it is antibiotic, antimicrobial, antiseptic, analgesic, and anti-inflammatory. It prevents infections in the respiratory, urinary, and digestive systems if used correctly and early.

GARLIC Garlic may lower the risk of ovarian, colorectal, and other cancers, and it helps decrease blood pressure and prevent strokes by slowing arterial blockages. It helps lower blood sugar and blood cholesterol levels, and its antimicrobial and antibiotic actions make it an excellent cold and flu fighter. Crushed, fresh raw garlic is best, so enjoy it in spreads, dips, and other dishes once a day if possible.

LEMON BALM It soothes nervous tension and anxiety, promotes sleep, and speeds the healing of cold sores. It is antioxidant, antiviral, and antibiotic, so use it in cough syrups and teas for insomnia.

LEMON BALM

PARSLEY Great for the immune system, parsley acts as a tonic by flushing excess fluid from the body. It heals the nervous system and tones the bones, and is also a powerful breath freshener and a rich source of vitamin C.

PARSLEY

ROSEMARY It contains caffeic acid and rosmarinic acid, both of which are potent antioxidants as well as anti-inflammatory agents. It is a good source of antioxidant vitamin E (*Alpha tocopherol*), and it improves mood and helps improve concentration and memory. Rubbing grilled meat with rosemary and eating it with a rosemary sauce will help reduce carcinogenic effects from the charred meat.

ROSEMARY

TURMERIC A tropical plant, turmeric contains *curcumin*, a powerful anti-inflammatory that helps relieve the pain and swelling of arthritis. Turmeric helps prevent colon cancer when taken with *quercetin*, another powerful antioxidant found in onions, apples, and cabbage. It helps clear the brain of plaques that are characteristic of Alzheimer's disease. Anti-inflammatory, antioxidant, antimicrobial, antibacterial, antifungal, and antiviral, this is a powerful herb that helps lower blood cholesterol and protects liver cells.

TURMERIC

VALERIAN

VALERIAN (*Valeriana officinalis*) Antispasmodic and sedative, valerian calms nerves, relaxes, and helps with sleep. It works well when taken as a tincture or tea. Not all people can take valerian due to adverse reactions.

SPICES

Like most edible plants, spices offer specific healing properties that can ease some health conditions for humans. Here is a very short list of some kitchen herbs that have strong medicinal benefits. Except for ginger, which is used fresh, preserved in syrup, or dried, these herbs are generally dried before using them medicinally. If fresh herbs are used instead of dried, you will need to double the amount called for in the recipe.

CINNAMON (*Cinnamomum*) A warming carminative, cinnamon is used to promote digestion and relieve nausea, vomiting, and diarrhea. It has been shown to help the body use insulin more effectively, and it stabilizes blood sugar and reduces cholesterol if taken in a controlled extract daily.

CLOVES (*Syzygium aromaticum*) The dried flower buds of the tree are high in antioxidants and provide effective emergency relief of toothache. Cloves are antiseptic and anti-inflammatory, and are both an anodyne as well as a digestive. Cloves also help to relieve bloating and flatulence.

CORIANDER It is anti-inflammatory and may help control blood sugar and cholesterol. Coriander is soothing and acts as a digestive and appetite stimulant, helping the body to absorb nutrients.

FENNEL SEEDS Fennel can ease colic in babies and digestive problems (bloating and gas) in adults. Fennel seed infusion is safe to treat colic and coughs in babies and children.

FENUGREEK (*Trigonella foenum-graecum*) An expectorant and a soothing digestive, fenugreek is used to ease diverticular disease and ulcerative colitis. It lowers cholesterol and triglycerides (blood sugar) and may protect against cancer.

GINGER It prevents nausea, helps regulate blood flow, is an anti-inflammatory, and may help reduce ovarian and other cancers. If you suffer from arthritis, ginger may ease the pain and swelling.

LICORICE ROOT (*Glycyrrhiza glabra*) Herbalists consider licorice to be one of the best tonic herbs because it supplies nutrients to most body systems. An expectorant that soothes and coats tissue, it is used to ease asthma and other lung/breathing issues, sore throat, cough, bronchitis, gastritis, urinary tract infection, and constipation.

STAR ANISE (*Illicium verum*) Star anise combines well with fennel to ease colic in babies and digestive problems (bloating and gas) in adults.

Calendula-Infused Oil

Herbalists and other natural healers use several techniques to infuse or extract the healing properties of herbs into water (tisane or decoction), alcohol (tincture), vinegars, or fats (oils or butter). Salt and sugar are also a medium for extracting the flavor and medicinal constituents, but they're used mostly as flavorings for cooking.

When you make your own herbal oil for either culinary or medicinal purposes, you employ the same method; the only difference is in the choice of herb for the oil. In medicinal oils, usually only one herb is used, but two or more complementary herbs may be combined in culinary oils. Homemade infused oils are safe to use full strength directly on the skin, whereas many distilled essential oils must be diluted before being ingested or used topically.

You can use any dried medicinal herb in this recipe. If using fresh herbs, use the same amount, coarsely chop, and lightly press into a measuring cup. You can halve or double these infused oil recipes as your needs dictate.

The process of infusing oil is simple and requires little equipment. It does take a minimum of two weeks to draw the healing components out of the herbs, but it is done with little work on your part. Infused oils will keep for up to a year if fine quality, extra-virgin, organic, raw coconut or olive or almond oil is used and if the oil is stored in the refrigerator. Using coconut oil allows for longer storage of infused oils (longer than two years); and because it is very stable, it is not necessary to store coconut oil or products made with coconut oil in the refrigerator. On pages 42–43 I outline two ways to infuse oil.

DRYING CALENDULA FLOWERS

Harvest just-opened flower heads in the morning after the dew has evaporated. Arrange in a single layer on drying racks and set aside in a warm, dry, dark place with good air circulation until crackling dry—this may take two days or two weeks, depending on the location and weather.

Once the flowers are dry, pull the edible petals away from the bitter green sepals (the protective leaves at the base of the flower) and the center cone, and transfer them to a dark-glass or opaque (stainless steel or porcelain) container with a lid. Never use plastic, tin, or aluminum to store herbs and spices. If the container is clear glass, store in a dark cupboard. Label and keep in a cool, dry place for one winter and replace with fresh flowers the next summer.

CALENDULA-INFUSED COCONUT OIL

Because of its inherent healing properties, I always use coconut oil for both medicinal and culinary infused oils. Coconut oil is stable at room temperature and will not break down into unhealthful free radicals, as do polyunsaturated oils if they are overheated or not stored properly. For a simple salve, coconut oil is easy to use because it is solid if stored below 76°F, so beeswax is not required as a setting agent.

Makes 2 cups

2 cups melted extra-virgin coconut
    oil (see step 1)
2 cups dried calendula petals
1 pint glass jar with lid, preferably
    dark in color

At Four Elements Herb Farm in North Freedom, Wisconsin, large jars of medicinal oils are set outside every day in direct sunlight to infuse.

1. If the oil is solid, set the jar in a saucepan with 1 to 2 inches of simmering water. Swirl the jar around from time to time and remove when the oil has melted. This works for glass jars only. If your coconut oil is in a plastic jar, transfer some to a glass jar before melting in simmering water, then measure 2 cups.

2. Pour the petals into the empty jar. Pour melted oil over petals, filling the jar to within one or two inches of the top. Loosely cap, label, and set in a sunny window or other warm spot to steep for 2 weeks or up to 1 month. Gently swirl the jar a couple of times a day. Secure the cap and store in a cool, dark place.

3. To use, bring the oil back to liquid if it is solid, using the method in step 1. Strain through a cheesecloth-lined metal strainer into a glass measuring cup or jug. Gather up the four corners of the cheesecloth, twist, and squeeze the petals to release all of the oil. Discard petals and cheesecloth. Pour calendula-infused oil into smaller jars. Cap, label, and store jars in a cool, dark cupboard or refrigerator.

CALENDULA-INFUSED VEGETABLE OIL

Always use fine quality, organic, extra-virgin oil for making external skin preparations because the skin is porous and will absorb everything. You can use olive, avocado, hemp, or some other high-quality vegetable oil for hand and body creams. I prefer to use almond oil for face creams because it is lighter than olive oil.

Makes 2 cups

2 cups dried calendula petals

2 cups extra-virgin vegetable oil
(see headnote)

1 glass pint jar with lid, preferably
dark in color

1. Pour the petals into the jar. Pour oil over petals, filling the jar to within 1 or 2 inches of the top. Loosely cap, label, and set in a sunny window or other warm spot to steep for 2 weeks or up to 1 month. Gently swirl the jar a couple of times a day. Secure the cap and store in a cool, dark place.

2. To use, strain through cheesecloth-lined metal strainer into a glass measuring cup or jug. Gather up the four corners of the cheesecloth, twist, and squeeze the petals to release all of the oil. Pour into smaller jars. Cap, label, and store jars in a cool, dark cupboard or refrigerator.

Medicinal Herb Salves

Medicinal salves or ointments use infused oil as the carrier of an herb's medicinal properties, and some have a few drops of essential oil for added strength. Soothing salves are made with calendula-infused oil; salves used to treat bruises are made with arnica-infused oil. Knowing the healing properties of herbs helps when choosing herbs with which to infuse oils. Vitamin E acts as a stabilizer and preservative for a salve made with olive oil or any oil other than coconut oil.

With its anti-inflammatory, healing, and soothing properties, calendula oil and salve are popular products among herbalists. Use this salve to soothe cuts, burns, rough or dry skin and lips, rashes, and other minor skin problems. As an option, you can add eight to ten drops of lavender essential oil to the strained, liquid calendula oil before pouring it into small jars. Lavender is particularly soothing for burns.

Use any size small jar that suits your needs—I prefer the small, ¼ cup (2-ounce) size for salve, but ½ cup (4-ounce) or slightly larger size jars will also work.

COCONUT HERB SALVE

Makes about 2 cups

2 cups strained Calendula-Infused Coconut Oil (page 42)
Small, clean jars with lids

1. Bring oil back to a liquid by setting the jar in a large saucepan with 2 to 4 inches of simmering water. Swirl the jar around from time to time and remove when the oil has melted.

2. Pour into small jars, cap, label, and store in a cool, dark place.

VEGETABLE OIL HERB SALVE

Makes about 2 cups

2 cups strained Calendula-Infused Vegetable Oil (page 43)
1 teaspoon liquid vitamin E
½ cup grated beeswax
Small, clean jars with lids

1. Pour the oil into a nonreactive saucepan. Add the vitamin E to the oil in the pan. Gently heat over medium-low heat and stir in beeswax, heating and stirring until the wax has melted.

2. Transfer mixture to a glass measuring cup or jug. Pour into small jars, cap, label, and set aside to cool completely. Store in the refrigerator or a cool, dark cupboard.

Summer Flower Frittata

Makes 6 servings

2 tablespoons Calendula-Infused
  Oil (page 43) or extra-virgin
  olive oil

2 small yellow squash or zucchini,
  chopped

1 red onion, chopped

½ cup summer herb flowers or
  petals, fresh or dried (see note)

12 large eggs

1 cup milk

1 cup heavy whipping cream
  (36% butterfat)

½ cup Pesto (page 13) or
  chopped fresh basil

1 teaspoon sea salt

8 ounces chilled soft goat cheese,
  broken into small pieces

½ cup chopped green or black
  olives

1 loaf country-style bread, torn
  into 1-inch pieces

½ cup grated Parmesan cheese

NOTE: Use calendula, rose, violet,
bergamot, borage, or any other
organic edible flowers.

1. Preheat oven to 350°F. Lightly oil a 13 × 9-inch baking pan.

2. In a skillet, heat oil over medium heat. Sauté squash and onions for 5 minutes or until soft. Stir in flowers and set aside to cool.

3. Meanwhile, in a bowl, whisk together eggs, milk, cream, pesto, and salt.

4. Toss goat cheese and olives with the cooled squash mixture.

5. Spread bread cubes in one layer in the bottom of the prepared baking pan. Spread squash mixture evenly over the bread, and pour egg mixture over top of vegetables.

6. Sprinkle top with Parmesan cheese. Bake in preheated oven for 45 minutes or until a knife inserted in the center comes out clean. Let stand for 10 minutes before cutting and serving.

Root Slaw

Makes 4 servings

3 cups shredded red cabbage

1 cup daikon radish or turnip matchsticks

1 carrot, shredded

¼ cup shredded beet

2 green onions, sliced

¾ cup Summer Flower Vinaigrette (recipe follows)

¼ cup fresh or dried calendula petals, for garnish

¼ cup pecans, for garnish

In a salad bowl, combine cabbage, radish, carrot, beet, and onions. Drizzle dressing over and toss to combine. Divide among 4 salad plates or bowls, and garnish with calendula and pecans.

SUMMER FLOWER VINAIGRETTE

Makes ¾ cup

½ cup extra-virgin olive oil or grapeseed oil

2 teaspoons toasted sesame oil

3 tablespoons freshly squeezed lime juice

1 tablespoon fresh or dried calendula petals

½ teaspoon sea salt

In a bowl, whisk together olive oil, sesame oil, lime juice, calendula, and salt until well combined.

Chamomile

German *Matricaria recutita* or Roman *Chamaemelum nobile*

I am sorry to say that Peter was not very well during the evening,
in consequence of having eaten too much in Mr. McGregor's garden.
His mother put him to bed, and made some camomile tea. And she gave
a dose of it to Peter! "One table-spoonful to be taken at bed-time."

—Beatrix Potter, *The Tale of Peter Rabbit*, 1902

As Art Tucker explains in *The Encyclopedia of Herbs*, "German chamomile, alias Hungarian chamomile, is widely confused with Roman chamomile, *Chamaemelum nobile*, and the two have been used almost interchangeably." Lower-growing perennial Roman chamomile, or *lawn chamomile* as it may be called, makes a good ground carpet and fills in pathways, releasing its fresh apple scent as it is trod upon, and the nonflowering variety, *C. nobile* 'Treneague', is used in place of grass for lawns because it can be mowed often. Upright-growing German chamomile (*Matricaria recutita*) is an annual and is generally used for medicinal preparations.

Chamomile can soothe and pamper the body inside and out. After sipping a soothing cup of chamomile tea, you can remove and chill the used tea bags. When you take a nap, rest the chilled tea bags over closed eyes to reduce inflammation and dark shadows. You can freeze used tea bags (between waxed paper to keep them separate) to have on hand when the need for a nap strikes. In fact, lavender and chamomile in a hot bath can be enough to put you to sleep after you towel off. A hair rinse with strong chamomile tea or 3 or 4 drops of chamomile essential oil added to baby shampoo can even brighten blond hair or bring out fair highlights.

FLAVOR

The fresh chamomile flower is very aromatic, with a refreshing, green apple smell. When dried, chamomile tastes strong, green, and herbaceous; some people describe the taste of the dried herb as cloying or soapy.

PARTS TO USE

Only the flower heads (centers and petals) of chamomile are used.

CULINARY USES

Chamomile is commonly used dried, in herbal tea blends and in liqueurs. It can be added fresh or dried to salads, desserts, and other dishes as you would calendula. One way to add chamomile's aroma and flavor to dishes is to make a strong tea and substitute it for the liquid ingredient in sauces, baked products, puddings, or other dishes.

You can also powder dried flower heads and whisk them into liquids or add to the dry ingredients in recipes. (See page 93 for directions on making powdered petals, but use the whole flower head when powdering chamomile.) Powdered chamomile can also be added to spice blends, puddings, egg and cream dishes, soups, dressings, and sauces. Sprinkle it over salads and vegetable dishes as a garnish.

Chamomile, an important market herb, clings to the rock face in the Andes, near Cusco, Peru.

❤ HEALTH BENEFITS

The traditional use of German chamomile has been for calming anxiety, for assisting sleep, and for easing stomachaches. Both German and Roman chamomile have been used to treat heartburn, nausea, gas, and vomiting. Brilliant blue *chamazulene*, a constituent that appears in the process of distilling chamomile essential oil, is anti-inflammatory and eases skin rash, insect bites, mild eczema, and other minor irritations when applied to the skin in a carrier oil or cream. Medical herbalists and aromatherapists use the essential oil of German and Roman chamomile as a grounding antidepressant and sedative compound and to reduce stress symptoms.

Because of chamomile's astringent properties, chamomile tinctures and tisanes are used in face cleansers, face packs, and conditioners, and in a facial steam to treat problem skin of all ages and types. Chamomile is also mixed with calendula for healing salves or for anti-inflammatory hand and face cream.

GROWING CHAMOMILE

Often called the "physician plant," chamomile improves the health of most plants grown around it. Both the annual and perennial varieties are easy to grow from seed. Chamomile prefers a dry sunny location and reseeds easily. A hardy, upright annual, the German variety (*M. recutita*) grows 15 inches tall. Roman chamomile (*C. nobile*) is a low-growing (6 inches) perennial that spreads quickly. This variety makes a very nice ornamental edging or ground cover for hot, dry, sunny sites due to its low-growing, matted, evergreen habit. Both species display gray-green, feathery leaves and yellow-centered flowers with white petals. Harvest once the petals shrink back and expose the rounded yellow center. The aroma of chamomile attracts bees, so it's a good choice for a bee garden.

To use *C. nobile* 'Treneague' as a lawn substitute, mow after blooming to keep the plants compact. Divide in the spring by digging up the shallow roots, ripping apart into smaller pieces, and replanting to widen the area covered.

AN HERBAL TEA PRIMER

In North America, the phrase *herbal tea* is used to describe a non-caffeinated drink that is made by infusing the aerial parts of edible herbs in boiled water for a specified time. The French use the word *tisane* to mean the same thing. However, herbal teas (or tisanes) are significantly different from what we know as *tea*, because that word denotes a drink that is made by steeping or infusing only green or black tea leaves from the *Camellia sinensis* plant. The word *tisane* is often confused with *decoction*, which, by contrast, is a liquid infused by simmering the woody parts of plants in water to extract their active medicinal constituents.

TEA HERBS

Many fragrant and medicinal herbs offer gentle, caffeine-free, calming, and therapeutic effects. Some soothe, some revive and stimulate, and others have constituents that calm tummy troubles, headaches, or other minor health issues. All herbal teas are safe to use in moderation; but if you are pregnant or wishing to use them for medicinal purposes, it is wise to follow the advice of a medical practitioner.

BERGAMOT It has a fresh citrus flavor with warm, spicy-minty notes, making it a great blending herb to use in digestive teas. Its flowers, fresh or dried, are milder in taste than the leaves but are used because they add color to beverages.

BERGAMOT

CHAMOMILE A significant ingredient in "sleepy" teas, its calming properties soothe your nerves and help you to relax. Use fresh or dried flower heads for teas.

CHAMOMILE

COSTMARY (*Chrysanthemum balsamita*) The leaves and flowers have a balsamic bite that adds a rich tone to milder herbs such as *Pelargonium*, rose, lemon balm, and bergamot.

COSTMARY

HOPS (*Humulus*) Hops is bitter tasting, so team it with sweet cicely, stevia, cinnamon, or bergamot if you want to soften the bitter taste. Combine with chamomile for a calming, sedative effect and relief from hangover headaches.

HOPS

LEMON BALM The taste is pleasantly lemon, and it blends well with other citrus herbs and sweet spices. Take lemon balm tea as a stress reducer because it calms nerves.

LEMON BALM

MINT Refreshing mint aids digestion, stomach cramps, nausea, and abdominal pains. Try different mint varieties in teas including orange (*M. aquatica* var *citrata*), apple (*M. suaveolens*) and ginger (*M. arvensis*), and, of course, peppermint (*M. ×piperita*).

MINT

RASPBERRY (*Rubus idaeus*) Midwives have long known that drinking a tea made from raspberry leaves relaxes the uterus, relieves morning sickness, and, if taken throughout pregnancy, helps carry the baby to term, according to James Duke's *The Green Pharmacy*.

RASPBERRY

ROSE/ROSE HIPS Rose petals may be used in teas, but the fruit or "hip" is more common. High in vitamin C, rose hips lend a tart, citrus flavor to tea blends. Dried rose hips are processed using a blender or food processor due to tiny hairs in the core that irritate the throat if not finely ground.

ROSE HIPS

SWEET CICELY The anise-scented leaves and stems are dried, which brings out a faint vanilla taste that is sweetly pleasant in teas. Fresh or dried sweet cicely may be used to infuse honey or granulated sugar, which is also used to sweeten teas as well as other beverages.

SWEET CICELY

TEA HERB BLENDS

Blending herbs for teas is part art but mostly trial and error. It's fun and easy to do, but it helps if you are organized: write the proportions on the airtight container so that you can easily make more of your favorite blends each season. Try these blends using dried herbs to get started.

Lemon Blend

1 part lemon balm
1 part lemon verbena
1 part lemon thyme

½ part sweet cicely
¼ part pineapple sage, optional

Citrus Spice Blend

8 parts lemon balm	1 part calendula petals
4 parts sweet cicely	⅛ part crushed licorice
3 parts ground rose hips	⅛ part crushed cinnamon

Raspberry Blend

1 part raspberry leaves	¼ part ground rose hips
½ part lemongrass or lemon thyme	⅛ part bergamot flowers, optional

Sore Throat Blend

Because of their bacteria-fighting and throat-soothing constituents, the following herbs make comforting teas. Sweeten them with throat-settling honey.

1 part sage	½ part rosemary
1 part thyme	½ part ginger
½ part horehound	

DRYING, STORING, AND USING HERBS FOR TEAS

The optimum time to harvest herbs is around midmorning after the dew has evaporated, but before the hot midday sun leaches out essential oils. Cut tea herbs for drying when stems are fairly long, rinse, and pat dry. Gather bunches together, secure with twine, and hang upside down in a dark, hot, dry place for a day or two. Herbs tend to look the same when dried, so label each bundle. They also shrink when dried, so tighten the twine after a day or two and rehang for a week or more until crackling dry. Strip the leaves from the stems, but try to keep them whole for storage.

Store in an airtight container or dark-colored jar in a dark, dry cupboard.

When ready to use in teas, rub the leaves between your palms into a fine powder (spices are already crushed in the blends) and measure 1 tablespoon for every cup of tea you are making.

THE PERFECT POT OF TEA

Making tea is a ritual in Japan. For Western cultures, it serves as a means to end a good meal or to simply relax and enjoy a quiet moment. Whatever the occasion, taking the time to make tea properly pays off in taste and ultimate enjoyment.

To make herbal or green tea, bring fresh, cold water to a boil. Use a nonreactive teapot, such as glass, ceramic, stainless steel, or porcelain. Pour some of the boiling water into the teapot, place the lid on, and set aside for 3 minutes to warm the pot.

Because boiling water will burn delicate herb leaves and flower petals as well as white or green tea leaves, let boiling water in the kettle rest for 3 minutes off the heat.

Pour out the hot water from the teapot just before adding the herbs. Into the warmed pot, measure 1 tablespoon of dried herb blend for every cup of water. Add 1 extra tablespoon "for the pot." Pour the boiled water over herbs, replace the teapot lid, and let steep for 3 to 5 minutes or until fragrant. Pour tea through a strainer into cups.

Herbed Soft Cheese

Soft cheese is often combined with herbs, as much for the herbs' preservative qualities as for their flavor. This cheese is adapted (with permission) from a recipe by Kathy Kinghorn, a garden volunteer who served it at a reception in the Minnesota Landscape Arboretum one year when I was privileged to speak at an herb event. To this day, when I make this cheese, it takes me right back to a sun-filled terrace at the Minnesota Landscape Arboretum and I am reminded of the blessings of having garden/herb friends.

It is light and so incredibly delicious, you might want to double the recipe and serve it at your own garden soirées. Keep utensils and countertops scrupulously clean and keep the cheese chilled after it is made. It will keep for up to three days in the refrigerator. This method uses no acid to accelerate the separation of curds from whey, so it must stand at room temperature for two days. If you add 2 tablespoons of freshly squeezed lemon juice to the warm cream in step 1, the curds will separate out in less than an hour and the taste will be slightly fresher.

You can omit the garlic, but it adds such a subtle flavor, it really adds to the flavor. Use ¼ cup of one green herb, mix two or more herbs with the chamomile, or omit the chamomile and use ¼ cup fresh chopped herbs. It is worth experimenting to find your favorite combination. Try serving it with the Chamomile Syrup (facing page).

Makes 1 cup soft herb cheese

4 cups half and half cream
   (10% butterfat)
2 tablespoons dried buttermilk
2 cloves garlic
2 tablespoons crushed dried
   chamomile

2 tablespoons chopped fresh herbs (sage,
   thyme, rosemary, French tarragon)
1 teaspoon sea salt
Fresh herb sprigs and/or flowers for
   garnish, optional
Cheesecloth

1. In a heavy saucepan, scald the cream: bring it almost to a boil. Remove from heat when bubbles start to form at the edges around the inside of the pan. Set aside on a cooling rack to cool to lukewarm (90–100°F).

2. Meanwhile, tie the garlic cloves in a large square of cheesecloth and smash with a rolling pin. Stir buttermilk into the cooled cream and suspend the garlic cheesecloth from the handle of the saucepan so that it is immersed in the cream. Cover the pan with a tea towel and set aside to stand at room temperature for 48 hours or until soft curds form. The whey will be clear as it separates from the cream—discard or use it as the liquid in baked goods or soup. (It will keep in the refrigerator for up to 3 days.)

3. Line a strainer with several layers of cheesecloth and place over a large bowl. Remove and discard garlic. Pour curds into the lined strainer and set aside to drain for one hour.

4. Spoon soft curds into a bowl and add chamomile, herbs, and salt. Reline a strainer with 2 fresh layers of cheesecloth and set over a bowl. Spoon herbed cheese into the strainer. Cover with plastic wrap and set aside in the refrigerator to drain and chill. Chill overnight or for 2 days—the longer the curds drain, the firmer the cheese will be. Turn out onto a platter, and garnish with fresh herb sprigs and flowers.

CHAMOMILE SYRUP

Serve this herbed syrup drizzled over the Herbed Soft Cheese. It is delicious in cocktails, over ice cream or pancakes, or with fresh fruit.

Makes 3 cups

3 cups water

2 cups sugar

3 tablespoons crushed or powdered dried chamomile

3 to 4 drops chamomile essential oil, optional (see Caution, page 91)

In a saucepan, bring the water to a simmer over medium-high heat. Stir in the sugar and chamomile and simmer, stirring frequently for 5 to 7 minutes to thicken slightly. Remove from heat and stir in essential oil if using. Store in a lidded jar in the refrigerator for up to 2 weeks.

Chamomile Beurre Blanc

Makes 3/4 cup

5 chamomile tea bags or ¼ cup
dried chamomile, crushed or
powdered
¾ cup boiled water
1 tablespoon freshly squeezed
lemon juice
¾ cup chilled unsalted butter, cut
into pieces

NOTE: Serve with vegetables,
fish, chicken, or egg dishes, or as
a fragrant topping for scones or
other baked goods.

1. Cut off the tops of the tea bags and empty
the chamomile into a teapot. Add the boiled
water, stir, cover with the lid, and set aside for
5 minutes to steep.

2. Strain chamomile tea through a fine mesh
metal strainer into a saucepan. Add lemon
juice and bring to a gentle boil. Reduce heat
to medium and add butter, a piece at a time,
whisking constantly to incorporate before
adding the next piece. Whisk until the
mixture is emulsified into a smooth sauce.

Raisin and Chamomile Scones

Makes 12 to 14 scones

2 cups all-purpose flour
1 tablespoon powdered chamomile
or crushed dried chamomile
1 teaspoon baking powder
½ teaspoon baking soda
Pinch of salt
¼ cup cool extra-virgin coconut oil
or chilled vegetable shortening
⅓ cup golden raisins
¼ cup milk
¼ cup strong chamomile tea,
strained and cooled
1 large egg, beaten
¾ cup Chamomile Beurre Blanc,
optional

1. Preheat oven to 450°F. Position an oven rack
in the top third of the oven.

2. In a large bowl, combine flour, chamomile,
baking powder, baking soda, and salt. Whisk
well to combine. Using a pastry blender or
two knives, cut the coconut oil into the flour
mixture until it is the size of peas. Toss the
raisins with the flour mixture.

3. In a measuring cup, combine milk and
chamomile tea. Slowly stir the liquid into the
flour mixture, stirring with a fork until a soft
dough forms.

4. On a lightly floured surface, knead the dough gently with floured fingertips to form a smooth ball of dough. Roll the dough out to ¼ inch thick. Using a 2-inch cookie cutter, cut round shapes out of the dough and place on an ungreased baking sheet. Lightly brush the tops with beaten egg.

5. Bake on the top shelf in preheated oven for 7 to 10 minutes or until lightly browned. Remove to a cooling rack. Store in an airtight container for up to 3 days. Serve with Chamomile Beurre Blanc if desired.

Chamomile Cooler

Makes 2 drinks

2 chamomile tea bags or 2 tablespoons dried chamomile flowers
1 cup boiled water
1 cup plain Greek-style yogurt
¾ cup fresh sliced strawberries or blueberries
2 tablespoons plain or herbed honey

1. In a teapot, pour hot water over chamomile. Cover and set aside for 10 minutes to steep. Remove and discard tea bags or strain tea made from loose chamomile into a small jug or bowl. Cover and chill chamomile tea in the refrigerator.

2. In a blender container, combine yogurt, berries, and honey. Blend for 30 seconds or until smooth. Add chamomile tea and blend for 10 seconds or until combined. Serve over ice.

Chervil

Anthriscus cerefolium

Chervil, whose tender tops are never wanting from our sallets.

—John Evelyn, *Acetaria: A Discourse of Sallets*, 1699

Native to Asia and Eastern Europe, chervil has been grown and used for a very long time, mostly for food, but also for medicine. Indeed, first-century nobleman Pliny (23–79 CE) held that the seed in vinegar stops hiccups and, not long after, Marcus Gavius Apicius, a Roman epicure who lived at the time of the emperor Tiberius, included a green chervil sauce in his *De Re Coquinaria* (The Art of Cooking), perhaps the oldest surviving collection of recipes— compiled in the late fourth or early fifth century under its current name.

Around 1640, John Parkinson advised that chervil leaves included in "a sallet gives a marvelous relish to the rest" and he said of the seeds, "some recommend the green seeds sliced and put in a sallet of herbs and eaten with vinegar and oil, to comfort a cold stomach of the aged." While chervil has few medicinal uses today, it is traditionally used as part of the well-known French fines herbes blend, and its delicate flavor makes it suitable for many culinary uses both savory and sweet.

FLAVOR

Chervil has a delicate, mild parsley-green taste with subtle hints of anise and caraway.

PARTS TO USE

The leaves and flowers of chervil are most widely used, but the roots have been boiled and eaten as a vegetable in the past.

CULINARY USES

French cooks combine chervil with chives, parsley, and French tarragon for their classic Fines Herbes Blend (page 62). Fresh whole or chopped leaves can be used liberally in raw fruit or vegetable salads. On its own, chervil complements egg, milk, cheese, and seafood dishes. It can also be used in soups made with light broth or bland vegetables such as potatoes. Its mild flavor makes it a good choice for vinaigrettes and cream sauces. It pairs particularly well with spring peas, leeks, carrots, potatoes, strawberries, and asparagus. Always add chervil at the very end of cooking. The dainty, fern-like leaves make beautiful garnishes, especially for desserts.

Chervil pops up and enjoys a sunny spot at the entrance to the tool shed in the beautiful herb and vegetable gardens of Lori and Dave Schaeffer, Douglassville, Pennsylvania.

♥ HEALTH BENEFITS

Chervil juice was once taken as a tonic for the blood; but without scientific research, it is not thought to be an important medicinal herb.

GROWING CHERVIL

Chervil is easy to grow from seed and should be planted in fertile, moist, well-drained soil. It prefers full sun in winter or part shade in late spring or fall (it does not fare well in the heat of summer) in the northern hemisphere. It can also be planted under taller plants. Choose the location carefully because chervil, with its long taproot, does not transplant well. Press fresh seeds into the soil about 12 inches apart and keep moist until they sprout. Chervil prefers cooler weather, so in cold climates, fall sowings or self-sowings from earlier plantings often survive the winter to yield early spring crops. In warm climates, fall and winter sowings do well. At its best in June, this early annual reseeds quickly after flowering, so harvest chervil when the plants are about 4 inches high to delay flowering. Plant it again in late summer for another crop in the fall. Cutting off the flowers prolongs the life of the plant, but a few heads should be left to set seed for the next year.

Because it only ever grows to a height of 2 feet maximum, and usually to 1 foot, with its lacy, fern-like leaves and dainty white flowers, it is beautiful around taller-growing plants such as angelica, elecampane, and lovage.

A FRESH AND MILD HERB PRIMER

If you are discovering herbs and wish to start incorporating their fragrance and flavor in recipes, my advice is to start with clean, fresh-tasting, and mild herbs. The herbs in this group are easily blended with fruit, vegetables, mild cheese, and dairy dishes along with other herbs, and it's hard to overuse them, so experimenting is fun and yields great results. (For tips on using strong and spicy herbs, see page 142.)

There are very few rules to enjoying herbs and I encourage you to jump right in and have fun learning about these amazing plants, but there are some tips I can share:

* Always, if possible, use *fresh* herbs, especially when using mild herbs, because they will deliver the pure essence of the herb.

* Don't be timid with the fresh and mild herbs; use them in handfuls, *not* the stingy ½ to 1 teaspoon still called for in many recipes. Taste and add more until you can detect the subtle effect of the herbs in the dish, and always trust your own palate.

* Add woody and aromatic herbs anytime during cooking; all other herbs, especially fresh and mild herbs, should be added in the last few seconds of cooking because their essential oils are soon lost when heated.

* The herbs in this group help to bring out the flavors of other herbs, and they make good balancing herbs for the stronger, more aromatic herbs.

* Use these fresh and mild herbs in brothy soups and light vinaigrette dressings; toss with abandon into raw salads and with spring leeks, asparagus, and peas; their subtle flavors complement poultry, mild fish (such as tilapia and perch), and seafood; add to omelets, quiches, and other egg dishes; use in cream and mild cheese dips, sauces, and desserts; add their flowers to beverages and garnish all your summer foods with their leaves, sprigs, and flowers.

BORAGE The flowers add a mild, cool, and fresh cucumber taste to dishes. Use the brilliant star-shaped flowers in drinks and as a garnish.

CHERVIL The leaves and flowers have a subtle, green-licorice-caraway flavor. Cut before flowering and use the leaves in every spring dish you make.

LEMON BALM With its light lemon fragrance and flavor, lemon balm can enhance savory and dessert dishes. You can also use the leaves in teas.

MARJORAM Its sweet and milder oregano flavor earns marjoram a place in this group of herbs.

PARSLEY Spikes of lemon, mint, and spice combine to give parsley a light, peppery taste.

PURSLANE The fleshy leaves and stems have a refreshing, tangy citrus flavor and juicy texture. Chop and mix with yogurt for an easy dip or sauce for grilled lamb or fish.

SALAD BURNET (*Sanguisorba minor*) A mild and slightly nutty cucumber taste to the leaves makes salad burnet a natural for yogurt and mild cheeses.

SUMMER SAVORY Milder and less peppery than winter savory, summer savory has subtle thyme, mint, and marjoram tones.

Fines Herbes

Unlike French Bouquet Garni (page 21), the herb blend known as fines herbes is a loose mixture (not bundled), and the herbs that comprise it are well defined and not usually substituted. Chervil is central to fines herbes, adding a sweet, balancing quality to the chives, parsley, and French tarragon that make up the rest of the blend.

Fresh herbs are essential. I have stored the blend for a few weeks with limited success—the herbs will fade upon drying and the flavor will weaken; but if not tightly packed, the blend will still be useable for up to 1 month. However, it is best if made with fresh herbs (not dried) and used immediately or within two or three days. You can halve or double this recipe as needed.

This blend of fresh spring and early summer herbs is exceptional on asparagus, leeks, artichokes, peas, and new potatoes. It flavors light soups, dressings, and salads as well as dips and glazes and savory egg dishes; a pinch brightens desserts and puddings.

Makes a scant cup

¼ cup chopped fresh chervil
¼ cup chopped fresh parsley
¼ cup chopped fresh chives
2 tablespoons chopped fresh French tarragon
4-inch square of cheesecloth

In a bowl, combine chervil, parsley, chives, and French tarragon. Transfer to a jar, label, and cover loosely with cheesecloth. Use immediately or store in a cool, dark place for up to 2 weeks.

Fines Herbes Pesto

Makes 2 cups

¼ cup sesame seeds

3 tablespoons crumbled feta
cheese

½ cup chopped fresh chervil

½ cup chopped fresh chives

½ cup chopped fresh parsley

¼ cup chopped fresh French
tarragon

½ teaspoons sea salt

About ½ cup extra-virgin
grapeseed oil (see note)

NOTE: The subtle flavor of
chervil is best fresh, and it fades
considerably on drying; so to
preserve it, mix chopped fresh
chervil with butter and freeze,
or use this pesto to preserve the
delicate spring fines herbes well
after the season is past. Use an
extra-virgin but light-tasting oil
such as grapeseed or hemp oil
in order to let the fines herbes
shine. Pesto keeps for up to three
weeks in the refrigerator, but you
can double or triple the recipe
and freeze extra in zip-top freezer
bags for up to four months.

1. In the bowl of a food processor, pulse sesame
   seeds and feta for 10 seconds to combine. Add
   chervil, chives, parsley, French tarragon, and
   salt and pulse 3 or 4 times to combine.

2. With the machine running, add oil through
   the opening in the lid in a slow, steady stream,
   stopping to scrape down the sides of the bowl
   once. Continue to process and add oil until the
   pesto reaches the desired consistency. As you
   add more oil, the pesto will progress from a
   chopped, dry sauce to a smooth, creamy one.

Apricot and Anise Frangipane Tart

This recipe has been adapted with permission from Charmian Christie (themessybaker.com), author of *The Messy Baker* (HarperCollins).

Makes one 10-inch tart

Pastry dough, enough to line a
    10-inch tart pan
6 ounces dark chocolate
½ cup ground almonds
½ cup sugar
2 eggs, divided
2 teaspoons pure vanilla, divided
¾ cup heavy whipping cream
    (36% butterfat)
¼ cup chopped fresh chervil
1½ cups raspberries, fresh or
    frozen
1 cup diced apricots or peaches,
    fresh or frozen, drained
Several fresh chervil fronds for
    garnish, optional

1. Preheat oven to 400°F.

2. Roll pastry dough to ¼ inch thick and press into a 10-inch tart pan. Set aside in the refrigerator until needed.

3. Shave the chocolate into a bowl and set aside.

4. **TO MAKE THE FRANGIPANE:** Using a blender or food processor, blend almonds, sugar, 1 egg, and 1 teaspoon vanilla until they form a paste.

5. **TO MAKE THE CUSTARD:** In a small bowl, whisk together whipping cream, remaining egg, chervil, and remaining vanilla.

6. **TO ASSEMBLE THE TART:** sprinkle chocolate over the bottom of the chilled crust. Drizzle frangipane over the chocolate layer. Spread raspberries and apricots on top, distributing them evenly over the frangipane. Pour custard over the dish.

7. Place the tart pan in the center of the preheated oven and bake for 10 minutes. Reduce the heat to 350°F and bake for 45 minutes or until the pie is golden and set.

8. Set aside on a cooling rack to cool thoroughly before serving. Serve each slice on top of a chervil frond if using.

Chervil Lemon Cream Sauce

I tend to make this light and easy sauce in the spring to complement new peas, potatoes, and asparagus. It's positively divine with poached or smoked fish and chicken or as a hollandaise substitute over poached eggs.

Makes a scant 1½ cups

3 tablespoons freshly squeezed lemon juice

1 tablespoon finely grated lemon zest

¼ cup chicken or vegetable broth

1 cup heavy whipping cream (36% butterfat)

Sea salt to taste

¼ cup finely chopped fresh chervil

In a saucepan, combine lemon juice, lemon zest, and broth. Bring to a slow simmer over medium heat. Slowly whisk in cream and gently simmer for 10 minutes. Remove from heat, add salt to taste, and stir in chervil.

Chile Peppers

Capsicum species

It [cayenne] is no doubt the most powerful stimulant known;
its power is entirely congenial to nature, being powerful in raising and
maintaining heat, on which life depends . . . I consider it essentially a
benefit, for its effect on the glands causes the saliva to flow freely
and leaves the mouth clean and moist.

—Samuel Thompson, herbalist, 1832

Why do Chileheads brave the searing, red-hot flames of chile peppers? It's because *capsaicin* irritates the pain receptors on the tongue, which ignite the pain center in the brain, triggering a release of morphine-like natural painkillers—endorphins. Endophins try to douse the fire by setting off a sense of well-being throughout the body, and we ride the wave of euphoria through to dessert.

But that's not the only reason people are all fired up over chiles. In addition to their distinctive aroma and taste, a quarter cup of the fresh, diced scorching orbs yields 4,031 IUs of vitamin A, which becomes even more concentrated as the pod turns red and dries. Simply eating one teaspoon of red chili sauce supplies the body with the recommended dietary allowance for vitamin A.

The same quarter cup of chopped fresh chile pepper delivers 91 milligrams of vitamin C (as compared to 66 milligrams in one orange). And while the vitamin C diminishes by more than half in the dried red pods, the effect is still more than a flash in the pan.

Factor in the medicinal tonic, warming, and stimulating, circulatory, mucus-expelling properties, and all in all, using chile peppers to ignite the taste and heat of foods is a very good thing for one's overall health.

But not all chile peppers are hot. Sweet (or bell) peppers do not produce capsaicin, but they still pack a nutritional punch with high levels of vitamin C and vitamin A. Peppers are native to Mexico, Central, and South America and are members of the nightshade family of plants and, as such, are relatives of potatoes, tomatoes, and eggplant.

Purple, yellow, red, orange, and chocolate-colored bell peppers sit on display at the Farmers' Market, Terminal Building, San Francisco, California.

FLAVOR

Depending on the variety, chile flavors may be fruity, floral, smoky, nutty, tobacco, or licorice and their level of heat ranges from sweet, mild, and slightly peppery (generally *C. annuum*) to fiery hot (usually *C. frutescens*) or incendiary (*C. chinense*).

PARTS TO USE

The fruit or pepper pods of chiles are used.

CULINARY USES

Fresh chiles can be served raw in salads or as a topping for dishes, or they can be cooked in soups, bean or lentil stews, or casseroles. Sweet or hot chiles can be stuffed with cheese, grains, mild vegetables, and herbs and served as appetizers, salads, or main-dish accompaniments.

To preserve them, chiles are dried, pickled, or smoked. Dried chile peppers are ground to a powder for adding heat to foods, especially Mexican, Indian, Asian, and African dishes and drinks. Flakes (or seeds) can be used as a condiment and fresh or dried threads (thinly cut strips) as a garnish.

One whole, fresh, or dried hot Mexican or Poblano chile pepper with its ribs and seeds removed will be hot enough for a recipe serving 2 to 4 people. If using dried, ground chile powder, a pinch and up to ¼ teaspoon is sufficient for 2 to 4 servings. Start with small amounts, taste, and add more if required.

♥ HEALTH BENEFITS

Chiles are an excellent source of the antioxidant vitamins A and C. The hot, pungent flavor comes from capsaicin, which is found in varying degrees of intensity in the seeds, white fleshy parts, and skin. Capsaicin acts as a digestive stimulant and tonic and it purifies the blood and promotes fluid (mucus) elimination and sweating.

Topical capsicum liniment, ointment, or cream preparations are used to ease painful arm, shoulder, and spine muscle spasms, and to treat arthritis, rheumatism, neuralgia, lumbago, and chilblains.

CAUTION: The active components that fire up chiles are the *capsaicinoids*, which are concentrated in the placenta (the thin white membrane surrounding a spongy white center found in the middle of the pepper, where the seeds are attached). According to Arthur O. Tucker and Thomas DeBaggio in *The Encyclopedia of Herbs*, "The pure seeds themselves contain none or up to 10 percent of the total capsaicinoids; the heat on the seeds primarily arises from contamination from the placenta."

These extremely irritating components transfer easily not only to the seeds, but also to your hands, the knife, the cutting surface, and anywhere you touch with your hands, such as your eyes or lips. When harvesting, handling, and cooking hot chiles, use disposable gloves and avoid touching your face and eyes. After handling, wash hands, knives, and countertops thoroughly in hot, soapy water and rinse well.

GROWING CHILE PEPPERS

Peppers require a long growing season and enjoy well-drained, mulched soil in full sun except in the South and Southwest, where partial shade protects the tender pods from burning. They should be started early indoors from seed. Transplant seedlings after the soil has reached 65°F and the threat of frost has passed.

Harissa

A key flavoring and condiment in Middle Eastern and North African cuisine, harissa is never far from a Moroccan, Libyan, Algerian, Turkish, or Tunisian table. In fact, it is the go-to seasoning for many cooks in the region. Often it is added during cooking of soups, stews, and curry dishes or tagines. It is also used with meatballs, or rubbed into kebabs and other meats before grilling. The main ingredient is hot chile peppers, and while it is easy to make from fresh or dried hot chiles, harissa is widely available in cans or tubes or freshly prepared in tubs in Middle Eastern or North African markets.

Dairy products (especially yogurt) and starchy foods such as pastas and couscous are often paired with harissa and other hot chile dishes to help dial down the heat.

Makes ½ cup

12 cayenne, serrano, or jalapeño chile peppers, fresh or dried
¾ cup boiled water, for dried chiles
1 tablespoon cumin seeds
2 teaspoons coriander seeds
1 teaspoon fennel seeds
1 piece (2 inches) cinnamon, crushed
½ teaspoon fenugreek seeds, optional
2 cloves garlic
½ teaspoon sea salt
½ cup extra-virgin olive oil

1. Trim and discard the stems and seeds from the chiles. Using kitchen scissors, cut the chiles crosswise into thin strips into a bowl. If using dried chiles, pour water over and soak for 30 minutes or until softened.

2. Meanwhile, in a small, heavy pan or spice wok, dry-fry the cumin, coriander, fennel, cinnamon, and fenugreek seeds (if using) over medium heat, for 3 minutes or until fragrant and light brown. Set aside to cool.

3. Using a food processor or blender, chop the garlic with the salt. If using dried chiles, drain them, discarding or reserving the soaking water for another use. Add the chiles to the garlic in the bowl of the food processor and process until smooth. Add the toasted spices and process to incorporate them into the mixture.

4. With motor running, gradually drizzle in the oil through the opening in the lid, processing the mixture until the sauce is well blended to the consistency of mayonnaise.

A HOT AND SWEET CHILE PRIMER

HOT CHILE VARIETIES

There are five cultivated species of the *Capsicum* genus and hundreds of varieties with a wide range of potency and heat. Hot chiles can be found among any of the following species: *C. annuum*, *C. baccatum*, *C. chinense*, *C. frutescens*, or *C. pubescens*.

The Scoville scale is a standard measure of the heat that is generated by the capsaicin in a chile pepper. The number of Scoville heat units (SHU) ranges from zero—the rating for a sweet red bell pepper—to more than 200,000 for a habanero and more than a million for new varieties of hot chiles. The rating reflects the number of times the capsaicin in a chile pepper would have to be diluted before being undetected. Here are just some of the varieties of hot chile peppers, listed from mild to hot.

NEW MEXICAN (*C. annuum* 'New Mexican') Formerly called Anaheim, these long, green, mild chiles are available fresh, canned, and roasted. They are often left on the bush to turn red. Mild and tingly hot (around 1,000 units on the Scoville scale), they are widely used in many classic Mexican dishes. They are a good choice for novice hot chile users.

NEW MEXICAN

POBLANO (*C. a.* 'Poblano') Poblano is the name of the fresh version of this broad, heart-shaped flat pepper, the widest of all hot chiles. *Poblano* means "people" in Spanish, and these chiles are relatively mild, so they make a great jumping-off point for training your palate to accept some heat. They are the most commonly used variety in Mexico. Poblanos acquire a nutty taste and raisin-like appearance when dried; in the dried form, they're called *ancho*. The terms *mulato* (brown) and *negro* (black) refer to different varieties of poblano chile.

POBLANO

JALAPEÑO

JALAPEÑO (*C. a.* 'Jalapeño') At between 2,000 and 8,000 on the Scoville heat unit scale, jalapeño peppers lend a meaty texture and rich, mildly hot flavor to dishes. Their thick flesh makes them an excellent roasting chile. They are called chipotles when smoked and dried.

SERRANO

SERRANO (*C. a.* 'Serrano') Meaning "from the mountains" in Spanish, serrano chiles are more flavorful than jalapeño, and they are often pickled or used fresh in salsa, stews, and moles.

CAYENNE (*C. a.* 'Cayenne') It is grown commercially in New Mexico, Africa, India, Japan, and Mexico. The most common form of cayenne is dried (powdered or flakes), and herbalists use this chile pepper most in preparations. Referred to as a *crisis herb* by herbalists, cayenne is used for treating inflammation. Its Scoville measure is 25,000 to 50,000.

CAYENNE

CHERRY BOMB (*C. a.* 'Cherry Bomb') They may look like small round red (or green) bell peppers, but cherry bomb peppers are extremely hot, between 100,000 and 250,000 on the Scoville heat index.

CHERRY BOMB

THAI HOT (*C. a.* 'Thai Hot') Grown and used in Thailand and throughout Asia, they are hot, but still only half as hot as habanero.

THAI HOT

HABANERO (*C. chinense* 'Habanero') Habanero chiles (also known as Scotch Bonnet) are rated at between 200,000 and 300,000 Scoville units. They really pack a punch in hot pepper sauce and Caribbean jerk sauces, where they impart a unique fruity, apricot-like flavor.

HABANERO

TRINIDAD CONGO (*C. c.* 'Trinidad Congo') This very hot habanero-type pepper is round and deeply ribbed.

TRINIDAD CONGO

GHOST (*C. c.* 'Bhut Jolokia') Ghost peppers (also known as *C. c.* 'Naga Jolokia') have a Scoville heat index rating of more than 1,000,000. This pepper, shown dried, is considered to share the spotlight with Naga Morich (*C. c.* 'Naga Morich') and a few other habanero-type varieties as one of the hottest peppers in the world. Too hot for me, just a tiny piece would be enough to set off a Three-Alarm Barbecue Sauce.

GHOST

SWEET CHILE VARIETIES (*CAPSICUM ANNUUM*)

Sweet peppers, also referred to as bell peppers, rank zero on the Scoville heat index because they are the only *Capsicums* that do not produce capsaicin.

Sweet peppers may be round and shaped like a bell or they may be long and thin.

All *Capsicum* pods start out green and change color as the chlorophyll deteriorates and they ripen to red, yellow, orange, purple, brown, or even white. As the pods mature, levels of vitamin C may double, and sugars as well as anthocyanins become concentrated, which accounts for the flavor difference from green to red. Some varieties of sweet bell peppers follow.

BANANA SWEET Long, thin banana-like peppers start out light yellow and mature to crimson red. Their flavor is mild and they are often pickled or chopped for salads. Don't confuse the sweet banana pepper with the hot banana pepper, which rates between 5,000 to 10,000 SHU.

BANANA SWEET

BISCAYNE A cylindrical shape makes Biscayne peppers easy to cut into strips for frying and for including in salads and cooked dishes.

BISCAYNE

CARMEN A rich, sweet, fruity flavor and elongated shape makes this a good roasting pepper.

CARMEN

MINI BELL CHOCOLATE The word *Chocolate* used in this name refers to the ripened color only, not the taste of these peppers. They are very sweet and great raw on salads and vegetable platters or stuffed with salad and served as an appetizer. The color dissipates when the peppers are cooked.

MINI BELL CHOCOLATE

MINI RED BELL The sweet-tasting thick red flesh makes these tiny peppers excellent snacks or a stunning appetizer when stuffed with vegetable or seafood salad.

MINI RED BELL

PURPLE The purple varieties range in color from light lavender to black-purple in intensity. Their sweet, fruity flavor makes them a good addition to a raw vegetable platter.

PURPLE

● PAPRIKA

Paprika is a common flavoring blend of dried and ground sweet *Capsicum annuum* peppers. While there may be several different types of peppers used in the blend, paprika is usually made from sweet peppers. Middle Eastern paprika blends may be hot. If the peppers are exposed to smoke during the drying process, the flavor of the resulting paprika will have a mild or strong smokiness to the taste. Use paprika to add flavor and color to dishes, such as soups, casseroles, and vegetables, and use as a garnish sprinkled over potato, egg, or tuna salad.

In some European countries, notably Holland, sweet peppers are called "paprika."

CHILE VS. CHILI

The Aztecs used the word *chil* in their native language of Nahuatl to describe red peppers as well as the color red. The original Spanish and the current Mexican word for pepper is *chile* (from that Nahuatl word), and I prefer to use *chile* as the spelling for the plant and the pod.

Chili (corruption, *chilli*) refers to an all-bean or bean- and meat-dish (*Chili con Carne*) or to a type of sweet hot sauce used as a condiment (chili sauce). However, you would not be altogether incorrect in using *chili* as the spelling of the plant or pod, since it is the Anglicized version of *chile*. But in this book chile peppers are spelled with an *e*, not an *i*.

Pulled Chicken and Beans

Makes 6 to 8 servings

2 tablespoons extra-virgin olive oil

1 onion, chopped

1 poblano or bell pepper, chopped

4 cloves garlic, finely chopped

1 tablespoon ground cumin

1 can (28 ounces) diced tomatoes
  and juices

2 cups chicken broth

4 boneless, skinless chicken breasts

2 cups cooked or 1 can (15 ounces)
  navy beans, drained and rinsed

2 cups Roasted Red Pepper slices
  (page 76) or canned

¼ cup chopped fresh cilantro or
  parsley

1 tablespoon freshly squeezed
  lime juice

Pinch to ½ teaspoon cayenne
  chile powder, or to taste

Sea salt and pepper

1. In a soup pot, heat oil over medium heat. Sauté onion for 5 minutes. Add pepper, garlic, and cumin. Cook, stirring frequently, for 3 minutes or until vegetables are soft.

2. Add tomatoes and their juice and broth and bring to a boil. Add chicken breasts, cover, reduce heat to medium-low, and simmer for 20 minutes or until a thermometer inserted into the meatiest part of a chicken breast registers 165°F. Lift out breasts and pull the meat apart using 2 forks, or slice very thinly. Return the pulled chicken to the pot.

3. Add beans, red pepper slices, cilantro, lime juice, and chile powder. Bring to a simmer to heat through. Season to taste with salt and pepper.

Grilled Vegetables with Peppers

Makes 4 servings

2 zucchini squash, cut into
    1-inch cubes
2 onions, quartered
12 mushrooms
1 Japanese eggplant, cut into
    1-inch cubes
2 pears, quartered
8 cloves garlic
Extra-virgin olive oil
2 cups Roasted Red Pepper slices
    (page 76)
2 tablespoons balsamic vinegar
Sea salt and pepper

1. Preheat the barbecue grill to high.

2. Thread zucchini, onions, mushrooms, and eggplant onto separate metal skewers. Alternately thread pear quarters and garlic onto a metal skewer. Brush vegetables with oil.

3. In a large bowl, combine red pepper slices and vinegar and set aside.

4. Grill zucchini and onions for 2 minutes, flip over and add pear (with garlic), mushroom, and eggplant skewers to the grill. Grill vegetables, turning the skewers at regular intervals, for 2 to 3 minutes or until tender and slightly charred. Remove each skewer from the grill as the vegetables finish cooking and, using a kitchen knife, slide vegetables from the skewer into the bowl with the pepper mixture.

5. When all the vegetables are removed to the bowl, toss and season to taste with salt and pepper. Serve hot or at room temperature.

Roasted Peppers

Roasted peppers are divine. In the fall, when they are in abundance, I buy them at the farmers market by the green garbage bag. If you can find a thick-fleshed variety, make sure to tell the farmer that you want the same variety next year, because the thicker the flesh, the better the roasted pepper. Have a bottle of good-quality extra-virgin olive oil on hand and for added flavor, fresh chiffonade basil (page 46) by the handful for every dozen peppers.

Red peppers, hot or sweet
Extra-virgin olive oil
Fresh basil leaves, chopped or cut
    into chiffonade
Balsamic vinegar
Coarse salt

1. Cut the peppers in half and seed them. Arrange in one layer, cut side up on the grill, and grill until charred. Transfer to a bowl and cover with a towel or a lid. Set aside to cool. Repeat this step until all the peppers are grilled.

2. Using a paring knife, pull the skin off grilled peppers and discard. Slice peppers into ½ inch-wide strips and transfer to a bowl. When all of the peppers are sliced, drizzle with olive oil and toss with basil and vinegar. Sprinkle with salt.

3. Transfer to jars, cap, label, and store in the refrigerator for up to 3 weeks, or transfer to freezer bags, seal, label, and freeze for up to 3 months.

Roasted Corn Salsa

Makes 3 cups

2 ears corn, kernels removed, or
    1 can (12 ounces) corn kernels,
    drained
2 carrots, diced
½ poblano chile or red bell pepper,
    diced
2 tablespoons extra-virgin olive oil
1 avocado
3 tablespoons freshly squeezed
    lemon juice
2 green onions, thinly sliced
¼ cup chopped fresh cilantro
    or parsley
1 tablespoon fresh thyme
½ teaspoon sea salt

1. Preheat oven to 400°F.

2. On a rimmed baking sheet, combine corn, carrots, and pepper. Spread out in one layer. Drizzle with oil and roast in preheated oven for 35 minutes or until carrots are tender when pierced with a knife. The corn and red pepper may be a bit charred at the edges. Set aside to cool.

3. Peel and dice the avocado into a bowl. Add lemon juice and toss. Add roasted vegetables, green onions, cilantro, and thyme and toss well to combine. Add salt to taste.

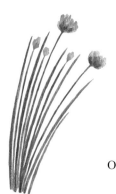

Chives

Allium schoenoprasum

Once we have grown chives, we shall never like to be without them.

—Frances A. Bardwell, *The Herb Garden*, 1930

I n her book *Herbs*, Mary Forsell writes, "When the Venetian traveller Marco Polo first encountered chives on an extended journey to China in the late thirteenth century, they had already been a culinary staple of life there for at least three thousand years." And we know from herbals that chives were used as a vegetable for the pot, not daintily snipped to crown a soup or to delicately flavor an egg dish as they often are today.

The Flemish physician and botanist Rembert Dodoens (1517–1585) used the old French name, *Petit poureau*, to describe chives; and throughout the Middle Ages, this term, which means "rush-leek," was widely used. In fact, the Latin *schoenoprasm* comes from two Greek words: *schoinos* for "rush" and *prason* meaning "leek." From Maud Grieve, author of *A Modern Herbal*, we learn that John Parkinson (1567–1650)—himself author of two great monumental works on plants, *Paradisi in Sole Paradisus Terrestris* (1629) and *Theatrum Botanicum* (1640)—"mentions Chives as being cultivated in his garden, among other herbs." We have to assume that Dodoens had some influence on this great botanist and apothecary.

FLAVOR

The leaves and flowers of chives emit a faint onion aroma and have a nippy, slightly spicy onion flavor.

PARTS TO USE

The leaves and flowers of chives are used.

CULINARY USES

Chives are best used raw, and both the long, thinly tapered and hollow leaves and the delicate buds or fully opened flowers may be used to artfully garnish plates. They can be snipped using scissors into soups, salads, sauces, and all other dishes. When chives are added to cooked dishes for texture, color, and mild onion taste, it is always at the very end of cooking. Chives are one of the ingredients in Fines Herbes blend (page 62).

A bright clump of chives along the border entrance greets visitors to the tidal island castle on Saint Michael's Mount, near Penzance in Cornwall, England.

♥ HEALTH BENEFITS

Chives are used in Chinese medicine to promote sweating and male fertility. The active components of chives are *alkyl sulfides* and *alkyl sulfoxides*, which are weaker in chives than they are in garlic but are still thought to be beneficial to circulation and have some diuretic and antiseptic properties. Chives are also high in iron and calcium as well as antioxidants (vitamins A and C, kaempferol, and quercetin).

GROWING CHIVES

An easy perennial to grow, chives prefer sun but will survive in light partial shade. They need to be watered well to feed the shallow-growing bulbs. Once established, one compact clump may be separated over and over, so starting with one plant is a good idea. They self-seed easily and because the flowers may be used in vinegars and oils and other summer dishes, they can be harvested in the bud and just-opened stage to keep the plants from invading.

GARLIC CHIVES (*A. tuberosum*) Also known as Chinese chives, garlic chives are large-blossomed, beautiful herbs that are native to central and northern Asia. With wide, flat leaves and white, star-like flowers, garlic chives make a pretty addition to a border or herb garden. Like garlic scapes, the leaves and buds with their stems are eaten as a vegetable in Asian cuisine, finding their way into spring rolls and stir-fry dishes while the flower heads are battered and deep-fried. Their flavor is mildly garlic-onion, so they are perfect for omelets and other mild-flavored dishes.

MAUVE GARLIC CHIVES (*A. tuberosum*) Similar to the white-flowered garlic chives, this variety has large pink-mauve flowers and is just as beautiful. Use it in cooking as you would the white-flowered garlic chives or regular chives (*A. schoenoprasm*).

Herb-Infused Vinegar

Herb vinegars are one of the oldest herbal preparations, dating to a time even before the Middle Ages, when antibiotics, refrigeration, and greenhouse growing were unknown luxuries. Indeed, infusing wine or its counterpart—vinegar—with not only the flavors but also the healing attributes of various herbs was a significant tool in the ancient healer's medicine chest. Due to its acidic composition, which is proven to slow bacterial growth, vinegar is a preservative and so it provided a very simple way to concentrate and keep the medicinal constituents of fresh plants on a shelf over long periods. Using plain or herbed vinegar as an antibacterial and antiseptic wash was one of the key crisis responses to wounds.

Lavender and rosemary were important herbs in medieval vinegars, and during the plagues, looters were said to have employed a magic concoction called Four Thieves' Vinegar, thought to protect them while they plundered the houses of the victims of the Black Death. Accounts vary, but it is thought that garlic, rosemary, rue, sage, wormwood, mint, and lavender were central to the brew, and perhaps cinnamon, cloves, and nutmeg were added when available.

Even with the dramatic changes in medicines in modern times, there is still a place for infused vinegar in the kitchen. When fresh herbs are harvested at their growing peak and at midmorning, they offer valuable essential oils for flavoring and, as an added benefit, for assisting healing. I love chive vinegar in particular, because the lavender-pink flowers tint it, making it a beautiful as well as tasty culinary ingredient.

If you want to make your own herb-infused vinegars, start with naturally fermented vinegar from wine (champagne vinegar is perfect), fruit, berries, honey, molasses, cereal grains (malt vinegars), or coconut nectar preferably with at least 5 percent acidity. You can encourage leftover wine to turn to vinegar by adding some "mother" starter from natural vinegar. Never use the common and widely available white, chemically acidized vinegar—save it for washing windows. Apple cider and coconut vinegars can be very strong tasting and require a greater amount of herbs than the milder vinegars.

With the exception of thyme (too strong) and parsley (too green tasting), almost any aromatic herb—rosemary, sage, opal basil, rose, lemon verbena, lavender, chives—may be used.

To make herb-infused vinegar the traditional way, stuff (not too tightly) a wide-mouth jar with sprigs of a fresh herb (start with single herbs and then try a blend of two herbs) and pour vinegar into the jar, leaving a 1-inch headspace. Cap, label, and set in a sunny place for two weeks or up to one month. Strain into smaller jars, cap, label, and store in a cool, dark place indefinitely. The color from floral vinegars will fade, but the vinegar will still be viable.

There's also a quick-and-easy method that can be used just before a vinegar is needed and at the spur of the moment when herbs are at their peak. For every cup of tightly packed, coarsely chopped fresh herbs, you will need 1 cup champagne or other white wine vinegar. Combine the vinegar and herbs in a blender container and add a pinch of sea salt. Blend on high for about 30 seconds. Strain the vinegar through a fine-mesh strainer into a glass jar, pressing on the herbs to release as much flavor as possible. Taste and add more vinegar if needed. Use immediately or cap, label, and store in a cool, dark place.

BRIGHT PINK CHIVE VINEGAR

Cut the stems of the chive flowers at a length so that they will stand upright in the jar. Insert with the blossoms at the bottom of the jar. Pour vinegar over, leaving a 1-inch headspace. Loosely cap the jar and set it aside just until the color has infused the vinegar (the flowers will be white). Grasp the stems, squeeze the flower heads, and discard them. Insert a fresh batch of the same length, long-stemmed chive flowers upside down into the vinegar and set aside for up to two weeks. Remove and discard the flowers, strain the vinegar into smaller jars, cap, label, and store in a cool, dark place indefinitely. The color will fade over time, but the vinegar will still be viable.

WILD LEEKS (*ALLIUM TRICOCCUM*)

Wild leeks are native to and grow abundantly in deciduous forests in northeastern Canada and the United States. However, with the increasing numbers of chefs seeking to use local produce, their numbers are dwindling due to inappropriate and indiscriminate harvesting. Once the bulbs are dug up, those plants will never grow back. If you know of a cache of wild leeks and wish to dig some for a bright spring meal, be sure that the colony is well established and that you only gather less than one-fifth of the growth (and only on the edge of the colony), leaving almost all plants to reproduce and keep the species alive.

Should you happen to find wild leeks for sale at a farmers market, be sure to question the method of collection and only buy from growers, not wildcrafters, because these and other delightful herbs are fast becoming rare. It's one thing to wildcraft for one meal and quite a disturbing practice to collect enough to sell at a market.

The wild leeks in these photos and those used in the Couscous Leek and Pepper Loaf were gathered from a large colony very close to my home in southwestern Ontario. I am fairly certain that because I live more than an hour from an urban area, the wild leeks on my patch are safe from being exploited, but I still practice good harvesting techniques and I treat them like the delicacy they truly are by taking a tiny amount and only once a season.

What's in a name? Well, in the case of wild leeks, a lot of confusion. Our wild leek (*A. tricoccum*) is commonly called *ramp, ramson, wild onion, wild garlic, bear's garlic, wood garlic*; take your pick. Many of these names, especially *ramp*, are the same common names that are used for the wild leek (*A. ursinum*) that grows in many parts of Great Britain and Europe. That wild leek has a similar, slightly garlic taste but differs from the North American variety with a broader leaf and smaller flower.

To clean wild leeks, grasp the leek in one hand, close to the start of the bulb; pull the short, dirty outer layers of white skin back over the rootlets; snap off the root end along with most of the dirt, and discard; then wash bulbs and leaves in cool running water, drain, and pat dry.

CAUTION: Wild leeks look like and can easily be mistaken for another woodland plant, lily of the valley (*Convallaria majalis*), which is poisonous.

Couscous Leek and Pepper Loaf

Makes 1 loaf

6 whole wild or 3 whole domestic
  leeks, halved, with leaves for
  garnish

2 cups chicken broth

½ teaspoon sea salt

1½ cups couscous

3 tablespoons extra-virgin olive oil,
  divided

1 onion, chopped

4 cloves garlic, chopped

⅓ cup chopped wild or domestic
  leeks, white and light green
  parts

3 tablespoons chopped chives

1 tablespoon Curry Spice blend
  (page 104), or store-bought

2 teaspoons ground coriander

½ teaspoon red pepper flakes,
  optional

1 small zucchini, diced

8 ounces mushrooms, chopped

½ cup chopped Roasted Red Bell
  Pepper (page 76), or store-
  bought

1. Clean and trim the leeks. Line an 8-cup loaf
   tin with plastic wrap, letting it overhang on
   the long sides. Arrange 1 or 2 wild leek(s) or
   1 domestic leek half, trimmed to size, on the
   base of the tin; set aside in a cool place. Set
   aside remaining whole wild or halved domestic
   leeks for garnish later.

2. In a saucepan, bring broth to a boil over high
   heat. Remove from heat and stir in salt and
   couscous. Cover and let stand for 10 minutes.
   Fluff with a fork and transfer to a large bowl.

3. Meanwhile heat 2 tablespoons oil in a skillet over medium heat. Sauté the onion for 5 minutes. Add garlic, chopped leeks, chives, garam masala, coriander, and red pepper flakes if using. Cook, stirring frequently, for 1 minute. Add the remaining oil, zucchini, and mushrooms. Cook, stirring frequently, for 7 minutes, or until vegetables are soft. Set aside to cool.

4. Stir the onion-mushroom mixture and roasted pepper into the couscous. Cover and chill for an hour. Press the mixture into the prepared tin, pressing it in and around the leek on the bottom of the tin. Fold the plastic wrap over to cover.

5. Weigh down with food cans: Place a slightly smaller loaf pan on top of the plastic wrap over the loaf in the original pan. Place 2 full cans of food in the empty pan and chill overnight.

6. Serve hot or at room temperature.

Shallot, Onion, and Chive Tart

Makes one 9-inch tart

Pastry
1 cup all-purpose flour
Pinch of sea salt
¼ cup chilled butter, cut into
　　rough pieces
¼ cup firm extra-virgin coconut
　　oil or shortening, cut into
　　rough pieces

Filling
1 tablespoon extra-virgin
　　coconut oil or olive oil
1 tablespoon butter
8 shallots, thinly sliced
3 onions, thinly sliced
Sea salt
4 large eggs
2 large egg yolks
¾ cup heavy whipping cream
　　(36% butterfat)
1 tablespoon Dijon mustard
¼ cup chopped fresh chives

1. **TO MAKE THE PASTRY:** Combine flour, salt, butter, and oil in the bowl of a food processor. Pulse until the mixture resembles fine bread crumbs. With the motor running, slowly add 3 or 4 tablespoons very cold water, pulsing just until the dough comes together in clumps. Turn out the dough onto a lightly floured surface and gently press into a smooth ball. Wrap tightly with plastic wrap and set aside in the refrigerator while preparing the filling, about 30 minutes.

2. **TO START THE FILLING:** In a skillet, heat the oil and butter over medium-low heat. Add the shallots and onions. Cook, stirring occasionally, for 20 minutes, or until soft and golden brown. Season to taste with salt and set aside to cool.

3. Heat the oven to 400°F and lightly flour a 9-inch tart pan.

4. On a lightly floured surface, roll out the chilled pastry to ¼ inch thick. Drape the pastry over the prepared tart pan, leaving excess pastry hanging over the edges. Gently guide some of the excess pastry down around the sides of the pan. Cover the bottom of the pastry with parchment paper and fill the pan with dried beans, uncooked rice, or lentils. Bake for 15 minutes in a preheated oven. Remove the parchment and beans and trim away any excess pastry from the edges. Return the pan to the oven for 8 minutes or until the pastry is lightly browned. Leave the oven on.

5. Meanwhile, in a large bowl, whisk the eggs, egg yolks, cream, mustard, and chives together. Season with salt and add the cooled onion mixture. Stir well to combine. Pour into the baked pastry in the tart pan and bake for 25 to 30 minutes, or until the filling is just set and golden brown. Set aside in the pan for five minutes before serving.

Clove Pink

Dianthus species

For beauty and delicious smels and excellent properties
[these flowers] deserve letters of gold.

—Stephen Blake, *The Compleat Gardeners Practice, Directing the Exact Way of Gardening in Three Parts*, 1664

Pinks often evoke a nostalgic response when their fragrance swirls around the herb garden. They maintain a sentimental grip on many gardeners' hearts due to their use as border flowers into the early twentieth century by garden designers such as Capability Brown and Vita Sackville-West. The name comes from pinking shears, a tailor's tool that cuts cloth in a zigzag pattern, as is found on the edges of these small, brilliant flowers.

From illustrations found in Stephen Blake's 1664 *The Compleat Gardeners Practice*, we can determine that many varieties have existed for centuries. In fact, wild forms of pinks were evident in ancient Greece, from whence the name comes: *dios* means God or Zeus and *anthos* denotes flower. Writing in the mid-fourteenth century, Chaucer called pinks *girofle*, meaning "clove." *Gillyflower* is a surviving common name for them even today.

FLAVOR

Pinks have a sweet floral essence with hints of cloves and allspice.

PARTS TO USE

The petals of pinks are used in cooking.

CULINARY USES

Clove pinks are most commonly used in simple syrup—pink, coral, or red pinks turn syrup and other mixtures red. The petals can be used in herbed oils or vinegars, jellies and jams, or served with fruit or fruit-based sauces. Clove pink petals can also be used to flavor crème fraîche or other milk/cream dishes, and they can be added to puddings and sweet soufflés. Like violets, clove pinks can be crystallized and used as decoration for baked goods and dessert.

D. chinensis features front and center in the John Blair Garden, Williamsburg Colonial Village, Virginia.

♥ HEALTH BENEFITS

Eastern medicine methods use *Dianthus* to treat bladder stones, bladder obstructions, and urinary tract infections. Pinks have also been attributed with having diuretic and cardiovascular effects, while generous eugenol levels give these plants bacteriostatic properties.

CAUTION: Don't use pinks to self-medicate, and avoid use during pregnancy.

GROWING PINKS

Pinks are perennials that grow from seed or may be divided after flowering in the autumn. Pinks prefer full sun and are easily grown in average, medium-moisture, well-drained soil. They should be deadheaded to prolong the bloom period.

CLOVE PINKS VS. CARNATIONS

Dianthus refers to a genus in the family *Caryophyllaceae*, in which there are some 300 species native to Asia, Europe, Africa, and arctic North America. These include carnations (*D. caryophyllus*), sweet William (*D. barbatus*), and pinks (*D. plumarius*, *D. superbus*, *D. gratianopolitanus*, and *D. chinensis*). All *Dianthus* plants have edible petals. Pinks look like miniature carnations, and they can tough it through even this Canadian's Zone 5b winter, but they flower only once in late summer and their gray-blue foliage and narrow leaves help to set them apart from carnations. The larger carnations are long-blooming and can be very showy, but they are not winter hardy. Now, however, the long-blooming carnation has been crossed with the hardy pink, and the best of both are found in the new hybrids.

D. CHINENSIS

USING AND COOKING WITH ESSENTIAL OILS: A PRIMER

Herbs have tiny sacs, mostly on the leaves, but also on the petals, stems, and other parts that contain aromatic, healing oils that can be distilled into essential oils. Essential oils hold potent, concentrated active components and are usually diluted and (mainly) used topically. Except for citrus oils, which are pressed from the rind, all other essential oils are distilled from fresh plant material, and the resulting concentrated essence of the plant itself is widely used in aromatherapy.

Aromatherapists add a few drops to massage oil, and these oils can also be used in relaxing baths or in salts or soap for the bath. Oils may be breathed in with the help of a diffuser, which combines tiny amounts of essential oil with steam. A few drops of lavender essential oil mixed with ¼ cup almond oil, for example, may be massaged into the nape of the neck and temples to relieve headaches and to soothe burns, scalds, and sunburn.

Recently, however, essential oils and hydrosols (infused water by-products of essential oil distillation, see facing page) have gained popularity with innovative chefs.

I like to keep a few basic essential oils in my pantry, just as I maintain a good stock of whole spices and dried herbs. And as I experiment more and more with them in different recipes, I've found essential oils to be fresher, clearer, and truer-tasting than dried herbs, and I'm learning to rely on them when fresh herbs are not available.

● TO MAKE ESSENTIAL OILS

A still is required similar to the one operated by George Frazier (photo, right) in a demonstration at the Ozark Folk Center in Arkansas. Large quantities of fresh herb or flower material are used in order to produce a very small amount of pure essential oil, and this is why they may seem to be costly. In George's still, small snips of fresh rosemary are in a glass beaker suspended above a beaker of boiling water. Steam rises and passes through the rosemary, collecting with it small amounts of the essential oils from glands on the leaves. The mixture of steam and oil vapor then passes through a condenser, causing them both to return to liquid oil and water (hydrosol), which are collected separately.

Infused oils (like my recipes found on pages 42–43) are not the same as distilled essential oils, because they carry a smaller and unquantifiable amount of the plant's essential oils. Pure, distilled essential oils are available in very small quantities in natural food stores. Here are some guidelines for using essential oils:

* Use only pure and natural, organic herb or herb-flower essential oils, never synthetic oils (sometimes called fragrance oils).
* Do not taste or topically apply undiluted pure essential oils.
* Always use essential oils sparingly, a drop at a time.
* Always dilute essential oils in the stock, liquid, batter, or fat (butter or oil) in a recipe.

CAUTION: Essential oils are not usually taken internally or used for cooking except in tiny amounts (a drop or two) or diluted in other ingredients. Check labels to be sure that the oil is 100 percent herb-based (not synthetic) and preferably organic.

Pink Petals Jam

Makes 2½ to 3 cups

1 cup clove pink petals or
   rose petals
1 cup sliced, peeled fresh apricots
   or peaches
¾ cup freshly squeezed orange
   juice
1 tablespoon grated lemon zest
1 tablespoon freshly squeezed
   lemon juice
2 teaspoons crushed coriander
   seeds, optional
2½ cups sugar
2 teaspoons pure almond extract

1. In a large canning kettle or pot, arrange three 1-cup canning jars on a rack. Add water to 1 inch over the tops of the jars. Cover and bring to a boil over high heat. Turn the heat off and keep the pot covered until jam is ready to fill the jars. In a shallow pan, pour boiling water over flat metal lids and set aside until jam is ready.

2. In a canning kettle or Maslin pan, combine pink petals, apricots, orange juice, lemon zest, lemon juice, and coriander if using. Bring to a boil over high heat. Stir in the sugar, 1 cup at a time, stirring to dissolve before adding the next cup. Boil, stirring frequently, until the mixture becomes thick and coats the back of a wooden spoon, about 15 minutes or until it reaches the jelly stage (212°F) on a candy thermometer. Skim off and discard any foam, remove the pan from the heat, and stir in almond extract.

3. Fill hot jars, one at a time, leaving a ¼-inch headspace. Run a thin non-metallic utensil around the inside of the jar to allow air to escape. Add more hot jam, if necessary, to leave the ¼-inch headspace. Wipe the rim, top the jar with a flat lid, and screw on a metal ring. Return the filled jar to the hot water in the canning kettle and continue to fill jars until all are filled. Cover the canning kettle and return the water to a full rolling boil. Boil jars for 10 minutes, keeping the water vigorously boiling the entire time.

4. Turn the heat off and wait for 5 minutes before removing the canning lid and the jars to a towel or rack to cool completely. Check seals, label, and store jam in a cool place for up to 1 year.

● TECHNIQUES: DRYING AND POWDERING PETALS

DRYING FLOWERS AND PETALS

Flowers and petals retain their color if dried in a dark, well-ventilated, warm place such as a closet.

If using whole flowers for cooking, rinse them well in cool water and pat dry. Hang upside down by the stems to dry. Cut the flowers from the stems and store in a sealed, dark-glass container in a dry place for up to one year.

If using petals for cooking, rinse the flowers well in cool water and pat dry. Remove petals from the inedible center (except chamomile, which is edible) and pinch or cut away the white bitter heel at the base of each petal. Spread in a single layer on a mesh screen, and set aside in a dark, warm, well-ventilated place until crackling dry. Store in a sealed, dark-glass container in a dry place for up to one year.

POWDERING PETALS

Use an electric spice grinder, small food processor, or mortar and pestle to pulverize dried flower petals. Using a fine-wire mesh sieve, sift pulverized petals into a bowl and transfer to a dark-glass jar. Tighten the lid, label, and store in a warm, dry place for up to one year.

Roses, lavender, and pinks are the most highly perfumed and therefore the most widely used in their powdered state. Use powdered petals in spice blends, puddings, egg and cream dishes, soups, dressings, and sauces. Sprinkle over salads and vegetable dishes as a garnish.

Clove Pink Panna Cotta

Makes 6 servings

1 tablespoon powdered gelatin
2½ cups whole milk
¾ cup heavy whipping cream
    (36% butterfat)
⅓ cup honey
2 tablespoons powdered clove
    pink or rose petals
2 tablespoons sugar
1 teaspoon freshly squeezed
    lemon juice
Pinch of salt
Handful clove pink petals for
    garnish, optional

1. In a small bowl, combine gelatin with 3 tablespoons warm water. Set aside for 10 minutes.

2. In a saucepan, combine milk and cream and heat over medium-high heat until bubbles form around the inside of the pan. Stir in gelatin mixture and set aside to cool. When milk mixture is cool, whisk in honey, pink petals, sugar, lemon juice, and salt.

3. Pour milk-gelatin mixture into a medium bowl and set over a larger bowl of ice. Gently stir until it starts to thicken.

4. Pour into 6 small serving bowls or ramekins, cover, and refrigerate until set, about 3 hours or overnight. Serve chilled, and garnish each bowl with clove pink petals, if using.

Honeyed Petals Dressing

Makes 1½ cups

1 cup extra-virgin almond or
   olive oil
⅓ cup liquid clover or herb
   honey
⅓ cup lightly packed clove
   pink petals
¼ cup freshly squeezed
   lemon juice
Pinch sea salt, or to taste

In a jar with a tight-fitting lid, combine the oil, honey, petals, and lemon juice. Shake to mix well. Taste and add salt if required. Cap, label, and store in the refrigerator for up to 2 weeks. Shake well before using.

Fruited Clove Sauce

Makes 1½ cups

1 cup lightly packed clove
   pink petals
1 cup fresh strawberries
¼ cup liquid floral honey
Pinch ground cloves
½ cup boiled water

In a blender container, combine pink petals and strawberries. Drizzle honey over and sprinkle with cloves. With the motor running, add hot water through the opening in the lid slowly until the sauce is the desired consistency. Use more or less water as required to achieve a thick, spoonable sauce or one that is thinner and pourable.

Clove-Glazed Carrots

Makes 4 to 6 servings

2 cups vegetable broth or
    water
5 medium carrots, sliced
    crosswise into coins
3 tablespoons butter
2 drops clove essential oil
3 tablespoons honey
1 tablespoon cornstarch
Pinch sea salt

1. In a saucepan, bring broth to a boil over medium-high heat. Add carrots, reduce heat, and simmer for 6 minutes or until fork-tender. Drain, reserving ¼ cup of the cooking liquid.

2. In the same saucepan, melt butter over medium heat. Stir in the essential oil and honey. In a small bowl, combine cornstarch with the reserved cooking liquid and add to the mixture in the pan. Cook, stirring constantly, for 3 minutes or until mixture is thickened. Taste and add salt if required. Add carrots and toss to coat well.

Coriander/Cilantro

Coriandrum sativum

A real love-it-or-hate-it herb, the *Coriandrum sativum* plant is commonly known as coriander. The fruit—berries, but often called seeds—of the plant is also called coriander. The fresh leaves, however, are referred to as cilantro in North America. In an interview, herb researcher Rex Talbert explained, "In the *Apiaceae* family the term for the seed is fruit. The name *cilantro* and its use is recent, [the] last 20-plus years. I learned it first as just coriander leaf or Chinese parsley—this was typical in English herb books then."

Cilantro leaves change shape as the plant matures in a process called *heterophylly*.

Coriander leaves go through three distinct leaf shapes. When the plant is in the vegetative state its first green leaves are flat and parsley-like. These bright, young leaves, called cilantro, are at their peak flavor and aroma and are harvested for use in salsa, Thai dishes, and other cooking applications.

As the plant prepares to bloom, the flower-stem leaf shape emerges as a fern-like shape. Once this happens, the typical cilantro flavor is not as evident and the leaves, although edible, are not usually used in cooking.

Finally, as the berries ripen, the leaves again change into a different shape, one that is three-lobed, with each lobe having five points.

The fruit itself initially develops as green berries. Moroccan coriander (*C. sativum* var. *microcarpum*) matures to small, round berries, and Indian coriander (*C. sativum* var. *sativum*) to oblong, tan-colored fruits, called seeds.

FLAVOR

Many people describe the aroma and taste of fresh cilantro leaves as refreshing and gingery-citrus, with hints of thyme or sage. Others can't tolerate what they call the stinky, soapy, or dirty socks taste. The reason for such widely diverse reactions to cilantro leaves is described in the Misocoriandrists box (facing page). Coriander seeds are pleasantly sweet, spicy, and floral with orange overtones.

PARTS TO USE

The leaves, roots, and seeds of the coriander plant are used.

Coriander is in bloom in the herb garden at Shady Acres Herb Farm, Chaska, Minnesota.

CULINARY USES

Fresh cilantro leaves are key ingredients in raw and cooked salsas, chutney, relish, and other sauces. They should be added at the very end of cooking. Cilantro blends with chives, basil, mint, and lemon herbs but clashes with rosemary, oregano, thyme, and savory. The roots are more pungent than the leaves, and they are used as a vegetable in Asia or mashed and added as a flavoring to Thai soups. Coriander seeds are dried and ground and used as a spice in Middle Eastern, Indian, and Thai spice blends, including curry and garam masala. They can be used whole in pickling spice and sausages, or ground for use in vegetable dishes, stews, and chili dishes. Coriander seeds combine well with other sweet spices for baked goods or fruit compotes. I use a small cast iron mortar and pestle to coarsely grind coriander seeds. An electric spice grinder will produce a finer power.

♥ HEALTH BENEFITS

Cilantro leaves and fruit are antioxidant-rich. The leaves are a good source of potassium, calcium, manganese, iron, and magnesium, are high in folic acid, vitamins A and C, and are one of the best herb sources of vitamin K. Cilantro is antiseptic and analgesic (relieves pain).

GROWING CORIANDER/CILANTRO

An annual that requires sun, coriander grows easily from seed and if left to flower and fruit, it will reseed.

● MISOCORIANDRISTS

Are you like me, someone who abhors the smell and taste of coriander? When you eat at Thai or other Asian restaurants, do you ask that cilantro not be added to your plate? Do you cringe if a tiny piece of it accidentally finds its way anywhere near your fork and—horrors!—into your food? If so, you are a true *misocoriandrist*.

In fact, you are not alone. John Gerard called cilantro "a very stinking herbe" with leaves of "venomous quality." If it's any comfort, you can't actually alter the fact that you hate cilantro, because it all comes down to your genes, specifically to genetic variants in your olfactory receptors. A genetics firm based in Mountain View, California, identified one olfactory-receptor gene in a study of 14,604 individuals that makes some people sensitive to the aldehyde chemicals that cause cilantro to smell, well, like soap or doll hair or something burnt. It seems that people who love the fragrance and taste of cilantro (and there are a lot more who love cilantro than those who hate it) simply do not have the nose for those specific aldehydes. And because they can't detect the offending constituents, they can't smell or taste their equally offending properties.

A SALSA HERB PRIMER

Originating from Mexico and Latin America, *salsa* is the Spanish word for "sauce." But a salsa isn't just any sauce—it's always spicy, tangy, zippy, and often hot, with lots of flavor and texture not only from the fresh, picante vegetables or fruits but also from the herbs. Traditional tomato salsa demands fresh cilantro, but salsas made with fresh fruits (or beans or nuts and seeds) are complemented by a wide range of green herbs and even some spices.

CHILE PEPPERS Hot fresh peppers (jalapeño, habanero, serrano), smoked (chipotle), and dried cayenne peppers add heat to salsa. Sweet peppers are flavorful and add texture and color, so both hot and sweet peppers are often called for in a salsa recipe.

CHIVES Try substituting the milder-tasting chives in place of onion in fruit or other delicately flavored salsas.

CILANTRO AND CILANTRO MIMICS Many people consider cilantro to be essential for any kind of salsa, and it certainly is central to many Mexican sauces. I substitute flat-leaf parsley whenever cilantro is called for. Cilantro mimics, plants that smell and taste like cilantro, including chameleon, culantro, papalo, pepicha, and Vietnamese coriander, can also be used in place of cilantro.

CORIANDER While the fresh green leaves (cilantro) are a staple in many salsa recipes, the seeds of the plant are slightly sweet, with spice, floral, and orange notes. Grind and use coriander seeds in fruit, nut, and some milder vegetable salsas.

CUMIN (*Cuminum cyminum*) Used crushed, ground, or whole, the rich, slightly bitter, and earthy flavor of cumin seeds teams well with beans, nuts, and seeds in salsa.

EPAZOTE (*Dyphania ambrosioides*) Native to central and southern Mexico, this herb is almost as popular in salsa as cilantro due to its pungent, earthy, and slightly minty flavor.

GARLIC AND ONIONS Most often diced and added raw to salsa, garlic and/or onions may be sautéed or roasted to sweeten them.

GINGER Grated fresh ginger or ginger syrup is added to fruit and mild vegetable salsas.

LEMON HERBS Lemon balm, lemongrass, and lemon verbena add the citrus zing to both fruit and vegetable salsa.

MINT Most spearmint varieties are great with tropical fruit (mangoes, papaya, pineapple) and some vegetable salsas. Use peppermint for a stronger mint taste.

OREGANO Use it with fresh tomatoes, tomatillos, and peppers. Oregano adds a rounded spicy flavor with hints of anise and cloves.

PARSLEY Curly parsley is fine in salsa, but the stronger-tasting flat-leaf variety is preferred if replacing cilantro.

ROSEMARY Its pine and aromatic camphor taste is perfect for tomato, pepper, and some fruit salsas.

Roasted Pepper Salsa

Some would say that salsa isn't salsa unless fresh cilantro is a key ingredient, so if you are a cilantro lover, use it in this sauce. For those who cannot abide cilantro, omit it and go with parsley. I use flat-leaf (Italian) parsley as a cilantro substitute because it is stronger in taste than the curly-leaf variety and because it is similar in appearance.

Roasting the peppers gives this sauce an extra, nutty dimension to the mild heat of the peppers. This salsa is not only highly flavorful, but it is also nutritious, being high in vitamins A and C as well as having antioxidant power. Use it as an accompaniment for nachos, fish, chicken, and barbecued pork or beef or as a sauce for burritos, rice, or pasta. It is best if set aside for up to 2 hours to allow the flavors to blend and ripen. It may be stored, covered, in the refrigerator for six to eight hours, but the liquids may separate from the tomatoes. If this happens, strain and discard the juices.

Makes 2 cups

2 tablespoons extra-virgin olive oil
1 tablespoon freshly squeezed
    lime juice
1 teaspoon ground coriander
½ teaspoon ground cumin
Pinch ground cloves
6 fresh New Mexican or poblano
    chile peppers, roasted (page 76)
4 tomatoes, chopped
1 red onion, chopped
2 cloves garlic, finely chopped
½ cup chopped fresh cilantro or
    flat-leaf parsley

1. In a bowl, combine oil, lime juice, coriander, cumin, and cloves and set aside.

2. In a separate bowl, combine peppers, tomatoes, onion, garlic, and cilantro. Drizzle with oil mixture and toss to coat the ingredients. Cover and set aside at room temperature for up to 2 hours before serving.

Thai Nut Sauce

Makes 3 cups

2 tablespoons melted extra-virgin
    coconut oil
1 onion, finely chopped
1 clove garlic, minced
1 tablespoon Curry Spice Blend
    (page 104)
1 can (15 ounces) full-fat
    coconut milk
1 cup natural peanut, almond,
    or cashew butter
¼ cup coconut nectar or honey
Juice of 1 lime
½ cup chopped fresh cilantro
    or parsley

1. In a saucepan, heat oil over medium heat. Sauté onion for 5 minutes. Add garlic and curry. Cook, stirring frequently, for 2 minutes or until onions are soft and mixture is fragrant.

2. Add coconut milk and bring to a boil over medium-high heat. Add nut butter, nectar, and lime juice. Cook, stirring constantly, for 1 to 2 minutes or until incorporated and smooth. Add water, if necessary, to thin the sauce to the desired consistency: thin for a satay or dipping sauce, thicker for a fish or vegetable sauce. Stir in cilantro.

3. Transfer to a bowl. Use immediately or store, covered, in the refrigerator for up to 3 days. Bring to room temperature before serving.

Curry Spice Blend

Makes ½ cup

3 tablespoons coriander seeds

2 tablespoons fenugreek seeds

1 tablespoon allspice berries

1 stick (4 inches) cinnamon,
   crushed

10 cardamom pods

2 (or to taste) dried cayenne
   peppers or other hot chiles,
   crushed

2 to 3 tablespoons chopped fresh
   coriander root, optional

2 tablespoons ground turmeric

1 small dark-glass jar (½-cup
   capacity) and lid

1. In a small skillet or spice wok, combine the coriander, fenugreek, allspice,
   cinnamon, cardamom, chiles, and coriander root if using. Toast over medium
   heat, stirring frequently, for 3 to 4 minutes or until lightly colored and fragrant.
   Remove from heat just as the seeds begin to pop. Do not let spices smoke and
   burn. Set aside to cool.

2. In a mortar, using a pestle, or in a small electric grinder, pound or grind toasted
   spices to the preferred consistency: coarse or finely ground. Transfer to a
   bowl, add turmeric, and mix well. Spoon into a jar, cap, label, and store in the
   refrigerator for up to 1 month.

Coriander Pear Bread

Makes 1 loaf

Bread
1 cup all-purpose flour
⅔ cup coconut flour
1½ teaspoons baking powder
1 teaspoon ground coriander
1 teaspoon orange zest
1 teaspoon sea salt
2 pears, coarsely chopped
3 large eggs
¾ cup sugar
¼ cup melted extra-virgin
    coconut oil or olive oil
Juice of 1 orange

Glaze
½ cup confectioners' sugar
1 teaspoon ground coriander
2 tablespoons orange juice, as
    required

1. Preheat oven to 350°F. Grease the bottom and sides of an 8 × 4-inch loaf pan.

2. **TO MAKE THE BREAD:** In a large bowl, combine all-purpose flour, coconut flour, baking powder, coriander, zest, and salt. Add pears and toss to coat.

3. In a medium bowl, whisk eggs and sugar together until light and creamy. Whisk in oil and orange juice.

4. Stir the egg mixture into the flour mixture and mix just until combined. Scrape into the prepared pan and bake in preheated oven for 55 to 65 minutes, or until a cake tester inserted into the middle comes out clean. Set aside on a cooling rack for 15 minutes.

5. **TO MAKE THE GLAZE:** In a bowl, combine sugar and coriander. Slowly add orange juice and mix until the glaze is thin enough to drizzle over the loaf.

6. Remove the loaf to a serving platter and drizzle with glaze.

Dandelion

Taraxacum officinale

It is one of the drugs overrated, derogated, extirpated, and
reinstated time and time again from Theophrastus' time to to-day.

—C. F. Millspaugh, *Medicinal Plants*, Philadelphia, 1892

Dandelion never started out as a noxious weed. It was its success as a "footprint herb," one that became a weed and spread wherever humans went, that helped to define it as common and, worse, useless.

Arab physicians introduced dandelion to Europe around the tenth century, and by the late fifteenth century dandelion was well known as a tonic; a cleansing herb for the liver, gallbladder, and spleen; and as a powerful diuretic, which was also known as *pissenlit*, French for "piss in bed." Later, when Culpeper echoed, "You see here what virtues this common herb hath, and that is the reason the French and Dutch so often eat them in the spring," sometime in the seventeenth century, dandelion was already well established as an effective medicinal herb.

The Chinese were using dandelion as early as 659 CE, according to records of medical texts. Today, Eastern medicine uses dandelion for lung and breast tumors, jaundice and hepatitis, mastitis, abscesses, and urinary tract infections. In *The Green Pharmacy*, James Duke suggests that it is effective in preventing osteoporosis and for treating a wide range of ailments, including Alzheimer's disease, bladder infections, breastfeeding and liver problems, pneumonia, swelling, tonsillitis, and warts.

Today, while millions of homeowners try to eradicate dandelion from their lawns, herbalists are still using it as a diuretic, as a digestive, and to help cleanse digestive organs (see Health Benefits and A Detoxifying Herbs Primer, page 108). The leaves support the kidneys and the roots support the liver.

FLAVOR

Dandelion leaves are slightly bitter with refreshing citrus notes. This bitterness increases as the leaves mature. The flower petals are sweetly floral. The roots are earthy and slightly bitter.

PARTS TO USE

The young leaves, the flowers, and the roots are all used.

Dandelions are encouraged and the yellow flowers spring up along with tulips and daffodils in the spring garden of Deb Knapke, Columbus, Ohio.

CULINARY USES

Fresh, young dandelion leaves are delicious in salads or lightly steamed as a green leaf vegetable. The sweet flower petals can be used in the same way as calendula petals: in salads or as a garnish and in wine and jelly-making. The roots can be steamed or sautéed as a vegetable, candied, or used in a medicinal preparation.

♥ HEALTH BENEFITS

The leaves are rich in iron, zinc, and potassium, high in B-complex vitamins, vitamin D and antioxidants (vitamins A and C), and are a powerful diuretic. A tea or tincture of the leaves and aerial parts may relieve bloating and the feeling of abdominal fullness. The roots stimulate the appetite, assist the liver, and help treat jaundice and spleen ailments. Dandelion's leaves and roots are used to treat liver, gallbladder, kidney, and bladder ailments, including hepatitis and jaundice. The flowers are an excellent source of lecithin and a good source of choline, both thought to improve brain activity.

CAUTION: Do not take dandelion if you are pregnant or have any acute gastric inflammation.

GROWING DANDELION

As most homeowners know, dandelion is a prolific, perennial weed with a long taproot that is difficult to eradicate once established. Gathering dandelion from lawns and waste spaces is easy, but be sure that the plants have not been treated with pesticides.

A DETOXIFYING HERBS PRIMER

The goal of cleansing or detoxifying is to flush out toxins stored in the tissues, blood, organs of elimination (especially the liver and colon), and the fat cells, where they are stored. During cleansing, toxic elements are released from these areas and are free to unleash their nasty effects again, causing headache, irritability, and catarrh, so it is important not only to flush the toxins out of the tissues, but also to eliminate them through soaking in herbal baths and by flushing and diluting them by drinking herbal teas and plenty of water.

Cleansing, fasting, or detoxifying programs will ultimately produce a calm feeling, a clear-headed and focused brain, a sense of well-being, as well as an abundance of energy. There are several ways to cleanse, but the easiest is to eat only raw, fresh vegetables and vegetable soups, whole grains and legumes, vegetable and herb juices, blended drinks made with vegetables and herbs and a small amount of fruit, and lots of herbal teas made with detoxifying herbs. While cleansing, it is essential to drink eight to ten glasses of water per day and to refrain from all other foods, including fats (fried foods, red meats, and cheeses), dairy products, alcohol, soft drinks, caffeine, refined grains, processed foods, fast foods and snacks, and sugar or other sweeteners.

During cleansing, the main organs of elimination, the liver, kidneys, respiratory, and lymph systems, and the skin must be supported. Fresh, raw juice is a natural choice for cleansing because the concentrated nutrients are assimilated quickly without putting stress on these organs, so they can rest and be nourished. The antioxidants in vegetables, fruits, and herbs are necessary for eliminating toxins and neutralizing free radicals, so fresh, raw juices are key to a successful cleansing program.

The following herbs provide support for cells and organs and the process of elimination and cleansing. Many whole or natural food stores carry them, and some are easily grown. Use one or more of them fresh in juices, or add a tincture to juice, or make herbal teas and bath infusions from the dried herbs.

ASTRAGALUS ROOT (*Astragalus membranaceus*) A tonic and immune-building herb, you can add the dried root to soup broths or whisk a tablespoon of the powder into drinks.

ASTRAGALUS

BURDOCK ROOT (*Arctium lappa*) Burdock cleanses the skin and blood, and it stimulates urine flow and sweating and supports the organs of elimination. Use the fresh leaves and root in soups and a tincture (5 to 20 drops) or a teaspoon of the powdered root in herbal teas and juices.

BURDOCK

CHILE PEPPER It stimulates blood circulation, purifies the blood, expels mucus, and promotes fluid elimination and sweating. Juice fresh chile peppers with other vegetables, or whisk a pinch of cayenne, powder into juice or herbal teas.

CHILE PEPPER

DANDELION ROOT Dandelion root cleans the liver and blood, filters toxins, acts as a mild laxative, and increases the flow of urine. Juice the fresh root or add a tincture (5 to 20 drops) to juices and herbal teas.

DANDELION ROOT

ELDERBERRY Elderberries support detoxification by promoting bowel movements, urination, sweating, and secretion of mucus. Cook, mash, and juice fresh berries, or add a tincture (5 to 20 drops) to drinks.

ELDERBERRY

GINGER It stimulates circulation and sweating and because it is widely available, ginger is a good cleansing herb to grate fresh into food and juice and to use in herbal teas.

GINGER

LICORICE (*Glycyrrhiza glabra*) With its gentle laxative effect, licorice root is often included in cleansing juices and teas.

LICORICE

MILK THISTLE (*Silybum marianum*) A potent liver cleanser, milk thistle is a good herb to use not only during cleansing, but also periodically in herbal teas or juices because it protects and rejuvenates the liver.

MILK THISTLE

Herbalist Simple: Tincture

A tincture is a concentration of the medicinal properties found in herbs dissolved in a solvent. In this case, the menstruum (or solvent) is alcohol, which serves to extract the active components and to preserve them. Apple cider or coconut vinegar may be used in place of alcohol to make tinctures. Dried or fresh herbs may be used; however, the proportion of alcohol to herb will be higher if dried herbs are used. Any part—leaves and stems, flowers, roots, bark, and seeds—may be used to make a tincture, and it is the active constituents that determine what parts to use. For example, the roots of *Astragalus*, comfrey, and *Echinacea* are more powerful than the leaves, so it is likely that a tincture would be made from mostly the roots of those plants.

To make dandelion tincture, all parts of the plant may be used together in one tincture, or each part may be used to make a separate tincture. Due to their sweet flavor and exceptional levels of lecithin and that they are a good source of choline, whenever available, I always include dandelion flowers with leaves and/or roots.

You can use 80- or 90-proof vodka, gin, or rum, or 190-proof grain alcohol or brandy as the menstruum. Gather the herbs in midmorning, after the dew has evaporated and before the afternoon sun is high.

For every 100 grams (about 3½ ounces) of fresh herbs, use 200 mL (about ¾ cup) alcohol. This makes what is known as a 1:2 tincture.

If using dried herbs: For every 100 grams of dried herbs, use 300 to 400 mL (about 1¼ to 1½ cups) alcohol.

SIMPLE METHOD:
USE FOR AERIAL PARTS (LEAVES, STEMS, AND FLOWERS)

1. Wash fresh leaves and flowers, if using, in cool water, pat dry, and coarsely chop.

2. Pack into a wide-mouth jar and cover with alcohol, leaving a 1-inch headspace. Cap, label, and store in a warm place, shaking the jar once or twice per day for at least 4 weeks. (Note: If using vinegar, use a plastic lid or a layer of plastic film over the opening before capping, because the vinegar will corrode metal lids.)

3. Strain mixture through several layers of cheesecloth into a large liquid measuring cup or bowl. Gather the ends of the cheesecloth around the herbs, and squeeze them to release as much infused alcohol as possible. Pour into several small dropper jars. Cap, label, and store in a cool, dark place. Tinctures will store indefinitely.

4. To use, unless otherwise directed by a health-care professional, take 1 teaspoon three times per day, diluted in a small amount of water or juice.

BLENDER METHOD:
USE FOR AERIAL PARTS AND ROOTS OR ROOTS ONLY
OR SEEDS OR BARK

1. Wash fresh leaves, flowers, and seeds in cool water and scrub bark and roots using a vegetable brush. Pat dry and coarsely chop.

2. Combine equal parts herb material and alcohol in a blender container and process on high until herbs are finely chopped. Pour into a wide-mouth glass jar, adding more alcohol if necessary, and leaving a 1-inch headspace. Cap, label, and store in a warm place, shaking the jar once or twice per day, for at least 6 weeks. (Note: If using vinegar, use a plastic lid or a layer of plastic film over the opening before capping, because the vinegar will corrode metal lids.)

3. Strain mixture through several layers of cheesecloth into a large liquid measuring cup or bowl. Gather the ends of the cheesecloth around the herbs and squeeze them to release as much infused alcohol as possible. Pour into several small dropper jars. Cap, label, and store in a cool, dark place. Tinctures will store indefinitely.

4. To use, unless otherwise directed by a health-care professional, take 1 teaspoon three times per day, diluted in a small amount of water or juice.

Dill

Anethum graveolens

I am always pleased with that particular time of the year which is
proper for the pickling of dill and cucumbers.

—Joseph Addison, *The Spectator*, England, circa 1711

My delight in the natural world is always renewed every time I discover another of the plant world's coincidences. Did we first use dill leaf and seed with cucumbers simply because both plants were maturing at the same time in the garden? Was it serendipitous or simply convenience that the marriage of dill and summer's most celebrated vegetable was consummated a very long time ago?

Cucumber didn't earn its "cool" reputation without a good reason: it is about 95 percent water, which is efficient in keeping it about 20°F cooler than the outer skin. Dill, on the other hand, is warming and provides a perfect counterbalance when the two take the plunge together into the pickle jar.

Dill pickles aside, the feathery dillweed and its flavorful oil add zest to dishes from Russia (root vegetables, especially borscht, a beet and dill soup), Scandinavia (herring marinated with dill), Greece (stuffed grape leaves with dill), India (lentils and spinach with dill leaves and seeds) and Iran (dill, spinach, and shallots). Capers, thickened cream, and chopped fresh dill are spectacular with poached fish of any kind, and potato or egg salads, and fresh spring vegetables are enhanced by it.

FLAVOR

Dill's feathery leaves (also known as dillweed) have a refreshingly clean taste of citrus with slight anise and parsley notes, while the seeds are warm, with caraway and anise flavors.

PARTS TO USE

The leaves, flowers, and seeds are used.

CULINARY USES

Fresh dill leaves are best known as an accompaniment for fish and seafood in marinades, sauces (notably tartar sauce), and basting liquids, or as a garnish or rub for grilled fish, chicken, vegetables, and seafood. Fresh or dried leaves are used as a pickle ingredient and in light vinaigrettes for salads and with root vegetables. The fresh leaves make a delicate ferny garnish for savory dishes or desserts and they are also good with chicken,

Dill thrives in a sunny location in the historic garden at the Whitehorse Inn (circa 1762) in Douglassville, Pennsylvania.

soups (especially beet soup), in cream sauces, and in salads. Dill is often blended with yogurt and capers or mustard as a sauce for roasted beets (and other root vegetables) as well as vegetable soups and stews. Dill is always added at the very end of cooking in order to retain its aroma and flavor.

Dill and lemon are often used together for rice, couscous, potatoes, and in light pasta dishes. Dill leaves and seeds combine with lentils for pulses of northern India. In baked goods, dill seeds are used alone or in combination with other seeds such as sesame, coriander, poppy, and cumin. The seeds can also be used whole in pickle spice or as a digestive tea, or ground in herb or spice blends.

The delicate flavor of dill leaves dissipates when the herb is dried, so like parsley, fennel, chervil, and basil, dill is best frozen to preserve it. Wash fresh stems, pat dry, and freeze whole in an airtight bag and simply snip off sprigs as needed.

❤ HEALTH BENEFITS

Perhaps best known as a digestive, dill seeds are used to treat heartburn, colic, and gas. Dill is antimicrobial and a good source of calcium, iron, and magnesium. It has also been shown to reduce cholesterol in animal studies.

GROWING DILL

Dill is easy to grow from seed. Plant directly into the ground after the last threat of frost; it reseeds easily. As a hardy annual, dill must be allowed to go to seed to ensure a crop for the next year.

SEED HERBS

Growing aromatic plants for their seeds is just as easy and rewarding as growing them for their leaves, flowers, or roots. You simply let the plant flower and go to seed and harvest once the seeds are mature. Fresh seeds are stunningly flavorful, much more so than seeds that have been transported from faraway places, stored, packaged, and sold at supermarkets or spice stores. See page 117 for directions on harvesting, drying, and storing herb seeds. Dill seeds are, of course, a significant part of pickling spice blends, and they may be used alone or blended with fennel and aniseed for a pleasant and effective digestive eaten after meals or taken in an herbal tea. Here are some other herb seeds you might enjoy.

ANISEED (*Pimpinella anisum*) Similar in appearance to dill, with feather-like leaves and umbel white flowers, aniseed is used as a digestive in teas and liqueurs and is eaten whole after meals.

CARAWAY (*Carum carvi*) The plant fares well in northern gardens if treated as a biennial and sown in autumn. The foliage resembles carrot and the roots are sometimes cooked and eaten as a root vegetable. Caraway seeds taste sweet and spicy with a slight hint of licorice and are used in seedcakes, breads, soups, and preserves; see cumin.

CORIANDER An annual that grows to about 2 feet high with white flowers, smaller but similar in shape to those of dill. Coriander seeds are an essential ingredient in curry and garam masala spice blends.

CUMIN (*Cuminum cyminum*) A staple seasoning in chili con carne and other lentil or bean dishes, this long, thin, and dark brown seed is pungent and slightly bitter. Both cumin and caraway help indigestion by easing hiccups, belching, swelling, and flatulence due to blockage in the lower intestines.

FENNEL All parts of the plant have a sweet licorice flavor, with the seeds having the strongest taste and effect on the body. Chew seeds whole or in a tea (strained) as a digestive for colic in infants and flatulence in adults.

FENUGREEK (*Trigonella foenum-graecum*) Fenugreek grows well in North America; the seeds give the characteristic curry flavor to spice blends. Very nutritious, it balances blood sugar levels and contains choline, which aids the thinking process.

MUSTARD Grown for both the leaves and seeds, mustard is a peppery-hot herb that adds punch to salads and spice blends.

SWEET CICELY Sweet and strongly anise-flavored, the long, dark brown mature seeds of sweet cicely are chopped and used in cookies, muffins, sweet breads, and cakes or as a garnish for chicken or fish dishes.

Pickling Spice Blend

Garlicky Polish, Russian, and Iranian as well as New York City deli-style pickled cucumbers all employ the leaves and seeds of dill for their classic flavor. In contrast to that singular dill-pickle taste, this spice blend is sweetened by cinnamon, allspice, and cloves; warmed by mustard, ginger, and hot pepper seeds; and brightened by coriander and anise. It is designed to be used for not only cucumbers but also other vegetables, so try it in a brine for preserved carrots, cauliflower, bell peppers, or beans.

Makes about 1 cup

6 bay leaves
1 star anise
1 stick (3 inches) cinnamon
2 tablespoons allspice berries
2 tablespoons dill seeds
2 tablespoons brown or yellow
    mustard seeds
1 tablespoon coriander seeds
1 tablespoon ground dried ginger
1 tablespoon hot pepper seeds
2 teaspoons cumin seeds
1 teaspoon cloves

1. Stack the bay leaves and, using scissors, snip thin strips crossways through the stack. Using a mortar and pestle or rolling pin, crush the star anise and cinnamon.

2. In a bowl, combine allspice, dill, mustard, coriander, ginger, hot pepper, cumin, and cloves. Add bay, star anise, and cinnamon and toss to mix well. Transfer to a dark-glass jar with a tight-fitting lid. Cap, label, and store in a dry, dark, cool place.

3. To use the pickling spice, cut a 10-inch square of doubled cheesecloth and a 24-inch length of thin string. Spoon a tablespoon or more of pickling spice, as required, into the center of the square.

4. Bring up the edges of the cloth around the spices to make a pouch. Secure with the string, leaving one long end to tie around the handle of the pot for easy removal after boiling with the pickling liquids.

● TECHNIQUES: DRYING SEEDS

As one means of propagation, most plants produce fruit, which contain anywhere from one to thousands of seeds. Dill's umbel flower heads, for example, produce tens of thousands of seeds on one plant. Almost all herb seeds are edible and contain a concentrated dose of the herb's nutrients and essential oils. As an indication of the value of seeds for future crops, baskets of coriander and dill seeds were found in Tutankhamun's tomb, put there as nourishment for his journey to, or to sustain him once he reached, the afterworld.

In order to harvest seeds at their peak, wait for them to mature and change color from green—dill seeds turn light tan when ready. Some seeds will show signs of bursting from pods or seed heads; others will be encased in overripe fruit. Get to know the growing cycle of the plants you love so that you can save their seeds and plant them every year.

Snip the whole flower heads from the stalk and encase them in a paper bag. Label and set aside in a warm, airy place to dry. Drying may take up to a week depending on the weather, longer if it is damp and rainy. When the seeds are crackling dry, rub the seed heads between your palms to separate the seeds from the husks. Store the seeds in dark-glass jars in a cool, dry spot for up to two years. Discard saved seeds after that and replace them with fresh.

Saving seeds is a basic and time-honored right of people all over the world. One way that we can preserve heritage plant species is to join Seed Savers Exchange. We can also help protect native medicinal plants of Canada and the United States by becoming a member of United Plant Savers. See Resources (page 397) for more on these associations.

Dill-Spiked Grilled Salmon

Makes 4 servings

¼ cup extra-virgin olive oil

¼ cup chopped fresh dill

2 tablespoons freshly squeezed
  lemon juice

1 tablespoon honey

1 teaspoon sea salt

1 pound boneless salmon fillets

1 to 2 cups Dill Cream Sauce
  (facing page)

1. Heat barbecue grill to high.

2. In a saucepan, combine oil, dill, lemon juice, honey, and salt. Bring to a boil over high heat. Remove from heat and set aside to use as a basting sauce.

3. Lay fillets on the grill, skin side down, and brush the tops liberally with the basting sauce. Close the grill lid and cook for 15 to 20 minutes, brushing liberally with basting sauce every few minutes. Do not flip fish. The skin will stick to the grill when you gently lift the fillets off to a heated platter. Fish is cooked when it turns opaque and flakes easily with a fork.

4. Discard remaining basting mixture and serve with Dill Cream Sauce.

DILL CREAM SAUCE

Makes 2 cups

1 tablespoon dill seeds
1 tablespoon coriander seeds
2 cups strained plain yogurt
    (see note)
¼ cup chopped fresh dill
2 tablespoons drained capers
1 green onion, finely chopped

NOTE: To strain yogurt, line a fine-mesh strainer with cheesecloth and set over a bowl. Empty a container (23 ounces) of plain yogurt into the strainer and set the strainer and bowl in the refrigerator to drain for 15 minutes. Use the clear drained liquid in soups or baked goods, or discard.

1. Using a mortar and pestle, crush dill and coriander seeds to desired consistency, fine or coarse.

2. In a bowl, combine yogurt, dill, capers, green onion, and crushed seeds.

Dilled Cream Cheese Dates

Makes 24 appetizers

4 ounces chèvre (goat cheese),
at room temperature

4 ounces cream cheese, at room
temperature

3 tablespoons finely chopped
fresh dill

24 large fresh dates, pitted

6 slices bacon

Fresh dill sprigs, for garnish

NOTE: To wrap all of the dates
with bacon, increase the bacon
to 12 slices. If you wish to make
the stuffed dates ahead of time,
after step 1, cover the stuffed
dates tightly and refrigerate for
up to 2 days. About an hour
before serving, bring to room
temperature and continue with
step 2.

1. In a bowl, combine chèvre, cream cheese,
   and dill. Using a teaspoon, scoop some cheese
   and stuff into a date. Place the date on a
   rimless baking sheet. Repeat until all of the
   dates are stuffed with the cheese mixture. Chill
   for 30 minutes.

2. In a skillet, cook bacon for 2 to 3 minutes or
   until crisp on both sides. Remove and drain on
   paper towels. Cut each bacon slice in half.

3. Wrap 12 of the stuffed dates with the bacon
   and secure with a toothpick. Transfer both
   the bacon-wrapped and the plain cheese-
   stuffed dates to a serving platter and serve
   immediately.

Elder

American (or Eastern) Elder *Sambucus canadensis*
and European Elder *Sambucus nigra*

The common people formerly gathered the Leaves of Elder upon the
last day of April, which to disappoint the charmes of Witches they
had affixed to their Doores and Windowes. I doe not desire any to pin
their Faiths upon these reports, but only let them know there are
such which they may believe as they please.

–William Coles, *The Art of Simpling*, 1656

Elder as protector is a concept that is woven through history in many cultures, including the pre-Christian Germanic legends of Frau Holle, goddess of life and death, who lived in an elder tree; the Danish Hylde-mikoer (elder tree mother-spirit); the Scandinavian Mother Elder; and the Russian belief in the power of elder to expunge evil spirits. The Danes never made furniture, especially cradles, from its wood and in the English countryside elder was respectfully asked before its wood was removed. The mother spirit is clearly embodied in elder throughout time.

Magic, superstition, and enchantment aside, elder wood was prized for making musical instruments; in fact the name *Sambucus* is sometimes said to be from the Greek *sambuke*, a stringed musical instrument made of elder wood whose music was believed to heal the spirit. It is more likely that, as in Pliny's time (23–79 CE), pipes, not stringed instruments, were made from hollow elder wood. Native Americans, living without benefit of ancient or European tradition, referred to elder as "tree of music" and fashioned flutes from the wood.

FLAVOR

Elderflowers are fragrant and faintly muscatel, while the berries are tart and astringent, like a cranberry.

PARTS TO USE

Elderflowers and berries are both used for food, but all parts of the plant are used for medicine (see Caution).

CULINARY USES

Elderflowers do not contain the glycosides found in elderberries or other parts, and so they are not poisonous even when eaten raw. Fresh elderflowers are used to make elderflower waters, syrups, pickles, fritters, and teas. Most recipes call for one flower head or more. This means use

The Climatron (first geodesic dome to be used as a conservatory) is barely seen over the top of elderberry in the Missouri Botanical Garden, St. Louis, Missouri.

the whole umbel from which you may glean hundreds of the individual flowers. The rest of the plant must be cooked in order to be safely consumed. The flowers can also be battered in fritters and pancakes or added to baked goods. Elderberry syrup is excellent in cordials and added to wine. The berries work well in pies, jams, jellies, syrups, liqueurs, and other drinks.

TO HARVEST FLOWERS FOR COOKING: Plan to do it on the day that you expect to use them. Snip the whole flower head, gently shake to remove any insects, and keep at least a 1- to 2-inch length of stem to make it easy to dip the flower heads into batter. Gently swish in cool water and pat dry or set aside to dry.

If you wish to use only the tiny white flower blossoms (as you would petals in a recipe), after rinsing and drying, remove the flower blossoms using herb snips and discard the stems or twigs.

If you can catch the buds just before they flower, you can harvest and pickle them and use them as you would capers.

♥ HEALTH BENEFITS

Antioxidant, anti-inflammatory, antiviral, expectorant, and laxative, elderberry is very effective in preventing and shortening the effects of viral infections—especially flu and cold but also herpes and shingles—and it reduces fever and strengthens the cardiovascular system.

Elderflower is used to treat colds, specifically catarrh and feverish, flu-like conditions. It is also used as a diuretic.

CAUTION: Elderflowers are edible when raw, but only fully ripe, purple elderberries are used and they *must* be cooked, never eaten raw. Leaves, twigs, stems, branches, bark, roots, seeds, and raw (green or red) berries contain cyanogenic glycosides, precursors to hydrocyanic acid, which is poisonous, but they are neutralized and safe to eat when heated.

GROWING ELDER

S. canadensis, a tall (3 to 15 foot), weedy shrub, is native to eastern Canada and the United States and is adaptable and hardy in Zones 3 to 10. It is easy to grow from seed and offshoots in full sun or partial shade. Larger flowers and more berries result from having two bushes (plant 6 to 10 feet apart). Compact varieties, including some with striking purple leaves and pink flowers (*S. nigra* 'Black Lace'™), are available at nurseries and herb farms.

◗ LIQUEUR HERBS

Liqueurs—herb- and fruit-flavored alcohols—have their roots in medieval monasteries when wine was used to extract aromatic oils from herbs and spices. As their herb gardens flourished and the spice trade brought new plants from Asia, China, and India in the 1600s, monks developed more complex blends, and these potent medicinal drinks became a source of income. Now the recipes of the famous Carthusian Chartreuse and Bénédictine monks' liqueur of the same name are closely guarded.

While the Egyptians and other cultures fermented mostly fruit for beverages, it was the Persians and later the conquering Arabs who distilled alcohol from other plants. Even today, all alcoholic spirits are plant-based, distilled from grains, fruits, or vegetables. Some also rely on extractions of essential oils from herbs for flavoring. Many of the mixes we use to dilute or flavor alcohol are or were originally made from plants: for example, tonic water was once (some brands still are) made from the bark of the *Cinchona* tree, containing fever-reducing quinine, which is why the British in India began combining it with gin to mute the bitter taste of their malaria tonic. Ginger ale was, in fact, ginger syrup or extract with soda water added for carbonation, which is why we were given it as children when nausea threatened.

As Amy Stewart puts it in *The Drunken Botanist*, "Around the world, it seems, there is not a tree or shrub or delicate wildflower that has not been harvested, brewed, and bottled. Every advance in botanical exploration or horticultural science brought with it a corresponding uptick in the quality of our spirituous liquors." The following list gives some of the herbs that have been and continue to be used in alcohol or spirits.

HERB	LIQUOR
Agave (*Agave tequilana*)	Tequila
Angelica	Chartreuse, Fernet, Galliano, Strega, vermouth, Bénédictine, and Drambuie
Bay	gin, vermouth, some liqueurs, some brands of Bay Rum (not the aftershave)
Elder	cordials, wine, St. Germain, Sambuca
Elecampane (*Inula helenium*)	bitters, herbal liquors, vermouth
Ginger	ginger ale, ginger beer, shandy
Hops (*Humulus lupulus*)	key flavoring in beer
Juniper (*Juniperus communis*)	key ingredient in gin
Lemon balm	absinthe, herbal liqueurs, vermouth, and perhaps Chartreuse and Bénédictine
Licorice (*Glycyrrhiza glabra*)	absinthe, aguardiente, anis, anisette, mistrà, ouzo, pastis, raki, and sambuca, among others
Mint	crème de menthe, Hesperidina, Menthe-Pastille, menthe vert, peppermint schnapps
Rose	crème de rose, My Rose, rosolio, Shan rose
Sweet woodruff (*Gallium odoratum*)	the fresh leaves are used to flavor immature white spring wines for May Day celebrations
Violet (*Viola odorata*)	crème de violette, Crème Yvette, parfait amour
Wormwood (*Artemisia absinthium*)	Absinthe

Herbalist Simple: Herb-Infused Syrup

While we might think of simple syrup as a sweetener for desserts or drinks (mainly cocktails), centuries ago, herbalists, monks, and healers were using herb-infused honey or herbed sugar and water as medicine. Called *rob* or *roy*, syrup was another tool—along with herb-infused vinegar, salts, and alcohol—that extracted the medicinal components from an herb's essential oil and acted as a preservative so that the essence of the herbs could be stored at room temperature for a very long time.

Any fresh medicinal or culinary herb leaf and flower may be used to make syrups. The flavor of the syrup will depend on the amount of herbs used. Be sure to bruise the herbs—rub them between your palms—before adding them to the sugar water. If you insert one sprig of the fresh herb in the syrup before capping the bottle, it will continue to infuse the mixture, causing the taste to intensify over time. Experiment with different herbs and amounts. The following is a guideline for using herbs in syrups. The recipe may be cut in half or doubled.

To serve as a cordial, fill a glass with ice. Pour ¼ cup of Herb-Infused Syrup over the ice and top with a splash of soda water. Taste and add more cordial or soda as desired.

Makes 2 cups

2 cups water

2 cups sugar

2 cups individual elderflowers
removed from the head

NOTE: The elderflowers may be replaced by any one of the following fresh herbs: about 10 basil sprigs, 8 rosemary sprigs, 2 large handfuls of mint, 12 thyme sprigs, or 16 fresh or dried bay leaves. Use sprigs that are about 6 inches in length.

1. In a saucepan, bring the water to a boil over high heat. Add sugar, reduce the heat, and simmer, stirring constantly, until dissolved. Add elderflowers and simmer for 1 minute.

2. Remove from heat, cover, and set aside to cool for 30 minutes or up to 1 hour. Taste, and if the flavor is too weak, replace lid and let sit for up to 24 hours.

3. Strain through a fine-mesh strainer into a pint or two 1-cup sterilized jars. (See directions, page 243, for sterilizing jars or step 7, page 129, for processing syrup in a water bath.) Cap, label, and store in a very cool place.

Eldercello

Makes 1 quart

2 cups individual elderflowers
1/2 cup fresh lemon balm leaves
2 organic lemons, rind on,
    thinly sliced
1 quart vodka
2 cups Herb-Infused Syrup
    (facing page)

1. In a wide-mouth 6-cup jar, combine elderflowers, lemon balm, and lemons. Pour vodka over, leaving a ½-inch headspace. Cap, label, and set aside in a sunny window for 1 month, shaking the jar once a day. The vodka will turn a deep amber color.

2. Strain through a cheesecloth-lined strainer into a wide-mouth 6-cup jar, pressing on the herbs and lemons to extract as much flavor as possible. Discard the solids.

3. Cap and set the strained vodka aside for 2 weeks. Decant (transfer) into smaller jars: two pint jars or four 1-cup jars. Cap, label, and store in a cool place. To serve, chill in the freezer for 30 minutes or until very cold.

Eldercello Cocktail

Makes 4 drinks

1 cup chilled Eldercello (above)
1 to 2 tablespoons Herb-Infused
    Syrup (facing page), optional

NOTE: You can dilute this even more by adding carbonated water to taste.

Add ice to 4 short glasses. Pour about ¼ cup Eldercello over ice in the glasses. Taste and add syrup if using, as required.

Elderberry and Gooseberry Jelly

Makes 8 cups

3 pounds fresh ripe elderberries

2 pounds fresh red gooseberries

½ cup water

6 cups sugar

½ cup freshly squeezed
    lemon juice

2 pouches (3 ounces each)
    liquid pectin

1. In a canning kettle or Maslin pan, combine elderberries, gooseberries, and water. Bring to a boil over high heat, reduce heat, and simmer for 25 minutes or until fruit is very soft. Using a potato masher, mash berries.

2. Line a cone strainer with cheesecloth, or use a jelly bag or clean cotton pillowcase to extract the juice. Place the strainer over a large bowl and tip the elderberries and liquid into the strainer. Let the pure juice drip into the bowl overnight or at least 12 hours. If you force the fruit or squeeze the strainer, the juice and resulting jelly will be cloudy.

3. Stand canning jars upright in a preserving canner or stockpot. Cover them with water, 1 inch over the top of the jars. Cover and bring to a boil over high heat. Turn off the heat when water has boiled. Place the 2-piece canning lids in a shallow pan and pour boiling water over; set aside until needed.

4. Meanwhile, measure the strained juice. You should have 3 cups. If not, add enough water to the juice to measure 3 cups.

5. In a canning kettle or Maslin pan, combine the juice, sugar, and lemon juice. Bring to a boil over low heat, stirring constantly to dissolve the sugar. Boil for 1 minute. Remove from heat and add pectin.

6. Using a jar lifter or tongs, remove and fill one jar at a time. Wipe the tops clean and center a flat lid disc over the top. Twist one ring on the jar and tighten with fingers. Place the jar back into the canner. Continue to fill, cap, and return remaining jars to the hot water.

7. Cover the canner, bring water to a rolling boil, and boil for 15 minutes. Turn heat off, remove lid, and let the canner sit for 5 minutes before removing the jars to a cooling rack or tea towel. Lids should snap shut with a distinctive "pop," which indicates that the contents are sterile and there is no air in the jar. Jars may be stored at room temperature for 1 year or longer.

Elderberry Chicken Tagine

Makes 4 servings

1 tablespoon paprika

1 teaspoon ground cinnamon

½ teaspoon sea salt

4 boneless, skinless chicken breasts

4 tablespoons extra-virgin avocado oil or melted coconut oil, divided

1 onion, quartered

3 red or black plums, seeded and quartered

1 or 2 hot chile peppers, finely chopped

½ cup dried cherries

¼ cup chicken broth

¼ cup Elderberry Jelly (page 128) or cranberry jelly

2 tablespoons elderberry vinegar or balsamic vinegar

1. In a bowl, combine paprika, cinnamon, and salt. Place chicken in a shallow pan and brush with 1 tablespoon of the oil. Rub spice mixture into chicken. Set aside.

2. In the bottom of a large tagine or Dutch oven, heat remaining oil over medium-high heat. Add onion and sauté for 5 minutes. Add chicken and brown for 2 to 3 minutes on each side. Using tongs, remove chicken to a plate and set aside.

3. Add plums, peppers, cherries, broth, jelly, and vinegar and bring to a boil. Reduce heat and simmer, stirring frequently, for 3 minutes. Add chicken, cover, reduce heat to low, and simmer for 30 minutes or until a thermometer registers 165°F when inserted into the thickest part of the chicken.

Fennel

Foeniculum vulgare

The fact that it is a mild diuretic most probably led the ancient Greeks
to think of it as an effective slimming agent.

—Sarah Hollis, *The Country Diary Herbal*

Florence fennel (*F. vulgare* var. *dulce* or
F. vulgare var. *azoricum*) is a hardy,
perennial Mediterranean vegetable
that is very popular in Italy, where it has been
a culinary specialty since the seventeenth
century. Italians call it *finocchio*. Growing
conditions are the same as *F. vulgare*, with
the exception that the bulb plants should be
fertilized during growth. Sometimes mis-
labeled as "anise," the fennel bulb is lightly
anise-licorice in aroma and flavor.

When fennel is used as a vegetable, all
plant parts are used. Treat the seeds and
leaves as you would *F. vulgare*.

FLAVOR
All parts of fennel are sweetly anise or licorice flavored.

PARTS TO USE
Fennel leaves, flowers, flower pollen, seeds, and bulbs (especially the bulbs of *F. vulgare* var. *dulce* and *F. vulgare* var. *azoricum*) are all used.

CULINARY USES
Fennel leaves and flowers are used in salads, sauces, and dips as well as in marinades
for chicken or fish. They can also be used to stuff fish or whole poultry. Bright yellow

pollen from the flowers makes an unusual garnish. The fresh or, more often, dried seeds are found in spice blends, notably the Chinese five-spice blend and some curry blends. Fennel seeds are used as a digestive and breath freshener.

Hollow green fennel stems are tied together to flavor the poaching liquid of chicken or fish and can be added to the wood in smokers. With a texture similar to celery, the swollen, white stem bases that form the bulb are often chilled in a bowl of water in the refrigerator for 20 minutes before being used raw in sal-

Feathery fennel blooms in the "Doctrine of Signatures" garden at Sudeley Castle, Winchcombe, Gloustershire, England.

ads. Stem bases are also sliced crosswise and baked in a cheese sauce (au gratin) and cooked in a variety of dishes, including soups, stews, and stir-fry dishes.

♥ HEALTH BENEFITS

A digestive, fennel seed relieves gas. Fennel essential oil (distilled from seeds) is used to expel mucus and treat catarrh of the upper respiratory tract in children; it eases dyspepsia, mild spastic disorders of the gastrointestinal tract, and the feeling of fullness and flatulence, and it is a diuretic.

CAUTION: Fennel oil is not recommended for use during pregnancy.

GROWING FENNEL

A self-seeding perennial, fennel prefers well-drained, sunny locations. According to Francesco DeBaggio in *Dill, Herb of the Year 2010*, it is a gardening myth that dill and fennel will cross-pollinate if planted too close together.

A feathery ornamental, fennel makes an effective backdrop for the herb garden. It grows to 5 feet and when in bloom, its broad, golden yellow umbel flowers make a stunning show. When planted in drifts, it makes a dramatic stand, especially when plants with contrasting textured leaves and complementary flowers are integrated into the bed's design. Sprays (stems and ferny leaves) of fresh fennel are also used in floral arrangements.

A DIGESTIVE HERB PRIMER

BITTERS TO JUMP-START DIGESTION

Bitter herbs trigger taste buds at the back of the tongue to signal the central nervous system to stimulate the flow of digestive juices from the mouth, stomach, pancreas, duodenum, gallbladder, and liver. Bile and other liquids such as hydrochloric acid help in the process of breaking down, absorbing, and eliminating food. The following is a list of some bitter herbs.

ANGELICA It stimulates digestion and acts as a tonic—make a tea or tincture (add drops to water) and drink about 30 minutes before meals.

DANDELION A mild bitter, it is also a blood cleanser and diuretic.

HOREHOUND (*Marrubium vulgare*) Horehound is mentioned in the Bible, and it is used to treat cough and respiratory problems.

YARROW (*Achillea millefolium*) It has astringent and bitter properties and is used in cough syrups.

CAUTION: Diabetics should be aware that bitter herbs can change blood sugar balance, so use with caution or professional help.

CARMINATIVES TO DISPEL GAS

Some herbs provide relief from the pain of gas in the intestines. The first signs of gas may be pain and swelling in the lower abdomen. This is the time to take a digestive tea. Examples of carminative herbs follow.

FENNEL Mild enough for children with colic, fennel leaf is made into tea, and adults either chew on fennel seeds or sip a strained fennel seed tea to help digest fat.

MINT Most widely used after meals, mint may be taken as a tea or liqueur but may also be served in a sauce. Chopped fresh mint in vinegar is an excellent accompaniment for lamb and beef. Mint relieves stomachache due to gas and indigestion.

ROSEMARY Include rosemary with lamb and beef dishes to help digest the saturated fats. Rosemary is also helpful in stimulating the digestive organs.

ANTISPASMODICS TO RELAX MUSCLE SPASMS

Cramps may be mild or severe when digestive problems present themselves. Antispasmodic herbs help to dispel cramps. The following antispasmodic herbs aid in calming stomach and abdominal pain.

CHAMOMILE A mildly bitter herb, it helps relieve cramps.

LEMON BALM Generally calming, lemon balm relieves cramps and gastrointestinal disorders and is mildly sedative.

DEMULCENT HERBS TO SOOTHE, COAT, AND LUBRICATE STOMACH AND INTESTINES

When fats and acids wear away the stomach lining, demulcent herbs help to soothe the irritated tissue.

MARSHMALLOW (*Althaea officinalis*) Relieves stomach ulcers and soothes inflammatory bowel diseases.

SLIPPERY ELM BARK (*Ulmus rubra*) Soothes irritated mucous membranes.

Herbalist Simple: Herb Bitters

Herbs that help relieve the pain of gas and indigestion or bitter herbs that stimulate digestion or those that soothe inflammation were—and still are—a valuable medicine. There are several ways to effect relief: take herbal bitters as a predinner cocktail; brew bitter herbs in a tea and sip before and after meals; enjoy a few drops of bitter-herb tincture in water or juice; or eat a bitter salad of radicchio or arugula before a meal to stimulate digestion.

After a meal, take herbs that relieve gas, pain, and inflammation (see Digestive Herbs, page 133). Chewing fennel, dill, and coriander seeds is popular in India, but you can take an herbal tea or tincture in water or juice after eating. It also helps to add digestive herbs to dishes that are fatty—for example, rub lamb with rosemary before cooking, and serve mint in a jelly or sauce with it.

Tonic and digestive herbs were often extracted in alcohol. These tonics or digestives were called "bitters," which were later used as ingredients in cocktails. Now bitters have become widely popular among mixologists, and many small-batch bitters brewers have popped up. The following is loosely based on Stoughton's Bitters, without the red cochineal or carmine dye.

Makes 4 cups

½ ounce chopped dried gentian root (*Gentiana lutea*; see note)
½ ounce dried orange zest
½ ounce crushed cinnamon
½ ounce chopped dried angelica root
¼ ounce fennel seeds
2 cups brandy
1 to 2 cups grain alcohol or vodka

NOTE: Use dandelion or burdock root in place of gentian.

1. In a wide-mouth quart jar, combine gentian, orange zest, cinnamon, angelica, and fennel. Add brandy and alcohol, leaving a 1-inch headspace. Cap, label, and shake the jar. Set aside in a warm place, shaking the bottle once a day, for 2 to 3 weeks or longer.

2. Strain through a cheesecloth-lined sieve into four 1-cup jars. Discard solids. Cap, label, and store in a cool place for up to 2 years.

3. To use, pour 2 ounces into a small glass and sip slowly 30 minutes before meals.

Predinner Bitter Tea Blend

Dried herbs are best for tea blends. A half cup of tea, warm or at room temperature, taken 30 minutes before a meal will help to stimulate digestion. The point is that the herbs are bitter, and, as such, they do a good job at kick-starting digestion, so it is not advised to add sweetener of any kind. The herbs in this recipe are dried.

Makes 1¾ cups blend

1 cup fennel seeds, crushed
½ cup coarsely crushed dandelion leaves
¼ cup coarsely crushed yarrow leaves and flowers
1 teaspoon cloves, crushed

1. In a bowl, combine fennel, dandelion, yarrow, and cloves. Toss to mix well. Transfer to an airtight container, label, and store in a cool, dry, dark place.

2. **TO MAKE A PREDINNER TEA FOR ONE PERSON:** Finely crush 1 teaspoon of the blend into a small teapot. Pour ½ cup of boiled water over blend. Cover and set aside to steep for 5 minutes. Strain into a cup or small glass. Take immediately, or cover and set aside to cool slightly. Sip slowly about 30 minutes before eating.

Chicken Salad on Fennel Boats

Makes 6 appetizer servings

2 cups chopped cooked chicken
¼ cup chopped fresh basil
2 stalks celery, thinly sliced
½ cup Fennel Aioli (below)
      or prepared mayonnaise
1 tablespoon freshly squeezed
      lemon juice
Sea salt and pepper
6 white fennel stalk bases
2 fennel leaf sprays, for garnish

1. In a bowl, combine chicken, basil, celery, aioli, and lemon juice. Season to taste with salt and pepper.

2. Cut green stalk away from each white fennel stalk base. Divide the chicken salad evenly into 6 portions. Pile each portion onto a fennel base. Snip a few fennel leaves on the top or side as a garnish. Repeat with remaining salad and fennel bases.

FENNEL AIOLI

Makes ½ cup

½ cup extra-virgin olive oil
1 clove garlic, finely chopped
¼ teaspoon finely ground fennel
      seeds
2 egg yolks
1 tablespoon white wine vinegar
1 tablespoon freshly squeezed
      lemon juice
1 teaspoon Dijon mustard
½ teaspoon sea salt

1. In a bowl, combine olive oil, garlic, and fennel.

2. In a blender container, combine yolks, vinegar, lemon juice, mustard, and salt. Pulse or process on medium for 10 seconds to mix well.

3. With the motor running, add the oil mixture in a slow, steady stream and stop when all the oil has been added. Transfer aioli to a container, cover, and refrigerate. Aioli will thicken upon chilling. Store for up to 3 days in the refrigerator.

Radish, Fennel, and Avocado Toss

Makes 4 servings

2 tablespoons freshly squeezed
    lemon juice
2 tablespoons chopped fresh
    fennel leaves
1 tablespoon white wine vinegar
1 ripe avocado, pitted and diced
2 cups mixed spring greens
1 cup thinly sliced fennel bulb
1 watermelon radish, thinly
    sliced (see note)
¼ cup extra-virgin olive oil or
    avocado oil
Sea salt and pepper
1 fennel spray, for garnish

NOTE: Watermelon radish is a
large round or oval radish with
bright pink flesh. The taste is sweet
and the crisp texture adds extra
dimension to raw summer salads.
Sometimes found at supermarkets,
they are making a presence at
farmers markets. If you can't find
watermelon radish, substitute 4 to
6 French breakfast radishes or
regular radishes in this recipe.

1. In a glass or nonreactive bowl, combine lemon juice, fennel leaves, and vinegar. Add avocado and toss to coat. Set aside until ready to serve the salad.

2. In a bowl, combine greens, fennel slices, and radish slices. Toss to mix well. Divide evenly among 4 salad plates.

3. Using a fork, whisk oil into avocado mixture just until incorporated, keeping avocado slices whole. Spoon over vegetables and season to taste with salt and pepper. Snip 4 small pieces of fennel from the larger spray and use to garnish each plate.

French Tarragon

Artemisia dracunculus 'Sativa'

It is well to warn the cooks who have been given the key of the Herb-garden
to be cautious how they use Tarragon.

—Frances Bardswell, *The Herb Garden*, 1930

H ad I known Frances Bardwell or even read her advice about French tarragon, I might have saved myself a few stressful moments just before a dinner party I hosted for a group of friends who were "into" food. It was the late 1970s, long before the term *foodie* was coined. My first culinary herb garden was proving to be the inspiration for new dishes, and I was young and up for any challenge. I had heaps of French tarragon, so I chose Chicken Kiev, a new recipe for me. I've since found many recipes online that are similar. Not many have the same international name, but most call for about two tablespoons of chopped fresh French tarragon, not the heaping handful that I added—I love licorice!—to a half-cup of butter. That was the night I learned that if herbed butter is divided and frozen in separate portions, it will slowly release its flavor into fish or chicken as it cooks.

I also learned how potent fresh French tarragon can be, and it is one lesson that is as vivid now as it was forty years ago. After I browned and popped the French tarragon-stuffed chicken into the oven, the kitchen air was sweetly, invitingly scented with anise—and almost as quickly, it became cloyingly, densely methanol-like, and then it just reeked, overwhelmingly, sickeningly heavy with a medicinal smell that didn't bode well for the chicken.

What to do? The guests were happily sipping on white wine spritzers, noses twitching with curiosity with every swing of the restaurant-style kitchen door. I pulled that door tight and did what first came to mind. I ran outside with the pan of perfectly browned Chicken Kiev, hurled it into the trash, ran back in, opened all the windows, popped a frozen pizza into the oven, topped it with the roasted asparagus that had been selected as the perfect side dish for Chicken Kiev, and created a whole new trend in "gourmet pizza dinners" among my friends.

It was a long time before I invited French tarragon to dinner again, but the promise of sweet licorice won out and I was careful to start with a small amount in recipes. And I never gave French tarragon permission to run, free-rein and unchecked, in any of my own recipes.

French tarragon takes center place in a tiny urban community garden in Pittsburgh, Pennsylvania.

There are a number of herbs that display varying degrees of anise or licorice fragrance and flavor that may be substituted for French tarragon. The list on page 5 provides some alternatives. But I love the buzz that French tarragon gives to the end of my tongue and its combination of pine and licorice, so I tend to use it to gently spike the flavor of mild fish or poultry, egg, cream, and mild cheese dishes that benefit from its zippy character.

FLAVOR

Used to flavor white wine vinegars and olive oils, French tarragon adds a peppery, anise fragrance and taste. Due to its strong licorice flavor with hints of pine and spice, French tarragon can overpower dishes if overused, so taste and adjust the amount for recipes accordingly. Cooking *may* diminish French tarragon's aroma, but the flavor is sometimes intensified, especially if teamed with fats such as butter, oil, or cream cheese.

PARTS TO USE

Only the leaves are used in cooking; however, stems and leaves are used for infusing oil or vinegar.

CULINARY USES

Fish, poultry, egg, cream, and dairy dishes benefit from the discreet use of French tarragon. It combines well with mustard, tomatoes, seafood, and potatoes and is essential to béarnaise sauce. It is widely used to flavor butter, vinegars, and olive oils, and it is the signature flavor of the stuffed rolls known as Chicken Kiev.

♥ HEALTH BENEFITS

Early herbals from the ninth century employed French tarragon as a general tonic for assisting the heart, liver, and digestion. James Duke cites French tarragon as beneficial for treating amenorrhea (irregular menstrual cycles) and assisting in lowering blood pressure. The oil is antifungal, according to Tucker and DeBaggio.

GROWING FRENCH TARRAGON

A hardy perennial, French tarragon does not grow from seed but is propagated from root or stem cuttings. It does best in full sun, in well-drained soil.

While there are other types of tarragon, most notably Russian (*A. dracunculus*), be sure to plant and use French tarragon (*A. dracunculus* 'Sativa') for cooking because Russian tarragon has none of the zip and characteristic licorice flavor.

A STRONG AND SPICY HERB PRIMER

My advice for starting to explore the incredible gifts of fresh herbs is to start with clean, fresh-tasting, mild herbs (see A Fresh and Mild Herb Primer, page 60) because they blend easily with other herbs as well as a wide range of ingredients. Once you've experimented with the milder herbs, working with stronger, spicy herbs is the next logical step. Because their flavor is more assertive—some may be pungent or resinous—use them in robust dishes and with stronger meats and try blending one of them with milder herbs.

Tips for cooking with pungent herbs:

* Fresh is best; but when fresh is not available, you may find that adding a few drops of pure essential oil (see page 90) distilled from the strong and spicy herbs in the following list is a good substitute because it adds the pure, clear essence of the herb.

* Strong and spicy herbs demand respect, so use them by the sprig or, if chopped, by the tablespoon. Start with a small amount, taste, and add more until they begin to assert their own personality.

* While fresh and mild herbs blend easily with other herbs, the pungent herbs need to be balanced with the sweet or mild ones, so using them in blends takes some experience—it's not hard to do, but it takes some trial and error to find the combinations that you like.

* Use one strong and spicy herb from the following list first to see how it tastes in food and drinks, then begin to combine one pungent herb with one or more sweet, fresh, and mild herbs (page 60) to help balance out their stronger flavors.

* In the following chart, I give a couple of suggestions of ingredients that combine well with each strong and spicy herb, but treat this as a starting point because you will find many combinations that you love simply by applying these tips and experimenting.

* Use strong and spicy herbs whole or coarsely chopped so that they yield their flavors slowly to a dish as it cooks. For long-simmering soups and stews, whole sprigs of woody herbs such as thyme, sage, and rosemary may be added from the start of cooking; all others should be added any time after the halfway point— with tender herbs such as arugula, watercress, cilantro, and culantro stirred in at the very last moment.

HERB	COMPLEMENTS	BLEND WITH
Arugula (*Eruca vesicaria* var. *sativa*)	nuts, especially walnuts, creamy cheeses such as goat cheese, iceberg lettuce, potatoes, tomatoes, raspberries	basil, borage, cilantro, dill, lovage, parsley, salad burnet, watercress
Cilantro	avocado, coconut, fish, poultry and seafood, rice and pastas, cucumber, citrus dishes, salsa, guacamole, chermoula, ceviche	basil, lemon balm, lemon grass, mint, parsley, chile peppers, chives, dill, galangal, garlic, ginger, salad burnet
French Tarragon	avocados, artichokes, asparagus, eggs, fish, seafood, cream cheeses, tomatoes, zucchini, aioli and vinaigrette dressings	bay, basil, chervil, dill, parsley, lemon herbs, poultry, salad herbs
Hyssop	game meats, legumes, beets, cabbage, mushrooms, peaches, melon, apricots	chervil, lemon balm, marjoram, mint, parsley
Oregano	tomatoes, squash, sweet peppers, beans, carrots, cauliflower, cabbage, cheese dishes	chile peppers, parsley, rosemary, sage, thyme
Rosemary	mild and creamy cheeses, apricots, eggs, fish, tomatoes and tomato sauces, parsnips, lamb and other red meats and game, mushrooms, onions, leeks	bay, chervil, chives, garlic, lovage, mint, oregano, parsley, sage, savory (winter), thyme

HERB	COMPLEMENTS	BLEND WITH
Sage	apples, mild and creamy cheeses, legumes, onions, breads and pastas, tomatoes, eggs, poultry and stuffing, especially poultry stuffing	bay, caraway, ginger, lovage, paprika, parsley, rosemary, savory (winter or summer), thyme
Savory, Winter	fresh and dried beans, beets, cabbage, potatoes, tomatoes, sweet peppers, fish, eggs, poultry	basil, bay, cumin, garlic, rosemary, thyme
Thyme	corn, eggplant, tomatoes, legumes, onions, garlic, leeks, potatoes, mushrooms, egg and cheese dishes	allspice, basil, oregano, parsley, rosemary, sage, savory
Watercress (*Nasturtium officinale*)	chicken, fish, seafood, oranges, peaches, apricots, cucumber, potatoes, raisins and other dried fruit	arugula, fennel, ginger, lemon balm, parsley, savory (winter or summer)

French Tarragon Nut Paste

Like pesto or salsa verde, this herbed nut paste is extremely versatile—you will find yourself reaching for it often. Spread it on crackers or crostini for an appetizer; toss with cooked pasta or vegetables as a sauce; stuff into zucchini or peppers or chicken breasts before baking; toss with rice as a stuffing for roast chicken; and use as a seasoning—add a couple of tablespoons (or to taste) to soups and stews. Cover tightly and refrigerate and use it fresh within a week or freeze it in an airtight container for up to three months.

Makes 2¼ cups

1¼ cups pecan halves or pieces
2 tablespoons extra-virgin olive
    oil or coconut oil
1 onion, chopped
3 cloves garlic
1 pound button or cremini
    mushrooms
3 tablespoons butter
½ cup sliced green olives
2 tablespoons fresh French
    tarragon or rosemary
½ teaspoon coarse sea salt or
    to taste

NOTE: Any nut may be used—almonds, walnuts, pine nuts, pistachios, or cashews—and you can substitute sage, basil, thyme, rosemary, or cilantro for the French tarragon.

1. Preheat oven to 400°F. Spread out pecans in one layer on a rimmed baking sheet. Toast in preheated oven for 3 to 5 minutes or until lightly browned. Set aside to cool.

2. In a skillet, heat oil over medium heat. Sauté onion for 5 minutes or until soft.

3. Meanwhile, using a food processor, chop garlic. Add mushrooms to the food processor bowl and pulse until coarsely chopped.

4. Add butter to onions in the skillet. Stir in chopped mushrooms and garlic. Reduce heat and cook, stirring often, for 15 minutes or until mushrooms are soft and have released their juices. Increase heat to medium and cook for 3 to 5 minutes or until juices have evaporated (mixture should still be moist). Set aside to cool.

5. Using a food processor, finely chop toasted pecans and French tarragon. Add cooled mushroom mixture and the olives and process until smooth. Taste and add salt as desired. Scrape into a bowl, cover tightly, and refrigerate until ready to serve.

Easy French Tarragon Fettuccini

Makes 4 servings

1 pound fettuccini

½ cup French Tarragon Nut Paste
    (page 145)

About ¼ cup extra-virgin olive oil

1. Bring a large pot of salted water to a boil over high heat. Add fettuccini and bring back to the boil. Reduce the heat and simmer for 5 to 7 minutes or until al dente. Drain well.

2. Transfer fettuccini to a large bowl and toss with French Tarragon Nut Paste, adding olive oil as required to make a moist dressing.

French Tarragon Chicken Cassoulet

Makes 4 servings

¼ cup chopped fresh French
tarragon, divided
3 tablespoons all-purpose flour
3 pounds chicken (breasts
or whole chicken, cut into
8 pieces)
4 tablespoons extra-virgin
coconut oil or olive oil,
divided
1 onion, chopped
2 cloves garlic, finely chopped
1 red or green pepper, chopped
1 cup long-grain rice
5 ounces chorizo sausage,
peeled and coarsely chopped
2 tablespoons freshly squeezed
lemon juice
2½ cups chicken broth
12 pitted black or green olives

1. In a zip-top bag, combine 3 tablespoons of
French tarragon and the flour. Add chicken
and shake to coat chicken well.

2. In a Dutch oven or flameproof tagine, heat
2 tablespoons of oil over medium-high heat.
Add coated chicken and brown it in oil for about
6 minutes on each side, working in batches and
adding more oil if necessary. Remove chicken to
a shallow dish and set aside.

3. Add remaining oil to the pot and sauté onion
for 5 minutes, scraping up the browned bits
and stirring them into the onion. Add garlic
and pepper. Cook, stirring frequently, for 3
to 5 minutes or until pepper is crisp-tender.
Stir in rice, sausage, and lemon juice. Cook,
stirring frequently, for 2 minutes or until the
rice is translucent. Add any remaining French
tarragon flour from the bag used to coat the
chicken in step 1.

4. Add broth and bring to a boil. Return chicken
to the pot, pushing it gently into the rice and
vegetables. Cover, reduce heat to low, and
simmer, stirring once or twice, for 45 minutes
or until chicken is cooked and rice is tender.
Chicken is done when it registers 165°F on
a meat thermometer. Sprinkle olives and
remaining French tarragon over cassoulet,
stir, and serve.

Garlic

Allium sativum

Tomatoes and oregano make it Italian; wine and tarragon
make it French. Sour cream makes it Russian; lemon and cinnamon
make it Greek . . . Garlic makes it good.

—Alice May Brock, *Alice's Restaurant Cookbook*, 1969

From subtle to superior, garlic's flavor power is almost as wide-ranging as the number of its varieties. Its taste can go from sweet and delicately mild, to robust, to heated and zingy. One tiny raw, fresh garlic clove delivers a powerful punch, yet a handful of whole bulbs, when roasted or gently "sweated" in olive oil, morphs into a sweet and meltingly tender pulpy mass with a deceptively mellow flavor. Feisty or fragile, sweet, hot, or loaded with sulfur, as Alice May Brock asserts, garlic is the secret to making food taste good.

As part of the lily plant family (*Amaryllidaceae*), garlic shares its ancient lineage with leeks, onions, shallots, and chives. Like its pungent relatives, garlic is more vegetable than seasoning, actually a fleshy, edible bulb that separates into cloves each neatly wrapped in paper-thin skin. Knowing even a little bit about the subspecies (there are two: softneck and hardneck), the varieties (there are seven), and some of the sub-varieties (over 600) gives you a garlic master's edge in the kitchen (see Varieties, page 150).

Garlic is thought to have originated in the Great Steppe region of northern and central Asia and was cultivated in Early Dynastic Egypt from around 3050 BCE. Greek historian Herodotus (484–425 BCE) noted that garlic was the daily food of Egyptian laborers for a thousand years. The active component, *allicin* (which is high in garlic, lower in onions, and mild in leeks and chives), destroys various bacteria, fungi, and yeast, making it a strong tool against infection. Allicin has some antiviral benefits, and it lowers blood pressure and strengthens blood vessels.

With an impeccable medicinal legacy and its legendary use by cooks and chefs all over the world, I nominate garlic as the *King of Herbs*.

FLAVOR

Depending on the variety, garlic ranges from hot and bold to sweet and mellow. Scapes are mildly garlic in flavor.

PARTS TO USE

The cloves, young green leaves, and tender, green scapes are used.

CULINARY USES

Young spring garlic greens are delightful in salads as one of the first green leaves of spring. Add the raw cloves to as many recipes as possible, including salad dressings and dips. Gently sauté minced, finely chopped, sliced, crushed, or whole cloves in olive oil, or roast the whole head for a nutty, mild garlic flavor. Scapes are used in dishes as you would fresh green onions or beans. Use scapes blanched or raw in potato salads or with pasta, toss with cooked vegetables, or add to stir-fry dishes and casseroles.

Garlic, just before scapes are removed, grows in a Pennsylvania home vegetable garden.

❤ HEALTH BENEFITS

One of the best plant medicines with the potential to help more than 200 conditions, garlic is antibiotic and antifungal and thus fights infection. Antioxidants help prevent colon, intestinal, and stomach cancers; antioxidants and liver enzyme boosters help detoxify by reducing levels of toxic heavy metals. Garlic helps to lower blood pressure and prevent blood clotting to keep the heart healthy. For optimum health benefits, take one raw clove of garlic, crushed or minced, daily. Allicin is the compound responsible for garlic's pungent taste and its healing ability.

CAUTION: Garlic thins the blood, so consult your medical professional before self-medicating with garlic.

GROWING GARLIC

Northern gardeners plant garlic in the fall, before the first frost; those in semi-temperate growing zones (like Ohio) plant it in early spring. Use large bulbs for seed, separate into individual cloves, and plant in a sunny location 2 inches deep and 4 to 6 inches apart. Position the wide, flat end (with roots if visible) down and the pointed end up. Garlic does well with plenty of compost or humus and likes manure. Water well in the first few days and then just keep the soil from drying out. Around mid- to late June a 2-foot green stem called a scape will grow on hardneck garlic. Scapes are usually removed (see page 154). Mature garlic plants grow 1 or 2 feet tall, and as they mature, the one clove divides into a cluster, called a bulb or head.

VARIETIES

According to information in their book *The Garlic Farmers' Cookbook*, the Garlic Seed Foundation agrees with Dr. Gayle Volk and a team of USDA/ARS researchers that there are basically two subspecies (types) of garlic: hardneck (*Allium sativum* sp. *ophioscorodon*) and softneck (*Allium sativum* sp. *sativum*). Within each type there are a few groups, into which the hundreds of cultivars fall.

Garlic adapts to its environment, taking on shape, size, color, and flavor characteristics based on its location, so for example, the 'Music' cultivar grown in southwestern Ontario will have slightly different characteristics from the same 'Music' grown in Vermont or Pennsylvania . . . or northern Ontario.

Hardneck Garlic

The hardneck types are so called because of the hard central stalk or scape that sprouts from the center of the bulb to hold the seed head that sits atop the scape. The photo shows the thick, dried, hard stems, cut to about 2 inches above the dried bulbs. Hardneck varieties thrive in cooler temperatures and are divided into three groups: Rocambole, Porcelain, and Purple Stripe. Other, minor groups within the hardneck type are Creole, Asiatic, and Turban. What follows are some examples of garlic cultivars from each of the five hardneck groups.

Rocambole

Rocambole is the most common of the hardneck groups. Garlic varieties in this group have complex, full-bodied flavors that chefs love. The cloves are large and they peel easily and store well. Notable varieties include German Red, Russian Renegade, and Spanish Roja.

Porcelain

Bulbs in this group are smooth-skinned, with larger but fewer cloves per bulb. Continental, Georgian Crystal, German White, Romanian are all Porcelain cultivars.

Purple Stripe

These hardneck types are perhaps the most beautiful, with pink, maroon, or brilliant purple stripes on the outside skin. Cloves are straight and narrow, most bulbs producing eight to ten cloves. Try Chesnok Red or Persian Star.

Marbled Purple Stripe

Along with Glazed Purple Stripe, the Marbled types, such as Siberian, have recently been reclassified from a subspecies of Purple Stripe. Both Glazed and Marbled have fewer, fatter cloves than those of Purple Stripe.

Glazed Purple Stripe

A newly designated hardneck category, Glazed Purple Stripe types, such as Purple Glazer, have delicate wrappers that require careful handling, making them a poor commercial variety but great for the home gardener.

Softneck Garlic

Softneck bulbs tend to be larger than hardneck types, with more cloves, but the cloves tend to be smaller than those in the hardneck group. Overall, softneck varieties are milder in flavor and they store longer than hardneck types. There are two groups of softneck garlic types, Artichoke and Silverskin.

Artichoke

Generally, these types of garlic, such as Italian and Polish, are mild-flavored but can become pungent when grown in cold climates.

Silverskin

These tend to taste very strong and often lack the complexity of other types. They are a popular type for braiding because of their smooth, shiny skin and symmetrical shape. New York White, Nootka Rose, and Silver White are three common Silverskin varieties.

🌿 A GARLIC PRIMER

I curtsy to garlic as the King of Herbs for many reasons, not least because of all food plants, garlic alone is infused into world history, culture, literature, and folklore. It has affected the culinary and medicinal practices of people globally and throughout history, and continues to do so right up to the present. The humble bulb reigns over recipes: raw, baked, roasted, minced, chopped, slivered, sliced, squeezed, and even juiced. Its long list of medicinal benefits sets it above all other herbs in the realm of health and healing. In production, garlic alone is sovereign: no other culinary herb comes close to the estimated 10 million metric tons produced annually (according to the United Nations Food and Agriculture Organization). I invite you to plant garlic, revel in its healing properties, and ultimately cook with it, starting with the following garlic tips.

PEELING AND CRUSHING

As part of preparing garlic for storage, garlic growers spread harvested garlic on the ground or on flat wagons and leave them in the field for a few days. Then the bulbs, usually with their dried stalks intact, are hung in a warm, dark, sheltered area with good air circulation to allow the bulbs to "cure" or dry slightly so that they will store without allowing mildew or mold to invade them. Dried garlic cloves are easier to peel than fresh (directly out of the soil), because the flesh has had time to shrink away from the skin.

To peel a handful of fresh cloves, soak them in lukewarm water for 15 minutes. The skin should rub off with little effort.

To peel and crush a single clove, flatten it with the side of a French knife and then gently press the knife with the palm of your hand. Alternatively, you can pound a clove or two in a mortar using a pestle, remove the skin, and continue pounding until crushed.

CHOPPING

Slice, crush, chop, or mince garlic for increasingly pungent results. The finer the garlic is cut, the more intense the flavor becomes. This is why some recipes in this book call for minced garlic, others for chopped.

INFUSING OIL TO DRESS GREENS

Use garlic-kissed oil for salad dressings or to sauté greens or dress pasta. To infuse oil with garlic: heat ¼ cup of extra-virgin olive oil in a skillet over medium heat. Add 3 or 4 crushed garlic cloves and swirl. Cook until cloves are aromatic and very lightly golden. Remove, slice, and set aside the sweet cloves to garnish the greens or pasta.

Add about 3 cups coarsely chopped kale, Swiss chard, spinach, or other greens to the pan and heat until wilted. Add 2 tablespoons of wine vinegar or freshly squeezed lemon juice and toss with greens. Serve as is or add cooked pasta. You can also substitute cooked vegetables for the greens.

SPRING GREEN GARLIC

In the spring, when fresh, mild garlic greens are barely 4 inches above the ground, cut the tender leaves (or pull, as in the photograph), and use fresh in smoothies or as you would chives in salads and to garnish spring dishes. Fresh greens will keep in water for up to one week.

SPRING GREEN GARLIC

SPRING BULB

Once the shoots grow about a foot high, if you pull hard enough, the tiny pearl-like bulbs will come out with the greens and you can use them as you would a mildly garlicky green onion (scallion).

SPRING BULB

GREEN POWDER

To preserve spring green garlic, dry the young garlic greens using a dehydrator or in the oven at a very low temperature. Powder the dried greens in an electric spice grinder. Transfer to a dark-glass jar, cap, label, and store in a cool, dark place for up to one year. To use the powder, whisk 1 or 2 tablespoons into juice or smoothies, or use as a garnish for soups, salads, or cooked dishes.

GREEN POWDER

GARLIC SCAPES

The tall, firm stem that supports a hardneck garlic seed head is called a *scape*. Around the end of June it is cut off, 2 to 4 inches up from the base of the stem, in order to send more energy to the bulb for larger growth. Most growers remove the scapes by hand to encourage large bulbs, but some have found that leaving the scape on the bulb and drying the bulbs with the scape still attached extends their storage time.

GARLIC SCAPES

Scapes are used in dishes as you would fresh green onions or green beans. To cook scapes, wash them under cool running water, drain, and pat dry. Cut into 1- to 4-inch lengths and use as you would green beans. You can steam or lightly boil them as a green vegetable or add them to soups, stews, stir-fry dishes, or casseroles. Use scapes in warm potato salad by sautéing them with onion and bacon and tossing them with cooked diced potatoes.

Raw scapes freeze well. Chop or cut into 1- to 4-inch lengths and pack into a freezer bag. Seal, label, and freeze for up to six months. Add frozen to soups, stews, stir-fry dishes, or casseroles, or use as you would fresh scapes.

BLACK GARLIC

When garlic is fermented using heat and humidity, it softens, caramelizes, and turns black and sticky. The taste is fruity, slightly tinny, and sweet, with a hint of balsamic vinegar. Use black garlic in soups, sauces, dressings, dips, risottos, and pastas and with butter as a spread for chicken or with bread as a stuffing.

BLACK GARLIC

Roasted Garlic

To coax a sweet, mild taste from garlic, you can slowly sauté individual garlic cloves in olive oil or roast whole heads of garlic in a hot oven. The carbohydrates turn to sugar and the pungent taste morphs into a nutty, mellow flavor with a creamy, soft texture so that the whole head can be used in sauces, dressings, spreads, marinades, and dips. Roasting is easy. Here's how.

1. Preheat oven to 400°F. Rub loose skin off bulb(s). Cut a ¼-inch slice off the top of each bulb. Set root ends down on a small, ovenproof baking dish or sheet. Drizzle 1 tablespoon extra-virgin olive oil over the top of each bulb. Cover the dish with foil. Roast in the preheated oven for 45 to 60 minutes, or until cloves are tender. Cool.

2. Squeeze roasted garlic cloves out of their skins and into a bowl. Use as directed in the recipe.

Lamb Brochettes with Artichoke Spread

Makes 4 servings

1 pound boneless leg of lamb, trimmed

1½ cups Roasted Garlic and Artichoke Spread (facing page), divided

5 tablespoons extra-virgin olive oil, divided

1 tablespoon balsamic vinegar

2 cloves garlic, chopped

2 zucchini squash, cut into 1-inch chunks

2 red onions, quartered

1 thin eggplant, cut into 1-inch chunks

8 metal skewers, lightly oiled

1. Cut lamb into cubes about 1¾ inches square. In a zip-top bag, combine ½ cup of the spread, 3 tablespoons of oil, the vinegar, and garlic. Add lamb cubes, seal the bag, and squeeze to combine the ingredients. Set aside in the refrigerator to marinate for 2 hours or overnight.

2. In a bowl, toss zucchini, onions, and eggplant with ½ cup of the spread.

3. Oil the grill rack and position it about 6 inches above the heat source. Preheat a charcoal or gas grill to medium-high heat.

4. Remove lamb from the marinade and thread the cubes onto 4 skewers. Reserve marinade in a small bowl for basting the lamb. Alternately thread zucchini, onion, and eggplant on the remaining skewers.

5. Position lamb skewers in the center of the grill over the hottest part of the fire and grill, basting and turning every few minutes. Grill lamb alone on the grill for 3 minutes.

6. Add vegetable skewers to the grill and position them around the outside of the grill. Grill vegetables, turning every few minutes to cook evenly on all sides, for 8 to 12 minutes or until tender. Continue to grill lamb, basting and turning every few minutes, for 8 to 12 minutes or until a thermometer registers 130–140°F for medium-rare, or 140–150°F for medium. Serve on a heated platter with remaining Artichoke Spread.

ROASTED GARLIC AND ARTICHOKE SPREAD

Makes 1½ cups

2 heads Roasted Garlic
  (page 155)
1 can (14 ounces) artichokes,
  drained
1 tablespoon chopped fresh
  rosemary
3 tablespoons extra-virgin olive oil
Sea salt and pepper

Squeeze garlic out of the skins into a blender container or bowl of a food processor. Add artichokes and rosemary. Blend on high, adding oil through opening in the lid. Process until soft and creamy. Season to taste with salt and pepper.

Scape Pesto Potatoes

Makes 4 servings

Extra-virgin olive oil
12 small new potatoes
¾ cup Scape Pesto (below)
Sea salt and pepper

1. Preheat oven to 375°F. Lightly oil a rimmed baking sheet.

2. Combine potatoes and pesto on the prepared baking sheet. Grind salt and pepper over top. Roast in preheated oven for 35 minutes or until potatoes are tender and golden.

NOTE: Any pesto may be used in place of the Scape Pesto.

SCAPE PESTO

Makes 4 cups

4 cups roughly chopped garlic scapes
4 cloves garlic
⅓ cup roughly chopped walnuts
⅓ cup grated Parmesan cheese
About 1 cup extra-virgin olive oil
Sea salt to taste

1. In the bowl of a food processor, combine scapes, garlic, and nuts. Process for 30 seconds. Add cheese; process for 10 seconds to blend. With the motor running, add olive oil in a steady stream through the opening in the lid until the pesto reaches the desired consistency. Add salt to taste.

2. Scrape into a clean jar, cap, label, and refrigerate for up to a week or freeze in measured ½ cup or 1 cup amounts for up to 6 months.

Garlic and Greens Soup

Makes 4 servings

¼ cup extra-virgin olive oil

12 cloves garlic

1 cup 1-inch bread cubes

12 fresh sage leaves

1 leek, chopped

5 cups chicken or vegetable broth

½ cup black or Scotch barley

2 tablespoons freshly squeezed
  lemon juice

2 cups chopped fresh or frozen
  spinach

1. In a large saucepan, heat oil over medium-high heat. Sauté garlic for 5 to 7 minutes or until lightly browned. Using tongs or a slotted spoon, remove to a paper towel–lined plate and set aside.

2. Add bread cubes to hot oil and toast, turning to brown on all sides. Remove to a paper towel–lined plate.

3. Add sage leaves to hot oil and fry until crisp. Remove to a paper towel–lined plate.

4. Add leek to hot oil and sauté for 5 minutes or until soft. Add broth and bring to a boil over high heat. Stir in barley, cover, reduce heat, and simmer for 50 minutes or until barley is tender. Stir in lemon juice and spinach and simmer until greens are wilted.

5. Chop reserved garlic and divide into 4 portions. Ladle the soup into 4 bowls and garnish each with reserved garlic, bread cubes, and sage.

Baked Cauliflower and Garlic

Makes 4 servings

4 slices dark rye bread
5 tablespoons Garlic Butter Spread
    (below), divided
1 leek, sliced
2 cloves garlic, chopped
1 teaspoon caraway seeds
1 head cauliflower, cut into
    bite-size pieces
2 cups grated Cheddar cheese
4 large eggs
¾ cup milk
1 tablespoon Dijon mustard
Sea salt and pepper to taste

1. Preheat oven to 325°F. Butter a 2-quart casserole dish.

2. Butter both sides of bread with garlic butter. Arrange in one layer on a baking sheet. Bake in preheated oven for 5 minutes. Flip slices, return to oven and bake for 5 minutes or until both sides are crisp. Cut into 1-inch cubes and set aside. Increase the oven temperature to 350°F.

3. In a skillet, heat remaining garlic butter over medium-high heat. Sauté leek for 5 minutes or until soft. Add garlic and caraway seeds. Cook, stirring frequently, for 2 minutes or until fragrant. Add cauliflower and sauté for 6 minutes or until just tender but not soft. In prepared casserole dish, combine cauliflower mixture with toasted bread cubes and cheese and toss to mix well.

4. In a bowl, whisk together eggs, milk, mustard, salt, and pepper. Pour over cauliflower mixture and stir to combine. Bake in preheated oven for 25 to 30 minutes or until the casserole puffs up and is golden and the center is set.

GARLIC BUTTER SPREAD

Makes ½ cup

½ cup butter, at room temperature
3 cloves garlic, minced, or 1 head
    Roasted Garlic (page 155)
1 tablespoon extra-virgin olive oil

In a bowl, combine butter, garlic, and oil.

Ginger

Zingiber officinale

In New England, until very late, many of the herb gatherers were
squaws who brought various roots and barks to market to
serve as flavorings for the colonial beers.

—Helen Morgenthau Fox, *Gardening with Herbs*, 1938

Ginger beer? Yes! In fact, in England from around the middle of the eighteenth century, ginger was fermented with sugar, water, and a "starter culture" to make an alcoholic beverage that quenched thirst and quelled stomachs at the same time. So it is entirely possible that indigenous herb gatherers brought the woody rhizomes of North American native wild ginger (*Asarum canadense*) to market for colonists to add to homemade brews.

Nowadays, most "ginger beer" drinks on the market are nonalcoholic but still spicy, with the kick and zing of ginger. Ginger ale, on the other hand, is a sweet, mildly ginger-tasting, and heavily carbonated soft drink. Many people of my generation actually remember being given, when sick or nauseous, a serving of "flat" ginger ale (the sweet beverage was decanted to a glass and allowed to rest until all of the bubbles disappeared, leaving a syrupy-sweet liquid). Our mothers got it half right: ginger is effective at settling upset stomachs, but the sugar likely sent our blood sugar skyrocketing while providing a banquet upon which bacteria feasted.

With the recent "discovery" and foment around fermented foods came a modern take on the ginger beer or ginger ale drinks. It's called "Ginger Bug" (page 168), and it is made by combining grated fresh ginger with a small amount of sugar and water. It's easy and fun to make. I keep mine in the refrigerator, and I always have freshly grated and preserved ginger on hand for Asian-style recipes as well as a great base for punch and homemade sodas.

FLAVOR
Ginger is hot and nippy with tangy citrus tones.

PARTS TO USE
The fleshy rhizome, often called gingerroot, is widely used, but the fresh young shoots and leaves are also edible and are used in salads and for garnish.

Ginger is sold in many forms.
Clockwise from top, center: fresh, candied, whole, and dried powdered.

CULINARY USES
Fresh gingerroot is sliced, chopped, or grated into fish, seafood, meat, and poultry dishes or used in soups, dips, marinades, dressings, sauces, glazes, pickles, chutneys, and relishes. It is also used to make ginger beer and ginger ale. Use fresh, young shoots in herbal teas, soups, and stews or anywhere you would use lemongrass or bay leaves; remove at the end of cooking. Fresh young leaves are used as a wrap to poach, steam, or grill chicken, fish, rice, and vegetables. Soak leaves overnight or at least an hour for using to wrap foods for grilling. For baked goods, powdered ginger is often preferred. Chopped candied ginger or powdered ginger is used in spice blends.

♥ HEALTH BENEFITS
A circulatory stimulant, ginger is a warming herb that relaxes blood vessels and promotes sweating and is an expectorant. It is an excellent anti-nausea agent for treating travel sickness and vomiting in pregnancy, fresh ginger being the most potent. It is antispasmodic, carminative, and antiseptic, so it is an essential ingredient in bronchitis, cold, and flu medicine because it is warming and the leaves are high in antioxidants. It is effective in treating chronic inflammation and may help to prevent colorectal and ovarian cancers. Gingerroot, blessed thistle, and gentian root are used to treat anorexia.

GROWING GINGER

A tropical plant, ginger may be grown from a piece of root in rich, moist soil in a sheltered spot. If you live in a tropical area (Zone 7 or higher), plant ginger directly in the ground. If not, start it indoors in a container. It is being grown in Massachusetts as an annual and harvested while still very tender (see Resources, page 395).

🌿 A GINGER PRIMER

From fresh and powdered to pickled and candied, ginger can take many forms and be used in preparations both sweet and savory. Here's how to use the various kinds.

FRESH GINGER

The fresh, fleshy gingerroot adds a warm, Asian flavor to foods. Use it as they do in China to minimize the fishy smell and taste of fresh fish or seafood. Fresh ginger brightens vegetable dishes and all kinds of sauces, including Thai dipping sauces and Korean kimchi pickles. Ginger and garlic are a natural combination, and ginger also complements chile pepper, coconut, lime and lemon, mint, basil, and turmeric.

Organic ginger need only be scrubbed and used without peeling (you may find that the skin is actually thinner than on commercially grown ginger). Like other nonorganic fruit and vegetables, ginger is always peeled before using. I have found that using a regular kitchen spoon to scrape away the peel is the easiest method for peeling ginger.

Fresh ginger freezes easily and is convenient to use from the frozen state. Simply seal whole fresh ginger in a freezer bag and store on the door of the freezer. When needed, remove and grate it right into the dish using a micro grater (a handheld zester/grater for grating citrus peel, cheese, nutmeg, and other spices) or slice using a mandolin. Reseal and pop back into the freezer for the next time.

GINGER JUICE

To make ginger juice, grate fresh ginger using a micro grater or chop using a food processor or blender. Transfer the grated ginger to a square of cheesecloth, twist the four corners together, and squeeze the juice into a small bowl. Use ginger juice in smoothies, sauces, dips, dressings, and marinades.

DRIED GINGER

Various forms of dried ginger are found online or in Asian markets. It is available cracked, chopped, sliced, or in small whole pieces that look petrified. Use cracked, chopped, or sliced ginger in tea blends; grate whole dried pieces into batter or dough, beverages, or stir-fry dishes and desserts.

POWDERED DRIED GINGER

The powdered form of ginger has more bite than the fresh, and the sweet citrus flavor is gone, leaving a slightly bitter taste. The medicinal benefit is not as strong as in fresh ginger, but it is still effective for nausea, indigestion, sore throat, cold, and cough. Powdered ginger is used in some dried seasoning blends, drinks, and baked goods.

CANDIED OR CRYSTALIZED GINGER

Also called glacé ginger, candied ginger is made by boiling fresh ginger in sugar syrup. The strips are dried and coated in sugar and will keep for months in a jar at room temperature. Chop and use as you would fresh ginger. See Candied Angelica or Ginger (page 6) for how to candy or crystallize ginger.

PICKLED GINGER

Called *Gari* or *Amazu shoga* in Japan, pickled ginger is made by covering thinly sliced fresh ginger with a brine of sea salt, granulated sugar, and rice vinegar. The ginger is bottled and processed in a hot water bath to preserve it. This form of ginger is traditionally served with sushi and other forms of raw fish, and it serves to protect against microorganisms in the raw ingredients.

● WILD GINGER
(*ASARUM CANADENSE*)

The *Asarum* genus is native to the temperate zones of the Northern Hemisphere. *A. canadense*, or wild ginger as it is commonly called, is found in deciduous and cedar woods across much of North America. It has a low-growing habit and kidney-shaped leaves. A single, bugle-like burgundy flower emerges at the base of young, pale leaves in the spring. This plant is commonly called wild ginger because the thin, surface-growing rhizomes smell and taste like *Zingiber*, but it is not what most people think of as "true" ginger and it does not have the same medicinal qualities as *Zingiber*.

If you gather it from the wild, take small amounts and be sure that the patch is large and not in danger of being denuded. Wash the rhizomes well. Remove smaller rhizomes and candy the rhizome whole or chop and dry for use in teas.

COLTSFOOT

GINGER

HOREHOUND

HYSSOP

PEPPERMINT

Herbalist Simple: Ginger Cough Syrup

A good cough syrup is meant to soothe the itch of a sore throat and to help expel mucus and phlegm. It should also neutralize harmful bacteria and reduce inflammation while at the same time warming the system. I've included a note about the effectiveness of each of the following herbs in this preparation. The sugar makes the syrup and acts as a preservative for the active ingredients in the decoction, so don't reduce the amount.

See Resources (page 395) for information on where to purchase fresh and dried medicinal herbs. Here is what each herb adds to the cough syrup.

COLTSFOOT (*Tussilago farfara*) Its principal active ingredient is a throat-soothing mucilage.

GINGER A warming herb that promotes sweating, it is antiseptic and an expectorant.

HOREHOUND (*Marrubium vulgare*) Soothes coughs and is an expectorant, which makes it an important herb in cough medicines.

HYSSOP Its antibiotic action is due to a penicillin-producing mold that grows naturally on the leaves.

PEPPERMINT Because it is antiseptic and a decongestant (relieves stuffiness and catarrh), it is useful for relieving cold and flu symptoms.

You can use either chopped fresh or dried whole (or coarsely chopped) herbs in the following recipe without changing the quantities—using dried herbs will make the syrup more potent—but be sure to use fresh ginger.

Makes 4½ cups

½ cup peppermint
¼ cup horehound
¼ cup hyssop or thyme
¼ cup coltsfoot
3 cups boiled water
¼ cup chopped fresh gingerroot
2 cups sugar

1. In a heatproof jug or bowl, combine peppermint, horehound, hyssop, and coltsfoot. Pour boiled water over herbs, cover, and set aside to steep for 1 hour.

2. Strain the tisane (herb tea) into a large saucepan, pressing on the herbs. Discard herbs and add ginger to the infused water. Bring to a boil, cover, reduce heat, and simmer for 1 hour. Turn heat off and set aside (with the lid on) for 24 hours.

3. The next day, return to a boil over medium-high heat and stir in sugar. Reduce heat and gently boil for 2 or 3 minutes or until the syrup is thick and coats a metal spoon. Remove from heat and set aside to cool.

4. Transfer to sterilized jars (see page 243). You can leave the pieces of ginger in the syrup or strain them out before pouring the syrup into jars. Cap, label, and store jars in a cool place for a year or more.

Ginger Bug

This drink is, well, buggy . . . probiotic if you want to get scientific. It uses friendly bacteria, like bacteria that are already inside your body, especially your gut, to produce a slightly sour-tasting, naturally carbonated drink. Probiotics boost the immune system, prevent and help heal urinary tract infections, improve digestion, and help treat inflammatory bowel conditions. Like other fermented foods (tea, coffee, yogurt, sourdough bread, sauerkraut), ginger bug provides food in the form of sugar for the wild microorganisms floating around and on us at all times; and in return, they multiply and replenish the microorganisms that live in our insides, performing all kinds of minute tasks to keep us well. I love the taste of this drink on its own or mixed with juice; some people sweeten it with honey.

Makes about 2 cups

2 large pieces (2 inches long, each) fresh gingerroot, divided

½ cup sugar, divided

2 cups cold, non-chlorinated water

1. Wash your hands and start with clean utensils and a quart glass jar, but there is no need to sterilize since the culture comes from bacteria on you, in the air, and in your kitchen.

2. Peel (if the ginger is not organic) and grate 1 piece of ginger into the quart glass jar. Add roughly the same amount of sugar (about 3 tablespoons). Add water and stir with a wooden spoon. Cover the jar with a piece of cheesecloth or a coffee filter secured with a rubber band. Set aside on your countertop (do not refrigerate).

3. Each day for the next 5 days, stir the mixture, and add 1 tablespoon grated ginger and 1 tablespoon sugar. The mixture will start to ferment—bubbles form at the top and the mixture smells slightly sweet and yeasty—usually within 5 days, but it could take as long as 7 to 8 days of adding grated ginger and sugar to start the fermentation. Mold should not appear, but if it does, scrape it off and if it reoccurs, start the process again. If the mixture doesn't fizz and bubble by the eighth day, discard it and start again.

4. Refrigerate the "bug," adding 1 teaspoon grated ginger and 1 teaspoon sugar once per week.

TO USE GINGER BUG FOR FIZZY DRINKS: In a jug, combine ¼ cup strained Ginger Bug and 4 cups herbal tea or fresh fruit juice. The fermentation of the ginger makes these drinks lightly fizzy.

TO USE GRATED GINGER IN RECIPES: Scoop the grated ginger out of the jar, drain, measure, and use in recipes as you would freshly grated ginger.

Gingerbread with Pears in Ginger Syrup

Makes 1 loaf

2½ cups all-purpose flour
½ cup packed brown sugar
2 teaspoons baking soda
1 teaspoon ground ginger
1 teaspoon ground cinnamon
½ teaspoon sea salt
¾ cup dark molasses
½ cup hot water
½ cup applesauce
1 large egg, lightly beaten
½ cup butter, softened
Pears in Ginger Syrup (facing page)
½ to ¼ cup slivered almonds,
    optional
Whipped cream, optional

1. Preheat oven to 350°F and grease a 9 × 5-inch loaf pan.

2. In a large bowl or the bowl of a stand mixer, combine flour, sugar, baking soda, ginger, cinnamon, and salt.

3. In a batter bowl or large measuring cup, combine molasses, hot water, and applesauce. Pour molasses mixture into dry ingredients all at once and beat using a wooden spoon or on low speed of the mixer. Add egg and butter and beat until combined. Beat by hand for 5 minutes or increase mixer speed to medium and beat for 2 minutes.

4. Scrape batter into prepared baking pan. Bake in preheated oven for 55 to 60 minutes or until a cake tester inserted into the center comes out clean. Set aside on a cooling rack for 15 minutes before removing from the pan. Cool completely and wrap tightly with plastic wrap. Store in a sealed container for up to 5 days in the refrigerator.

5. To serve, cut slices of gingerbread and arrange on dessert plates. Remove pears from syrup, letting the syrup drain back into the bowl. Cut in half and remove core but leave the stem intact on one half. Slice from the base toward the top of the pear halves, leaving the slices intact one inch from the top. Fan each pear half out on the gingerbread. Drizzle with syrup, garnish with slivered almonds, and top with whipped cream if desired.

PEARS IN GINGER SYRUP

Makes 2 pears (4 pear halves) and about ½ cup syrup

¼ cup freshly squeezed orange juice

¼ cup white wine

⅓ cup sugar

2 tablespoons packed brown sugar

2 tablespoons finely grated fresh ginger

2 pears

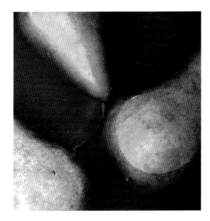

1. In a saucepan, combine orange juice, wine, sugar, and brown sugar. Bring to a boil over medium-high heat. Add ginger, reduce heat, and gently boil for 5 minutes.

2. Using a large spoon, ease pears into the syrup. Cover, reduce heat, and simmer, gently rolling the pears over a few times, for 8 minutes or until crisp-tender. Remove the pan from the heat and set aside to cool. Transfer pears and syrup to a bowl, cover, and refrigerate for up to 48 hours. Bring to room temperature before using.

Gingered Sweet-Sour Onions

Makes 4 servings

1 pound small red and white
   onions, root and stem ends
   trimmed, skin on
½ cup freshly squeezed orange
   juice
¾ cup dry red wine
3 tablespoons red wine vinegar
2 tablespoons finely grated
   fresh ginger
2 tablespoons packed brown
   sugar, or more to taste
2 tablespoons extra-virgin olive oil
Sea salt and pepper to taste

1. In a saucepan, cover onions with water and
   bring to a boil over high heat. Boil for 1 minute
   and drain. Set aside until cool enough to
   handle and rub skins off, leaving onions whole.
   Discard skins and water or reserve water for
   another use.

2. Meanwhile, in a bowl, combine orange juice,
   wine, vinegar, ginger, and sugar. Set aside.

3. In a skillet, heat oil over medium-high heat.
   Add onions and cook, stirring frequently, for
   5 minutes. Add orange juice mixture and bring
   to a boil. Reduce heat and simmer, stirring
   occasionally, for 15 minutes or until onions
   are tender.

4. Use as a garnish for roast meats or vegetables
   or with cheese as an appetizer. Store tightly
   covered in the refrigerator, for up to 2 weeks.

Horseradish

Armoracia rusticana

(Use) . . . with good ventilation to avoid asphyxiation.
—Art Tucker, on grating horseradish, *Horseradish, Herb of the Year*, 2011

Native to southern Russia and eastern Ukraine, horseradish isn't called "stingnose" because it is a sweetly perfumed herb. In fact, grating the root, especially if it's from a second-year crop harvested after the first frost, irritates the eyes, nose, and skin. And that's just as you are preparing it. Eating horseradish prepared with only lemon juice or vinegar can take your breath away, which is why it is often sweetened and teamed with cream, yogurt, or sweet vegetables such as beets.

From the Middle Ages (*ca.* 1215–1293) onward, horseradish has been used as a bitter herb during the Jewish Passover holiday, which celebrates the Hebrews' exodus from Egypt. The word *seder* means "order," and the evening ceremony, which includes a meal, is divided into fifteen parts. One of them is *maror*, or bitter herbs (sometimes endive, now often horseradish), symbolizing the bitterness of slavery. After the blessing and breaking of the unleavened bread (matzah), a blessing is recited over *maror* and it is eaten.

Horseradish became popular in England in the late 1600s and was transported from there to North America. Its use as a condiment may have originated in Central Europe.

Commercial horseradish cultivation in North America started by the early 1800s, and later in the century a horseradish production area sprung up around Collinsville, Illinois, where the rich soil around the Illinois River east of St. Louis offered the perfect growing conditions. This area in southwestern Illinois now produces more than half of the entire U.S. supply of horseradish roots.

According to the Ministry of Alberta Agriculture and Rural Development, most of the Canadian horseradish production in Manitoba and Ontario is used for extracting the peroxidase enzyme for medical applications, while much of the U.S. crop still goes to household use as whole roots or is further processed into grated horseradish or bottled horseradish sauce.

Planted away from the main herb and vegetable gardens, horseradish thrives in full sun at the back of a barn in Pennsylvania.

FLAVOR

Horseradish is sharply pungent, hot, and mustard-like.

PARTS TO USE

Horseradish roots are most popular, but the fresh, young and tender leaves are also edible.

CULINARY USES

Horseradish is one herb that is always used raw. This is because cooking or storing horseradish (fresh or bottled) at room temperature will cause the flavor and pungency to dissipate. Vinegar is added to commercially prepared horseradish to help stabilize its biting aroma and taste and keep it from turning brown. (Vinegar or lemon juice is added in home-prepared horseradish.) Commercially bottled horseradish should be bought in small quantities and stored in the refrigerator. For use, spoon it into small glass or ceramic bowls for serving, recap the jar, and return it to the refrigerator immediately. Never return leftover horseradish to the jar. Roots are packaged and shipped to supermarkets. They will keep for months in the refrigerator (at or just below 40°F) if stored in plastic bags to retain humidity and water.

Use the fresh root grated as a condiment or combined with vinegar, lemon juice, ketchup, mayonnaise, mustard, sour cream, cream cheese, or drained yogurt to make a sauce to accompany beef, fried fish, shrimp, clams, oysters, mussels, and vegetables (especially potatoes). It can also be added to drinks such as the cocktail known as Bloody Mary, which combines horseradish with spices and tomato juice.

Fresh young horseradish leaves are best served raw in salads or cooked as you would spinach. They can also be used to make a mildly hot pesto.

❤ HEALTH BENEFITS

Horseradish is antidepressant, antibacterial, anticancer, and antioxidant; and its enzyme peroxidase is used to diagnose the AIDS virus. High in calcium and vitamins C and K and acting as a non-potassium-deleting diuretic, it is used to treat some kidney disorders. It is a circulatory and digestive stimulant, which is why it is often combined with fatty meats. It has antimicrobial properties for preserving meat.

CAUTION: Ingesting large amounts of the mustard oil glycosides in horseradish may depress thyroid function; beware if you have hypothyroidism (underactive thyroid).

GROWING HORSERADISH

A tall (up to 3 foot), herbaceous perennial, horseradish can be planted from thin branches or from root cuttings in early autumn or spring. Choose a sunny, damp location where you can manage it because it is difficult to remove—even after digging up, a tiny piece of root will grow a new plant. Horseradish likes cool weather and rotted manure or compost. Harvest it as needed but only after the first frost when the flavor is at its peak. Always harvest before the third year because the roots are woody and tough after that.

A WARM AND PEPPERY HERBS PRIMER

WARM OR HOT HERBS

Warming herbs work, in general, to speed up some body processes. They improve circulation and bring blood to the surface of the skin, which warms the area through which the blood is pulsing. Warming herbs also tend to soothe the stomach, aid digestion, and keep your blood sugar from spiking and crashing. What follows is a short list of warming herbs.

CAYENNE PEPPER The hot, pungent flavor comes from *capsaicin*, which is found in the seeds, the white fleshy parts, and the skin. Capsaicin acts as a stimulant and tonic; it purifies the blood; and it promotes fluid (mucus) elimination and sweating.

GINGER A circulatory stimulant, ginger is a warming herb that relaxes blood vessels, promotes sweating, and is an expectorant. It also boosts the immune system, fights allergies, lowers cholesterol, eases arthritis pain, fights nausea, and promotes digestion.

HORSERADISH A circulatory and digestive stimulant, this warming herb is antidepressant, antibacterial, anticancer, and antioxidant.

NIPPY OR PEPPERY HERBS

Peppery herbs dance on the tongue. They nip and sometimes bark, and they make you pay attention to the food you are eating. A good way to test the pepper punch in herbs is to take a bite of the leaf and see if it bites back as you chew. Peppery herbs are added to recipes as you would black pepper (*Piper nigrum*)—mindfully, in small amounts, and tasting as you add, so that you get just the right amount. Sometimes they leave your mouth and throat humming with delight, so taste and wait a bit before adding more. The following are some of the herbs with a bite.

ARUGULA (*Eruca vesicaria* var. *sativa*) As part of the *Brassicaceae* family of plants, arugula has a nutritional resemblance to cabbage, broccoli, and other members of that important group. Use alone as the Italians do—simply dressed with a splash of vinaigrette—and you will enjoy its digestive bitter benefits.

NASTURTIUM Both the flowers and leaves are colorful and edible, but the leaves add the zing to salads and other dishes. High in vitamin C, nasturtium has been used in herbal medicine for chest colds and as an expectorant. It is also antiseptic and is used for respiratory and urinary tract infections.

ROSEMARY Its pine and slight menthol taste requires judicial use, but when used with skill, rosemary adds flair to tomato sauces, casseroles, and many other dishes. A powerful antioxidant; the *carnosic acid* can protect the brain from stroke and neurodegeneration that comes from toxins and free radicals.

SAGE Fresh sage leaves make a bitter digestive stimulant so include raw sage leaves in salads. It helps to restore memory and its antiseptic qualities make it an ideal gargle or mouthwash.

SAVORY Similar to rosemary and sage, savory has some resinous pine flavor but with more of a bite. Add it to salads and use with beans, kale, and spinach and in legume and potato dishes.

WASABI (*Eutrema japonica*) Use with caution because the fumes go up your nose and it has a fiery bite. A root similar to horseradish, wasabi is bright green in color. It is grated and used as a sushi and fish accompaniment. It is widely available dried and powdered and can be made into a paste by adding water. Some specialty shops offer wasabi in premixed paste form.

WATERCRESS (*Nasturtium officinale*) Like the herb we call nasturtium, watercress adds a green and pleasant zest to salads and soup. It teams well with creamy and soft cheese for watercress sandwiches and chopped fresh watercress may be used in place of spinach in casseroles.

Horseradish Sauce

Like any root, horseradish should be scrubbed and peeled (if not organic) as you would a potato. It may be grated using a box or hand grater, the grater disc of a food processor, or chopped using a blender. If grating by hand, do it in a well-ventilated area or even outside. Freshly prepared horseradish sauce is pure white and piquant and it is advisable to use it immediately because once exposed to air, the mixture begins to brown and lose its powerful punch.

If you grow horseradish, clean, trim, and store whole roots tightly wrapped in plastic in the refrigerator. Make only as much grated sauce as you need for a meal, but if you make more, store it in a tightly capped glass container in the refrigerator and use as soon as possible. To horseradish lovers, the following recipe is the easiest way to enjoy the piquant root, but beware: it is not creamy or mellow. It is one that Charles Voigt contributed to *Horseradish, Herb of the Year 2011*, and I've adapted it here with permission. Use a mature, two-year root (harvested after the first frost if possible).

Makes about 3 cups

Cold water

½ cup crushed ice

1 fresh mature horseradish root, coarsely chopped (about 3 cups)

3 tablespoons vinegar or freshly squeezed lemon juice

2 tablespoons sugar, optional

1 teaspoon sea salt

1. Add water to a blender container until the blades are covered. Add ice, horseradish, vinegar, sugar if using, and salt. Add water up to about half of the volume of the container.

2. Cover with blender lid and process from low to high for about 30 seconds. Check the consistency and add more water if necessary. Process until as fine as desired. Spoon into a sterilized jar; cap, label, and refrigerate. Freshly prepared horseradish will keep for several months, but its pungency and flavor will decline over time.

Herb and Lemon-Baked Whitefish with Horseradish Cream

Makes 4 servings

8 sprigs fresh thyme or savory
4 cloves garlic
¼ cup extra-virgin avocado oil
   or olive oil
4 fillets (4 to 6 ounces each)
   whitefish
1 lemon, thinly sliced
¼ cup capers
Coarsely ground sea salt
1 cup Horseradish Cream (below)

SERVING SUGGESTION: As in the photo, serve with roasted potatoes and steamed greens such as spinach or kale.

1. Preheat oven to 350°F.

2. In a baking pan, arrange thyme and garlic in one layer in the bottom of the pan. Add oil, and heat in the preheated oven for 2 minutes.

3. Add whitefish to the pan and spoon hot oil and thyme sprigs over. Lay lemon slices over fish and sprinkle with capers and salt.

4. Bake for 9 minutes, remove, and turn fish over. Return to the oven and bake for 9 more minutes or until the fish is cooked (it turns opaque and flakes easily with a knife). Lift out of the pan with a slotted spoon, discard thyme and garlic, and serve with Horseradish Cream.

HORSERADISH CREAM

Makes 1 cup

1 cup sour cream
⅓ cup drained prepared horseradish
3 tablespoons finely chopped shallots
1 teaspoon freshly squeezed lemon
   juice
2 tablespoons chopped chives for
   garnish, optional

In a bowl, combine sour cream, horseradish, shallots, and lemon juice. Scrape into a serving bowl and garnish with chives if using.

Broccoli Sauté with Dried Cherries and Horseradish

Makes 4 servings

2 tablespoons extra-virgin
coconut oil

3 cups broccoli florets

½ cup dried cherries

1 tablespoon freshly grated or
drained prepared horseradish

2 teaspoons butter

In a wok or skillet, heat oil over medium-high heat. Add broccoli and stir-fry for 6 minutes or until crisp-tender. Add cherries, horseradish, and butter and stir-fry for 1 minute or until heated through.

● SUBSTITUTING PREPARED HORSERADISH FOR FRESH

In all recipes except for the basic prepared horseradish (page 178) you may substitute drained, bottled prepared horseradish for freshly grated horseradish. When a recipe calls for prepared horseradish and you wish to use freshly grated, taste the sauce or mixture and add freshly squeezed lemon juice or vinegar, a teaspoon at a time, because prepared horseradish always contains vinegar.

When a recipe calls for freshly grated horseradish (this is less common), and you wish to use prepared horseradish, use 4 teaspoons of prepared for every tablespoon of fresh horseradish called for and taste before adding vinegar or lemon even if called for, because prepared horseradish already contains vinegar.

A Trio of Zippy Sauces

To make each of these simple and yet very popular sauces, just combine the ingredients in a bowl and enjoy! They will keep for up to three weeks in a jar in the refrigerator. Each makes about 1½ cups.

COCKTAIL SAUCE

1½ cups bottled chili sauce or ketchup
3 tablespoons freshly grated or drained
    prepared horseradish
1 tablespoon freshly squeezed lemon juice

HORSERADISH MAYONNAISE

1½ cups mayonnaise (bottled or homemade)
¼ cup freshly grated or drained prepared
    horseradish
1 tablespoon freshly squeezed lemon juice

TARTAR SAUCE

1½ cups Horseradish Mayonnaise (above)
¼ cup drained and chopped sweet or dill
    pickles

Hyssop

Hyssopus officinalis

Purge me with hyssop, and I shall be clean: wash me, and
I shall be whiter than snow.

—Psalms 51:7

Scholars have argued over which herbs were meant by the term *hyssop*, which is used in the Bible, with marjoram, savory, even thyme being among the dozen or more herbs put forth as possibilities. But it wouldn't be surprising if *H. officinalis* were the actual plant mentioned in Psalms since its healing, anti-inflammatory, and infection-fighting qualities are pretty impressive. Indeed, John 19:29 explains that a sponge soaked in vinegar and hyssop was given to Jesus as he hung on the cross, and again, *H. officinalis* would be my choice as the herb in question.

Hyssop has been cultivated in English gardens since 1658. In her book *A Garden of Herbs*, Eleanour Sinclair Rohde says, "when kept well clipped, hyssop makes an excellent dwarf hedge." Hyssop is like honey (nectar, actually) to pollinators and hummingbirds and butterflies. It is also heat- and drought-tolerant. Gardeners, cooks, and herbalists agree: it's a great plant for the herb garden.

Hyssop (*H. officinalis*) and Anise hyssop (*A. foeniculum*) are actually two separate genera within the *Lamiaceae* family. Anise hyssop is included here because it is a delightful herb for culinary uses; for that reason, it is more common in herb gardens than *H. officinalis*. While *H. officinalis* has more medicinal attributes and a slightly biting taste and *A. foeniculum* is slightly sweeter, with a whisper of anise, you can use either in these and most other recipes that call for "hyssop." Because it blooms for a long time and the spikes are so showy and striking with lavender-blue color and licorice scents, anise hyssop is also outstanding for landscape designs.

FLAVOR

Slightly bitter spikes of mint and camphor make hyssop potent and nippy. Anise hyssop (*A. foeniculum*), which is not hyssop at all but often used in the same way, is sweetly licorice in aroma and flavor.

Anise hyssop stands tall at a bend in the path at Scotney Castle in Kent, England.

PARTS TO USE

Use the leaves, flowers, and young shoots of hyssop.

CULINARY USES

Use the fresh hyssop leaves and flowers raw in fruit or vegetable salads and dips, or include in pesto or green sauce to use with game meats. Hyssop is often used fresh or dried with lentils, stuffings, marinades, and roasted meats. It acts as a digestive and can be used to flavor nonalcoholic drinks (especially bitters), liqueurs, and teas.

♥ HEALTH BENEFITS

Antioxidant, bitter, and slightly warming, hyssop treats colds and asthma because it is expectorant, carminative, and antiviral and it reduces phlegm and promotes sweating. It is also used as a topical anti-inflammatory to ease swelling.

GROWING HYSSOP

Grown from seeds or cuttings planted in spring, hyssop prefers a light, sandy soil and partial shade. Divide two- or three-year-old plants to keep them from turning woody.

What follows are three varieties of anise hyssop (*Agastache*) and one other plant named hyssop.

ANISE HYSSOP (*A. foeniculum*) Long, fat, purple spikes bloom on plants that are 2 to 5 feet tall. This cultivar is the most popular, with good reason.

GIANT (*A. f.* 'Giant') This variety sports striking, pink-lavender flowers with long, showy flowerets.

GOLDEN JUBILEE (*A. f.* 'Golden Jubilee') A stunning plant with chartreuse foliage and lavender flower spikes; use it as a focal plant.

HEDGE HYSSOP (*Gratiola officinalis*) This genus is low-growing—great for knot garden borders and as a ground cover. Used mostly as a medicinal herb (it is a laxative, among other properties), it is not widely used as a culinary herb.

A BITTER HERB PRIMER

Herbalists and other natural healers champion the bitter taste of some herbs and garden greens because although aggressive, bitter flavors are also fresh and stimulating to the body and the brain. It is generally agreed that bitters support the heart, small intestines, and liver as well as reduce fever. As one of the four official tastes—sweet, salty, bitter, and sour— bitter is just now getting some respect and beginning to take its rightful place at the table.

Some ancient traditions link the four tastes to mental as well as physical effects on the body. For example, a balanced intake of bitter flavors is thought to encourage honesty, integrity, optimism, and a loving heart. Not bad for a friend that started out as a bully in the kitchen.

The astringent taste of herbs and greens such as those in the following list awakens the palate and poises it for more balanced tastes in the meal to come. The digestive tonic action promotes the secretion of hydrochloric acid, which aids digestion, so take bitter greens at the start of a meal. A small light salad or a few drops of bitter tincture or sips of bitter tea are excellent tools for whetting the appetite.

Leafy bitter greens and herbs not only positively affect our body and brain, but they also deliver vitamins A and C, fiber, iron, and calcium, all with low caloric impact. Toss any of the following bitter herbs into an appetizer salad or use in the water recipe (page 186) and sip just before a meal.

ARUGULA · HOREHOUND · HYSSOP · NASTURTIUM · RUE

ARUGULA (*Eruca vesicaria* var. *sativa*) A nutty, peppery, hot, and sharp-tasting oak-shaped leaf that may be green or red.

HOREHOUND (*Marrubium vulgare*) Its minty flavor is sharp but not unpleasant. Horehound has been used in lozenges to relieve respiratory and bronchial illnesses such as sore throat, bronchitis, cough, and asthma.

HYSSOP (*H. officinalis*) Slightly bitter spikes of mint and camphor make hyssop potent and nippy. Anise hyssop is sweetly licorice in aroma and flavor.

NASTURTIUM The flowers and leaves are colorful and edible, and the leaves add a peppery, citrusy zing to salads and other dishes.

RUE (*Ruta graveolens*) Rue is often overlooked but its soft, blue-green, rounded leaves and small yellow flowers make it a dainty addition to border or herb gardens. The flavor of the leaves is biting and hotly bitter. Handling the plant, especially in sunlight, may cause skin irritation.

SORREL

SORREL (*Rumex acetosa*) Its fruity, sour flavor blends well with other leafy vegetables and you can use sorrel in place of spinach in recipes. The sharp taste is due to oxalic acid, which is harmless in small quantities for most people except those that suffer from gout, arthritis, or kidney stones.

TANSY

TANSY (*Tanacetum vulgare*) The fragrant, strong-tasting leaves are bright green and feathery in shape. Use chopped fresh leaves to flavor puddings and butter cakes or add to smoothies.

WATERCRESS

WATERCRESS (*Nasturtium officinale*) Hot and peppery with hints of citrus, this makes a good salad addition.

WORMWOOD (*Artemisia absinthium*) One of the most bitter herbs known, it is a key ingredient in absinthe, a liqueur that was wildly popular in pre–World War I France. Its dusty white, lacy leaves add silver color and texture in a garden.

WORMWOOD

Herbalist Simple: Hyssop Herb Water

When herbs are at their peak and abundant, an infusion of water is made for immediate consumption or for use in other longer-lasting herbal preparations, such as syrups or cosmetics. This hyssop water makes a very refreshing drink for hot summer days, especially for athletes and people who work outside. Serve chilled with a slice of lemon.

As a medicine, make the following recipe using ½ cup chopped fresh hyssop and ½ cup fresh or dried elderflowers or cooked elderberries (in place of the 1 cup chopped fresh hyssop). Sip the warm hyssop/elder water during the early stages of a cold and influenza or use to ease digestive upsets and nervous stomach. Use the infused water to make a cough syrup (below) and take as needed to ease chest colds.

Makes 6 cups infused water

6 cups filtered water
1 cup chopped fresh hyssop or
   ½ cup dried hyssop
1 cup barley
½ cup chopped figs
½ cup chopped dates
½ cup raisins

1. In a large pot, bring the water to a boil over high heat. Add hyssop, barley, figs, dates, and raisins. Cover and boil lightly for 35 minutes or until barley is soft. Strain the water through a sieve into a jug. Discard the solids or toss them with vinaigrette, chill, and use as a salad. Set the water aside to cool.

2. When cool, cover the water in the jug, and chill in the refrigerator. Use within 2 days or to make Hyssop Cough Syrup.

HYSSOP COUGH SYRUP

3 cups strained Hyssop Water
   (above)
2 cups sugar

In a saucepan, combine water and sugar. Bring to a boil over high heat. Reduce heat and boil lightly, stirring occasionally, for 30 minutes. Set aside to cool. Pour into three 1-cup bottles. Cap, label, and store in the refrigerator for up to 1 month or in the freezer for up to 1 year.

● TECHNIQUES: DRYING HERBS

Drying is a traditional way to preserve herbs for use all year, and while most of the essential oils remain in dried herbs, which makes them viable for medicines and cooking, it is always best to use fresh herbs for cooking whenever possible. The only exception to this is sweet woodruff (*Galium odoratum*), which actually improves upon drying, since it has no fragrance when fresh. Some herbs, such as chives, parsley, and basil, just do not dry well, and even freezing these particular herbs isn't ideal.

The method of drying depends on the amount of herbs you are working with. Always gather herbs midmorning, after the dew has evaporated, but before the noon sun draws out the essential oils. Rinse in cool water and pat dry with a towel.

For sprigs in small batches, use a dehydrator or arrange in one layer on a cooling rack (or parchment paper) and loosely cover with a sheet of parchment paper. Set aside in a warm, dark, and airy place for a few days until the leaves are crackling dry. The length of time depends on the dryness of the air; it could take a week or more. For a faster method, arrange herbs on a baking sheet and set in an oven between 77°F and 95°F. Check after 24 hours; this method could take up to 48 hours.

When you have large bunches of herbs and bushels of flowers, a barn or shed is ideal for hanging herbs to dry. A homemade drying cupboard with wire shelves and a steady flow of warm air works well too. An extracting fan helps exhaust moist air, an essential consideration for a closed cupboard.

To store dried herbs, remove the leaves from the stems and keep whole in an airtight container—glass or porcelain—with a tight-fitting lid. Keep for one season only. You can use the dried stems, if thick enough, as skewers for grilled vegetables or to flavor soup stocks, or as kindling for the fireplace.

Peppery Zucchini Gratin

Makes 4 servings

2 tablespoons melted extra-virgin
    coconut or olive oil
1 red onion, sliced
3 cloves garlic, chopped
½ red bell pepper, sliced
1 fresh hot chile pepper, finely
    chopped
2 tablespoons chopped fresh
    hyssop
2 zucchini squash, sliced thinly,
    crosswise
4 tomatoes, sliced crosswise
¼ cup chicken broth or water

1. Preheat oven to 375°F and butter a 2-quart baking dish or four 2-cup individual baking dishes.

2. In a skillet, heat the oil over medium-high heat. Sauté onion for 5 minutes. Add garlic and sweet and hot peppers and cook, stirring, for 4 or 5 minutes or until vegetables are soft. Add the hyssop to the vegetables and toss to mix well.

3. Meanwhile, arrange zucchini and tomato slices alternately in the prepared baking dish. Spread the onion mixture evenly over the zucchini-tomato layer and pour the broth over. Bake in the preheated oven for 40 minutes (less if using individual dishes) or until zucchini is tender.

Mixed Rice and Cranberries

Makes 6 servings

3 tablespoons extra-virgin olive oil
1 onion, chopped
1 leek, green and white parts,
    chopped
1 cup short-grain brown rice
1 cup wild rice
5 cups chicken or vegetable broth
1 tablespoon butter
½ cup dried cranberries or cherries
2 tablespoons chopped fresh chives
2 tablespoons chopped fresh hyssop

1. In a large skillet, heat oil over medium-high heat. Sauté onion and leek for 8 minutes or until soft. Add brown and wild rice and cook, stirring constantly, for 1 minute. Add the broth and bring to a boil. Cover, reduce heat, and simmer for 50 minutes or until rice is tender.

2. Add butter, cranberries, chives, and hyssop and toss to mix.

Lavender

Lavandula species

Let's go to that house, for the linen looks white and smells of lavender,
and I long to lie in a pair of sheets that smell so.

—Izaak Walton, *The Compleat Angler*, 1653

Lavender, thought to be from the Latin *lavare*, meaning "to wash," was used by the Romans as a bath perfume, and ever since, its honest and pleasant fragrance has been associated with cleanliness and purity. Science has proved its antiseptic properties and has made lavender's timeless household use as a disinfectant appropriate, even for today. In his book *The Country Housewife's Garden* (1617), William Lawson tells us to "Boil it [lavender] in water, wet thy shirt in it, dry it again and wear it." And gentle folk everywhere and throughout time have done just that.

With more than 2,500 years of recorded use, lavender is one herb that people cultivated, tended, and utilized to the fullest. The Egyptians included lavender in their mummification ritual and it is believed that they were perhaps the first to extract lavender's essential oils through distillation. People learned that lavender could calm the mind, and they used it as a "mood enhancer" by dabbing a lavender-steeped handkerchief to the temples or brow or inhaling its scented essence to revive from a faint or relieve a headache. In the Middle Ages, it was popular as a "strewing herb" (literally to walk on) for keeping insects, moths, and other pests under control and to add a lingering freshness to the air. Nineteenth-century English novelist Elizabeth Gaskell writes of using it in the drawers of cabinets or to "burn in the room of some invalid" in her book *Cranford*.

Aromatherapists and chemists now know that lavender's distinctly aromatic and sweetly hay-like scent is derived from about 180 different constituents found only in the essential oil of lavender plants. This is the chemistry behind lavender's enduring allure and usefulness to the perfume industry and to ordinary folk who would, I'm sure, still love to slip between the evocative yet soothing comfort of lavender-scented sheets.

Grosso (*L.* ×*i.* 'Grosso') is a large plant that is popular at Purple Haze Lavender Farm, Sequim, Washington.

FLAVOR

Every variety is slightly different, but overall, lavender's floral flavor is laced with lemon, mint, and camphor overtones.

PARTS TO USE

The buds, flowers, and leaves are used.

CULINARY USES

There are many varieties of lavender; but for cooking, English and Lavandin types are the best, with Hidcote and Munstead specifically being the most widely used. The flavor of fresh or dried lavender buds is quite potent and has a tendency to overpower a dish, so start with small quantities, taste, and add more as needed.

Use fresh or dried lavender leaves and flowers sparingly in salads, dips, and sauces. Lavender can also be used to infuse sugar or to flavor baked goods or desserts. Lavender ice cream or frozen yogurt is sweetly floral. The flowers make a beautiful garnish for cakes and other desserts. If adding buds to a cake batter, try 1 teaspoon or no more than 1 tablespoon. Make a note on the recipe of the variety, whether fresh or dried, and the amount you used so that, depending on the results, you can duplicate or alter the amount next time.

Lavender teams well with cream, eggs, chocolate, honey, lemons, macadamia nuts, almonds, hazelnuts, pears, and berry fruits and also works well in marinades and rubs for chicken, lamb, and fish. It adds a blue-purple tinge to vinegar. Combine it with chives, marjoram, thyme, parsley, rosemary, and savory in spice blends.

Aromatherapists dilute lavender essential oil in their own blends for use topically, but for cooking it is diluted in vegetable oil by the manufacturer to make an edible flavoring known as culinary lavender essence. It is used in very small amounts (drops) for flavoring baked goods, puddings (crème brûlée), sauces, sweet dips, ice creams (*glace à la lavande*), chocolates, honeys, and candies. It is potent and clear in color, and it blends easily into recipes without adding dried bits of the actual bud.

Many herb farms sell culinary lavender "grains" or flower buds, lavender sugar, and lavender essence; others sell lavender products such as tea bags, cookies, and fudge—check the Internet for sources.

CAUTION: Flowers, including lavender and roses, sold in florist shops are inedible because they have been grown and sprayed with chemicals.

❤ HEALTH BENEFITS

Lavender is calming and lifts spirits. In Germany, it is used as a medicinal tea for sleep disorders (restlessness and insomnia) and nervous stomach. It was used in ancient Greek, Roman, and Arabian medicine as an antiseptic. The diluted essential oil is effective for treating burns, cuts, and bruises, for cleaning wounds, and for soothing bites and stings. *CAUTION:* Some people are allergic to lavender.

GROWING LAVENDER

Because it is a shrub that is native to the Mediterranean region, lavender does best in hot, dry, sunny places. Its attractive, blue-green foliage and fragrant flowers range from white and pink to mauve and deep purple, and make it a popular choice for all kinds of gardens and landscapes.

Plant cuttings or seedlings in a sunny place that is well drained, has good air circulation, and is covered in reflective mulch. Shelter from wind by planting lavender close to a wall or protect with hay or straw. Harvesting flower stems and pruning keep the shrub compact and vigorous.

VARIETIES

There are more than fifteen species of lavender with each species containing several varieties. Listed here are the four most popular species of the lavender genus

(*Lavandula*) into which many varieties fall. Note that the common names for the species may be, for example, English or French, but this does not mean that lavenders in these species come from or are grown exclusively in those countries. This is another example of common names being misleading and causing confusion.

All of the following varieties are hardy in Zones 8 to 11. Some cultivars of English lavender are hardy, with winter protection, to Zone 5.

English Types (*Lavandula angustifolia*)

This species is clearly the most popular, with more than forty varieties, making it the most widely known and available. This group tolerates some humidity and winter moisture and is hardy from Zones 5 to 11, which makes it the most sought-after type in North America. Its sweet soft fragrance and lighter taste make it an excellent culinary lavender for baked goods, sauces, puddings, and dips. Some popular English lavender cultivars follow.

ARCTIC SNOW (*L. a.* 'Arctic Snow') The pure white flowers are stunning when planted next to deep purple varieties or in a white garden.

LADY ANN (*L. a.* 'Lady Ann') Its pale pink flowers are set off by the deep green foliage.

ROYAL PURPLE (*L. a.* 'Royal Purple') Long stems appear in early summer, and deeply scented dark purple flowers hold the color well after drying. It is a good border variety.

Lavandin Types (*Lavandula ×intermedia*)

A hybrid cross between English and spike lavender, these types tend to be the cultivars grown in France. They are taller than most English varieties and generally paler in color. They are grown for perfume and prefer dry, hot climates. A few Lavandin cultivars follow.

GROSSO (*L. ×i.* 'Grosso') Its strongly scented, rich purple flowers bloom in midsummer and may bloom again in the fall. Grosso is a large plant and is popular in Sequim, Washington.

PROVENCE (*L. ×i.* 'Provence') With its light lavender flowers on long stems, Provence is grown commercially for its oil and strong scent. It is a good variety for making lavender wands.

PROVENCE

HIDCOTE GIANT (*L. ×i.* 'Hidcote Giant') This variety sports long spikes of medium blue–violet flowers and gray-green leaves. Like Provence, it is also good for making lavender wands.

HIDCOTE GIANT

Spanish Types (*Lavandula stoechas*)

Cultivars in this group sport shorter, fat, pinecone-shaped flower heads topped with bracts that look like large petals. Native to the Mediterranean and northern Africa, Spanish lavender cultivars do not like the cold but are excellent for containers in northern climates. This group of lavenders is sometimes—confusingly—called French lavender. Some examples of Spanish varieties follow.

BALLERINA

BALLERINA (*L. s.* 'Ballerina') Small, dark purple flower buds and flowers with frilly white bracts that mature to light pink are the features of this plant.

CURLY TOP (*L. s.* 'Curly Top') This exceptional variety grows fat, rather stubby clusters of deep purple flowers that are topped by two or three fluted, arching purple bracts.

CURLY TOP

French Types (*Lavandula dentata*)

The lacy, gray-green notched leaves are the main attraction of the cultivars in this group. The flowers are not as sweetly lavender-scented as English or Lavandin, being more like camphor. French lavenders are grown mainly as an ornamental plant and are often used in sachets. These types are also sometimes incorrectly called Spanish lavender.

FRINGED LAVENDER

FRINGED LAVENDER (*L. d.*) Dark green leaves are deeply toothed.

● TECHNIQUES: USING AND PRESERVING LAVENDER

To dry lavender, harvest the lavender spikes before the buds open and snip the long flower stems at their base, where the leaves begin. Secure a bunch and hang upside down in a warm, dark, and airy place to dry. When crackling dry, strip the buds off the stem into a jar. Cap, label, and store in a cool, dark place for one year.

To powder lavender once the buds are dry, pound in a mortar using a pestle or grind in an electric spice grinder to a fine powder. Store as you would dried lavender buds. Add a tiny amount to the dry or wet ingredients in baked goods, puddings, sauces, dips, dressings, and vinaigrettes.

Lavender can also be frozen. Keep the stems whole or break in half and freeze in a freezer bag. You can use one or two stems under the skin of chicken or pressed into lamb or stuffed into fish or under fish as it grills. Dried stems may also be used for smoking fish and vegetables.

Herb/Floral Water

Because flowers were important to medicines and toilette as well as food, cookbooks dating from the sixteenth, seventeenth, and eighteenth centuries include recipes for using flowers with sugar, butter, honey, oils, syrups, vinegars—and floral waters. These ancient recipes are the source for all of our modern techniques.

If you grow fragrant herb flowers, you don't need a homemade steam method or a still to make floral waters, but keep in mind that hydrosols from steam distillation, as outlined on page 91, are stronger in floral/herb essence because they contain a small amount of oil and other plant properties that are not extracted from Floral Water using the following method.

Follow directions for using and preparing edible flowers in the Edible Flower Primer (page 261). Choose only aromatic flowers (roses, lavender, pinks, violets, jasmine,

Pelagonium) or herbs (rosemary, mint, dill, lemon verbena) for this water. See also Rose-Scented Leaf Water, page 295.

Makes about 2 cups

1 pound fresh petals and/or herbs, divided (see headnote)

Pure spring or filtered water

1. In a nonreactive saucepan, place about 3 cups of the petals. Add enough water to cover the petals. Cover and bring to a gentle simmer over medium-low heat. Simmer for 40 minutes.

2. Using a slotted spoon, lift out the petals and discard. Add about 3 cups of fresh petals but do not add more water to the pan. Cover and bring to a gentle simmer over medium-low heat. Simmer for 40 minutes.

3. Repeat step 2 until all of the petals have been simmered in the water.

4. Strain the water through a fine-mesh strainer lined with cheesecloth into a pint glass jar. Cap, label, and store in the refrigerator and use within 2 weeks.

Herb Leaf and Floral Hydrosols

It was skilled tenth-century Persians (from the area known today as Iran) who mastered the art of distillation, or separating essential oils, alcohols, and water from plants—most notably roses. With these and other exotic ingredients, one of the world's most sophisticated cuisines evolved.

Hydrosol is the name for the water (along with minute plant particles and essential oils) that collects as a by-product of the steam distillation of flowers, roots, bark, needles, and leaves of plants for essential oil. These herbal distillates are aromatic—although perhaps somewhere around one-hundredth as strong as the actual essential oil—and are used as flavoring in baked products such as cookies or cakes, for adding to teas for flavor, as ingredients for spa products such as bath water supplements and refreshing body misters, as room fresheners, and in some medicines. You can only get pure herbal hydrosols using a steam distillation process or by purchasing them from producers who steam-distill essential oils using professional distilling equipment.

The good news is that you can collect small amounts of hydrosols using kitchen equipment. Here is how to do it.

Fresh aromatic flowers (roses, lavender, pinks, violets, jasmine, *Pelagonium*) or herbs (rosemary, mint, dill, lemon verbena)

Pure spring or filtered water
Ice

1. In a large pot with a lid, place a rack or a heatproof ramekin or brick to elevate the collection container (a 2-cup or larger heatproof measuring cup). Stand the collection container on the rack. It will collect the distilled hydrosol, so it must be higher than the water used to steam the plant material.

2. Fill the bottom of the pot with plant material. The herbs or flowers should reach up to within 1 inch of the top of the empty measuring cup. Add water to the pot until the plant material is just covered.

3. Put the lid on the pot upside down and fill it with ice. Bring the water in the pot to a simmer. The water surrounding the plant material should simmer but not boil. Simmer for 20 to 30 minutes. Check the hydrosol collected in the measuring cup and if you have enough, pour it into a glass jar. Cap, label, and store in the refrigerator for up to 1 week.

4. If you want more hydrosol, repeat steps 2 and 3 using fresh plant material.

Perfumed Sugar

Rose, mint, *Pelargonium*, calendula, pinks, jasmine, and lavender make sweetly fragrant, slightly exotic sugars for chefs and cooks to use in desserts, sauces, mousses, and puddings. Some savory dishes, such as Moroccan-spiced chicken or baked fish, are brightened by a sprinkling of rose or calendula sugar.

To make perfumed sugar, use only crackling dry herbs (see Drying Herbs, page 187) because any moisture from the plant material will melt the sugar and cause it to form a sticky paste. Use 1 part freshly dried rose, calendula, pinks, jasmine petals, mint, or *Pelargonium* leaves for every 2 parts granulated or powdered (fruit) sugar. For lavender, the ratio is 1 part freshly dried lavender buds for every 9 or 10 parts sugar. As always, taste and adjust the ratio to your preference.

Combine herb and sugar in a blender container or bowl of a food processor. Secure lid and process on high for 40 seconds or until the herb is powdered and evenly distributed in the sugar. Transfer to a jar. Cap, label, and store in a cool, dark place for up to one year.

Lavender Lemonade

Makes 4 servings

Lavender buds from 3 fresh
    sprigs lavender or 1 tablespoon
    dried lavender buds
1 cup sugar
2 cups boiling water
1½ cups freshly squeezed
    lemon juice
2 cups cold water
1 cup ice cubes

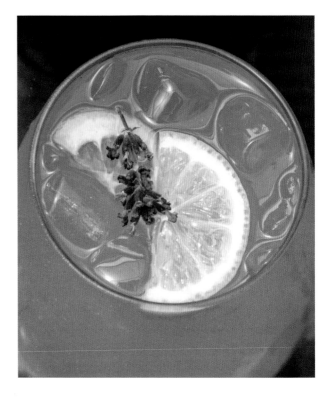

1. In a large bowl, combine lavender and sugar. Rub the buds and sugar between your fingers to mix well. Pour boiling water over and stir to melt the sugar. Cover and set aside for a minimum of 30 minutes and up to 4 hours to infuse the water. The longer the mixture steeps, the stronger the lavender taste will be.

2. Strain the water through a fine-mesh strainer into a jug and discard the lavender. Add lemon juice and cold water. Taste and add more sugar or lemon if necessary. Divide the ice among 4 glasses and pour lemonade over.

Herbes de Provence Spice Blend

Makes about ¾ cup

3 tablespoons dried marjoram

3 tablespoons dried thyme

3 tablespoons dried savory

1 tablespoon dried rosemary

1 tablespoon dried lavender buds

1 tablespoon fennel seeds

In a bowl, combine marjoram, thyme, savory, rosemary, lavender, and fennel. Toss to mix well. Transfer to a glass jar. Cap, label, and store in a dry, dark place for up to 1 year.

Lavender Garlic Paste

Makes about ¼ cup

2 cloves garlic

1 tablespoon crushed fresh lavender buds (see Note)

1 piece (2 inches) cinnamon

1 slice candied ginger

½ teaspoon sea salt

3 to 4 tablespoons extra-virgin olive oil

NOTE: If using dried or powdered lavender, use 1 teaspoon. Smear this fragrant paste over chicken breasts or fish for grilling or baking; add to stir-fry dishes or toss with roasted or steamed vegetables.

In a mortar or blender container, combine garlic, lavender, cinnamon, ginger, and sea salt. Pound using a pestle or process to a thick paste. Add olive oil slowly until a spreadable paste is formed. Scrape into a glass container, cover, and refrigerate for up to 1 week.

Lemon Balm

Melissa officinalis

The herb without all question is an excellent helpe to comfort the heart
as the very smell may induce any so to believe.

—John Parkinson, *Paradiso*, 1629

While the ancient Greeks and Romans found many uses for lemon balm, it may have been early Arabs who used it to lift the spirits, believing that hidden in its heart-shaped, lemony-green leaves lay lemon balm's power to ease heart disorders. Add to that the fact that the Persian "prince of physicians," Avicenna (born Abū ʿAlī al-Ḥusayn ibn ʿAbd Allāh ibn Sīnā, 980–1037) recommended lemon balm "to make the heart merry" and we begin to see a pattern of use for merry little *Melissa*.

Were those learned men, plant pushers in the most honorable sense, actually ahead of their time? James Duke (1929-2017), author of *The Green Pharmacy* and USDA ethnobotanist, believed so. According to Duke, "Since 2002, our lemon balm has been shown to help, more with dementia than with depression. For all I know, it is better than the $2 billion drug that proved no better than a placebo against major depression. Surely lemon balm is safer and cheaper to society, and just smelling it is anti-depressant to me, giving my spirits an aromatherapeutic jolt, almost better than a swig of fish oil." In an article appearing in *Lemon Balm Herb of the Year 2007* titled "Lemon Balm(y): The Evidence Please," Duke gave strong evidence for his belief in the ability of lemon balm to assist with Alzheimer's, anxiety, dementia, depression, dyspepsia, herpes, insomnia, stress, and virus.

With his feet firmly planted on both the scientific and the folk tradition perspectives of the efficacy of healing herbs, James Duke called for independent clinical trials comparing a pharmaceutical with a competing herb and a placebo and he stridently petitioned that such testing be applied to lemon balm.

The last word on Parkinson's observation that lemon balm is, indeed, an "excellent helpe to comfort the heart" came from Duke in *Lemon Balm Herb of the Year 2007*: "It's cheap, easy, efficacious ('evidence-based'), pleasing and safe; and it makes a good tea."

FLAVOR
Lemon balm tastes like fresh lemon with a hint of mint.

PARTS TO USE
The leaves and flowers are both used in medicinal and culinary preparations as well as spa applications.

A drift of lemon balm accents an Asian garden in Pennsylvania.

CULINARY USES
Use fresh or dried lemon balm leaves and flowers in sweet or savory dishes such as green or fruit salads, soups, salsas, and other sauces, tea, smoothies, punch, and other iced beverages. Lemon balm teams well with fish, chicken, and pork in sauces, stuffings, or marinades, as well as egg and pudding desserts. It complements yogurt and soft cheeses.

♥ HEALTH BENEFITS

Lemon balm has antibacterial, antioxidant, sedative, and calmative properties. It relieves restlessness, nervous tension, and digestive and gastrointestinal disorders, and calms the nervous system. It may be taken as a tea to stimulate appetite, for nervous sleep disorders, and it has been shown to be effective in a lip balm for sores associated with the herpes simplex virus. Fresh or dried lemon balm may be used in bathwater for easing tension and stress.

GROWING LEMON BALM

Easy to grow from seed or root stock division, lemon balm can be kept bushy and vigorous with regular harvesting or pruning, especially after blooming. It makes a good container plant.

Herbes Salée

Herbes Salée is the French term for salted herbs, a traditional way to preserve fresh herbs for winter use. Often made with equal parts parsley, chervil, lemon balm, onions, carrots, and either celery or lovage leaves as the "herb layer," herbs preserved in salt were often the only winter seasonings used by the early Canadian pioneers, Acadians, and North American colonists. Easy to make and easy to use, fresh herbs (or a mixture of fresh herbs and vegetables) were finely chopped and layered with salt in a canning jar.

Makes 4 cups

2 cups coarse sea salt

2 cups coarsely chopped herbs and vegetables (see headnote)

1. Start with about ½ inch sea salt in the bottom of a one-quart canning jar and alternate ½ inch herbs with a very thin layer of salt, ending with a ½ inch layer of salt on the top. Cap, label, and refrigerate or keep in a cold cupboard.

2. If liquid forms in the jar, drain it off. Salted herbs will keep in the refrigerator for several months.

PERFUMED FINISHING SALTS

Salts that are perfumed with herbs are a new twist on the traditional Herbes Salée. They are so versatile in the kitchen that I like to say they are worth their salt. Perfumed salts are different from Herbes Salée because the herbs are dry before mixing with the salt. I use them when a dish needs color or flavor-brightening after plating—even desserts, especially caramel or chocolate desserts! Sprinkling an herbed salt over both the food and the plate lends a professional finish to the dish. Another way to serve perfumed salts is to mound two or three different salts around the outside of a plate to let the diner lightly dust individual bites to experience different tastes as the dish is consumed.

To make perfumed salts, start with a good quality salt; never use table salt for perfumed salts. Depending on how I want to use the perfumed salt, I choose either kosher or white sea salt. (I have used Hiwa Kai black and Himalayan pink, among other gourmet salts, including apple-smoked brown salt, with spectacular effects, but generally I rely on white sea salt for my herbed salt blends.) Because of the crystal structure, it takes slightly more than twice as long to dissolve granulated salt as it does the same amount of kosher salt. Knowing this, if you want to cook with perfumed salts, use kosher, and if you want a salt that will add sparkle and granulated texture to the finished dish, use sea salt.

Always select medium-grind (or slightly larger-grind) salt, because the key to both aroma and flavor is processing the salt and the herb together in a blender container or spice grinder. If the salt is too fine, the end result will be a powder. Use an equal amount of salt and crackling dry herbs; the list on the facing page shows aromatic herbs for different colors and flavors. Try single-flavored salts, and then start blending two or three different herbs for a unique salt.

1 part dried herb or ½ part ground spice(s) (choose from the list on the facing page)
1 part medium-grind kosher or sea salt, divided

Use dried herbs for salt blends. Using a spice grinder or blender, process the herb until finely chopped or powdered. Add half of the salt and pulse to incorporate the salt and herb. Transfer to a bowl and add the remaining salt. Mix well and transfer to a jar. Cap, label, and store in a dry, cool place for up to 6 months.

GREEN SALTS: lemon balm, lemon verbena, thyme, sage, rosemary, dill, chervil, lovage, mint, scented geranium leaves, French tarragon, matcha (Japanese green tea leaves)

YELLOW/ORANGE SALTS: turmeric, calendula petals, saffron

RED SALTS: cayenne pepper, Sichuan peppercorn, rose petals, clove pink petals

PURPLE OR BLUE SALTS: lavender buds, chicory petals

BROWN SALTS: cinnamon, star anise, coriander, nutmeg, allspice, cumin

Citrus Salt

This salt is a favorite because it works with savory or sweet foods. Use it with poultry, fish, pork, and seafood or in sauces for those meats. It is an excellent match for chocolate mousses, puddings, brownies, cakes, ice creams, or fruit desserts—sprinkle just a pinch over the dessert and/or the plate just before serving, or pass in a salt cellar with a tiny, nonreactive spoon.

Makes about ½ cup

Grated zest of 1 lemon or lime
Grated zest of 1 orange
2 tablespoons dried lemon balm
⅓ cup medium-grind kosher or
    sea salt, divided

1. Dry the lemon and orange zest on a towel-lined cooling rack overnight or for up to 1 week.

2. Using a spice grinder or blender, process lemon and orange zest and lemon balm until fine. Add half of the salt and pulse to blend well. Transfer to a bowl and add remaining salt. Mix well and transfer to a jar. Cap, label, and store in a dry, cool place for up to 6 months.

CULINARY CITRUS RUB

Makes ½ cup

3 tablespoons coriander seeds
2 tablespoons cumin seeds
1 star anise
3 tablespoons Citrus Salt (above)

Using a spice grinder or blender, process coriander, cumin, and star anise until finely ground. Transfer to a bowl and add citrus salt. Mix well and transfer to a jar. Cap, label, and store in a dry, cool place for up to 6 months.

CULINARY HERB/SPICE RUBS

Rubs are meant to be just that: rubbed all over meat intended for the grill. They season the meat and help to keep juices in while it cooks over the flames and direct heat of the coals. Because the spices will be charred or toasted by the grilling process, I don't toast them for rub mixtures as I would for many of my regular spice blends.

For extra flavor, drizzle honey or coconut nectar over the rub mixture to form a stiff paste. Rub the paste all over the meat in the same way as you would the dry rub before grilling meat.

Tuscan Salt

The big, bold, Mediterranean aroma and taste of this salt blend is up to the challenge of lamb, beef, prosciutto, and root vegetables, and yet the smallest pinch is brilliant on sabayons or other eggy puddings. Use dried herbs for this salt.

Makes ½ cup

2 tablespoons rosemary
1 tablespoon lavender buds
1 tablespoon sage
¼ cup medium-grind kosher or sea salt, divided

Using a spice grinder or blender, process rosemary, lavender, and sage until fine. Add half of the salt and pulse to blend well. Transfer to a bowl and add remaining salt. Mix well and transfer to a jar. Cap, label, and store in a dry, cool place for up to 6 months.

Shrimp Cocktail Shooters

Makes 6 servings

1 pound peeled, deveined
shrimp

2 cups chicken broth

Juice of ½ lemon

3 breakfast radishes,
thinly sliced

2 stalks fennel, chopped

2 stalks celery, chopped

¼ cup chopped fresh
lemon balm

½ cup Lemon Aioli (facing page)

1 lemon or lime wedge

¼ cup Citrus Salt or Culinary
Citrus Rub (page 206),
divided

6 sprigs lemon balm or bay
leaves for garnish

NOTE: You can substitute an equal
amount of regular mayonnaise for
the aioli in this recipe.

1. In a saucepan, combine shrimp, broth, and lemon juice. Bring to a simmer over medium heat. Cover, reduce heat, and simmer for 3 to 4 minutes or until shrimp are cooked (they will turn bright pink). Using tongs or a slotted spoon, transfer shrimp to a colander, rinse with cold water, and set aside to drain and cool. Discard broth or use in another recipe.

2. Select 6 shrimp, wrap, and set aside in the refrigerator. Coarsely chop remaining shrimp.

3. In a bowl, combine chopped shrimp, radishes, fennel, celery, lemon balm, and aioli. Season to taste with a pinch of citrus salt.

4. Pour remaining citrus salt into a shallow plate or saucer. Rub lime around the outside of six 4-ounce shooter glasses. Invert glasses, one at a time, in the salt and twist to coat the edges.

5. Divide shrimp cocktail evenly between the rimmed shooter glasses and garnish each with whole shrimp and a sprig of lemon balm.

LEMON AIOLI

Makes ½ cup

½ cup extra-virgin olive oil
1 clove garlic, finely chopped
1 tablespoon chopped fresh
    lemon balm
2 egg yolks
1 tablespoon white wine vinegar
1 tablespoon freshly squeezed
    lemon juice
2 teaspoons Dijon mustard
½ teaspoon Citrus Salt
    (page 206) or regular sea salt

1. In a bowl, combine olive oil, garlic, and lemon balm.

2. In a blender container, combine yolks, vinegar, lemon juice, mustard, and salt. Pulse or process for 10 seconds to mix well.

3. With the motor running, add oil with garlic and lemon balm in a slow, steady stream and stop when all the oil has been added. Transfer aioli to a container, cover, and refrigerate for up to an hour. Aioli will thicken upon chilling.

Citrus Body Scrub

Salt is exfoliating when rubbed on feet, legs, and arms, leaving the skin soft and smooth. Citrus is refreshing, but you can also use coconut or aromatic herbs for their effect on the skin. For example, lavender soothes burns, cuts, and minor scrapes, so make a fragrant, healing lavender body scrub using the following method. Always use sea salt for body scrub mixtures.

Because of its incredible health benefits, I prefer coconut oil for cooking and cosmetics. It is solid at temperatures below 76°F, but melts in the palm of your hand. To melt coconut oil for this recipe, bring a small saucepan filled with about 3 inches of water to a simmer over medium heat. Place the glass jar of coconut oil in the water, turn the heat off, and wait until the coconut turns clear and liquid. Pour into a liquid measuring cup to measure and proceed with the recipe.

Makes about ½ cup

About ¼ cup melted extra-virgin coconut oil or almond oil
½ cup Citrus Salt (page 206)
6 drops citrus essential oil, optional

1. In a small jar, drizzle oil over citrus salt, mixing until the salt forms a soft paste. Add essential oil if using and stir well. Cap, label, and store beside a bathtub or sink.

2. To use, take a small amount of body scrub in the palm of your hand and rub it over feet, legs, hands, and arms. Keep rubbing until you feel a tingling sensation. Rinse off and pat dry.

Citrus Rubbed Pork

Makes 4 to 6 servings

2 pounds pork tenderloin
¼ cup Culinary Citrus Rub (page 206)

1. Preheat oven to 350°F. Arrange pork on a baking sheet, spread rub evenly over all sides, and rub into the meat.

2. Bake in preheated oven for 40 to 50 minutes or until the internal temperature reaches 155°F. Tent with foil and let rest for 10 minutes before slicing.

Roasted Pears with Citrus Salt

Makes 4 servings

4 pears

4 tablespoons Ginger Syrup
 (see note) or honey

¼ pound Camembert cheese

4 teaspoons Citrus Salt
 (page 206)

NOTE: To make Ginger Syrup, follow the recipe for Herb-Infused Syrup on page 126 and use ¼ cup grated fresh ginger in place of the elderflowers.

1. Preheat oven to 350°F. Line a rimmed baking sheet with parchment paper.

2. Arrange pears on prepared baking sheet and bake in preheated oven for 35 minutes or until browned on the outside and soft to the touch. Set aside to cool for 5 or 10 minutes. Leave the oven on.

3. Cut pears in half, leaving the stem intact on one half. Scoop out and discard the seeds and core. Return pear halves to the baking sheet with the cut side up. Drizzle syrup evenly over pear halves. Divide cheese into 8 equal slices and position on pear halves. Bake for 3 minutes or until cheese is soft. Transfer 2 pear halves to each dessert dish. Drizzle liquid, if any, from the baking sheet evenly over pear halves and sprinkle 1 teaspoon citrus salt evenly over each plate.

A SALAD HERB PRIMER

King James II's gardener advised that there should be at least thirty-five ingredients in an ordinary salad. The leaves (see below) and flowers (page 261), sometimes roots (see page 214), and stems of all fresh herbs—cultivated or wild—may be used in salads and the more you use, the more complex the taste will be and the greater the healing power. In fact, like the delicate art of perfumery or blending herbs and spices for tea or seasoning, combining herbs in a salad can be just as fun. The more you mix and taste, the more skillful you become. The following is a short list of the wide range of herbs that enliven fresh salads.

SALAD LEAF HERBS	QUALITIES	
Bloody Dock (*Rumex sanguineus*)	tangy and tart	
Chickweed (*Stellaria media*)	light citrus	
Chicory (*Cichorium intybus*)	flowers are lightly floral	
Good King Henry (*Chenopodium bonus-henricus*)	like spinach	

SALAD LEAF HERBS	QUALITIES	
Lemon balm	lemony, hint of mint	
Mustard Greens	slightly hot and peppery	
Nasturtium	leaves are peppery	
Orach (*Atriplex hortensis*)	red or green; mild, spinach-like	
Perilla (*Perilla frutescens*)	green is sweet and spicy; red is less aromatic	
Purslane (*Portulaca oleracea*)	mildly tart with citrus	
Salad Burnet (*Poterium sanguisorba*)	cucumber taste	
Watercress (*Nasturtium officinale*)	hot and peppery	

SALAD ROOT HERBS	QUALITIES	
Elecampane (*Inula helenium*)	tall, with sunflower-like flowers; root is candied and grated into salads	
Burdock (*Arctium*)	grate raw or chop candied root into salads	
Fennel (*Foeniculum vulgare*)	shave the white bulb thinly and toss with radishes, avocados, and artichokes as well as salad greens	
Angelica	roots are bitter and taste like anise; use sparingly, or candy and thinly slice for salads	
Beets (*Beta vulgaris*)	shred or slice raw, pickled, or cooked beets into salads; often served with soft or feta cheese. Young green leaves are edible.	
Daikon (*Raphanus sativus*)	a long, Japanese radish used raw or braised and added to warm and cold salads	
Coriander	root is often used in Thai foods; often sold in Asian markets	
Parsley	strong-tasting, usually steamed or simmered in water before adding to salads	

● DRESSING HERB SALADS:

Herbed Vinaigrette

Salad dressings are a blend of acid (vinegar or lemon juice) and oil. While there may be other herbs or flavorings added, a ratio of 1 part acid to 3 parts oil is the most widely used. For fresh herb-based salads, a light vinaigrette may be the best and simplest way to dress the ingredients. For slaws that include cabbage and root vegetables, aioli or mayonnaise may be a more suitable choice.

Experiment with organic, polyunsaturated oils such as hemp, sunflower, safflower, extra-virgin olive oil, or any of the nut oils to make dressings that are worthy of fresh herbs. Try freshly squeezed lime, grapefruit, or lemon juice or balsamic, coconut, apple cider vinegars or other interesting vinegars as the piquant punch. What follows is a recipe for vinaigrette that can serve as a template for any combination of ingredients that you wish to use.

Makes 1 cup

¾ cup oil (see headnote)
¼ cup vinegar or freshly squeezed citrus (see headnote)

3 tablespoons Ginger Syrup (see note, page 211) or honey
2 tablespoons chopped fresh herbs

In a jar, combine oil, vinegar, syrup, and herbs. Cap and shake vigorously. Drizzle over salad greens and toss.

Lemongrass

Cymbopogon citratus

The bulbous base imparts an elusive aromatic and lemon
fragrance to the cooking of Southeast Asia.

—Jill Norman, *Herbs & Spices*, 2002

My first delicious flirtation with lemongrass came some thirty-five years ago, when I discovered the sweetly scented, succulent bulbs in a fragrant Pad Thai dish. It was love at first lemony twang. And then, not to say that I stalked (pardon the pun) the scallion-like herb, but at that time it was a challenge to source these exotic and somewhat unknown fresh stems of pure culinary delight.

Happily, with awareness and demand came availability, and now Asian markets, farmers markets in cities with a large Asian population, and many regular supermarkets sell heaps of fresh lemongrass, all across North America. Look for white, soft but firm (not woody) bulbous bases with fresh green outer leaves. The leaves and stalk should not show signs of dryness, wrinkling, and/or yellowing.

Keep fresh lemongrass tightly wrapped in plastic in the refrigerator for up to three weeks. You can stand the stalks in a half-inch of water in a pail and keep in a cool place for about a week. Don't try to dry lemongrass because it loses fragrance and flavor, though freezing is actually a good way to preserve it: chop or finely slice the white and light-green base of the stalk and freeze in quarter-cup or half-cup amounts in zippered freezer bags. Label and freeze for up to six months.

FLAVOR

Lemongrass is tartly lemon with a slight heat.

PARTS TO USE

Discard the coarse outer dark-green leaves and use the tender, white and light-green inner leaf stalk.

CULINARY USES

Peel away the outer coarse, and very sharp, green leaves. Use the fresh white and pale green stalk whole, bruised, or finely chopped for teas, soups, stir-fry dishes, curries, or stews. Pound or purée the soft white part for spice pastes and sauces or dips.

To use the whole stalk for flavor, trim and discard tough outer leaves and leave the light green and white stalk whole or cut in half lengthwise. Bruise the stalk by hitting it with a meat tenderizer or rolling pin to release some of the volatile oils. Remove and discard at the end of cooking.

To cook with lemongrass as part of the ingredients, use only the tender white bulb and chop or slice very fine.

To make fragrant pastes, pound the soft, inner white bulb in a mortar, or purée using a blender with other herbs and spices.

Lemongrass gives height to a culinary herb bed at the Atlanta Botanical Gardens in Atlanta, Georgia.

♥ HEALTH BENEFITS

Lemongrass is sometimes used as a mild astringent and to treat symptoms of flu—fever, achy joints, itchy eyes, and scratchy throat. Lemongrass essential oil has antifungal properties and it also helps ease headaches, stomachaches, and abdominal, muscle, and joint pains.

GROWING LEMONGRASS

Lemongrass is a tropical plant that seeks warmth, full sun, and moist but well-drained soil. It is a grass and may grow up to 3 feet tall. Hardy only to Zone 10, it may be planted in containers or treated as an annual in northern gardens.

Citrus Red Curry Paste

This recipe seems like it has a lot of ingredients, and it does; but they all combine to make a rich, Thai-style curry that has lots of heat but is pleasantly fragrant and tasty. Of course, you may use more or less cayenne peppers to control the bite. Fenugreek (*Trigonella foenum-graecum*) is the key spice in Chinese and Indian curry blends, and it imparts the curry flavor, so do not omit it in this recipe.

Makes about 1½ cups

1 tablespoon coriander seeds

2 teaspoons cumin seeds

1 teaspoon fenugreek seeds

½ teaspoon green peppercorns

1 star anise

4 cloves garlic

2 shallots or ½ cup chopped onion

1 stalk lemongrass, white bulb and
  tender green parts, coarsely
  chopped

2 dried cayenne peppers, finely
  chopped

1 piece (1 inch) fresh galangal,
  or ginger

2 tablespoons chopped cilantro
  root, optional

1 tablespoon Ginger Syrup
  (see note, page 211) or
  coconut nectar

1 teaspoon grated lime zest
  (Makrut lime if possible)

1 tablespoon lime juice

1 teaspoon toasted sesame oil

1 teaspoon shrimp paste or
  fish sauce, optional

1 tablespoon coconut cream
  or milk

1. In a spice wok or small cast-iron skillet, toast coriander, cumin, fenugreek, peppercorns, and star anise over medium heat, stirring constantly, for 3 minutes or until fragrant and popping. Set aside to cool.

2. If using a mortar and pestle, be sure that it is large enough. Pound the cooled toasted spices until fine. Add garlic and shallots and pound until puréed. Add lemongrass, cayenne peppers, galangal, and cilantro root and pound until puréed. One at a time, work in syrup, lime zest, lime juice, sesame oil, and shrimp paste if using. Add coconut cream, a teaspoon at a time, until the paste is moist and spreadable but not thin.

3. If using a blender, combine coconut cream, syrup, lime zest, lime juice, sesame oil, and shrimp paste in the container and pulse to mix. Add garlic, shallots, lemongrass, cayenne peppers, galangal, cilantro root, and cooled toasted spices. Process, adding more coconut cream if needed, until smooth.

4. Transfer to a pint jar. Cap, label, and store in the refrigerator for up to 3 weeks.

Beef Pho

Makes 4 servings

7 ounces dried rice noodles

2 tablespoons extra-virgin
   coconut oil

1 onion, finely chopped

6 cups beef broth or consommé

½ cup Spicy Cashew Sauce
   (facing page) or peanut butter

½ pound beef fillet, thinly sliced
   (see note)

1 cup fresh bean sprouts

½ cup coarsely chopped salted
   cashews

¼ cup thinly sliced lemongrass,
   white bulb and tender green
   parts

Red Curry Paste for serving
   (page 218)

NOTE: For the beef to cook in a few minutes, it must be paper-thin. Wrap the fillet in plastic wrap and roll tightly into a cylinder. Place in the freezer for 30 minutes or until only just firm. Remove plastic and use a sharp French knife to slice the beef into paper-thin slices.

1. Place the noodles in a bowl and pour boiling water over. Set aside for 5 to 6 minutes or until tender. Drain and divide evenly among 4 soup bowls.

2. Meanwhile, in a soup pot, heat oil over medium heat. Sauté the onion for 5 minutes or until soft. Add broth and Spicy Cashew Sauce and bring to a boil. Add beef slices, reduce heat, and simmer for 2 or 3 minutes or until beef is cooked.

3. Divide bean sprouts evenly among the bowls, setting them on top of the noodles. Ladle broth and beef over noodles and sprouts in bowls. Divide cashews and lemongrass evenly among the 4 bowls to garnish each. Pass Red Curry Paste separately.

Spicy Cashew Sauce

Makes about 1 cup

1 cup chopped fresh basil

1 cup chopped fresh cilantro or
  flat leaf parsley

½ cup chopped fresh peppermint

2 to 4 tablespoons Red Curry
  Paste (page 218), or to taste

1 tablespoon melted extra-virgin
  coconut oil or olive oil

3 tablespoons fresh lime juice

½ cup cashew butter or peanut
  butter

1 to 2 tablespoons tamari or
  soy sauce

In a blender container, combine basil, cilantro, peppermint, curry paste, oil, lime juice, cashew butter, and 1 tablespoon of the tamari sauce. Secure the lid and blend (from low to high if using a variable-speed blender) until smooth. If the sauce is too thick, add remaining tamari and cold water, 1 tablespoon at a time, and blend until the sauce reaches the desired consistency.

NOTE: Use this sauce to flavor soups or stir-fry dishes, to toss with cooked vegetables, or as a dipping sauce for grilled kebabs. Make it as thin or as thick as you wish by adding more or less water.

Hot Lemon Toddy

Makes 1 drink

Grated zest and juice of 1 lemon
1 to 2 tablespoons Ginger Syrup
  (see note) or honey, to taste
1 to 2 teaspoons Red Curry Paste
  (page 218), to taste
1 cup boiling water
1 stalk lemongrass, bruised for
  garnish, optional

In a mug or heatproof glass, combine lemon zest and juice, syrup, and curry paste. Pour boiling water over and stir until syrup is dissolved. Garnish with lemongrass stalk if desired.

NOTE: To make Ginger Syrup, follow the recipe for Herb-Infused Syrup on page 126 and use ¼ cup grated fresh ginger in place of the elderflowers.

Lemon Seasoning

Lemon is a natural companion to fish and poultry, and this lemon blend may be combined with 1 part kosher or sea salt and used as a citrus rub or in rice or bread stuffing. Use 1 tablespoon in an herbal tea or add to sweet or savory sauces. It may be combined with the dry ingredients in baked goods or beaten into icing. For this blend, use dried herbs.

1 part dried lemon verbena
1 part dried lemon balm
1 part dried coarsely chopped
  lemongrass
½ part dried lemon zest
½ part dried lemon mint
½ part dried lemon thyme

1. In a bowl, combine lemon verbena, lemon balm, lemongrass, lemon zest, lemon mint, and lemon thyme. Transfer to a jar. Cap, label, and store in a cool, dark place.

2. To use, rub a small amount between your palms to powder the dried leaves. Measure and add to recipes.

Lemon Verbena

Aloysia citriodora

If you're a fan of lemon desserts, lemon verbena will be a star.

—Jerry Traunfeld, former executive chef and author of *The Herbfarm Cookbook*, 2000

Native to South America, Chile, and Argentina, lemon verbena has bright, shiny leaves that are prized for texture and scent. While glossy on the topside, the leaves are very rough to the touch and dull on the underside.

Lemon verbena is often trained as a topiary or standard and makes a very good container plant, except that being a deciduous tree, it loses its leaves with the arrival of cooler weather. If growing in zones colder than Zone 8, bring it inside and let the tree go dormant in a cool place—the basement is ideal—and water minimally. Transfer to a warmer area of the house around April and set outside when all threat of frost is past.

Romans used the word *verbenae* for aromatic plants that were used on altars. Lemon verbena is often confused with the wild plant called vervain (*Verbena officinalis*), native to the Americas, perhaps because the flowering tops are similar. Vervain is a bitter, digestive tonic herb that has been used traditionally for gout, kidney stones, and headache.

Dried lemon verbena leaves retain a fragrant lemon scent; as they dry, they curl and are easy to powder by rubbing between the palms of your hands. Prune just before the tree flowers (because this is the optimum time for essential oils in the leaves) and dry the leaves following the directions on page 187. When the tree reblooms, dry the flowers the same way once they are at their peak.

FLAVOR

The full lemon verbena taste is clear and sweet, not tart like a lemon.

PARTS TO USE

Both the leaves and flowers are used.

CULINARY USES

Use fresh or dried lemon verbena in teas and cold drinks; to season fish and poultry; to flavor sugar, salt, soups, sauces, dips, dressings, and baked goods; and in jellies and preserves. The flavor is best if the leaves are used fresh and added whole to sauces and other cooked dishes. If using dried leaves, be sure to rub or grind the leaves to a fine powder.

A tender plant, lemon verbena will do exceptionally well in northern gardens during summer months.

♥ HEALTH BENEFITS

The leaves contain vitamins A, B, and C and are antioxidant, antispasmodic, digestive, and sedative.

GROWING LEMON VERBENA

A deciduous shrub that grows to 15 feet, propagate lemon verbena by stem cuttings. It needs full sun and is hardy to Zone 8. For northern gardens, lemon verbena makes a good container herb.

Herb Sugar Paste

This is a very good way to use the fresh leaves of sweet herbs (angelica leaves, bergamot, fennel, gingerroot, lemon balm, lemongrass, mint, rose petals, and especially the tough and rough leaves of lemon verbena) in syrups, sauces, smoothies, puddings, sweet dips, and other desserts. If used whole or in a sprig, such herbs must be removed at the end of cooking, and, even if finely chopped, they will still need to be strained out of foods. However, by grinding some roots but mostly leaves with sugar to make a smooth herb paste, the leaves are fine enough to be incorporated into the dish.

In some of the recipes that follow, Lemon Verbena Herb Sugar Paste is called for. This simply means that the Herb Sugar Paste should be made using lemon verbena. If the recipe calls for another herb paste, make the Herb Sugar Paste using the specified herb (e.g., Lemon Balm Sugar Paste).

Use fresh herbs in this recipe.

2 parts lightly packed herb leaves
 (see headnote)

1 part sugar

1. In the bowl of a food processor, combine the herb and sugar. Process for 1 to 2 minutes or until a soft, green paste is formed. Transfer to an airtight container. Cap, label, and store for up to 2 weeks in a cool place or up to 3 months in the freezer.

TO USE HERB SUGAR PASTE: for sorbet, use 1 cup with every 3 cups water. Use equal parts herb sugar paste and granulated sugar in an herb syrup (page 126) or sauce, pudding, or dessert recipe.

Lemon Glazed Scallops with Citrus Salsa

1¼ pounds bay scallops
⅓ cup all-purpose flour
2 tablespoons butter
Juice of 1 lemon
¼ cup water
2 cups Citrus Salsa (below)

1. Preheat oven to 250°F.

2. Rinse and pat scallops dry, using a paper towel. Place in a shallow dish and dust all sides with flour. In a skillet, melt butter over medium-high heat. Working in batches, sear scallops in one layer for 1 to 2 minutes per side or until golden on both sides. Remove to a platter and keep warm in preheated oven.

3. Add lemon juice and water to the pan. Bring to a boil over high heat, scraping up the browned bits. Add salsa and cook, stirring constantly, for 2 minutes or until thickened. Serve scallops with hot salsa.

CITRUS SALSA

Makes 4 cups

2 tablespoons orange zest
4 oranges, sectioned
1 fresh jalapeño pepper, finely chopped
1 red onion, finely chopped
2 cloves garlic, finely chopped
¼ cup chopped fresh cilantro or flat-leaf parsley
2 tablespoons finely chopped lemon verbena or Lemon Verbena Herb Sugar Paste (page 225)

3 tablespoons freshly squeezed lime juice
1 tablespoon toasted sesame oil

In a large bowl, combine orange zest, orange sections, pepper, onion, garlic, cilantro, and lemon verbena paste. Drizzle lime juice and sesame oil over and toss to mix well.

Lemon Mousse

Makes 6 servings

⅓ cup cornstarch
1 cup sugar + ¼ cup Lemon
   Verbena Herb Sugar Paste
   (page 225) or 1¼ cups sugar
¼ teaspoon sea salt
1½ cups warm water
Zest and juice of 2 lemons
3 large egg yolks
3 tablespoons butter
1 cup heavy whipping cream
   (36% butterfat)
6 sprigs fresh lemon verbena,
   optional

1. In a saucepan, whisk together cornstarch, sugar, and salt. Gradually whisk in water and lemon juice and add herb paste if using. Bring to a light boil over medium high heat, stirring constantly, for about 5 minutes or until the mixture is thickened and clear.

2. In a bowl, whisk yolks together. Add about ¼ cup of the hot sugar mixture to the yolks, a little at a time, beating after each addition. When yolks are warmed up, scrape them back into the remaining sugar mixture in the saucepan. Cook, stirring constantly, for 2 minutes or until yolks are incorporated smoothly into the mixture.

3. Reduce heat to medium-low, add lemon zest and butter, and cook, stirring constantly, for 1 minute or until butter is melted. Transfer to a bowl, cover the surface of the lemon mixture with plastic wrap, and set aside to cool.

4. Meanwhile, in a bowl, using electric beaters or an immersion beater, beat whipping cream until soft peaks form. Fold into cooled lemon mixture. Spoon into individual ramekins, cover with plastic wrap, and refrigerate for at least 1 hour or overnight. Garnish with lemon verbena sprigs if desired.

Basic Tomato Salsa

Makes 4 cups

3 tablespoons freshly squeezed
   lemon juice
2 tablespoons Lemon Verbena
   or Lemon Balm Herb Sugar
   Paste (page 225)
4 tomatoes, seeded and chopped
2 cups chopped tomatillos
1 fresh serrano pepper, finely
   chopped
1 red onion, finely chopped
2 cloves garlic, finely chopped
½ cup chopped fresh cilantro
   or flat-leaf parsley

In a bowl, whisk together lemon juice and herb
paste. Add tomatoes, tomatillos, pepper, onion,
garlic, and cilantro. Toss to mix well.

Lovage

Levisticum officinale

This herbe for hys sweete savoure is used in bathe.

—Thomas Hyll (Hill), *The Gardener's Labyrinth*, 1577

We rarely bathe in herbs nowadays, lovage notwithstanding. But it's not just because many herbs are refreshing and calming or soothing and stimulating that I agree with Thomas Hyll. In a purely practical sense, what a sensible way to make use of those towering lovage stalks and mature (and, quite frankly, tough and bitter) leaves! How absolutely divine to slip into a not-too-hot bath and revel in the garden's endless bounty. And cleanup is easy if you cut the stalks to 6-inch lengths and keep leaves and buds intact on the sturdy stalks.

Lovage heightens the flavor of salad and soup herbs and vegetables, making it the essential herb for seasoning blends for these types of dishes. Use it fresh with spring and summer green salads and dried in winter root salads, potato salads, soups, and stews. It subtly complements fish dishes, chowders, and steamed mussels or clams and stands up to long-cooking dishes, adding a delicate and complex flavor. It is excellent in fruit preserves to serve with poultry, pork, lamb, and game meats. It's much stronger when added at the end of cooking, so adjust the amount to the cooking method.

Germans make the most of lovage in soups and stews. The German name for lovage is *Liebstöckel*, translated as "love stick," but they often call it *Maggikraut*, and in Holland, it is known as *Maggiplant*, both names originating from the well-known Maggi brand of dehydrated soup mix that relied on lovage as the base flavor. Today,

Nestlé owns the brand and while parsley plays a role, lovage is not an ingredient in any of the current Maggi products.

One lovage plant will produce enough leaves for a year. Lovage is used fresh, whole, or chopped from spring to fall and it is harvested for drying as soon as the plant is about one foot tall. Keep harvesting until midsummer, but taste to be sure the leaves are not mature and bitter. Cut back both leaf and flower stalks before they flower to promote a second growth of young leaf stalks.

Use lovage whenever celery is called for and add whole, young leaves to dishes by the scant handful. As the leaves mature, they become stronger, approaching bitter in flavor as they age. I don't use them in cooking but I do use older leaves, fresh or dried, in the bath by immersing them in large (4-inch-square) gauze or cheesecloth bags.

Rosemary (foreground), lovage (left), and flowering angelica (right) grow in the potager at Chamerolles Chateau, France.

FLAVOR

The whole lovage plant has a predominant celery flavor. The leaves and stem are spicy-sweet and have a strong celery flavor with parsley and angelica notes. The root is earthy-celery tasting with hints of mushroom, and the seeds are sharp tasting with an earthy, slightly turpentine flavor.

PARTS TO USE

The leaves, stem, and root are used for cooking, while the seeds work well in liqueurs and marinades and as a garnish in cooking. The root and seeds also have medicinal uses.

CULINARY USES

The fresh and dried leaves add a rich, slight spicy-celery flavor to stocks, soups, stews, and other long-simmering dishes, casseroles, stuffings, herb butters, vinegars, and salads. The hollow stem may be candied or used as a straw for cocktails. Both the stem and the root may be used, chopped, fresh, or dried, whenever celery is required, but add it in smaller quantities than celery. You can also cook fresh young root and leaf stalks as a vegetable.

♥ HEALTH BENEFITS

The root and seeds are carminative, reduce phlegm, and promote sweating. They can be used as a warming digestive tonic, expectorant, or diuretic. The active component, *falcarindiol*, in the roots makes them antibiotic, but root oil is too strong for topical use and should be used only under the care of a health practitioner.

GROWING LOVAGE

A hardy, easy-to-grow perennial that is very tall (up to 6 feet), lovage grows from seeds planted in spring. It likes rich, moist garden soil with good drainage. Harvest in the plant's second year, as soon as tender stalks with leaves appear. Cut older plants back in midsummer to encourage new growth and tender leaves for harvest, and prune again in the fall to about one foot.

● POTHERBS

The term *potherb* has evolved over time to mean leafy green plants that may be used in soups, but it actually comes from the very early use of leaves, roots, stems, and bulbs of plants, albeit mostly leafy green plants, in broths and soups or stews. Many plants that were destined for the pot such as cabbage, leeks, onions, and beet tops that we now call vegetables were gathered from hedgerows, fields, and woods and cultivated as *potherbs*.

If we lived in the Middle Ages (500–1500 CE), we would be very familiar with colewort. A leafy green plant that grew wild and was cultivated throughout Europe, colewort was a key potherb and through selective breeding, it became the ancestor of cabbage, kale, kohlrabi, cauliflower, broccoli, and Brussels sprouts.

Medieval *pottage* was a soupy, stew-like dish of colewort and other plants, lentils, peas or beans, and in rare times meat, boiled in broth. Pottage simmered all day, and the vegetables would reduce almost to a purée. Cooks sometimes added whole grains, eggs, or cheese to enrich and thicken the pottage. The vegetables would be served in a bread trencher that acted as the plate and broth saucer all in one.

A potherb can be any herbaceous plant cooked in broth with meat or vegetables. Around 1525, an alphabetical list of "Herbys necessary for a gardyn" was compiled for English landowner Thomas Fromond. Known as the Fromond List (see John Harvey, bibliography), it is important because it identifies plants popular at the end of the medieval period and it groups them into categories, such as herbs for pottage, for sauces, for salads, to distill, for ornament, and for beauty, along with other uses. Fromond's Herbs for Pottage list included these plants:

* Basil

* Beet (*Beta vulgaris*)

* Borage

* Cabbage (*Brassica oleracea*)

* Caraway (*Carum carvi*)

* Chervil

* Chives

* Coriander

* Dandelion

* Dill

* Fennel

* Leek (*Allium ampeloprasum*)

* Lettuce (*Lactuca sativa*)

* Marjoram

* Mint

* Nettle (*Urtica dioica*)

* Onion (*Allium*)

* Orach (*Atriplex hortensis*)

* Parsley

* Pot Marigold (*Calendula*)

* Radish (*Raphanus sativus*)

* Sage

* Spinach (*Spinacia oleracea*)

* Thyme

Soup Herb Blends

Some herbs have a natural affinity to soups, stews, and other simmering one-pot dishes. Most "soup herbs" are robust and stand up to long, slow cooking. Others add a singular taste, such as the celery flavor of lovage, and some are included because they offer carminative properties, especially in bean dishes (savory is the "bean herb").

Having a premixed blend on hand makes seasoning fall and winter dishes easy. Use the following blends as a guide for premixing herbs for the pot. Pottage Soup Herb Blend is designed for cruciferous vegetables (cabbage, cauliflower, Brussels sprouts) and potatoes, carrots, onions, leeks—any potherb vegetable. The Chowder Soup Herb Blend enhances fish and seafood soups. For tomato soups, sauces, or tomato-based casseroles, with or without meat, the Tomato Soup Herb Blend is the go-to combination.

Lovage is used in all of these blends because it is, quite simply, the ultimate soup herb. To use lovage in soup herb blends, dry the leaves whole, as instructed on page 187, and use them powdered or coarsely rubbed in blends.

Add up to 3 tablespoons of any of the following soup blends to replace herbs and salt in soups and stews, gratins, or casseroles as well as dips and sauces.

POTTAGE SOUP HERB BLEND

Makes about 1 cup

¼ cup dried lovage
¼ cup dried thyme
¼ cup dried savory

¼ cup dried parsley
¼ cup kosher salt or Citrus Salt
   (page 206)

CHOWDER SOUP HERB BLEND

Makes about 1¼ cups

⅓ cup dried savory
¼ cup dried lovage
¼ cup dried thyme

¼ cup dried lemon balm
¼ cup kosher salt or Citrus Salt
   (page 206)

TOMATO SOUP HERB BLEND

Makes about 1¼ cups

⅓ cup dried oregano
⅓ cup dried rosemary
¼ cup dried lovage
¼ cup dried thyme
¼ cup kosher salt

TO MAKE A POWDERED BLEND: In an electric herb/spice grinder or the bowl of a small food processor, combine herbs and process for 30 seconds or until powdered. Transfer to a bowl and stir in salt.

TO MAKE A RUBBED BLEND: Into a bowl, rub dried herbs between the palms of your hands or crush coarsely in the palm of one hand. Stir in salt and toss to mix well.

Store herb blends in a dark jar. Cap, label, and store in a cool, dark place for up to 8 months.

Whitefish Chowder

Makes 4 servings

4 slices side bacon, chopped

4 boneless, skinless whitefish
fillets (4 to 6 ounces each)

1 onion, chopped

2 cloves garlic, finely chopped

1 tablespoon Chowder Soup
Herb Blend (page 234)

1 can (5 ounces) clams and juices

1 cup light cream (18% butterfat)

1 large potato, cut in ½-inch dice

1 teaspoon cornstarch

¼ cup white wine, optional

4 sprig tops fresh lovage or ¼ cup
sliced green onions, bulb and
tops for garnish, optional

NOTE: You can add any potherb
such as chopped cabbage,
cauliflower, broccoli, Brussels
sprouts, spinach or kale to this
recipe.

1. In a large skillet over medium-high heat, cook bacon, stirring frequently, for 3 to 5 minutes or until evenly browned and crisp. Using a slotted spoon, lift out to a paper towel–lined plate and set aside.

2. Add fish to the hot fat and sear both sides for 1 to 2 minutes or until crusty and golden, turning carefully. Using a slotted spoon or spatula, transfer to a plate and set aside.

3. Add onion to the pan and sauté for 5 minutes or until soft. Add garlic and herb blend and cook, stirring constantly, for 1 minute. Add clams and their juices, cream, and potato and bring to a boil. Reduce heat and simmer for 12 minutes or until potato is tender, scraping up browned bits on the bottom of the pan.

4. Meanwhile, in a small bowl, whisk cornstarch into ¼ cup water. Add to the sauce in the skillet and cook over medium-low heat, whisking constantly, for 2 minutes or until thickened. Add fish and wine if using, cover, and cook for 5 to 7 minutes or until fish is cooked (it turns opaque and flakes easily with a fork). Lift fish into 4 flat soup bowls, ladle chowder evenly over, and sprinkle with reserved bacon. Garnish with lovage leaf tops or green onions.

Three-Cheese Gratin of Root Vegetables

Makes 4 servings

4 potatoes, cut into 1-inch pieces

3 parsnips, cut crosswise into 1-inch pieces

3 turnips, cut into 1-inch pieces or 1½ cups cubed rutabaga

2 carrots, cut crosswise into 1-inch pieces

2 tablespoons Pottage Soup Herb Blend (page 234), divided

1 can (13.5 ounces) coconut milk

4 ounces Brie cheese, sliced

¼ cup shredded Gruyère cheese

3 tablespoons grated Parmesan cheese

1. Preheat oven to 375°F and butter a 9 × 13-inch casserole dish.

2. Combine potatoes, parsnips, turnips, and carrots in a pot and cover with water. Add 1 tablespoon of the herb blend and bring to a boil. Reduce heat to medium-low and simmer for 25 minutes or until tender. Drain, reserving ½ cup of the liquid and discarding or reserving remaining liquid for another use. Transfer vegetables to a bowl and toss with remaining herb blend.

3. In the same pot, heat coconut milk over medium-high heat just until tiny bubbles form around the outside edge of the pot. Add vegetables and herbs and mash using a potato masher. Add reserved cooking water only as needed to keep the mashed vegetables moist.

4. Spoon half of the mashed vegetables into the prepared dish and top with slices of Brie cheese. Spoon remaining mashed vegetables over top of the Brie and smooth the surface. Sprinkle Gruyère and Parmesan cheeses over top. Bake in preheated oven for 15 minutes or until cheese is melted, top is golden, and the vegetable mixture is bubbly.

Mint

Mentha species

Mints are no longer the forgotten stalwarts of the herb garden.
They have risen to the top as one of the most exciting plants for flavor,
fragrance and landscape use to come along in many years.

—Jim Long, from "Freshly Minted Mints" in *The Herb Companion*, April/May, 2004

Mints join thyme, basil, horehound, hyssop, lavender, lemon balm, oregano, motherwort, sage, rosemary, savory, and other culinary herbs—as well as many wild and cultivated plants—in the *Lamiaceae* family. Not all relatives in this large family of plants have a strong menthol (minty) fragrance and taste, but most have slight mint notes.

Mint leaves are pointed or round ovals and grow opposite one another on square, four-sided stems. The flower heads are made up of hundreds of tiny, tubular blossoms with five petals fused together to give the appearance of an upper and lower "lip." The white, pink, lavender, or purple blossoms are clustered together, usually in terminal spikes but sometimes in round whorls at the leaf axils.

The best way to determine the difference between spearmint (*M. spicata*) and peppermint (*Mentha ×piperita*) is to smell and, especially, to taste them (see Flavor and Culinary Uses, facing page). Like the many other varieties of mint, including lemon mint and chocolate mint, they are all mints (*Mentha*) and they all display the same plant characteristics as outlined previously; but if you are really observant, you might notice that the leaves of spearmint are slightly softer and display a slight hairiness while those of peppermint are a bit more narrow, coarser, and shinier. The stems and the edges of the leaves of peppermint may be dark purple or burgundy-tinged as opposed to the lighter-green stems and leaves of spearmint. The photograph on the facing page is of peppermint.

FLAVOR

All *Mentha* mints are refreshingly clean tasting, with notes of menthol and slight lemon. Spearmint (*M. spicata*) is sweet and mildly menthol, while peppermint (*Mentha ×piperita*) is sharply menthol, hot, spicy, and sweet, with a cool aftertaste.

PARTS TO USE

Both the leaves and flowers are used.

CULINARY USES

Generally, all mints work well with lemon and chocolate.

Spearmint varieties are generally sweeter and milder than peppermints, and the best way to select the best mint for a recipe is to taste a fresh leaf and compare the minty tones.

Shade, plenty of water, and container growing help these mints survive desert conditions in the herb garden at the Desert Botanical Garden in Phoenix, Arizona.

The sweet, mild taste of spearmint is best used fresh muddled in drinks, especially juleps and mojitos, in sauces, salsas, and jellies, or added to puddings, fruit salads, and other desserts. Fresh leaves, sprigs, and flowers make a colorful garnish.

Peppermint has the strongest, clearest mint flavor and it is used in medicinal preparations. It may be used cooked, fresh, or dried. Fresh whole or chopped peppermint is best in teas, cold drinks, sauces, salsas, or jellies to accompany meats; in dips, rubs, marinades, and tabbouleh; tossed with peas, carrots, and new potatoes; and in vegetable and fruit salads.

Use fresh or dried peppermint in soups and lamb, chicken, fish, and curry dishes; in desserts, iced desserts, baked goods, and candies. Dried peppermint is most often used in teas, dips, and dressings and with other herbs such as oregano and cinnamon in seasoning for meatballs and other cooked vegetable or meat dishes.

♥ HEALTH BENEFITS

Peppermint is analgesic, antiseptic, antispasmodic, and digestive as well as a stimulant. Western herbalists use peppermint in teas or tinctures to treat nausea, indigestion, flatulence, colic, sore throat, fever, and migraines. A peppermint-soaked compress helps cool inflamed joints, rheumatism, or neuralgia. To ease nasal congestion, an infusion of peppermint in boiled water may be inhaled. To do this, place fresh or dried peppermint in a large, shallow bowl and pour boiled water over. Incline your head over the bowl close to the steam and cover your head and the bowl with a towel. Breathe in the medicinal steam. *CAUTION:* Do not give fresh herbs, herb tea, or essential oil to babies or young children under three years of age. Infants get all of their nutritional needs met by breast milk, and it is not advised that they consume excess liquid in the form of tea, herbal or otherwise.

GROWING MINT

A hardy perennial, mint prefers partial shade but tolerates sun and requires lots of water—in fact, it thrives in wet, well-drained areas. Invasive if left to spread, mints do well in containers. Start from nursery plants, stem cuttings, or root divisions and separate different varieties by at least 20 feet or prune before the flowers set seed to ensure that the plants do not cross-pollinate.

VARIETIES

According to Tucker and DeBaggio in *The Encyclopedia of Herbs*, there are eighteen "pure" mint species, and yet old and new cultivars (varieties) of mint could fill several pages of seed catalogs.

Mints with a fruity or distinct pineapple aroma and taste fall into the *M. suaveolens* group.

M. aquatica (water) mints are rare in the United States, but Bergamot Mint, Orange Mint, and Lime Mint are all part of this group.

The newest crop of trademarked, hybridized mints include Berries & Cream, Candied Fruit, Cotton Candy, Fruitasia, Italian Spice, Margarita, Marshmallow, Sweet Pear, and others that have been developed by Jim Westerfield, a long-time mint breeder from Freeburg, Illinois.

What follows are five species of *Mentha* and one non-*Mentha* mint worth considering for your garden.

HIMALAYAN SILVER MINT (*M.* 'Himalayan Silver') This plant has striking gray-blue or silver foliage, which makes it an excellent landscape plant. It has long terminal flower spikes. Not a great cooking mint; use it mostly for drinks or garnish only.

HIMALAYAN SILVER MINT

KENTUCKY COLONEL (*M. spicata* 'Kentucky Colonel') Sweet and mildly mint in flavor, this variety is used fresh in mint sauce for lamb, in salads, and in drinks. It is less susceptible than other varieties to mint rust disease.

KENTUCKY COLONEL

LIME MINT (*M. aquatica*) According to Tucker and DeBaggio's *Encyclopedia of Herbs*, "Lime Mint supposedly originated as a chance seedling from open-pollinated germplasm maintained by the U.S.D.A. Agricultural Research Service at Corvallis, Oregon, but is primarily *M. aquatica*."

LIME MINT

PENNYROYAL (*M. pulegium*) It is helpful as a repellant of insects, especially fleas (rub a handful directly on your pet's head and body, avoiding the face and eyes), and its low-growing habit makes it a fragrant ground cover plant.
CAUTION: The fresh plant is not edible and the essential oil is poisonous.

PENNYROYAL

PINEAPPLE MINT (*M. suaveolens*) A variant of Apple Mint, Pineapple Mint is fruity and has a delicate pineapple fragrance and taste. Some cultivars have the added visual bonus of white variegation on the leaves. Use fresh leaves whole in teas and salads or as a garnish.

PINEAPPLE MINT

VIRGINIA MOUNTAIN MINT (*Pycnanthemum virginianum*) A North American native, it is used as a *Mentha* mint substitute, fresh or dried, in tea and seasonings. It was used by Lakota people to treat cold and flu symptoms and by Cherokees to relieve headaches, according to Matthew Alfs in *Edible & Medicinal Wild Plants of Minnesota and Wisconsin*.

VIRGINIA MOUNTAIN MINT

Herb Jelly

Gem-like, jewel-toned, and glitteringly transparent, herb jellies may be subtle or substantial, depending on the herb or combination of herbs used. Any culinary herb may be used—basil, sage, French tarragon, mint, savory, oregano, cilantro, thyme, parsley, or the lemon-flavored herbs. If you wish to keep preserves for up to twelve months, you must process filled, capped jars in a boiling water bath as described in the recipe. If processing after filling, you do *not* need to sterilize jars. If you plan to make, refrigerate, and use the jelly immediately, processing is recommended but not essential and you may fill *sterilized* jars (see the following directions), store in the refrigerator, and use within two weeks.

Serve herb jelly with soft or hard cheese, crackers, or freshly baked bread; the lighter, sweetly flavored jellies (mint, parsley, marjoram, chervil, basil, lemon herbs) may be used to glaze cookies or as a filling for tarts. Toss savory, more robust jelly (French tarragon, sage, oregano, or thyme) with steamed or roasted vegetables for a glaze to lend a professional finish. Mint jelly complements lamb and pork; sage or a blend of sage and savory or oregano is good with poultry. Adding chopped chile pepper to any flavor herb jelly lends a tangy bite.

Makes slightly more than 6 cups

2 cups lightly packed coarsely
    chopped mint or other herbs
    (see headnote)
3 cups boiling water
1 cup unsweetened apple juice,
    plus more as needed
2 tablespoons rice vinegar or
    white wine vinegar
2 tablespoons freshly squeezed
    lemon juice
4½ cups sugar
1 packet (1¾ ounce) pectin crystals
¼ cup finely chopped hot chile
    pepper or to taste, optional

1. Place herbs in a large nonreactive teapot or pot with a lid. Pour boiling water over and cover with the lid. Let stand to steep until cool, an hour or longer.

2. Meanwhile, in a canner or large stockpot, stand seven 1-cup jars upright on a rack in the bottom of the pot. Cover with water to at least 1 inch above the jar tops. Cover and bring to a boil over high heat. Turn off heat and leave jars in the water until ready to fill. Arrange the lids, lifter, funnel, and tongs in a shallow pan and pour boiling water over.

3. Strain the herb infusion from step 1 through a cheesecloth-lined strainer into a 4-cup liquid measuring cup; discard the herbs.

4. Add enough apple juice to bring the total liquid to 4 cups. Pour the herb liquid into a Maslin pan or a large canning pot. Add vinegar and lemon juice. Bring to a boil over medium-high heat, stirring constantly.

5. Add sugar, 1 cup at a time, stirring after each addition. Bring to a full rolling boil. Add pectin and boil for 1 minute without stirring. Remove from the heat. Skim and discard any foam. If using chile pepper, let the jelly sit for up to 30 minutes before adding the chopped chile.

6. Remove the jars, one at a time, from the hot water and fill, leaving a ¼-inch headspace. Run a thin nonmetallic utensil around the inside of the jar to allow air to escape. Add more hot jelly if necessary, to leave a ¼-inch headspace. Wipe the rims, top with flat lids, and screw on metal rings. Return jars to the hot water bath. Cover and bring the water to a full rolling boil over high heat and process (boil) the jelly in the jars for 10 minutes.

7. Remove the canner lid and wait 5 minutes before removing jars to a towel or rack to cool completely. Check seals, label, and store in a cool place for up to 1 year.

● TECHNIQUES: STERILIZING CANNING JARS

This step is not required if you process preserves in a boiling water bath after filling jars as directed in the Herb Jelly recipe. Sterilizing jars is only required if you do not process the jelly, as detailed in steps 5, 6, and 7 in the Herb Jelly recipe.

To sterilize jars, in a canner or large stockpot, stand seven 1-cup jars—or the number of jars you need for your recipe—upright on a rack in the bottom of the pot. Add water to at least 1 inch above the jar tops. Cover and bring to a boil over high heat. Keep the water boiling steadily for 15 minutes. Leave the jars in the water until ready to fill.

Minted New Peas

Makes 4 servings

2½ cups shelled new peas

¼ cup chopped fresh mint or
mint jelly

Bring a medium pot of salted water to a boil over high heat. Add peas and cook for 1 minute or until tender. Drain peas and transfer to a bowl. Toss with mint and serve immediately.

Tabbouleh

Makes 4 to 6 servings

½ cup bulgur

3 tablespoons extra-virgin olive oil,
divided

1 cup boiling water

1½ cups chopped fresh parsley

1 cup chopped fresh mint

2 tomatoes, cut into ½-inch dice

½ cucumber, shredded

½ teaspoon sea salt

2 tablespoons freshly
squeezed lemon juice

1. In a bowl, combine bulgur and 1 tablespoon of the oil. Pour boiling water over, cover, and set aside for 15 minutes. Drain using a fine-mesh sieve and transfer to a serving bowl.

2. Add parsley, mint, tomatoes, cucumber, and salt. Drizzle remaining oil and lemon juice over and toss to mix well.

Mustard

Sinapis alba (yellow) *Brassica nigra* (black) *Brassica juncea* (brown)

They are pretty plants and, as with the dandelion, if they had
not multiplied so obtrusively but instead had thrown out a
challenge to the gardener's skill, they would be admired and valued
for their pale yellow flowers. As it is, one hesitates to advise
anyone to grow them, for they are a weed.

—Helen Morgenthau Fox, *Gardening with Herbs for Flavor & Fragrance*, 1938

Perhaps Fox's advice was well taken, or perhaps mustard simply fell out of favor on its own. Whatever the cause, it stopped showing up in gardens during the twentieth century. It's only just since the dawn of the twenty-first century that it has made a green and glorious comeback into our gardens and our salad bowls alike.

As a salad green, fresh sprouted shoots and young, tender mustard greens add zip and richness of taste. If we want to eat it all season, for a constant supply of young leaves for the kitchen, seeds should be sown several times throughout the season. Cut leaves back to keep the plant from flowering.

If allowed to flower, mustard seeds will ripen by the end of summer from a spring sowing. Cut the flower stalk, cover the pods with a paper bag, and hang upside down in a warm, airy, dark place (barn or garage). When dry, rub the seeds out of the pods. Store in a dark-glass jar in a cool, dry place. As with all herbs and spices, mustard seeds lose potency over time; store for one season only.

Yellow seeds, the mildest of all types, are used widely in pickling spice blends, rubs, and marinades. Brown seeds, native to India, have a long-lasting pungency and are used to add heat and piquancy to garam masala and other Indian spice blends. Black seeds are oblong and the heat is stronger than either yellow or brown—so hot, they can cause your eyes and nose to water.

Dry-roasting mustard seeds with other spices lends a nutty flavor to them. When dry-roasted seeds are ground with other ingredients into pastes, they make a hot condiment for fish, poultry, and beef and are often used in curry dishes.

Mustard seeds are also pressed for their oil; and the pungent oil from brown mustard seeds is used frequently as cooking oil in India. Mustard oil is also used to help stimulate hair growth and in the manufacture of soap. Whole seeds have no odor, but when powdered and soaked in water or other liquid, the fragrance and taste become very pungent due to the release of volatile oils that produce a deadly gas, which was unleashed in the First World War.

Blooming mustard towers over alliums in the Colonial Garden at Colonial Williamsburg Village in Virginia.

FLAVOR

Fresh young mustard leaves are hot, nippy, and mildly cabbage-like in taste. The seeds are fiery hot, piquant, and slightly bitter when cracked or powdered.

PARTS TO USE

Both the leaves and seeds are used.

CULINARY USES

Use fresh, young green mustard leaves and sprouted shoots in salads or smoothies, and steam or braise alone or with other greens. Mustard leaves can be chopped or shredded as a substitute for spinach, or as a bed for potato or chicken salads and cooked vegetable dishes. Larger leaves may also be used to wrap pork, chicken, beef, or vegetable fillings or to replace grape leaves.

The seeds are bruised, cracked, crushed, or ground and added in increasingly smaller amounts as they go from whole to finely ground. Mixed with vinegar or wine, crushed or powdered seeds are made into a paste used as a condiment for all kinds of meat and vegetable dishes.

Mustard oil derived from brown mustard seeds is widely used in India as a cooking oil.

❤ HEALTH BENEFITS

Like other *Brassica* plants, mustard seeds (and leaves to a lesser extent) contain powerful phytonutrients called *glucosinolates*, which protect against gastrointestinal tract and colorectal cancer. Mustard seeds are antioxidant; are high in selenium and magnesium, which give anti-inflammatory properties; are rich in B-complex vitamins (folate, niacin, thiamine, riboflavin) that stimulate metabolism; help digestion; relieve constipation; and may ease hemorrhoids. The powder from seeds is taken internally as an emetic and used externally in a poultice as a counterirritant.

GROWING MUSTARD

Mustard plants flower quickly from seed and grow to 3 feet. An annual, mustard easily escapes and naturalizes in the wild because the seeds may lie dormant on the ground for a long time before suddenly germinating.

Basic Mustard

For the ancient art of mustard making, seeds are bruised, cracked, ground, or powdered and soaked in water, vinegar, or wine. The bright yellow color of prepared mustard comes from the addition of turmeric. I use a mixture of yellow and brown seeds in most of my home-made mustard preparations. The liquids must be cold when added, because heating or cooking destroys the heat-producing chemical in the seeds. Adding acid—lemon juice, vinegar, or wine—keeps the heat-producing chemicals from dissipating. The combination of acid and salt is enough to preserve prepared mustard for a very long time.

This recipe produces a smooth paste and may be doubled or tripled. You can powder whole mustard seeds or purchase commercially powdered mustard. The paste will keep in a tightly sealed container in the refrigerator for up to six months. Sulfur in mustard oil causes discoloration of metal, so use glass or porcelain to make, store, and serve mustard.

Makes 1 cup

⅓ cup whole, yellow, or brown
    mustard seeds
½ cup mustard powder
1½ teaspoons sea salt
½ cup white wine or apple juice
3 tablespoons white wine vinegar

NOTE: For honey mustard, add ¼
to ⅓ cup of honey to the recipe.

Using a spice grinder or mortar and pestle, grind mustard seeds until coarsely cracked. Transfer to a bowl and add mustard powder and salt. Pour wine and vinegar over, stir well, and scrape into a jar. Cover and set aside for at least two days in the refrigerator before using.

Herbed Mustard Sauce

This versatile sauce is more rustic than the smooth Basic Mustard recipe. Use it as a marinade for meat, or substitute it for prepared mustard in recipes or at the table. Toss it with roasted or steamed root vegetables; use it as a glaze for stir-fry dishes or in casseroles and other hearty vegetable or meat dishes; add more lemon juice and use as a basting sauce for meat; add more olive oil and use as you would mayonnaise. Store in a glass jar in the refrigerator for up to 3 months.

Makes about 1 cup

2 cloves garlic
⅓ cup chopped fresh rosemary
¼ cup fresh thyme
3 tablespoons mustard seeds
1 tablespoon mustard powder
2 tablespoons freshly squeezed
    lemon juice
3 to 4 tablespoons extra-virgin
    olive oil, divided

1. In a mortar and pestle, pound the garlic, rosemary, thyme, and mustard seeds together until a coarse paste forms. Add mustard powder, lemon juice, and 1 tablespoon of the oil and set aside at room temperature for 1 hour or up to 24 hours, adding more lemon juice if the paste seems to dry out.

2. I like a rustic, chunky mustard, so I do not follow this step. You can grind the mixture to a finer paste if you prefer. Using an electric spice grinder or small food processor process mixture, adding more oil as required for the consistency you desire.

Stuffed Roasted Pork Loin with Herbed Mustard Sauce

Makes 6 servings

Stuffing

3 tablespoons extra-virgin
   olive oil, divided
1 onion, chopped
½ cup dried apricots
½ cup golden raisins
½ cup shredded mustard leaves
   or kale
3 tablespoons Herbed Mustard
   Sauce (page 249) or Dijon
   mustard

Pork Loin

1 boneless center-cut pork loin
   roast, about 3 pounds
1 tablespoon extra-virgin
   avocado oil
1 tablespoon cornstarch
3 tablespoons water
2 cups vegetable or chicken broth
2 cups mustard sprouts or
   shredded greens, optional

1. **TO MAKE THE STUFFING:** In a skillet, heat 2 tablespoons of the oil. Sauté onion for 5 minutes or until soft.

2. In the bowl of a food processor or blender container, combine apricots, raisins, mustard greens, and mustard sauce. Process on high, adding the remaining 1 tablespoon of the oil through the opening in the lid, for about 1 minute or until fruit is chopped and stuffing is well mixed. Scrape the sides of the bowl or blender container to return the mixture to the bottom. Pulse for 2 to 3 seconds or until incorporated.

3. **TO STUFF THE PORK LOIN:** Ask your butcher to butterfly the pork loin, or cut the loin so that it is butterflied to make one flat piece of meat (see Glossary). Preheat oven to 350°F. Lay out pork loin, fat side up, on a cutting board. Spread the puréed stuffing over the meat, leaving a ½-inch border all the way around. Gently fold one long side over the stuffing toward the opposite edge to enclose the stuffing. The roll will be open along the edge opposite the fold. Use bamboo or metal skewers crosswise in 3 or 4 places at regular intervals to hold the roll together without squeezing out the stuffing. Transfer any loose stuffing to a bowl and set aside.

4. In a large, ovenproof skillet or oval Dutch oven, heat avocado oil over medium-high heat. Add stuffed pork loin, skewered side up, and sear the top of the roll until browned, about 2 minutes. Turn the loin on one side, brown for 2 minutes, and flip to the other side and brown for 2 minutes.

5. Turn the roll so that the stuffing, skewered side is down if it will stand, if not, lay the roll down on one side. Transfer the skillet to preheated oven. Roast, uncovered, for about 60 minutes or until a meat thermometer inserted into the thickest part of the loin registers 155°F. Transfer loin to a cutting board, cover with foil or a lid, and set aside. Let stand for 6 to 10 minutes.

6. In a small bowl, whisk about 3 tablespoons of water into the cornstarch to make a smooth paste. Spoon off all but 2 tablespoons of the fat in the skillet and heat over medium-high heat. Whisk in cornstarch paste and cook, stirring constantly, for 30 seconds. Add the broth and whisk, stirring constantly, for 1 to 2 minutes or until the gravy thickens. Add any loose stuffing and heat through.

7. To serve, carve the roast into ½ inch-thick slices and transfer to a bed of mustard sprouts or greens, if using, on a warmed platter. Drizzle half of the sauce over the slices. Pass remaining sauce in a warmed gravy boat and any reserved stuffing at the table.

Pineapple Mustard-Glazed Onions and Beans

Makes 4 servings

2 pounds trimmed green beans

1 pound peeled pearl onions

3 tablespoons drained crushed pineapple

2 tablespoons Herbed Mustard Sauce (page 249) or Dijon mustard

1. Bring a pot of salted water to a boil over high heat. Add beans and onions, cover, reduce heat, and simmer for 6 to 8 minutes or until tender-crisp. Drain and return to the pot.

2. Meanwhile, in a bowl, combine pineapple with mustard sauce. Toss with cooked beans and onions in the pot. Transfer to a heated serving bowl.

Nasturtium

Tropaeolum majus

Cityfolk recently transplanted to the country would do well to
plant nasturtium as soon as the weather allows. . . . Nasturtium, a bright,
pleasant culinary herb, will make you look not only like a wonderful
gardener but also a competent country cook.

—Mary Forsell, *Herbs*, 1990

Mary Forsell maintained that because the long-blooming nasturtium grows almost any-where and without much intervention on the part of the gardener, it would turn the humblest of country properties into the prettiest of spaces. Her advice? Plant every color of nasturtium for display and snip the leaves and flowers to brighten a fresh summer salad or soup for a ladies' luncheon.

Nasturtiums are native to the Andes in South and Central America, where Spanish conquistadors discovered them and introduced them to Spain and from there to Europe in the sixteenth century. By the seventeenth century, nasturtiums had gained passage back to North America, where they became the darlings of North American colonial gardens.

In *The Complete Book of Flowers*, Denise Diamond tells of a strange observation by the daughter of the renowned Swedish botanist Carl Linnaeus. According to Diamond, it seems that the daughter described unusual flashes of light emanating at around dusk from nasturtium flowers that she had observed as a youth in 1762.

In the same year, the great German poet Goethe reported seeing similar flashes of light surrounding oriental poppies.

Nasturtium (*T. majus*) is often confused with the green, water-loving salad plant known as watercress, whose botanical name, *Nasturtium officinale*, offers a reason for the uncertainty. Even Maud Grieve, herbal educator of the early twentieth century, discusses the merits of "nasturtium," and we are left on our own to understand that she is actually describing watercress.

Nasturtium is featured front and center in a private Boston, Massachusetts, herb garden.

FLAVOR,

Nasturtium leaves have a peppery taste, similar to watercress, leaving the tongue tingling. The flowers are slightly floral and less nippy. The trumpet-like funnel at the base of the flowers contains a sweet nectar.

PARTS TO USE

Young leaves, flowers, and flower buds are used.

CULINARY USES

Use raw or lightly steamed young nasturtium leaves in green and vegetable salads, shredded as a bed for cooked meats and vegetables, or in a peppery pesto. Small leaves are floated in drinks and used as garnish for soups, dips, and other raw and cooked dishes. The flowers range in color from bright yellow and orange to red and burgundy, and are

used, as are other edible flowers, in salads, desserts, and ices and as a garnish for many dishes. The flower buds and seeds are pickled and used as you would capers.

♥ HEALTH BENEFITS

Nasturtium leaves are rich in vitamins A and C and were once used to prevent scurvy and treat kidney problems and urinary tract infections. Nasturtium is used as a counterirritant and an antibiotic for treating minor colds and flu. As a tea, it is an astringent toner for the skin, and it is also massaged into the scalp to help stimulate hair growth.

GROWING NASTURTIUM

A tender annual from South America, nasturtium grows easily from seed, either broadcast or in rows, in drifts, or interplanted with other flowering herbs. Choose a spot in full sun, do not amend the soil, and let it wander over rocks or ground.

Salmagundi

Salmagundi is mentioned by Hannah Glasse in her book, *The Art of Cookery, Made Plain and Easy* (1747). The term (noted as *Salamongundy* by Glasse) comes from the French word *salmigondis* and it refers to an elaborate salad with a generous number of ingredients—mostly raw but some cooked—that are artfully arranged and brightly garnished on one large platter. In her recipe titled "A third Salamongundy," Glasse calls for the following ingredients: mince veal or fowl, pickled herring, cucumber, apples, onion, pickled red cabbage, cold pork or cold duck or pigeons, boiled parsley, sellery (celery), the yolks of hard eggs and the whites, all "chopped small." She advises that the ingredients be set out "by themselves separate on saucers, or in heaps in a dish."

While she suggests dishing the salad out with sliced lemon "and if you can get Stertion-flowers (nasturtiums) lay round it," Glasse does not include a recipe for dressing or vinaigrette. She does concede that you can use "such things as you have, according to your fancy." So in this updated version, we follow Hannah Glasse's lead and go "salletting" with interesting flowers, greens, and herbs. While I often use whatever the garden is giving, nasturtiums are the one ingredient that I never substitute, because they are reminiscent of the eighteenth-century salmagundi.

Makes 4 servings

Salad

2 cups small, young nasturtium leaves
1 bunch (2 cups) watercress, pulled apart
1 cup mizuna lettuce
1 cup thinly sliced onions
1 cup thinly sliced radishes
⅓ cucumber, thinly sliced
8 to 12 water chestnuts, thinly sliced
½ cup cooked, toasted chickpeas
½ cup nasturtium flowers

Mustard Pesto Dressing

¼ cup toasted hazelnuts
2 cloves garlic
1 tablespoon Dijon mustard
2 cups mixed greens (mustard leaves, nasturtium, watercress, organic radish leaves)
About ½ cup extra-virgin olive oil
3 tablespoons freshly squeezed lemon juice
¼ teaspoon sea salt

(continued on following page)

1. In a bowl, toss together nasturtium leaves, watercress, lettuce, onions, radishes, cucumber, and water chestnuts. Cover and set aside in the refrigerator and bring to room temperature when ready to serve.

2. **TO MAKE THE DRESSING:** In the bowl of a food processor, combine hazelnuts, garlic, and mustard. Pulse for 30 seconds or until finely chopped. Add greens, and with the motor running, slowly add about ¼ cup oil through the opening in the lid. Stop and scrape the sides of the bowl and add lemon juice and salt. Cover, and with the motor running, slowly add enough of the rest of the oil to make a pourable dressing.

3. **TO MAKE THE SALAD:** On a large platter, spread out the greens mixture. Drizzle dressing over and garnish with chickpeas and nasturtium flowers.

Angel Flower Cake

Makes 1 cake

1 cup cake flour (see note)
½ cup confectioners' sugar
¼ teaspoon sea salt
12 large egg whites (1½ cups)
1½ teaspoons cream of tartar
1 teaspoon pure vanilla extract
1 cup granulated sugar
1¼ cup fresh nasturtium or other
    herb petals (see An Edible
    Flower Primer, page 261)
1 cup Rose Glaze (page 258)
¼ cup fresh nasturtium or
    other herb petals for garnish,
    optional

NOTE: Cake flour is preferred, but all-purpose flour may be substituted.

1. Preheat oven to 350°F.

2. Using a fine-mesh strainer, sift the flour, confectioners' sugar, and salt into a bowl. Stir well to combine, and set aside.

3. In a large bowl, beat egg whites and cream of tartar with a stand or portable electric mixer on high speed until frothy. Add vanilla extract and beat until soft peaks form. Gradually add the granulated sugar, ¼ cup at a time, beating until the whites are glossy and form stiff peaks.

4. Sprinkle about one third of the flour mixture over the whites and, using a rubber spatula, fold the flour mixture into the whites using a cutting and lifting motion.

5. Repeat step 4 once, until all but one third of the flour is incorporated into the egg whites. Toss remaining flour mixture with the petals, and fold into the egg white mixture, folding just enough to evenly distribute the petals throughout the batter.

6. Scrape the batter into an ungreased 10-inch tube pan. Bake in preheated oven for 45 minutes or until the top is golden brown and a cake tester comes out clean when inserted into the center of the cake.

(continued on following page)

7. Invert cake pan over a serving plate and set aside to cool completely. Run a knife around the edge of the cake, between the pan and the cake, and turn out onto the plate. Drizzle glaze over top and allow it to drip down the sides of the cake. Garnish with fresh petals if using.

ROSE GLAZE

Makes 1 cup

1½ cups confectioners' sugar
1 to 2 tablespoons rosewater

NOTE: For a lemon glaze, follow the Rose Glaze recipe but substitute strained freshly squeezed lemon juice for the rosewater and add 1 teaspoon finely grated lemon zest.

Sift the sugar into a bowl. Add rosewater gradually, stirring constantly, until the glaze has a spreadable or slightly thinner consistency.

Spring Flower and Seafood Cocktail

Makes 4 appetizers

1 cup Basil Aioli (page 260)
3 tablespoons extra-virgin olive oil
2 tablespoons white balsamic
  vinegar
½ pound crabmeat
½ cup fresh peas, steamed
1 cup fresh small nasturtium
  leaves or watercress
8 radishes, halved
12 fresh whole nasturtiums or
  other edible flowers

NOTE: This recipe was inspired by a dish served at Purslane Restaurant in Cheltenham, Gloucestershire, UK (see Resources, page 396), where this photo was taken.

1. Spoon ¼ cup of Basil Aioli into the bottoms of 4 clear cocktail glasses. Cover and set aside in the refrigerator until ready to assemble.

2. In a bowl, whisk together olive oil and vinegar. Add crabmeat and toss to mix well. Cover and set aside in the refrigerator until ready to assemble.

3. To assemble the cocktails, divide crabmeat evenly over aioli in the cocktail glasses. Sprinkle 4 portions of peas evenly over crabmeat. Add nasturtium leaves on top, interspersed with 4 radish halves in each glass. Top each cocktail with 3 flowers.

BASIL AIOLI

Makes 1 cup

1 large egg

1 egg yolk

2 tablespoons finely chopped
  fresh basil

8 drops basil essential oil, optional
  (See Caution, page 91)

1 tablespoon freshly squeezed
  lemon juice

1 teaspoon prepared mustard

1 to 1¼ cups extra-virgin olive oil

1. In a blender container, combine egg, egg yolk, basil, and basil essential oil if using. Process for 10 seconds. Add lemon juice and with the motor running, slowly pour oil through opening in the lid. Keep adding oil slowly and process for about 1 minute or until aioli begins to thicken and slap against the side of the blender.

2. Scrape into cocktail glasses, cover, and refrigerate until ready to assemble the cocktail, or store in a covered glass jar in the refrigerator for up to 3 days.

AN EDIBLE FLOWER PRIMER

Confucius was comfortable with chrysanthemums as a cooking ingredient, and Eisenhower (or his chef) served soup seasoned with nasturtium flowers. Our ancestors and their ancestors were eating cauliflower, artichokes, and broccoli, which are all flowers, long before flowers were trendy. Stuffed zucchini flowers were part of the Roman menu during Nero's time, and Shakespeare might have nibbled on lilac, nasturtium, and lavender blossoms.

Floral cuisine is well established in the world's food history. What's new today is the way inventive chefs and cooks are using flower petals, whole blossoms, and flower pollen to delight us with dishes that are not only delicious but also, in their own way, as beautiful as the gardens they come from.

Here are some guidelines for using flowers in food:

* Use organic flowers, not from a florist, because chemicals are a major part of the production of flowers for the florist trade.

* Avoid gathering flowers in public parks and along roadsides.

* Harvest flowers at their peak, just at the time of opening.

* Check flowers for insects, lightly rinse in cool water, and pat dry or drain on a towel.

* Pull petals off and discard bitter centers and stems.

* Set aside the stamens of flowers with abundant pollen, such as day lilies, and use either the whole stamens or grasp a couple of stamens and shake the pollen over a dish as a striking garnish.

* Use nonreactive cooking, storing, and serving utensils.

* Store fresh petals in the refrigerator: spread over a lightly moistened tea towel or square of absorbent paper in a sealed container.

* To dry, spread petals on a rack in a warm, dark room and store in a sealed opaque container for up to one year.

CAUTION: Never substitute unknown flowers in recipes, and do not experiment with wild flowers unless you are certain of the identity of the plant and know for sure that it is edible. Flowers from every herb featured in this book are edible; here is a list of wild or cultivated herb flowers for cooking and garnishing.

CHICORY (*Cichorium intybus*) Wedgwood blue petals and buds are plentiful in the fall, imparting an earthy flavor to both savory and sweet dishes.

CLOVER (*Trifolium*) Petals are white or pink and sweetly anise in flavor. Pull them away from the green center to use in recipes.

DAYLILY (*Hemerocallis*) Naturalized to the wild, a wide range of colors—pink, orange, red, burgundy, chocolate, striped, and variegated—make daylilies attractive for many different culinary applications, including beverages, desserts, appetizers, soups, and main dishes. Use the whole blossom and save the stamen for staining food or as a garnish. On their own, daylilies are delicate and bland tasting, so use in salads or stuff them with cooked vegetables or rice.

GLOBE AMARANTH (*Gomphrena globosa*) Tiny white, pink, mauve, and purple pompoms are used whole in teas, or pull the petals away from green center to use in cake and cookie batters. The taste is mild and slightly nutty.

HIBISCUS (*Hibiscus*) These flowers are large and provide a range of white, yellow, orange, pink, red, blue, or purple petals. Their flavor is tart, like cranberry. Use them in teas and sauces or syrups.

HOLLYHOCK (*Alcea*) Similar to hibiscus in size, hollyhock flowers range in color from pink to orange to red, burgundy, and chocolate. Devoid of flavor, they are mostly used as a garnish for drinks as well as savory and sweet dishes.

JASMINE (*Jasminum officinale*) Flowers are most often white and sweetly fragrant. Garnish teas and other drinks with them and use them in dessert sauces, syrups, and icings.

SUNFLOWER (*Helianthus annuus*) The yellow petals add a flash of gold to salads and stuffings and when used to garnish soups or other dishes. Steam the buds and use as you would artichokes. Fresh, raw petals are mild and the steamed buds are slightly nutty in flavor.

TULIP (*Tulipa*) The petals are rounded, pointed, ruffled, or grooved, and are found in a range of colors. Use them raw in salads or stuff and bake them as you would squash flowers. Depending on the variety, the flavor ranges from mild to tart.

VIOLET (*Viola odorata*) Flowers are light mauve to deep purple, sweetly violet in taste, and are used in teas, candies, desserts, sauces, syrups, icings, garnishes, and waters.

Pickled Flower Buds

Yield info 4 cups

3 cups fresh nasturtium or elderflower buds

2 cups sugar
4 cups white wine vinegar

1. Spread a ½- to 1-inch-thick layer of buds over the bottom of a quart jar with a lid. Cover the buds with a thin layer of sugar. Repeat the layering process, alternating buds and sugar and ending with a layer of sugar.

2. In a saucepan, bring vinegar to a boil over medium-high heat. Pour over buds and sugar in the jar until it just covers them. Cap, label, and set the jar aside in a sunny place for at least 10 days before using. Store in the refrigerator for several months.

Oregano and Marjoram

Oregano (*Origanum*) and Marjoram (*O. majorana*)

Italian Oregano is my favorite of all the Origanums since it combines
the sweet aroma of marjoram with the savory spiciness of oregano.
This is the one [cultivar] that is used in Italian recipes.

—Susan Belsinger, *Oregano: 2005 Herb of the Year*

Venus, goddess of love, adored sweet marjoram and grew it on Mount Olympus, naming it joy (*ganos*) of the mountains (*oros*). I picture oregano as a masculine, almost savage herb, standing ground on a steep hillside, fighting cypress trees and wild goats to claim a spot in the sun. It inhabits the ghoulish craters of the Canary Islands, grows in patches near Sicily's smoldering volcanoes, and clings to ditches along Moroccan roadsides. When I cook with oregano, I know I am adding a tenacious herb with bite and spunk, one worthy of hearty sauces and outdoor grills, one that can measure up to piquant olives, hot peppers, and hearty bean dishes.

On the other hand, feminine marjoram is pliant and adaptable, a proper descendant of the graceful nymph Menthe, unwitting founder of the mint family, to which *Origanum* belongs. Marjoram is an amiable herb, sympathetically relinquishing her fragrant, bittersweet oils. With undertones of pine and balsam, marjoram gives character to eggs, bland cheeses, pastas, and biscuits. But for all her daintiness, marjoram is surprisingly wily, keeping her aroma in all but the strongest of dishes.

Like all good mints, marjoram and oregano complement legumes (peas, beans, lentils, and chickpeas). In any country, in any language, rustic soups, stews, casseroles, stuffings, and meat loaf dishes—all the descendants of long-simmering cassoulets of the Mediterranean region—benefit from their dance with the joyous mountain herbs we know as oregano and marjoram.

FLAVOR

Oregano is warm, with a peppery bite and slight citrus notes, while marjoram has a subtler and sweetly spicy taste. The heat of both oregano and marjoram increases when they are grown in temperate regions.

PARTS TO USE

Both the leaves and flowers are used.

A misty summer morning reveals 'Gold Crisp' oregano in one corner of the herb garden.

CULINARY USES

Often called the "pizza herb," oregano is a key herb in Italian tomato sauce. Its hearty zip is used in salads, dips, and Greek souvlaki dishes and in fresh green rubs for grilled fish, vegetables, and chicken. Milder marjoram flavors egg, puddings and milk dishes and is good with mild and creamy cheeses.

♥ HEALTH BENEFITS

Oregano is a powerful antioxidant with potent antibacterial, antifungal, and antiparasitic properties. It is effective in treating acne, swollen glands, arthritis, asthma, insect bites and parasites, muscle pain, cough, *E. coli*, earache, and viral infections. The essential oil is antifungal, antibacterial, and a good antiseptic for internal and external use.

Marjoram improves blood circulation and speeds healing due to its ability to increase white blood corpuscles. It is antimicrobial and anti-inflammatory, and the essential oil is used in steam inhalation to treat bronchitis and colds. It also helps with insomnia, tension, high blood pressure, and headaches because of its strong sedative properties.

GROWING OREGANO

Oregano grows easily from seeds, by root division, and by cuttings. It craves full sun. Some of the best varieties are hardy in Zones 5 to 9, which means that much of North America can grow oregano as an overwintering perennial.

VARIETIES

While there are hundreds of varieties of oregano, what follows is a short list of some of my favorite types for ornamental, culinary, and medicinal uses.

The Edible Landscape

COMPACT (*O. vulgare* 'Compactum') With golden and dark green leaves, this oregano (sometimes called Creeping Oregano) is low growing, dense, and easily pruned into a round or square shape.

HERRENHAUSEN (*O.* 'Herrenhausen') This variety of oregano has a sweet, fruit scent. The deep green leaves are edible and dry well for crafts.

KENT BEAUTY (*O. rotundifolium* ×*Origanum scabrum* 'Kent Beauty') An edible, beautiful ornamental, Kent Beauty has round leaves on long, almost trailing branches and pretty pink or purple flowers. Because it is now thought to be a possible hybrid, I've added ×*Origanum scabrum* to the botanical name.

For the Kitchen

GREEK OR CHEF'S GREEK (*O. vulgare* subsp. *hirtum*) This is my favorite because it is a full-flavored, resinous, pungent, and peppery oregano that is a good variety for a wide range of dishes including tomato sauces, pizzas, and long-cooking dishes.

HOT & SPICY (*O. vulgare* subsp. *hirtum*) As the name says, this oregano is bold, nippy, and delivers lots of fiery heat along with zesty flavor.

ITALIAN (*O. vulgare* 'Italian') Italian oregano is Susan Belsinger's favorite oregano in the kitchen. It is warm and spicy, yet sweet and fragrant, an all-around great culinary oregano.

MEXICAN OREGANO (*Lippia graveolens*) This is not an *Origanum*, but is often sold as oregano in Mexico and the southern United States, where it is sometimes called Mexican oregano. The taste is similar to Italian oregano, and it is used in chili and other Mexican dishes.

For the Medicine Cabinet

WILD OR COMMON OR HARDY OREGANO (*O. vulgare* subsp. *vulgare*) This species is lacking true oregano fragrance or flavor and is not used in cooking, but it is beneficial as a medicinal to treat upset stomach, headache, cough, and diarrhea. It dries well so is often used in crafts, and bees love it.

Tomato Sauce

Makes 2 cups

3 tablespoons extra-virgin olive oil

1 onion, chopped

3 to 5 cloves garlic, finely chopped

8 medium tomatoes, skinned and chopped

2 tablespoons chopped fresh oregano

1 tablespoon chopped fresh rosemary

1 tablespoon fresh thyme

1 teaspoon sea salt

NOTE: For variations on this tomato sauce, sauté any of the following with the onion: 1 zucchini, chopped; 1 red pepper, chopped; and/or 1 cup sliced mushrooms. You can also add any one or two of the following: 1 cup packed spinach leaves; ½ cup whole fresh basil leaves; or 1 cup cooked, small meatballs.

In a saucepan, heat oil over medium-high heat. Sauté onion for 5 minutes or until soft. Add garlic and cook, stirring, for 1 minute. Add tomatoes, oregano, rosemary, thyme, and salt, and cook, stirring occasionally, for 10 minutes, or until the liquid has evaporated and the sauce is thick.

Vegetable Fritters

Makes 8 fritters

½ cup chickpea flour
½ teaspoon baking powder
¼ cup milk
1 egg
3 to 5 tablespoons extra-virgin
   olive oil or avocado oil,
   divided
Sea salt and cracked black
   pepper
1 small onion, chopped
1 zucchini, chopped
½ cup coarsely chopped
   mushrooms
1½ cups fresh, canned (drained),
   or frozen (thawed) corn
   kernels
2 tablespoons chopped fresh
   oregano
tips of 4 to 8 fresh oregano sprigs

1. Preheat oven to 350°F.

2. In a bowl, whisk together flour and baking powder. Whisk in milk, egg, and 1 tablespoon of the oil. Add a few grinds of salt and pepper to taste. Set aside.

3. In a skillet, heat 1 tablespoon of the oil over medium-high heat. Sauté onion for 3 minutes. Add zucchini and mushrooms, and cook, stirring frequently, for 3 minutes or until vegetables are soft. Let cool slightly and spoon into the batter. Add corn and oregano and stir well to combine.

4. In the same skillet, heat 1 tablespoon of the oil over medium-high heat. Using a quarter-cup dry measure, scoop the batter mixture into the skillet and add 2 or 3 more scoops to form 3 or 4 fritters. Flatten each slightly. Place an oregano tip on top of each fritter. Cook in batches, turning once, for 2 to 3 minutes on each side or until golden. Drain on absorbent paper. Transfer to a heatproof platter and keep fritters warm in the preheated oven while you cook the remaining batter mixture.

Grilled Eggplant Parmigiana

Makes 4 servings

Herbed Oil

½ cup extra-virgin olive oil
¼ cup chopped fresh basil
3 tablespoons chopped fresh
    marjoram
3 tablespoons freshly squeezed
    lemon juice
1 teaspoon Dijon mustard
1 clove garlic, finely chopped
Sea salt

Eggplant

2 large eggplants, trimmed
    and cut crosswise into
    ½-inch-thick slices
2 cups Tomato Sauce
    (page 268 or store-bought)
7 ounces fresh mozzarella,
    shredded, divided
¼ cup freshly grated Parmesan
    cheese

1. **TO MAKE THE HERBED OIL:** In a blender container or the bowl of a food processor, combine oil, basil, marjoram, lemon juice, mustard, and garlic. Add a couple of grinds of salt and process for 30 seconds or until smooth. Transfer to a liquid measuring cup.

2. **TO MAKE THE EGGPLANT:** Position an oven rack in the bottom third of the oven and preheat it to 400°F. Line 2 (or 3 if necessary) rimmed baking sheets with parchment paper. Brush eggplant slices on both sides with herbed oil and arrange in one layer on the prepared baking sheets.

3. Roast eggplant, one sheet at a time, for about 7 minutes or until brown on the bottom. Turn the slices over, brush the tops with oil, and roast for about 6 more minutes, or until both sides are browned. Remove the sheet from the oven. Stack browned slices on top of one another on the baking sheet and fold the parchment paper around them, enclosing them completely, allowing them to steam and soften completely.

4. Repeat step 3 with the second (and third if using) baking sheet of eggplant slices, steaming the last batch for at least 5 minutes.

5. Reduce oven to 375°F. Oil a 12½ × 13½-inch casserole dish. Arrange one third of the grilled eggplant slices in one layer on the bottom of the dish. Drizzle one third of the tomato sauce over. Sprinkle one third of the mozzarella over sauce.

6. Repeat the layers of eggplant, tomato sauce, and mozzarella until all have been used. Sprinkle Parmesan cheese evenly over the top. Bake in preheated oven for 12 minutes or until cheese is melted and tomato sauce is bubbling.

Smoked Chicken and Cabbage Salad

Makes 4 servings

Dressing

2 tablespoons extra-virgin olive oil
2 tablespoons walnut oil
2 tablespoons rice vinegar
1 teaspoon Dijon mustard
3 tablespoons chopped fresh
  oregano
Sea salt and freshly ground pepper

Salad

2 cups shredded green or red
  cabbage
1 cup shredded beet
½ cup thinly sliced fennel bulb
2 apples, diced
¼ pound boneless smoked
  chicken, cubed
½ cup toasted walnut halves

1. **TO MAKE THE DRESSING:** In a small bowl, whisk together olive oil, walnut oil, vinegar, mustard, and oregano. Season with salt and pepper, cover, and refrigerate until you are ready to serve, up to 4 hours ahead. Bring the dressing to room temperature before tossing with salad.

2. **TO MAKE THE SALAD:** In a serving bowl, combine cabbage, beet, fennel, apples, and chicken. Drizzle dressing over and toss well to coat. Sprinkle walnuts over top.

Herbed Cucumber Bites

Makes 16 bites

1 cup soft goat cheese

3 tablespoons chopped marjoram

1 tablespoon freshly squeezed lime
or lemon juice

2 peeled cucumbers, sliced
crosswise into 1-inch rounds
(about 8 rounds per cucumber)

12 radishes, each cut into 4 slices

16 fresh herb tips (oregano,
marjoram, savory, or thyme)

1. In a small bowl, combine cheese, marjoram, and lime juice.

2. To assemble bites, spread 2 teaspoons of the cheese mixture on a cucumber.
   Arrange 3 slices of radish over cheese. Spread 1 teaspoon of cheese on top of a
   radish slice and top with an herb tip. Serve immediately, or cover and refrigerate
   for up to 4 hours.

A SPA HERB PRIMER

The effects of tension, worry, and everyday stress can cause forgetfulness, exhaustion, impatience, and frustration, so it's not surprising that many people are turning to herbs, yoga, and meditation techniques to refresh, relax, and rejuvenate. Herbal essential oils and massage oils are of great benefit in helping to achieve inner and outer calmness and release tension.

One of the easiest ways to relax and refresh is to take a soaker herbal bath. A soaker bath is one in which your whole body from the neck down is immersed in water. Fresh or dried herbs, herb infusions, or herbal milk may be used in the water and herbal bath salts (see Lemon Citrus Salt, page 206), or sugars may be used afterward to exfoliate and stimulate blood flow.

USING HERBS IN BATHS

Select three to five fresh or dried herbs from the lists on page 274. Combine ¼ cup of each herb in a bowl. Pack ½ cup of the blended herbs into a 4- to 6-inch square net or cheesecloth bag, pull the string taut, and hang the bag from the spout while running the bath water. Allow herbs to steep in the bath water for a minimum of 15 minutes while soaking in the bath.

For a muscle-soothing soak, combine ⅓ cup blended herbs and 1 cup Epsom salts. Pack into a 4- to 6-inch square net or cheesecloth bag, pull the string taut, and hang the bag from the spout while running the bath water. The Epsom salts will melt into the water and the herbs will steep in the bath water and soothe you while you are soaking.

STIMULATING HERBS Use in cool water (70 to 85°F)	CALMING HERBS Use in warm water (96 to 98°F)
Basil	Catnip (*Nepeta cataria*)
Bay	Chamomile
Fennel	Elder
Lavender	Juniper berries (*Juniperus*)
Lemon verbena	Lemon balm
Marjoram	Mullein (*Verbascum thapsus*)
Mint	Rose petals
Nettle (*Urtica dioica*)	Tansy flowers (*Tanacetum vulgare*)
Pine needles (*Pinus*)	Valerian root (*Valerian officinalis*)
Rosemary	Vervain (*Verbena officinalis*)
Sage	Violet (*Viola*)

HERBAL BATH BLENDS

ACHING MUSCLE BATH BLEND: Equal parts sage, calendula, lemon balm, and Epsom salts.

TONIC BATH BLEND: Equal parts lavender, parsley, lemon peel, and baking soda.

STIMULATING BATH RUB: Equal parts rosemary, oregano, oats, and mint. Use as a bath soak and then rub the softened herbs in the bag over the body.

LAVENDER COCONUT BATH MILK: ¼ cup fresh or dried lavender buds and ½ cup powdered coconut milk. Pack into a muslin bag and hang the bag from the spout while running the bath water. The milk will dissolve in the water if the bag is swished around. Substitute powdered skim milk or powdered buttermilk for the coconut milk if desired.

SPA HERBS FOR BATH, SALVE, OR LOTION

CALENDULA Two properties make calendula an excellent spa herb: it's antibacterial and immunostimulant (it promotes healing by stimulating production of collagen at the site of wounds and minimizes scars).

CALENDULA

COMFREY (*Symphytum officinale*) An excellent spa herb because it softens skin and promotes skin cell healing. Comfrey root is more powerful than the leaves; chop or grate it to use in the bath, salves, and lotions.
CAUTION: In Canada, it is legal to grow comfrey for personal use; it is illegal to sell prepared comfrey in creams, ointment, pills, and teas, or other products. Oral comfrey products are banned in the United States, but topical comfrey skin products are legal to sell there.

COMFREY

HORSETAIL (*Equisetum arvense*) It contains silicon, which is used externally as a nail and hair strengthener.

HORSETAIL

LUFFA (*Luffa aegyptiaca* and *L. acutangula*) When the mature gourd is dried, its rough, fibrous shape is used as a body scrubber.

LUFFA

Herbal Body Lotion

Lotions may be thin or thick, depending on the amount of oils, beeswax, and water used to make them. Once you have made one batch, you can increase or decrease the amounts to get the consistency you want. Because lotions are lighter and have both an oil and a water component (unlike salves, which only use oils and beeswax), lotions are mechanically blended and are combined with an emulsifier (lanolin) to help keep the water in suspension. Use filtered water or any herb-infused water (see page 194) and any herb-infused oil (see pages 42–43) from the list on page 274.

Makes about 2 cups

Oil Component

1 cup Calendula-Infused Oil
(pages 42–43) or other herb-infused oil

⅓ cup extra-virgin coconut oil

1 teaspoon lanolin

1 teaspoon liquid vitamin E

¼ cup grated beeswax

Water Component

½ to ⅔ cup Herb or Floral Water
(page 194) or filtered water

⅓ cup pure aloe vera gel

10 to 20 drops essential oil, optional

1. **TO MAKE THE OIL COMPONENT:** In the top of a nonreactive (glass) double boiler, combine calendula oil, coconut oil, lanolin, vitamin E, and beeswax. Gently heat over enough simmering water to steam the top pan without allowing the water to touch it. Using a wooden spoon, stir until the wax is melted. Transfer to a 2-cup heatproof measuring cup or glass jar and set aside for 30 minutes or just until cooled but not enough that the wax has set.

2. **TO MAKE THE WATER COMPONENT:** In a blender container, combine aloe vera gel, herb water, and essential oil if using. Loosen the oil mixture by gently stirring with a wooden spoon. With the motor running on high speed, slowly pour the oil mixture through the opening in the lid into the water mixture. Blend until combined. Transfer to a 2-cup glass jar (or several smaller jars). Cap, label, and store in the refrigerator or a cool, dark cupboard.

Parsley

Petroselinum crispum

curled leaf (*P. crispum*) and flat leaf (*P. crispum* var. *neapolitanum*)

It is said that parsley seed goes seven times to the Devil and back before
it germinates, and that is why it is so slow in coming up!

—E. S. Rohde, *A Garden of Herbs*, 1936

In *The Herb Garden*, twentieth-century garden writer Frances Bardswell claims that garden parsley was not cultivated in England until 1548, the second year of the reign of King Edward VI. Almost four centuries later, in 1909, thirty-seven varieties of parsley were included in the *Royal Horticultural Society's Journal*.

It seems as though parsley was as slow to catch on in gardens and in recipes as it is to get itself established in the garden. Now, more than a century after those thirty-seven varieties were noted in Britain, we appear never to notice the sometimes limp, lonely lump of once-living green languishing on the dinner plate. In fact, one wonders why the cook bothers to add it.

In theory, adding a sprig of parsley to a dish is a thoughtful touch, given that it cleanses the palate and its chlorophyll freshens the breath. I for one never gave parsley its due until learning of its tonic properties and the ability of its medicinal oils to keep tumors from forming and cigarette smoke from delivering deadly carcinogens. Now my relationship with parsley is changed: I grow it in the summer, I buy it in the winter, and I use it raw in dips and dressings and add it to recipes even when it is not part of the ingredients. I reach for that bright green sprig on my plate (and lift it from the plates of my dinner companions) because I want parsley to bless me with its healing properties.

FLAVOR

Parsley has an earthy, green taste, with a hint of anise and lemon. Flat-leaf (also known as Italian) varieties are preferred by chefs because of their clean and lightly spiced flavor. The root tastes similar to celery.

PARTS TO USE

The leaves, stems, flowers, and root can all be used.

CULINARY USES

Parsley is an essential culinary herb. Use the fresh or dried leaves for herb season-

Flat-leaf parsley borders the culinary herb bed at the Minnesota Landscape Arboretum in Chaska, Minnesota.

ing blends, salsa verde, and other sauces, stuffings, salads, and fish and chicken dishes. Parsley is good with eggs, grains, and lentil dishes. An excellent herb for making pesto and seasoning blends, use it to round out the flavor of other herbs and when a large quantity of herbs is required. Curly parsley dries and freezes well.

The stems are stronger in flavor than the leaves and may be used in broths and stocks, soups, and stews. Hamburg, a different variety of parsley from the curled or flat leaf types (see page 280), is grown for its root, which is fleshy and similar in appearance to parsnip.

♥ HEALTH BENEFITS

Rich in vitamins A, C, and K, parsley also contains iron as well as folic acid for heart health. It is antioxidant and its volatile oils inhibit tumor formation, especially in the lungs, and they help neutralize the carcinogens in cigarette smoke. Parsley is usually included in spring tonics; and it is high in chlorophyll, which acts as a natural breath freshener. *P. crispum* is used as a diuretic (and to treat kidney stones, gravel, and urinary disorders); it is also carminative and spasmolytic.

CAUTION: Do not use parsley in medicinal amounts during pregnancy or if you are taking diuretics. Excessive amounts of parsley seed and oil can be toxic.

Parsley is a hardy biennial that produces leaves in the first year and flowers in the second. Plant a new crop from seed the second year to ensure a good supply of leaves. If you let each planting go to seed, you will always have it in the herb garden. Seeds are slow to germinate but if soaked in tepid water for three days and then drained and rinsed, the germination time may be shortened.

VARIETIES

All parsley varieties fall into one of the following three categories.

Curled Leaf (*P. crispum*)

Also called common parsley, this variety is indeed the most common, being widely used for garnish and in soups, stews, and other dishes. Some cultivars of this parsley type follow:

DECORATOR (*P. c.* 'Decorator') It has dark green, thick leaves and is used as an edging in herb beds.

FOREST GREEN (*P. c.* 'Forest Green') Heat-tolerant and pleasant tasting, it thrives in hot, dry weather and is excellent for both raw and cooked dishes.

EXTRA-TRIPLE CURLED (*P. c.* 'Extra-Triple Curled') The leaves are very curly, so it makes a pretty garnish and is a unique border plant.

Flat leaf (*P. crispum* var. *neapolitanum*)

Also known as Italian or plain-leaf parsley, the flat-leaf varieties have more flavor than the curled-leaf types, which is why most chefs prefer this type. Flat-leaf parsley is often used as a substitute for cilantro due to its strong taste and similarly shaped leaves. Cultivars include the following:

ARGON (*P. c.* var. *n.* 'Argon') With large, dark green leaves and strong flavor, it is considered to be a good all-round variety.

CICILIAN (*P. c.* var. *n.* 'Cicilian') This cultivar can be traced back to medieval times, and although it is not widely available, its lacy, delicate leaves and sweetly spiced aroma and taste make it worth seeking out.

GIGANTE CATALOGNO (*P. c.* var. *n.* 'Gigante Catalogno') It features long thick stems with large, dark leaves and is considered to be the true Italian parsley.

ITALIAN PLAIN LEAF (*P. c.* var. *n.* 'Plain Leaf') Dark green and fast growing, it's a good variety for a kitchen garden.

Root Parsley or Hamburg (*P. crispum* var. *tuberosum*)

Root parsley, also known as German parsley, is grown for the root, not the leaves, which tend to be sparse. Grate the raw root into salads and dips and use as you would carrot or parsley alone or in other dishes. Grow your own or look for it in ethnic and specialty markets. Cultivars available in North America include the following:

ARAT (*P. c.* var. *t.* 'Arat') Its slender, long roots grow straight and have the appearance of parsnips.

HILMAR (*P. c.* var. *t.* 'Hilmar') A productive and vigorous variety, harvest the roots after the first frost when the carbohydrates turn to sugar.

CURLED LEAF PARSLEY · FLAT LEAF PARSLEY · HAMBURG PARSLEY

Gremolata

Gremolata is the Italian version of persillade, and it relies on parsley and garlic, but other ingredients may also be added, including lemon zest, anchovies, or other herbs, such as rosemary or oregano. Use it with braised or slow-cooked veal or lamb and fish, as well as dishes that rely on persillade.

Makes 1 cup

2 cloves garlic
1 cup coarsely chopped fresh
    parsley
⅓ cup coarsely chopped toasted
    slivered almonds or walnuts
1 teaspoon sea salt

Using a food processor, process garlic until coarsely chopped. Add parsley, almonds, and salt. Pulse for 30 seconds or until mixture is chopped. I prefer the mixture to be slightly coarse, but you can process until it is finely chopped, depending on how you plan to use it.

● PERSILLADE

The French make a very simple seasoning of finely chopped parsley and garlic, which is added to dishes at the very last minute to impart a fresh, zippy taste and to garnish the plate. It is often used with cooked meats, poultry, and fish, soups, sauces, and stews. Dishes that have been garnished with this mixture are referred to as being *a la persillade*.

Chimichurri

This is a hot salsa that Argentinians use for barbecue, or *churrasco*. A little more elaborate and a lot hotter than the French or Italian garnishes previously mentioned, use it in the same way or try it with lamb or beef cooked over coals. Of course, cilantro may be used in this sauce, but either way, this sauce shouldn't be tamed.

Makes 1½ cups

½ cup extra-virgin olive oil
⅓ cup freshly squeezed
   lemon juice
2 tablespoons rice wine vinegar
4 jalapeño chiles, finely chopped
1 small red onion, finely chopped
4 cloves garlic, finely chopped
½ cup chopped fresh parsley
3 tablespoons chopped fresh
   oregano
2 tablespoons chopped fresh mint
Sea salt and pepper to taste

In a bowl, whisk together oil, lemon juice, and vinegar. Add chiles, onion, garlic, parsley, oregano, and mint. Toss to blend. Season to taste with salt and pepper.

● TOOLS: MEZZALUNA

From the Italian for "half moon," *mezzaluna* is the word used to describe a tool for chopping herbs and vegetables. It consists of one or two very sharp blades in a rounded arc or half-moon shape, with handles at the top of each end of the arc. The blade handles are held with two hands and the mezzaluna is rocked back and forth over the herbs until they are chopped to the desired consistency. Your hands aren't required to hold the herbs as they are being chopped, and the result is consistent and faster than using a French knife.

My personal preference for all knives is molded stainless steel handles because they are easy to clean. Wooden handles may harbor bacteria and require extra care in cleaning.

Three Grain Tabbouleh

Makes 3 cups

¼ cup pot barley

¼ cup rinsed red or black
   amaranth

¼ cup red or mahogany
   short-grain rice

⅓ cup freshly squeezed
   lemon juice

½ cup extra-virgin olive oil

½ teaspoon sea salt

2 cups chopped fresh parsley

¼ cup chopped fresh mint

4 tomatoes, seeded and
   chopped

1. In a saucepan, bring ¾ cup water to a boil.
   Add barley, cover, reduce heat, and simmer
   for 80 minutes or until tender. If using pearl
   barley, cooking time may be reduced to
   60 minutes. Drain, rinse, and set aside to cool.

2. Meanwhile, in a separate saucepan, bring
   ½ cup water to a boil. Add amaranth. Cover,
   reduce, heat and simmer for 20 minutes or
   until tender. Drain, rinse, and set aside to cool.

3. In the saucepan used to cook the amaranth,
   bring ½ cup water to a boil. Add rice. Cover,
   reduce heat, and lightly boil for 40 minutes or
   until tender. Drain, rinse, and set aside to cool.

4. In a bowl, combine lemon juice, oil, and salt,
   and whisk to blend. Add parsley, mint, and
   tomatoes, and toss well. Add barley, amaranth,
   and rice, and toss well to coat with lemon
   and oil.

Parslied Cheese Balls in Tomato Sauce

1 pound Swiss chard, stems
   removed
2 large egg yolks, lightly beaten
½ teaspoon sea salt
¼ teaspoon ground nutmeg
½ pound fresh ricotta cheese,
   drained
1 cup packed chopped fresh
   parsley or finely chopped
   Gremolata (page 281)
½ cup grated Parmesan cheese
¼ cup all-purpose flour
2 cups Tomato Sauce
   (page 268) or store-bought

1. Rinse chard leaves and shake to remove excess water. Place leaves with water still clinging to them in a saucepan. Cover and set over medium heat. Cook, turning the leaves with tongs once or twice, for 12 to 15 minutes or until tender and water has evaporated. Transfer to a colander and set aside to cool completely. Squeeze out as much water as possible and chop.

2. In a bowl, using a fork, whisk together egg yolks, salt, and nutmeg. Add chard, ricotta, parsley, and Parmesan cheese and mix well.

3. Line a rimmed baking sheet with parchment paper. Sprinkle flour over the bottom of a shallow plate. Using your hands, pinch off a small piece of the greens mixture about half the size of a golf ball. Roll in a ball, dust in the flour, and set aside on the prepared baking sheet. Repeat until all the greens mixture has been used.

4. Bring a large pot of salted water to a boil over high heat. In a saucepan, heat tomato sauce over medium-low heat. Carefully drop 8 to 10 cheese balls into the water. Cook for 6 minutes (they will float to the surface within about 1 minute) and using a slotted spoon, remove to the tomato sauce in the saucepan. Continue to cook cheese balls in batches until all are cooked.

A TONIC HERB PRIMER

By definition, a tonic is an infusion of herbs that invigorates or strengthens the system. Tonics often act as stimulants and alteratives as well. Taken either hot or cold, tonics restore tone to cells, purify the blood, and act as nutritive builders.

The common "tonic water" we now use mainly as a mixer for alcohol is a vestige of earlier times when bitter herbal tonics were widely used. By the 1500s, Europeans had learned of cinchona bark (*Cinchona officinalis*), which contains quinine, a substance that is extremely effective against malaria. The British living in colonial India began to add gin to the bitter-tasting quinine tonic to make the medicine more palatable. Most modern brands of tonic water still contain quinine for flavor but in amounts that are too small to be effective medicinally.

Tonic herbs support the body's systems in maintaining health. Depending on what herbs are used, they can support the whole body or specific systems or organs. They are able to do this because they contain opposing groups of constituents that can lower (or raise), stimulate (or depress), increase (or decrease) individual biological processes. Tonics increase the tone of the body tissues, imparting strength and vitality by promoting the digestive process, improving blood circulation, and increasing the supply of oxygen to the tissues.

Following is a list of tonic herbs that are safe to use daily except during pregnancy.

ALFALFA (*Medicago sativa*) It is a nutritive support for the musculoskeletal system and is safe for all ages to take on a daily basis.

ALFALFA

ASTRAGALUS (*Astragalus membranaceus*) The root promotes tissue regeneration and is a heart tonic as well as a powerful immune system stimulator for virtually every phase of immune system activity. It has proven effective for people recovering from chemotherapy and is safe for all ages to take on a daily basis.

ASTRAGALUS

DANDELION It is a detoxifying herb and a liver tonic. Its liver and kidney function stimulation gives it antirheumatic function and makes it an effective digestive.

DANDELION

DEVIL'S CLAW (*Harpagophytum procumbens*) In addition to being a liver tonic, the tubers are anti-inflammatory and antioxidant and they may help to lower blood pressure and heart rate. Devil's claw is used to relieve the pain and inflammation of arthritis and rheumatism.

DEVIL'S CLAW

ECHINACEA (*Echinacea purpurea or E. angustifolia*) An effective immune system tonic, to work properly *Echinacea* must be taken as soon as cold or flu symptoms are present and it must be taken in sufficient amounts every hour for several days.

GINSENG (*Panax quinquefolius*) Ginseng is a powerful adaptogen used to strengthen the immune system and relieve the symptoms of stress. As a tonic, it supports the body's energy, strength, and stamina.

LICORICE ROOT (*Glycyrrhiza glabra*) Licorice root is considered to be one of the best tonic herbs because it provides nutrients to almost all body systems. It is used to relieve inflammation of mucous membranes (asthma, bronchial, and lung congestion), as well as cough and sore throat. It teams well with other herbs to ease stomachache, ulcers, arthritis, bladder, and kidney ailments and for skin disorders.

PARSLEY Tea made from parsley seeds and leaves acts as a general tonic and treats gout, rheumatism, and arthritis as well as gallstones, kidney stones, and urinary infections. See Caution, page 278.

Tonic Tea

This tea feeds the cells of the body and boosts the immune system. It can be used every day with young and old (see Caution, page 278). Make it in bulk and store in a jar with a lid ideally every day but you can store for up to two days in the refrigerator. Add a cup or more of the tea to soups and stews and use in smoothies or in place of other liquids in cooking. This tonic may be used with cancer patients before, during, and after treatment.

1 part chopped dried Astragalus root
1 part dried parsley leaves
1 part dried alfalfa aerial parts

NOTE: You can make a day's worth of tonic tea at a time (about 5 cups). Cover tightly and store in the refrigerator and make fresh ideally every day but up to 2 days.

1. Blend and store the herbs in a labeled airtight container or dark-colored jar in a dark, cool, dry cupboard.

   TO MAKE THE TONIC TEA: crush a small amount of the blend to a fine powder. Measure 1 teaspoon per cup of water. Place in a warmed ceramic teapot, add 1 teaspoon of the crushed blend "for the pot," and pour boiled water over the herbs. Cover the pot and put a cork in the spout. Steep for about 5 minutes and strain into cups.

Spring Smoothie

Because of their pleasant taste, smoothies are the perfect drink for delivering the cleansing properties of spring tonic herbs. In this drink, you make a tea first using the Tonic Tea blend and then use the chilled tea as the liquid base for this cleansing drink.

Makes 2 servings

⅔ cup steeped Tonic Tea
   (page 287)
1 cup chopped kale or spinach
½ cup broccoli florets
½ cup green grapes
4 sprigs parsley

In a blender container, combine tea, kale, broccoli, grapes, and parsley. Secure lid and blend (from low to high if using a variable speed blender) until smooth.

Iron Builder

Young people experiencing puberty require extra iron to help them cope with the rapid changes within their bodies. This drink has a pleasant taste, is quite refreshing, and may be kept in the refrigerator for thirsty teens. Stinging nettle and burdock are abundant in wild areas, but you can use dried herbs, which are available in bulk from whole food stores or online. Sweet cicely is easy to grow and its sweet, anise flavor is delicious in tonics and teas.

Makes 2 servings

6 fresh peppermint sprigs
4 fresh stinging nettle tops
   (4 to 6 inches each)
1 fresh yellow dock or dandelion
   root, scrubbed
1 small fresh burdock leaf, chopped
1 cup chopped fresh parsley
½ cup chopped fresh sweet
   cicely, optional
4 cups boiled water

In a nonreactive teapot or heatproof jar, combine herbs and pour water over. Steep, covered, for at least 12 hours (the longer steeping time is necessary to extract the minerals from the herbs). Strain and drink ½ cup twice daily. Store tonic in a clean jar with a lid in the refrigerator for up to three days.

Wild Fresh Spring Tonic

If available, use fresh maple sap every day. It is possible to store sap in the refrigerator but not for more than two days, as it is prone to bacteria before it is "boiled off." This makes a pleasant spring celebration toast. Stinging nettle is commonly found in wild, even semi-wild, areas. Remember to wear gloves when harvesting and chopping it.

Makes 2 to 3 servings

3 cups filtered water

1 piece (2 inches) fresh burdock root, chopped

1 piece (2 inches) fresh dandelion root, chopped

1 piece (2 inches) fresh ginseng root, chopped

1 tablespoon chopped fresh parsley

1 tablespoon chopped fresh stinging nettle tops, optional

¼ cup fresh maple sap or 2 tablespoons maple syrup

1. In a nonreactive saucepan, pour water over burdock, dandelion, and ginseng. Cover and bring to a boil over medium heat. Turn off heat and steep, covered, for 15 minutes.

2. Stir in parsley and nettle. Steep, covered, for an hour or up to overnight. Strain into a clean jar and stir in maple sap. Use immediately, or cover tightly and keep in refrigerator for up to 2 days.

Stinging Nettle

Pelargonium

Pelargonium species

The Age of Discovery . . . opened the way for plant explorers—people like
John Tradescant (ca. 1570–1638), gardener to Charles I—to bring exotic botanical specimens to the great glass houses of Britain, Spain, and France.

—Pat Crocker, *Pelargonium: 2006 Herb of the Year*

The name *Pelargonium* comes from the Greek word *pelargos*, meaning "stork," because *Pelargonium* seedpods are similar in shape to that bird's beak. Once called geraniums (and still often referred to as scented geraniums) because they resemble the leaves of those hardy plants, *Pelargonium* plants are not to be confused with the genus *Geranium*.

Native to the southern part of the African continent, *Pelargonium* plants were unknown to Europeans until late in the fifteenth century, when the race to find spices led Portuguese and Dutch adventurers around Africa's southern tip. There they found exotic plants with geranium-like leaves that were highly perfumed and completely unknown in Europe. It was hoped that the plants they found would yield medicinal benefits along with their fruit, spice, and pungent scents.

For centuries, Zulu, Basuto, Xhosa, and Mfengi cultures treated coughs, upper respiratory tract irritations, and gastrointestinal issues with *umckaloabo*, a decoction of the roots of *P. sidoides* and *P. reniforme*. In 1897, Charles Stevens, an Englishman suffering from tuberculosis, traveled to southern Africa seeking a cure, which he found in the form of umckaloabo. Upon his return, Stevens sold the remedy as "Stevens' Consumption

Cure" throughout Europe until about 1930. According to Maria Lis-Balchin's book, *Geranium and Pelargonium*, Swiss missionary doctor Adrien Sechehaye treated a large number of patients with the original Basuto remedy. This remedy has since been proven by plant research to be effective and is currently being used by an increasing number of natural healers.

As the popularity of *P. graveolens*, or "rose geranium" as it was commonly called, grew in Victorian times, its use in the kitchen centered around cakes, jellies, and custards. Cooks were able to impart a rose flavor without the cost or trouble of making rosewater. When recipes called for rose geranium, the leaves of *P. graveolens* were strewn over the bottom of cake pans or wrapped around the sides of cakes after baking.

The leaves of *P.* 'Both's Snowflake' are soft gray-green and their scent is rose with an undertone of lemon.

The fragrance of scented-leaf *Pelargonium* is concentrated in small beads of oil produced by glands situated at the base of fine leaf hairs. Some leaves have unmistakable scents of apple, lemon, rose, mint, or spice. Others may smell like nutmeg to one individual or camphor to another, and so they are more difficult to categorize.

The adventure in cooking with *Pelargonium* plants comes from discovering their tantalizing perfumes—sharp lemon, tart fruit, exploding rose, or bold spice—that mimic the classic scents we love to apply to food. The reward comes from an unexpected, intense burst of flavor, or the mysterious, and mildly exotic note that intrigues yet defies description.

Explore *Pelargonium* plants with your nose first, and then with your fingertips and tongue. Let those senses direct the plants you choose to grow and enjoy in foods. Experiment with adding *Pelargonium* to various dishes to find ingredients that complement the plants' invigorating aromas.

FLAVOR

The fragrance and flavor of *Pelargonium* leaves may be mild or strongly rose, lemon, citrus, fruit, nut, spice, mint, or "pungent." The flowers may be bland or only very slightly tinged with the same taste as the leaves.

PARTS TO USE

The leaves and flowers are used.

CULINARY USES

Rub, chop, crush, or bruise a scented *Pelargonium* leaf to release its fragrance. Subtle rose and spice-scented leaves are highlighted in puddings, custards, and other egg dishes, while bold mint or citrus leaves are used in cake, cookie, scone, and muffin batters. The dainty leaves are often used as doilies for serving or for decorating baked goods.

♥ HEALTH BENEFITS

The roots of *P. sidoides* and *P. reniforme* are used in South African traditional medicine to treat upper respiratory tract infections (colds, cough, bronchitis, and inflammation of the sinuses) and diarrhea.

CAUTION: Some people may experience allergic reactions to *Pelargonium*.

GROWING *PELARGONIUM* PLANTS

Pelargonium plants are tender perennials easily grown from cuttings. They thrive in well-drained growing medium and plenty of light. Most will grow in full sun in the garden and must be watered regularly, but don't let them sit in water. Use a balanced fertilizer to bring out generous healthy foliage. Protect from frost and bring indoors in the fall.

VARIETIES

It is the leaves of *Pelargonium* plants that are used for their perfume in cooking. The flowers are delicate and delightful and may be candied or used in drinks or as garnish for dishes, but their scent is very mild. What follows are some popular cooking scents and flavors found in *Pelargonium* cultivars. This list contains just a fraction of the many fabulous *Pelargonium* plants available in each flavor group.

Rose

P. 'BOTH'S SNOWFLAKE' (cultivar) The taste is clear rose with lemon overtones, so it complements grains, fish, poultry, and tea blends.

P. 'CANDY DANCER' (cultivar) A lemon-rose flavor makes this variety useful in puddings and egg dishes, as well as with grains, fish, and baked goods.

P. 'ATTAR OF ROSES' (cultivar) It has an almost overpoweringly strong rose taste and smell. Use it in smaller amounts and to make Rose-Scented Leaf Water (page 295).

P. 'ROSE' (cultivar) With its classic rose scent and flavor, it is an all-round, versatile rose-scented leaf for cooking.

P. 'OLD-FASHIONED ROSE' (cultivar) Often the one most popular in culinary applications, this cultivar can be used in cake batters, jellies, sugars, puddings, and tea blends.

P. 'DR. LIVINGSTON' (cultivar) It has a more concentrated rose flavor that works in cakes and cookies as well as skin and hair preparations.

Lemon

P. CITRONELLUM (species) In the trade, the cultivar 'Mabel Grey' is considered the best lemon-scented leaf by many herbalists. It has a strong lemon scent and taste with some muskiness. Use it sparingly with grains, fish, and tea blends.

P. CRISPUM (species) One of the nicest lemon-scented *Pelargonium* leaves, its clear lemon taste works in baked goods, sauces, salads, and vinaigrettes.

P. 'FRENSHAM' (cultivar) A strong lemon essence makes this cultivar versatile for use with grains, fish, poultry, liqueurs, and salads.

Citrus

P. 'LIME' (cultivar) With its fresh, lime-citrus flavor, this variety is good in sauces, preserves, and salsas, and to accompany fish, poultry, and whole grains.

P. 'ORANGE' (cultivar) The delicate, mild citrus taste of this cultivar is used in sauces, syrups, batters for baked goods, salads, and tea blends. It goes well with fish.

Fruit

P. ODORATISSIMUM (species) With predominantly apple notes, its sweet, fruity taste and smell is best in sweet sauces, salads, and puddings.

P. 'GOOSEBERRY LEAF' (cultivar) The flavor resembles citrus-peach and complements desserts, sauces, and fruit salads.

Mint

P. 'MINT-SCENTED ROSE' (cultivar) A clear, strong mint essence with slight notes of rose makes this leaf an unusual addition to grains, sauces, and syrups.

P. 'PEPPERMINT LACE' (cultivar) It has a strong peppermint taste. You can use it in cake and cookie batters, icings, sauces, and for fudges or candies.

P. 'PUNGENT PEPPERMINT' (cultivar) This is another variety with strong peppermint scent and flavor. Experiment with it in sauces, salads, and tea blends.

Spice

P. 'ARDWICK CINNAMON' (cultivar) Its spice flavor can be pungent, so use it sparingly as you would allspice or cloves.

P. 'CREAMY NUTMEG' (cultivar) Spicy and pungent-tasting, the leaf is variegated, so it makes a beautiful garnish. Chop and use it as you would nutmeg in baked goods and vegetable sauces.

P. 'GINGER' (cultivar) Pleasantly ginger with citrus overtones, it is best added to sauces, or in fish and rice dishes.

Herbalist Simple: Rose-Scented Leaf Water

Often called the "mimic" herb, *Pelargonium* has the ability to impart its essence to other "carrier" substances and, through those mixtures, to food and beverages. Infusions require strong, clear leaf scents. Generally, rose, lemon, and peppermint are the best *Pelargonium* leaf scents for infusions. See Varieties (pages 293–294) for lemon, citrus, fruit, mint, or spice leaves to use in place of the rose called for in the recipe. Except in teas when a blend is desired, use only one flavor for an intense infusion.

Use this rose-scented infusion whenever rosewater is called for. To flavor cakes and other baked goods, replace up to half the liquid in the recipe with Rose-Scented Leaf Water. Use it as the liquid in hand cream or as a fragrant face or hair rinse. See also Floral Water, page 194.

Makes 2 cups

1½ cups chopped fresh
    rose-scented *Pelargonium*
    leaves
2 cups filtered water

1. In a nonreactive saucepan, combine leaves and water and bring to a boil over medium heat. Cover and adjust heat to gently simmer for 10 minutes. Turn the heat off and let stand on the element or gas burner for 30 to 60 minutes.

2. Strain the water into sterilized or clean jars. Cap, label, and store in the refrigerator for up to 4 days or up to 3 months in the freezer.

The leaves of P. 'Dr. Livingston' are skeletal, but they impart a distinct rose scent.

Creamy Lemon-Rose Gelato

Makes 4 servings

1 cup Rose-Scented Leaf Water
   (page 295)
1¼ cups sugar
Zest of 2 lemons, grated
Juice of 3 lemons
¾ cup heavy whipping cream
   (36% butterfat)

1. In a saucepan, combine Rose-Scented Leaf Water, sugar, lemon zest, and lemon juice. Bring to a simmer over medium heat and simmer, stirring constantly, for 2 to 3 minutes or until sugar dissolves. Set aside to cool completely.

2. In a bowl, beat whipping cream until thickened, but not firm. Stir into cooled lemon syrup. Pour into an ice cream machine and freeze, following the manufacturer's instructions.

Rose and Almond Apricot Tarts

Makes 4 tarts

½ cup unsalted butter, softened
3 tablespoons finely chopped
   rose-scented *Pelargonium* leaf
½ cup superfine (caster) sugar
2 eggs
½ teaspoon pure vanilla extract
¾ cup ground almonds
⅓ cup all-purpose flour
4 fresh apricots or peach halves,
   stones removed

1. Preheat oven to 400°F.

2. Lightly butter 4 ovenproof ramekins or small baking dishes.

3. In the bowl of a food processor or blender container, combine butter and Pelargonium leaf. Process until well blended. With the motor running, slowly add sugar through the opening in the lid and process until smooth.

4. Add eggs, vanilla, ground almonds, and flour and process for 30 seconds or just until combined.

5. Place an apricot in each ramekin. Divide the almond mixture into 4 portions and spoon each around the apricots. Bake in preheated oven for 15 to 20 minutes or until the almond mixture is puffed and golden.

Frisée, Pear, and Pistachio Salad with Rose and Pomegranate Vinaigrette

Makes 4 servings

1 ripe pear, cored and cut into
  thin slices
1 head frisée (3 cups), cored and
  torn into bite-size pieces
1 cup mesclun greens mix
½ cup shelled pistachio nuts
¼ cup pomegranate seeds
½ cup Rose and Pomegranate
  Vinaigrette (recipe follows)

1. In a large bowl, combine pear, frisée, and mesclun greens.

2. Shake or whisk vinaigrette to recombine and drizzle over greens. Toss to coat leaves well.

3. Divide evenly among 4 chilled salad plates and garnish each with 2 tablespoons of pistachio nuts and 1 tablespoon of pomegranate seeds.

ROSE AND POMEGRANATE VINAIGRETTE

Makes ½ cup

5 tablespoons sunflower oil or
  extra-virgin olive oil
2½ tablespoons pomegranate
  or raspberry vinegar
2 tablespoons finely chopped
  rose-scented *Pelargonium* leaf
½ teaspoon honey

In a jar with a tight-fitting lid or a small bowl, combine oil, vinegar, *Pelargonium* leaf, and honey. Cap and shake or whisk. Set aside and let stand for at least 60 minutes or up to 4 hours. Shake or whisk before using.

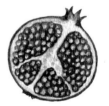

Purslane

Portulaca oleracea

Its name in Malawi translates as "buttocks of the wife of a chief,"
obviously referring to its succulent round leaves and juicy stems!

—Jekka McVicar, *Jekka's Herb Cookbook*, 2011

The earliest written use of purslane appeared in *The Forme of Cury*, an English recipe manuscript, published around 1390 by King Richard II's cook. The original "salat" recipe appeared as follows (purslane being spelled "purslarye"):

"Take persel, sawge, garlec, chibolles, oynouns, leek, borage, myntes, porrectes, fenel and ton tressis, rew, rosemarye, purslarye, laue and waische hem clene, pike hem, pluk hem small wiþ þyn honde and myng hem wel with rawe oile. Lay on vynegur and salt, and serue it forth."

A rough translation would be: "For salad, use parsley, sage, garlic, scallions, onions, leek, borage, mints, 'porrettes' (green onions, scallions, and very young leeks), fennel, and cress, rue, rosemary, and purslane. Rinse the ingredients well to clean. Trim and tear them into small pieces with your hands. Make a dressing of raw oil, vinegar and salt, toss with the greens and serve."

About 250 years later, around the same time that Louis XIV was enjoying golden purslane, a variety his gardeners cultivated for royal salads, Nicholas Culpeper (1616–1654) was writing in his book, *The Complete Herbal*, that purslane (or *purslain* as it is called in the book):

is good to allay the heat of the liver, blood, veins, stomach, and hot agues nothing better: it stays hot and choleric fluxes of the belly, women's courses, the whites, and gonorrhoea, or running of the reins, the distillation from the head, and pains therin proceeding from heat, want of sleep, or the frenzy, . . . The seed bruised and boiled in wine, and given to children, expels the worms. . . . The juice is singularly good in the inflammations and ulcers in the secret parts or man or woman, as well as in the bowels, and hemorrhoids, when they are ulcerous, or excoriations in them.

And American colonists, who knew a good herb when they ate one, were introducing purslane to Massachusetts around 1672. Now naturalized widely in the United States and southern Canada, it is creeping over open fields, gardens, and disturbed ground almost everywhere. This is one herb that proves my theory: the best way to control invasive herbs is to *eat them*.

FLAVOR

Purslane is refreshingly tart with lemon notes. The leaves add a juicy, crunchy texture to raw dishes.

PARTS TO USE

The leaves, stems, and flowers are all used.

CULINARY USES

Use the fresh, raw whole leaves and flowers in salads and chopped in yogurt or sour cream dips. Larger, older leaves may be blanched and tossed with other vegetables or added to soups or stews as a bright-tasting thickener. Leaves, stems, and flowers may be pickled.

Purslane is for sale (top row, far right), along with dozens of fresh herbs, behind the Ferry Building at Heirloom Organic Garden market stall in San Francisco, California.

♥ HEALTH BENEFITS

An important source of iron and vitamins A, B, and C, purslane is one of few vegetable sources of omega-3 fatty acids and it is important to the heart and the immune system. Because it is so nutritious and easy to grow or harvest from disturbed ground, it is an herb to learn to identify in the wild or to plant in an herb garden.

GROWING PURSLANE

This herb grows wild almost everywhere and it is easy to gather from bare ground, but you can grow it from seeds in the spring. A low-growing, mat-forming hardy annual, it will require more water than most herbs in very hot weather.

Herb Soup

This is a healthy, tonic soup, best if made in the spring when peas are fresh. It's meant to strengthen invalids, but the cream and eggs may be omitted. It is thick and flavorful and if you wish to thin it, add more broth at the end in step 2. The recipe is adapted from *Gardening with Herbs* by Helen Morgenthau Fox, but it dates at least to Dalgairns, 1830, and was once called Nun's Broth.

Makes 6 servings

½ cup extra-virgin coconut oil
   or butter
1 onion, chopped
3 small heads lettuce, chopped
2 cups fresh peas
1 cup coarsely chopped purslane
1 cup packed sorrel leaves
½ cup coarsely chopped chervil
6 green onions, sliced diagonally
4 cups chicken or vegetable broth
2 carrots, chopped
2 cucumbers, coarsely chopped
2 pieces of toast, coarsely chopped
1 teaspoon sea salt
Freshly ground pepper
½ cup light cream (18% butterfat)
2 egg yolks
6 tablespoons Gremolata
   (page 281), for garnish, optional

1. In a soup pot, heat oil over medium-high heat. Add onion, lettuce, peas, purslane, sorrel, chervil, and green onions. Reduce heat to medium-low and cook, stirring frequently, for 25 minutes or until vegetables are soft. Add broth, carrots, cucumbers, toast, salt, and pepper. Bring to a simmer, partially cover, and continue simmering, stirring occasionally, for 1 hour.

2. Transfer soup to a large bowl. Ladle soup into the blender container in batches and purée on high speed for 1 minute or until smooth, and return each batch to the soup pot. Repeat until all herbs, vegetables, and broth are puréed. Stir in the cream and egg yolks, heat to under the boiling point but do not boil, stirring constantly, over medium-high heat. Simmer, stirring frequently, for 3 minutes or until thickened. Taste and add more salt if necessary. Ladle into bowls and garnish each with 1 tablespoon of gremolata if using.

Pickled Purslane and Peppers

In times long past, herbs were salted, sugared, or pickled in vinegar to preserve them. Many of the surviving herbals and recipe books give instructions for preserves or pickling herbs. Because of its fleshy stems and leaves, purslane is a very good herb to include in vegetable pickles or to pickle on its own. I've read very old recipes that layer purslane and fennel (the bulb) in a white wine vinegar. Through the centuries comes this recipe for pickled purslane from John Evelyn's 1699 *Acetaria*. After that, you'll find my version.

> **21. Purfelan.** Lay the Stalks in an Earthen Pan; then cover them with Beer-Vinegar and Water, keeping them down with a competent Weight to imbibe, three Days: Being taken out, put them into a Pot with as much White-Wine Vinegar as will cover them again; and cloſe the Lid with Paſte to keep in the Steam: Then ſet them on the Fire for three or four Hours, often ſhaking and ſtirring them: Then open the Cover, and turn and remove thoſe Stalks which lie at the Bottom, to the Top, and boil them as before, till they are all of a Colour. When all is cold, pot them with freſh White-Wine Vinegar, and ſo you may preſerve them the whole Year round.

Makes 6 cups

1½ cups white wine vinegar
¼ cup bottled lemon juice
¾ cup sugar
6 cloves
2 cups purslane leaves and stems
1 pound red bell peppers, cut
    into 2-inch-wide strips
1 red onion, thinly sliced

1. Set a rack in the bottom of a canner or large pot. Set three 1-pint jars upright on the rack and fill the pot with water so that it reaches at least 1 inch over the top of the jars. Cover and bring the water to a boil. Turn the heat off and keep the lid on the pot until ready to fill the jars.

2. In a saucepan, combine vinegar, lemon juice, sugar, and cloves. Bring to a boil over high heat. Reduce heat to low and keep the brine warm.

3. Remove one jar from the water and set on a clean tea towel. Pack purslane, pepper strips, and onion slices into the jar. Pour the warm brine over, covering the vegetables but leaving a ½-inch headspace. Run a thin spatula around the inside of the jar to release any air bubbles. Wipe the rims of the jars.

4. Place the flat lid on the jar and screw the ring over the lid until finger-tight. Return the filled jar to the hot water. Repeat steps 3 and 4 until all the vegetables have been used to fill jars. Refrigerate any leftover small amount of vegetables and brine and use within a week.

5. Cover the canner and bring the water to a full boil over high heat. Boil the jars for 10 minutes. Turn the heat off, remove the lid, and let the pot sit for 5 minutes. Remove jars to a cooling rack and set aside to cool completely. Test for a proper seal and refrigerate any jars that have not snapped shut all the way around the lid. Label and store in a cool, dark cupboard for up to 1 year.

Quinoa and Sweet Potato Terrines

Makes 4 servings

3 cups chicken or vegetable broth

1½ cups quinoa, rinsed

2 cups diced sweet potatoes

3 tablespoons extra-virgin
   coconut oil

1 onion, chopped

1 cup sliced mushrooms

1 cup coarsely chopped purslane
   leaves and stems

1 tablespoon Curry Spice blend
   (page 104) or store-bought

1 tablespoon tamari or soy sauce

1 tablespoon rice vinegar

¼ cup grated Cheddar cheese

1. In a large saucepan, bring broth to a boil over high heat. Stir in quinoa and potatoes. Cover, reduce heat, and simmer for 25 minutes or until quinoa and potatoes are cooked. Drain any remaining liquid. Return quinoa and potatoes to the saucepan.

2. Meanwhile, in a skillet, heat oil over medium-high heat. Sauté onion for 5 minutes. Add mushrooms, purslane, garam masala, tamari, and vinegar and cook, stirring frequently, for 5 minutes or until vegetables are tender and the liquid has evaporated.

3. Preheat oven to 375°F. Set four 2-cup ramekins on a rimmed baking sheet. Using a potato masher, mash the quinoa and sweet potato mixture. Add cooked mushroom mixture and mix well. Divide mixture into four equal portions and spoon into ramekins. Sprinkle cheese evenly over each and bake in preheated oven for 15 minutes or until cheese has melted and the mixture is bubbly.

Tomato and Purslane Tarte Tatin

Makes 1 tart, 4 to 6 servings

5 tablespoons butter, divided
1 large onion, cut in half
    and sliced
2 teaspoons sugar, divided
1 tablespoon extra-virgin olive oil
2 cloves garlic, finely chopped
1 cup coarsely chopped fresh
    purslane
2 tablespoons chopped fresh
    thyme
5 Roma or plum tomatoes,
    halved lengthwise
2 cups cherry tomatoes
½ 14-ounce package puff pastry,
    thawed

1. Preheat oven to 375°F.

2. Melt 2 tablespoons of the butter in an 8-inch tart pan or ovenproof skillet over medium-low heat. Add onion and cook, stirring occasionally, for 10 minutes or until soft and golden. Stir in 1 teaspoon of the sugar and cook for 2 minutes. Transfer onion to a bowl and set aside.

3. Heat the remaining butter and the oil in the tart pan or skillet over medium-high heat. Sauté garlic, remaining sugar, purslane, and thyme for 2 minutes or until garlic is soft and lightly colored. Arrange plum tomatoes, cut side down, in the pan. Cook for 1 minute. Scatter cherry tomatoes evenly in the pan and remove the pan from the heat. Spread onions evenly over tomatoes and set the pan aside on a rimmed baking sheet.

4. Roll out one square (7 ounces) of puff pastry to about 9 inches square. Cover the vegetables in the tart pan with pastry, tucking in the edges all the way around. Bake in preheated oven for 25 to 30 minutes or until the pastry has puffed up and is evenly browned. Let the tart rest for 10 minutes. Serve from the tart pan (with pastry on the top), or flip the tart onto a serving plate following directions in step 5.

   TO SERVE: Position a serving plate over the tart pan and turn the plate and pan upside down so that the onions and tomatoes are on top of the pastry on the plate.

A FORAGER'S PRIMER TO WILD HERBS

With his 1966 book *Stalking the Healthful Herbs*, Euell Gibbons introduced a whole generation to the bounty of nature. In turn, over the next four decades, inspired foragers and writers produced books and recipes of their own for seeking and enjoying food from the wild. Now herbalists in almost every city in North America are leading small groups on "herb" or "edible weed" walks through parks and wild areas in order to rekindle our intimate relationship with plants in the wild.

Having myself hosted the "Riversong Herb Walk" program from an original 1857 log cabin in southern Ontario during the 1990s, I have seen firsthand the wonder that people experience as they learn there are indeed edible and medicinal plants thriving in the wild without any interference on the part of humans. For many people the supermarket is the only source of food, and they are unaware that our garden plants were first transplanted from the wild. In a very short time compared to our existence on Earth, many have lost the knowledge and the spiritual intimacy with nature that kept humans nourished in more ways than just mere survival. The following list is a very brief introduction to wild herbs. It is meant to whet your appetite for learning more about the plants around you.

CAUTION: Do not try to identify plants in the wild without expert guidance and do not take medicinal doses of herbs without the advice of a health-care professional or during pregnancy (see Glossary).

BURDOCK

BURDOCK (*Arctium lappa*) The roots are cooked and eaten as any root vegetable. In tincture form, it is used to cleanse the liver.

CLEAVERS

CLEAVERS (*Galium aparine*) Leaves and stems are eaten raw in salads, cooked as a green, or used in teas. It acts as a diuretic, cleanser, and lymphatic tonic.

BLACK COHOSH

BLACK COHOSH (*Actaea racemosa*) Its roots are used to relieve hot flashes and other menopausal symptoms.

BLUE COHOSH

BLUE COHOSH (*Caulophyllum thalictroides*) The purple seeds are roasted and infused in boiling water to make a healing tea, and the root is used in a decoction or infusion as an emmenagogue, antispasmodic, and diuretic and to treat other conditions.

COLTSFOOT (*Tussilago farfara*) A long-established cough and lung medicine, coltsfoot was used as the symbol for pharmacies in Europe. Use flowers or leaves in cough syrup.

FIDDLEHEAD OSTRICH FERN (*Matteuccia struthiopteris*) The unfurled ferns appear in early spring. Wash them well and steam or stir-fry as a green vegetable. They contribute omega-3 and omega-6 fatty acids, are a good source of fiber, and act as an antioxidant.

GARLIC MUSTARD (*Alliaria petiolata*) Like other plants in the mustard (*Brassicaceae*) family, it is a noxious weed when left unchecked. The leaves are mildly garlic flavored. Use garlic mustard leaf and flowers in salads and cook as you would leafy greens.

GINGER (*Asarum canadense*) This wild North American native grows in deciduous woods. The top-growing rhizome, which is used in teas, has a flavor similar to cultivated ginger. (See Wild Ginger, page 165.)

GOLDENSEAL (*Hydrastis canadensis*) A North American native, it is used by North American First Nations as a cancer remedy, and it has been shown to be antimicrobial, hepatic, and anti-inflammatory, among other properties.

WILD LEEKS (*Allium tricoccum*) These North American natives grow in deciduous woods, but be careful to identify them properly because their leaves resemble those of lily of the valley, a poisonous plant. Wild leeks must be dug up. Their characteristic fragrance and taste is garlic and onion. Use bulb, stem, and leaf in soups and stews or as you would onion or cultivated leeks. (See Wild Leeks, page 85.)

MOTHERWORT (*Leonurus cardiaca*) Herbalists use it to treat menstrual problems and to ease postpartum depression. Do not use during pregnancy, and use only on the advice of an herbal practitioner.

MULLEIN (*Verbascum thapsus*) A tall and stately herb known to First Nations people, the leaves are used in cough and cold syrup, and the flowers are infused in oil for use topically for skin problems and to ease earache.

STINGING NETTLE (*Urtica dioica*) It has almost invisible stinging hairs on the leaves and stem that cause a burning, itching sensation when they come into contact with skin. I use long rubber gloves when spring-cleaning my herb beds to remove the invading plants. Gather young leaves and steam them for a tasty warm salad or stir-fry, because the offending uric acid in the hairs is destroyed upon heating.

SAINT JOHN'S WORT (*Hypericum perforatum*) The blooms are bright yellow with five petals that stain the fingers red when rubbed. Herbalists use Saint John's wort in tea, oil, or salve for several ailments, most notably for easing depression.

VALERIAN (*Valeriana officinalis*) The odorous root is used in tincture to ease insomnia along with other ailments.

WILDCRAFTING GUIDELINES

* Learn from experts to properly identify plants, because several edible herbs resemble deadly ones.

* Take only one-tenth of a colony and leave new growth to establish itself.

* Only take what you know you will use and never harvest wild herbs to sell.

* Do not harvest from busy roads or highways, since plants take in pollutants from their surroundings.

* Approach all of nature with respect. Handle plants gently and bring a cooler so that aerial parts do not wilt or die during transportation.

Rose

Rosa species

Americans have always loved the flowers with which God decorates
our land. More often than any other flower, we hold the rose dear as the
symbol of life and love and devotion, of beauty and eternity. For the love of
man and woman, for the love of mankind and God, for the love of country,
Americans who would speak the language of the heart do so with a rose.

—President Ronald Reagan at the signing of the act adopting the rose as the national floral emblem
of the United States of America, October 7, 1986

Since proof abounds that the rose
has graced American soil longer
than any human, a better choice for
national flower of the United States could
not have been made. Indeed, rose imprints
on slate deposits in the Florissant Fossil
Beds near Cripple Creek, Colorado, have
been identified as being around 35 to 40
million years old—a lineage old enough
to warrant that this stately blossom be
crowned queen of the land.

The roses that were blooming near
Cripple Creek during the Oligocene epoch
were "wild species" roses that probably
originated in Central Asia. They were hardy, with simple single flowers growing on
shrubs or climbing cane-like shoots. Their rose hips were almost as big as the flower
itself. Wild species roses are the plants from which all modern roses descend. *Rosa
rugosa* is the best modern-day example of a wild species rose.

It is believed that some 5,000 years ago, the Chinese began cultivating the rose.
Throughout antiquity, the rose was associated with myths and legends and religious rit-
uals and ceremonies. Egyptian tombs dating to about 170 CE have revealed wreaths of
damask-like roses. Minoan frescoes (*ca.* 1700 BCE) in Crete at Knossos feature roses in

their design, and the Romans developed the first hothouses in order to feed their voracious appetite for the floral monarch.

The focus on religion and herbal medicine during the Middle Ages defined the use of the rose for medicinal purposes. Monks developed and perfected distillation techniques and were using rosewater for eye ointments and salves, syrups, powders, oils, conserves, scented rosary beads, and candied condiments and in baked products.

A deep, rose-colored rambling rose spills over the fence at Lavender Fleece Herb Farm in Midland, Michigan.

Royal connections to the rose were strengthened in the fifteenth century during England's War of the Roses. The House of York adopted a white rose as its emblem (possibly *R. alba*) and the House of Lancaster took a red rose (possibly *R. gallica*). After thirty years of civil war, Henry VII emerged victorious, married a York princess, and united the families in a new Tudor dynasty. He merged his Lancastrian rose with the white rose of his York bride and thus created the Tudor Rose, the rose of England.

The nineteenth century marked a dividing point between "old" roses and "modern" roses when the Dutch began systematically growing roses from seed and in the early part of the 1800s introduced the first hybrid roses, among them the *R. centifolia* varieties.

Around this time, the highly prized continuous-blooming roses were introduced to Europe from China and India. The Oriental roses arrived by ship along with another precious cargo—that of tea. It is because of this and the fact that their fragrance was similar to that of tea that they became known as *tea roses*. But the Eastern roses were far too tender to survive the temperate European climate and were crossbred with winter-hardy varieties, and in 1867, the first *hybrid tea roses* were introduced.

Today, breeders like British grower David Austin are bringing sensational roses to a worldwide market, while at the same time, because of their hardy nature, large hips, and strong fragrance, many herbalists and herb gardeners are insisting on the "old varieties" of *R. rugosa* as well as *R. gallica* such as the apothecary's rose, 'Rosamundi', and the York and Lancaster Rose.

FLAVOR

Rose petals are highly perfumed, especially the old varieties. (Some hybrids have no rose floral taste or aroma.)

PARTS TO USE

The buds, petals, and hips are used.

CULINARY USES

Fresh rose petals are used in making rose syrup or rosewater. Toss rose petals in salads, or use as a garnish for many dishes. Rosewater is a staple of Middle Eastern cooking, used in Turkish delight candy, other sweet desserts, drinks, and savory vegetable or rice dishes. Dried rose buds and petals are powdered or used whole in spice blends. Rose hips are used in tea blends.

❤ HEALTH BENEFITS

Rosewater and rose petal tea are soothing, mildly sedative, and antidepressant. Rose essential oil is used to treat stress and its symptoms and to help digestion and circulation. Rose hips are an excellent source of vitamins A, B_3, C, D, and E and other active constituents that soothe sore throat, diarrhea, and bladder infections.

Red rose petals from *R. gallica* have been the only recognized petals to be used in medicinal preparations—a fact reinforced by the British Pharmacopoeia of the early twentieth century. Maude Grieve, in her book *A Modern Herbal* (1931), notes that any scented roses of a deep red color may be used: "The main point is that the petals suitable for medicinal purposes must yield a deep rose-colored and somewhat astringent and fragrant infusion." Grieve advises that rose petals for medicine must be collected before they are about to open.

North American First Nations used rose bark and roots to treat dysentery, diarrhea, and worms. A tea of rose petals was taken as a tonic. Today herbalists consider the rose to be antispasmodic, astringent, digestive, nervine, diaphoretic, tonic, and antimicrobial and a uterine tonic. It is also used as a gargle for sore throat, an eyewash, and a skin tonic; it cools menopausal hot flushes and night sweats, reduces fever, and helps with insomnia.

A well-maintained rambling rose scrambles up
a château wall in Provence, France.

GROWING ROSES

Roses are grown from rootstalk. To plant, situate in full sun, and partially fill a hole larger than the root with peat moss and 2 ounces of bone meal. Place the root in the hole with the bud swelling at soil level. Refill with peat moss mixture, tamp down, and water thoroughly, keeping the soil moist by watering at ground level. Work in ½ cup of fertilizer mixture in the spring and again after blooming in July. Keep rose bushes at about 2 feet by pruning dead wood in the spring after the buds appear.

Advieh Seasoning

Advieh is the Iranian or Middle Eastern word for "fragrant spices," and the combination of spices for each blend is usually a well-guarded secret; however, most advieh blends include rose petals or rose buds. This is my personal blend for tagine cooking. Use 1 to 3 teaspoons with rice, vegetable, and chicken dishes.

Makes ½ cup

3 tablespoons coriander seeds

2 tablespoons cumin seeds

1 piece (2 inches) cinnamon, crushed

¼ cup crushed dried rose petals or buds

20 strands saffron

1. In the bottom of a small tagine, spice wok, or skillet, combine coriander, cumin, and cinnamon. Toast over medium heat, stirring frequently, for 3 to 4 minutes or until lightly colored and fragrant. Remove from direct heat just as the seeds pop; do not let the spices smoke and burn. Set aside to cool.

2. In a mortar using a pestle or using a small electric grinder, pound or grind toasted spices until coarse or finely ground. Stir in rose petals and saffron.

3. Store in an airtight dark-glass jar with a lid in a cool place for up to 3 months.

Rose Syrup

Makes 2 cups

1½ cups rosewater
3 cups sugar
1 cup fresh red rose petals

1. In a saucepan, combine rosewater, sugar, and rose petals. Bring to a boil over medium-high heat. Boil, stirring occasionally, for 12 minutes or until the syrup is thickened.

2. Strain into a pint jar. Cap, label, and store in the refrigerator for up to 1 month. Bring to room temperature before using.

Rose Hip Jelly

Makes 2 cups

1 pound rose hips
1 cup rosewater or filtered water
2 cups sugar
2 tablespoons freshly squeezed
   lemon juice

NOTE: See Clove Pink (pages 92, 94–95) for recipes for using petals in jams, dressings, and fruit sauces; you can substitute rose petals in these recipes. See directions on making Herb/Floral Water, page 194.

1. In a saucepan, combine hips and rosewater. Bring to a boil over medium-high heat. Cook, stirring occasionally, for 10 to 15 minutes or until hips are soft.

2. Pour water and hips into a cheesecloth-lined strainer or jelly strainer over a bowl. Set aside overnight for the juice to collect in the bowl. Return the juice to the saucepan and bring to a boil. Stir in sugar and boil, stirring frequently, for about 20 minutes or until it reaches the jelly stage on a candy thermometer.

3. Remove from heat and stir in lemon juice. Pour jelly into 4 dessert bowls to use as a dessert topped with Rose Cream (page 318) or pour into a jar. Cap, label, and store in the refrigerator for up to 4 weeks. Use jelly as an accompaniment to meat or as a glaze for vegetables, or as a topping for puddings, ice creams, or other desserts.

● ROSE HIPS

Seeds of dog rose hips were discovered in the skeleton of a 2,000-year-old Neolithic woman unearthed in Britain. This is one of the ways that we know the ancients used petals, bark, roots, and hips from the wild "brier" or "dog" rose (*R. canina*) in Britain and North America.

Rose hips are known for their vitamin C content—which is higher in hips than in citrus fruit—and have been brewed as a tea or made into wine, jams, jellies, preserves, conserves, and syrups for coughs and to treat scurvy. In Scandinavia, rose hip juice is as popular as orange juice is in North America, and it is also used in warm winter soups, puddings, and other desserts. Vitamin C is highest in hips from the dog rose (*R. canina*) and the farther north the plant is found, the higher the vitamin C content. Rose hips also contain a high level of calcium, phosphorus, and iron, making them ideal as winter tonics to help increase the body's resistance to infectious diseases.

Gather hips in the late fall just after the first frost. Handle gently, leave whole or coarsely chop, and use fresh in syrups, jellies, or preserves, or split and dry them rapidly in a well-ventilated place. Store in a dark-colored jar in a cool dry place and use within one year. Rose hips also freeze well. Take two cups of rose hip tea per day when colds or flu threaten.

Savory Rose Soufflés

Makes 8 (4-ounce) soufflés

Unsalted butter

¾ cup plus about 3 tablespoons
 sugar

1 cup large egg whites (from
 about 8 eggs; save 2 yolks
 for this recipe and reserve
 the remaining yolks for
 another use)

½ teaspoon cream of tartar

¼ teaspoon sea salt

1 cup plain whole-milk yogurt

2 large egg yolks

1 tablespoon rosewater

6 drops Moroccan rose
 absolute oil or rose essential
 oil (see Caution, page 91)

NOTE: Rose absolute oil is obtained
by using a solvent to extract the oil
from rose petals. It is more viscous
than rose essential oil and should
be warmed by rubbing the bottle
between your palms before adding
to the recipe.

1. Preheat oven to 325°F. Butter eight 4-ounce ramekins or soufflé molds. Sprinkle about 1 teaspoon of sugar over the sides and bottom, tapping out any loose sugar.

2. In the bowl of an electric stand mixer fitted with the whisk attachment, beat whites with half of the sugar, the cream of tartar, and salt until they form soft peaks. Continue to beat whites, adding remaining sugar slowly, until they form stiff, glossy (not dry) peaks.

3. In a large bowl, using a fork, beat together yogurt, egg yolks, rosewater, and rose absolute.

4. Using a spatula, fold one third of the whites into the yogurt mixture, being careful not to overmix. Fold in remaining whites just until combined and carefully ladle the mixture into prepared soufflé molds, filling the molds completely.

5. Bake in preheated oven for 10 minutes or until set but still moist inside (the soufflés will jiggle when gently tapped).

Buttered Advieh Chicken Tagine

Makes 4 servings

2 tablespoons extra-virgin avocado
   oil or olive oil
2 tablespoons butter, divided
1 onion, cut into quarters
1 tablespoon Advieh Seasoning
   (page 313)
4 skinless, boneless chicken breasts
   (about 2 pounds)
2 cups diced squash or pumpkin
¼ cup chopped dried apricots
2 cups cooked or 1 can (19 ounces)
   chickpeas, rinsed and drained

1. In the bottom of a flameproof tagine or Dutch oven, heat oil and melt 1 tablespoon of the butter over medium heat. Sauté onion and advieh for 5 minutes. Add chicken, moving vegetables away from bottom so that flesh is in direct contact with bottom of tagine. Cook for 4 to 5 minutes or until chicken is browned on the one side.

2. Using tongs, turn chicken over. Add remaining butter and squash, stirring until butter is melted. Cover with tagine lid, reduce heat to low, and simmer for 25 minutes without lifting the lid.

3. Stir in apricots and chickpeas. Replace the lid and simmer for 10 to 15 minutes or until apricots are plump, chickpeas are heated through, and vegetables are tender. Chicken is cooked when a meat thermometer inserted into the center registers 165°F. Season to taste at the table.

Baked Cherries and Plums with Rose Cream

Makes 4 to 6 servings

4 black plums, pitted and sliced
1 cup sweet cherries, pitted
¼ cup Rose Syrup (page 314)
    or rosewater
2 eggs
½ cup milk
½ cup all-purpose flour
½ teaspoon sea salt
¼ cup sugar
⅓ cup chopped almonds
2 tablespoons butter, cut into
    small pieces
¾ cup Rose Cream (below)

1. Preheat oven to 425°F and butter a 9-inch baking dish.

2. Arrange plum slices in one layer in the bottom of the dish and sprinkle cherries evenly over, filling up any bare areas in the dish. Drizzle syrup evenly over fruit.

3. In a bowl, using a whisk, beat eggs until lemon yellow in color. Beat in milk, flour, and salt to make a smooth batter. Pour evenly over fruit. Sprinkle sugar and almonds evenly over batter and dot top evenly with butter.

4. Bake in preheated oven for 15 minutes or until batter is puffed and golden and fruit is bubbly. Spoon into serving bowls and drizzle with Rose Cream.

ROSE CREAM

Makes about ¾ cup

1 cup heavy whipping cream
    (36% butterfat)
2 tablespoons Rose Syrup
    (page 314) or rosewater
1 teaspoon powdered dried
    rose petals

In a saucepan, combine cream, syrup, and rose petals. Bring to a simmer over medium-high heat. Cook, stirring constantly, for 7 minutes or until thickened and reduced by about one quarter. Strain into a heatproof measuring cup and set aside to cool. Cream may be made 24 hours in advance, cooled, covered tightly, and refrigerated. Serve at room temperature or heat in a saucepan before serving.

Rosemary

Rosmarinus officinalis

There's rosemary, that's for remembrance.

—Ophelia in Shakespeare's *Hamlet*, Act 4, Scene v

Rosemary is a heat- and sun-loving herb, and its generic name, *Rosmarinus*, actually translates to "dew of the sea," making rosemary the archetypical Mediterranean herb. In fact, it is often referred to as the "Tuscan herb."

Mediterranean herbs are sun- and wind-loving, drought-tolerant, aromatic plants that add zip and flavor to sauces (especially tomato sauce), pizzas, roasted meats, and grilled fish, poultry, and vegetables. Parsley, rosemary, thyme, French tarragon, oregano, lavender, sage, bay, borage, and basil are Mediterranean herbs that are big on flavor and easy to grow and use. When they are allowed to struggle in a dry, alkaline, and rocky soil similar to their native region, their flavor is more intense and the quality of their medicinal essential oils is higher than in a fertilized, well-watered, loamy soil.

FLAVOR

Rosemary is aromatic, warm, and slightly resinous with a hint of camphor and notes of pine and nutmeg.

PARTS TO USE

The evergreen, needle-like leaves are widely used; also the flowers, when available.

CULINARY USES

Use rosemary sparingly, because it can overpower ingredients and its flavor does not dissipate with long, slow cooking. Rosemary brightens roasted potatoes and other vegetables. It complements lamb, chicken, and veal. Use thick, woody rosemary stems as kabob skewers, and strew rosemary over the coals for grilling fish or meats.

♥ HEALTH BENEFITS

Ancient Greeks used rosemary to strengthen memory function. Now science has shown that it is a powerful antioxidant and its *carnosic acid* can protect the brain from stroke and the neurodegeneration that comes from toxins and free radicals. Rosemary extract inactivates excess estrogen, making it an effective estrogen blocker, helping to prevent breast cancer. Its warming properties (see Glossary) help to lower blood sugar levels and soothe aching muscles, joints, and arthritis pain.

Rosemary is used topically as an irritant to treat rheumatism, and rosemary tea is taken to relieve dyspepsia, flatulence, and gastrointestinal pain.

CAUTION: Rosemary tea, tincture, and topical preparations are generally safe to take, but do not take medicinal amounts without the guidance of a health-care professional.

GROWING ROSEMARY

A tender perennial, rosemary is propagated from cuttings or by layering in light, well-drained soil. Hard-prune it in the spring to keep plants bushy. Rosemary is a tender perennial, so in northern areas, grow it in containers and overwinter in a cool space with eight hours of eastern or southern light.

VARIETIES

Rosemary plants fall into two categories, upright (shrubs) and prostrate (creeping). Depending on the cultivar—and there are many that fall into each of the

Rosemary "trees" grow in raised beds outside the orangery at Boscobel House in the Hudson River Valley, New York.

two categories—rosemary leaves vary in length and width as well as in their shade of green from dark green to yellow- and blue-green. The edible blooms, attractive to bees, are generally blue, but may be pure white, pink, lavender, light, or dark blue to deep purple in color.

Interesting rosemary cultivars include the following:

ARP *(R. officinalis* 'Arp') An upright, winter-hardy (to Zone 6 with protection) plant with light green, lemon-scented leaves.

CORSICAN BLUE *(R. o.* 'Corsican Blue') It is upright with narrow, glossy dark green leaves and bright blue flowers.

SHADY ACRES *(R. o.* 'Shady Acres') Theresa Mieseler from Shady Acres Herb Farm (Chaska, Minnesota) introduced this excellent cooking rosemary in 1999. It has deep blue flowers and bright green leaves, strong upright growth with deep blue flowers, and a heavy aroma.

SISSINGHURST BLUE *(R. o.* 'Sissinghurst Blue') An upright with large, deep blue flowers, it holds the Royal Horticultural Society's Award of Garden Merit.

Culinary Herbalist Tool: Mediterranean Herb Paste

If you grow aromatic Mediterranean herbs, you can substitute any of them (except lavender, which should be added in 1-tablespoon amounts) for the fresh thyme leaves. Fall is the time to make this versatile Mediterranean flavor-paste and freeze it for use as a poultry or meat rub, toss it with roasted vegetables, or use it as an all-round herb blend in sauces, stuffings, soups, and stews.

Makes ¾ cup

1 large bunch fresh sage
¼ cup fresh rosemary
10 cloves garlic
½ cup fresh thyme
2 tablespoons Dijon mustard
1 tablespoon sea salt
¼ cup extra-virgin olive oil
1 tablespoon French tarragon
  or white wine vinegar

NOTE: You can use a food processor to make this paste and the consistency will be smoother, with fewer pieces of the individual herbs.

1. Using a mezzaluna or French knife, finely chop sage and rosemary leaves.

2. In a mortar, using a pestle, pound garlic into a pulp. Add sage, rosemary, and thyme leaves. Pound and grind until well mixed into the garlic.

3. Add mustard and salt and grind to a paste, adding oil by the tablespoon until a thick paste is achieved. Add vinegar just before the last of the oil is added.

4. Transfer to a jar with tight-fitting lid and store in the refrigerator for up to 2 months or freeze in zip-top freezer bags in ¼ cup or ½ cup amounts for up to 6 months.

Mediterranean Summer Soup with Herbed Croutons

Makes 6 to 8 servings

2 tablespoons extra-virgin
   avocado oil or olive oil
1 onion, chopped
2 cloves garlic
3 sprigs fresh rosemary
6 cups chicken or vegetable broth
2 cups cooked, peeled fava beans
1 cup 1-inch cut fresh green or
   yellow beans
1 cup coarsely chopped carrots
1 cup coarsely chopped sorrel
   or spinach
1 tablespoon chopped fresh savory
⅓ cup Mediterranean Herb Paste
   (facing page) or Basil and
   Walnut Pesto (page 13)
3 to 6 slices French bread

1. Preheat oven to 350°F.

2. In a saucepan or Dutch oven, heat oil over medium-high heat. Sauté onion for 5 minutes or until soft and fragrant.

3. Meanwhile, finely chop garlic and rosemary together. Add to onions and cook, stirring constantly, for 1 minute. Add broth, fava beans, green beans, carrots, and sorrel. Bring to a boil, reduce heat to medium-low, and cook for 15 to 20 minutes or until vegetables are tender. Stir in savory.

4. **TO MAKE CROUTONS:** while vegetables are cooking, spread paste evenly over one side of the bread slices. Place on an ungreased baking sheet and bake in preheated oven for 8 to 10 minutes or until bread is browned around the edges. Serve soup with croutons (toast slices) on the side or floating in the soup.

Rosemary-Roasted Vegetable Spaghetti

Makes 4 to 6 servings

1 head garlic
3 carrots, thickly sliced crosswise
2 onions, quartered
2 parsnips, thickly sliced crosswise
1 small eggplant, trimmed and
    sliced crosswise ½ inch thick
3 tablespoons extra-virgin olive
    oil or avocado oil
2 cups Tomato Sauce
    (page 268) or store-bought
8 to 12 ounces dried spaghetti
½ cup grated Parmesan cheese,
    for garnish
4 to 6 fresh sprigs rosemary for
    garnish, optional

1. Preheat oven to 475°F. Line a rimmed baking sheet with parchment paper.

2. Rub the loose outer layers of skin away from the head of garlic, slice ¼ inch off the top, and place on the baking sheet, cut side up.

3. Arrange carrots, onions, parsnips, and eggplant around garlic on the sheet and drizzle with oil. Roast in preheated oven for 25 minutes. Remove garlic, test vegetables, and remove if tender-crisp when pierced with the tip of a knife or continue to roast until done.

4. Meanwhile, in a saucepan, heat tomato sauce over medium-high heat. Squeeze soft, roasted garlic out of the skin into the sauce. Mash garlic with a fork and stir to mix well. Add roasted carrots, parsnips, onions, and chopped rosemary. Reduce heat to low and simmer, stirring occasionally, for 5 to 10 minutes or until the vegetables are tender.

5. Bring a large pot of salted water to a boil. Add spaghetti and bring the water back to a boil. Stir, adjust the heat so that the water is gently boiling, and cook for 8 minutes. Taste one noodle to test the consistency so that the noodles are cooked through to the center, but still "al dente" or firm. Drain and transfer to a serving bowl.

6. Ladle the vegetables in tomato sauce over the noodles and garnish with Parmesan cheese and sprigs of rosemary if using.

A BASIC KITCHEN HERB PRIMER

Fresh herbs add flavor in various ways: fresh or pungent, sweet or savory, aromatic or mild, lemony or resinous. Their variety meets any culinary use. Cooking with herbs releases tantalizing aromas that start your digestive juices flowing even before you reach the table. Herbs and spices literally dance on the tongue, increasing saliva, the first step in digesting food.

When you eat or drink fresh herbs in everyday meals, their medicinal constituents pass into the digestive tract and through the blood into your cells and organs, helping to repair tissue and rid the body of toxins or helping in myriad other ways. Herbs can have a profound effect on your overall health if taken along with a balanced diet of fruit, vegetables, whole grains, legumes, nuts, and seeds; small amounts of organic chicken and fish; and even smaller amounts of dairy, pork, beef, and lamb.

Use them raw in uncooked dips, salads, soups, and sauces. Add most fresh herbs at the very end of cooking, even if the recipe does not call for them. Only woody, aromatic herbs such as bay, thyme, rosemary, and sage can withstand long cooking times.

Cooking with herbs and spices is a great way to explore recipes from other cultures and to add more variety to everyday meals. An organic kitchen garden provides the freshest herbs. It's easy and can be done in very small spaces, including in containers on balconies. Drying your own herbs for winter use is one of the best ways to preserve their flavor for cooking (see page 187).

A good rule of thumb is to use about ⅓ part dried for 1 part fresh herbs. So for 1 tablespoon of fresh herbs called for in a recipe, use 1 teaspoon of the same dried herb.

The following herbs would be useful in a kitchen garden:

BASIL Essential to basil pesto, basil is best with Mediterranean herbs, tomatoes, eggplant, and fresh mozzarella cheese.

BASIL

BAY It is a key ingredient in béchamel sauce and bouquets garnis. It works for long-simmering dishes and adds a nutmeg-like flavor to rice, beans, tomatoes, fish, and chicken.

CHERVIL This delicate herb adds subtle flavor to light dishes with egg or fish and works well in soups and vegetable dishes. It combines well with parsley, basil, and chives.

CHIVES As a key ingredient in fines herbes, chives are good with cream cheese, potatoes, avocados, egg dishes, fish (including smoked salmon), and seafood. Chives combine well with other Mediterranean herbs.

CORIANDER The fresh leaf cilantro is essential to salsas, chermoula, and guacamole. It complements chile peppers, avocado, tomatoes, ginger, lemongrass, and mint.

DILL Classic in pickles, the leaves and seeds are also used with fish and chicken, in soups, and with eggplant and tomatoes. The seeds complement apple compotes, pies, and cakes.

FENNEL BULB Fennel bulb goes well with eggplant, tomatoes, and peppers and is used raw in salads. The leaf is used with beans, beets, cabbage, cucumber, fish, poultry, and cream cheese and egg dishes. The seeds are found in many spice or herbal tea blends because they act as a digestive.

FRENCH TARRAGON Essential to béarnaise sauce and fines herbes blend, French tarragon also complements fish, poultry, and egg dishes, as well as cream and feta cheeses. It is the most popular herb for oils and vinegars and it is good with potatoes, artichokes, asparagus, tomatoes, and zucchini. French tarragon in small quantities combines well with other Mediterranean herbs.

GARLIC Important in aioli, pesto, and other dips and sauces, garlic is an all-round savory herb for many recipes and ingredients. Use it fresh and raw as often as possible for health benefits.

LOVAGE An all-round soup herb, lovage is good with apples, vegetables (except celery and celeriac), cream cheese, ham, legumes, rice, fish, and poultry.

MINT A classic with lamb, mint also helps digest other fatty foods such as fatty fish, chicken, veal, and pork. Use it with fruit, cheeses, in salads, sauces, condiments, smoothies, and other drinks. It combines well with orange and chocolate, or use it on its own in desserts.

OREGANO/MARJORAM Essential to Italian dishes, oregano goes with anchovies, artichokes, cauliflower, tomato dishes and sauces, onions, and pork. It combines well with other Mediterranean herbs such as thyme, basil, rosemary, and bay.

PARSLEY A tonic herb that is essential to tabbouleh, persillade, gremolata, and salsa verde, parsley works with almost all savory herb blends and recipes. It also combines well with other Mediterranean herbs such as thyme, rosemary, sage, oregano and rosemary.

ROSEMARY Essential to the traditional Herbes de Provence blend, rosemary is a classic herb to use with lamb. It is also good with apricots, root vegetables, fish, lentils, pork, and winter squash dishes and combines well with other Mediterranean herbs.

SAGE A key herb in a poultry blend, sage is used in stuffings, soups, and stews. It is good with apples, legumes, cream cheese, onions, and tomato dishes and combines well with other Mediterranean herbs.

SAVORY The classic seasoning for beans and legumes because it helps reduce gas, savory also complements cabbage, tomatoes, and potatoes. Use it with basil, garlic, lavender, marjoram, and mint.

THYME Essential to bouquets garnis, thyme can be added to casseroles, stews, and soups. A standard herb for root vegetables, cabbage, lamb, and mushrooms, thyme combines well with other Mediterranean herbs.

Saffron

Crocus sativus

In 1444 Jobst Findeker of Nuremberg, was found guilty of adulteration of saffron. He was sentenced to be burned at the stake with his impure product.

—John Humphries, *The Essential Saffron Companion*, 1996

Too bad for Jobst Findeker that in 1358, the centrally located market town of Nuremberg passed the *Safranschou* code to govern the quality of saffron. Among other forms of adulteration, dried calendula petals were added or the saffron was coated in honey before it was dried to increase the weight. Offenders faced hanging or burning—with their impure saffron serving to fuel the flames.

I guess it comes as no surprise that a portion of the saffron sold today is adulterated, sometimes with dried safflower petals (*Carthamus tinctorius*). The orange petals are shorter and thicker than saffron, but may be dyed red to imitate saffron threads. Other devious suppliers include the white, tasteless styles that grow at the base of the red stigma. The threads with their white styles attached are treated with red dye and the styles turn pale yellow.

Excellent quality saffron is ⅜ to ½ inch in length because the styles have been snipped off and discarded. Saffron comprising only the stigma is much more potent than that which has the dyed styles attached.

Finding a reliable source for pure and potent saffron may take a bit of research; start in specialty-food or spice stores where the staff is knowledgeable about both their product and its source. Look for saffron that is dark, almost burgundy red, with no yellow. The strands must be dry and brittle to the touch (not soft) and the aroma strongly perfumed, never musty. The International Organization for Standardization

(ISO) sets minimum standards for saffron based on its ability to color food (or litmus paper in the lab). The higher the coloring strength, the higher its ability to release aroma and flavor. Minimum Category 1 ISO standard is 190, but some premium suppliers of pure, potent saffron guarantee coloring strength at 230 and higher.

Autumn in the Maryland garden of Dr. James Duke, where saffron blooms.

If you are buying and using saffron for the first time, you will need to be patient in determining the amount that is right for your taste. A "pinch" (10 to 15 strands) of good quality saffron is usually all that is necessary for most dishes, but experimenting is the only way to really get to know how potent your batch of saffron is and how strong you like the flavor it imparts to food. Be conservative to start, because while a small amount can make food luminous, too much makes a dish cloyingly bitter with a lingering medicinal bite.

FLAVOR
Saffron has a lingering, strong perfume that is hay-like, musky, and bittersweet.

PARTS TO USE
The three long, thin, trumpet-shaped, dark red stigmas from the flower are the only parts used, although the petals could be used in the same way as other herb petals.

CULINARY USES
French bouillabaisse, Spanish paellas, Italian risottos, English saffron cakes, and Indian kulfi (saffron-spiked ice cream) all rely on the perfumed flavor of saffron. Use it in egg custards and soufflés, fish and chicken dishes, and with seafood and vegetables.

Note that you can't just add saffron threads to recipes. The method that I prefer is to soak the threads for at least an hour (or as long as overnight) in three tablespoons of warm cooking liquid (broth, milk, or water, for example) from the recipe. The longer the saffron infuses the liquid, the stronger the flavor will be. You can also grind the threads using a mortar and pestle and add the powder to wet or dry ingredients. If your saffron is not crackling dry, you should dry-roast the threads before grinding them because doing so makes them crisp and easy to pulverize.

In sauces, soups, and rice dishes where it is easy to add saffron at the end of cooking, the flavor will be more potent than in dishes in which it is added at the beginning or even the middle of cooking. The taste is very mellow when saffron is baked in products such as scones, cakes, or biscuits.

While you can buy powdered saffron—chefs like it because it can be added directly to ingredients in recipes without presoaking—I have always been skeptical of the quality and potency, preferring the strands that I can identify as pure. If you can find a source that you trust, you may enjoy using the more versatile powder. See Resources (page 397) for some Internet sources of saffron.

♥ HEALTH BENEFITS

Saffron has been traditionally used for toothaches, kidney infections, stomach pains, and spasms; and research suggests that it may act as a preventive for stomach cancer. In homeopathic treatment, it is used as an antidepressant.

GROWING SAFFRON

Saffron favors well-drained soil and warm temperatures from June right up to October when it is harvested. It takes 200 mature corms to produce one half an ounce, a yearly supply for a busy kitchen.

Herb or Flower Butter

Fats—oil, butter, aioli or mayonnaise, or egg yolks—intensify the aroma and flavor of herbs. A blend of two or three different fresh herbs is ideal for herb butters.

Here are some herbs or their flowers to combine in a green butter. All except rosemary, sage, and French tarragon may be used in half-cup amounts per 1 cup butter.

- Basil
- Calendula petals
- Chervil
- Cilantro
- Clove Pink petals
- Dill

- French Tarragon (use ¼ cup)
- Lemon Balm
- Lovage
- Oregano/Marjoram
- Parsley

- Rosemary (use ¼ cup)
- Sage (use ¼ cup)
- Savory
- Sweet Cicely (best in a blend of other herbs)
- Thyme

GREEN HERB BUTTER

Makes 1 cup

1 cup unsalted, room temperature butter or softened extra-virgin coconut oil

Scant ½ cup chopped mixed fresh herbs from the list above

¼ cup chopped fresh chives

In a bowl, mix butter and herbs together using a fork. Use immediately, or cover and refrigerate for up to 4 weeks.

SAFFRON BUTTER

Makes 1 cup

1 small pinch (15 strands) saffron threads

2 tablespoons freshly squeezed lemon juice

1 cup unsalted, room temperature butter or softened extra-virgin coconut oil

1. Using a mortar and pestle, grind saffron roughly. In a small bowl, combine saffron with lemon juice. Set aside to infuse for at least 1 hour or as long as overnight.

2. In a bowl, whisk butter using a fork. Add saffron and lemon juice and beat well to incorporate. Use immediately, or cover and refrigerate for up to 4 weeks.

Ayurvedic Ghee (*Ghrita*)

Ghee is the name given to clarified butter. It originated in India as a method of preserving butter without refrigeration. Because the milky whey solids are skimmed away, clarified butter keeps without turning rancid, and the amount of milk protein is negligent.

In the Hindu tradition of India, the 5,000-year-old Ayurveda system of natural healing relies on body types and corresponding herbs, spices, and foods as pathways to healing. Ayurveda ghee, or ghee that is infused with medicinal herbs and/or spices, is called *Ghrita*, and it is an excellent way to deliver Ayurvedic herbs and spices to tissues because ghee actually facilitates the absorption of nutrients. It is also rich in antioxidants, and its short-chain fatty acids are beneficial to the body through antiviral activity.

Turmeric, neem (*Azadirachta indica*), cumin, coriander, holy basil, and licorice are some herbs that may be used alone or in combination in ghee.

Makes about 1½ cups

1 pound unsalted butter, cut into cubes

1 teaspoon finely cut or powdered dried herbs (see headnote or list in Green Herb Butter) or 1 teaspoon Curry Spice blend (page 104)

1. In a heavy-bottomed saucepan, melt butter over medium heat. Reduce heat to low and heat for 20 to 25 minutes or until lightly caramelized milk solids are visible on the bottom of the pan. The milk solids may be brown in color, but do not let them burn and turn black.

2. Set a fine-mesh strainer over a larger bowl and line it with two layers of cheesecloth. Pour the melted, caramelized butter through the strainer to remove the milk solids. Discard milk solids or use them in other recipes. Stir the herb or spice blend into the clear, bright yellow ghee and transfer to a covered glass jar. Stored in the refrigerator, ghee keeps indefinitely.

Chicken Paella

Makes 8 to 10 servings

6 cups chicken broth, divided
1 large pinch (30 strands) saffron
½ cup extra-virgin olive oil or
    coconut oil
2 onions, chopped
4 cloves garlic, finely chopped
2 slices pancetta, chopped
2 tomatoes, peeled, seeded,
    and chopped
3 cups Spanish bomba paella
    rice or basmati rice
1 teaspoon smoked Spanish
    paprika
8 skinless, boneless chicken thighs
8 ounces cooked chorizo sausage,
    sliced
1 cup shelled and peeled fava beans
¼ cup finely chopped fresh
    parsley

1. In a saucepan, gently heat ¼ cup of the broth over medium heat. Remove from the heat and add saffron. Set aside for at least 1 hour or as long as overnight.

2. Preheat oven to 400°F.

3. In a paella pan or ovenproof 18-inch pan, heat oil over medium heat. Add onions and sauté for 7 minutes or until soft. Add garlic and pancetta and cook, stirring frequently, for 3 minutes. Add tomatoes, rice, and paprika and cook, stirring constantly, for 3 minutes or until the rice turns opaque and resembles glass.

4. Add remaining broth and saffron-infused broth, increase heat to high, and bring to a boil. Add chicken and stir. Cover, reduce heat to medium-low, and simmer for 15 minutes.

5. Stir in sausage and fava beans and bake in preheated oven, uncovered, for 20 minutes or until the rice is al dente and chicken is cooked (a thermometer inserted into the center reads 165°F).

Honeyed Mango Saffron Ice Pops

Makes 6 large ice pops

2½ cups milk, divided

1 small pinch (15 to 20 strands)
saffron threads

3 or 4 fresh mangoes

½ cup honey

½ cup sweetened condensed milk

¼ cup skim milk powder

1. In a large saucepan over medium-high heat, warm ½ cup of the milk until bubbles form around the outside of the pan. Add saffron, stir, and set aside for at least 30 minutes, or cover and cool, then refrigerate in the saucepan overnight. Bring to room temperature before continuing with the recipe.

2. Peel, pit, and chop 3 mangoes. The flesh should measure 1 to 1¼ cups, so use the remaining mango if necessary.

3. In a blender container, combine mango and honey. Process until blended and smooth. Add mango-honey pulp, the remaining milk, the condensed milk, and skim milk powder to the saffron-infused milk in the saucepan.

4. Bring to a simmer over medium-high heat. Reduce heat and simmer, stirring constantly, for 10 minutes or until the mixture thickens. Set aside to cool completely.

5. Pour into ice pop molds, cover, and freeze for about 1 hour, or until the mixture is half frozen. Add popsicle sticks if desired and freeze for about another hour. The ice pops should be firm but not frozen into a solid block. If frozen too hard, set aside in the refrigerator or at room temperature to soften slightly before removing from molds to serve.

Sage

Salvia officinalis

Amongst my herbs, sage holds the place of honour;
of good scent it is and full of virtue for many ills.

—German monk Walafrid Strabo in *Hortulus* (*The Little Garden*)

Perhaps the unknown author of one of the best-known poems in the history of medicine and literature, *Regimen Sanitatis Salernitanum*, which was penned in the twelfth or thirteenth century, had read Strabo's *Hortulus*. One wonders only because one line from the *Regimen: Cur moriatur homo cui salvia crescit in horto?* ("Why should a man die who has sage growing in his garden?"), is a popular and often-quoted phrase.

But then, it is also entirely possible that Strabo was privy to the writings of Dioscorides, author of *De Materia Medica*, and Greek physician Galen, who explain that early Roman physicians used sage as a prescription for long life. In fact, it was the Roman word *salvere*, meaning "to be in good health," from which the Latin genus name *Salvia* is derived.

Too bad the venerable German monk Strabo (809–849 CE) only lived to see his fortieth birthday. And we pause to wonder if he perchance had taken a nightly nip of medicinal sage wine or sipped a soothing cup of sage tea with dinner, might those drinks have stood him in better health? For as the *Regimen* expands, "against the power of death there is not medicine in our gardens. But sage calms the nerves, takes away hand tremors, and helps cure fever."

FLAVOR

Sage is pungent and spicy, sometimes astringent, with warm camphor tones. When dried, sage becomes stronger and slightly bitter in flavor. Variegated species tend to be milder in taste and aroma.

PARTS TO USE
Both the leaves and flowers are used.

CULINARY USES
Sage has been traditionally used with poultry, pork, goose, and duck, perhaps due to its ability to aid digestion of these fatty meats. Now widely used to flavor poultry stuffing, sage also combines well with thyme, oregano, and parsley for Mediterranean dishes as well as pasta and rice.

Clary Sage blooms in the Petersfield Physic Garden, located in the center of the town of Petersfield, England.

♥ HEALTH BENEFITS

For sore throat, Pliny the Elder (*ca.* 23–79 CE) prescribed a decoction of sage, rosemary, honeysuckle, plantain (the herb *Plantago*), and honey boiled in water or wine.

Like other herbs in the *Lamiaceae* family, sage has antioxidant and anti-inflammatory properties and is a memory enhancer. Fresh sage makes a bitter digestive stimulant for oily or fatty foods and is used to treat dyspepsia and gallbladder disorders. Its antiseptic qualities make it an ideal gargle or mouthwash. Sage tea soothes a sore throat, in part due to its antimicrobial action. If taken internally, it relieves excessive perspiration. Several published studies indicate that sage may have a beneficial effect on Alzheimer's disease. *CAUTION:* Avoid internal medicinal doses and pure essential oil or alcoholic extracts during pregnancy.

GROWING SAGE
A hardy perennial, sage likes good drainage and air circulation. Like all herbs, it requires full sun for 8 hours per day. Sage may be propagated from cuttings or seeds sown directly in the garden in late spring.

VARIETIES
Salvia is the largest genus of plants in the mint family (*Lamiaceae*), with just under 1,000 species. Some salvia plants are herbaceous perennials, as mentioned here, while

others are shrubs and annuals. The Latin name *Salvia* reflects its healing properties, *salvere* meaning "to be well or healthy." A very short list of some varieties follows.

BLACK AND BLUE SAGE (*S. guaranitica* 'Black and Blue') Large, licorice-scented leaves make it popular as an edible ornamental. The dark blue/black flowers are striking against the acid green leaves.

CLARY SAGE (*S. sclarea*) It displays large leaves and pink-tinged, ornamental flowers, which make it a focal point in the herb bed. A deep musky odor makes it less desirable in the kitchen.

FORSYTHIA SAGE (*S. madrensis*) Tall (up to 10 feet) and large-leaved, with long, bright yellow flowering stems, this sage is bird- and bee-friendly and offers a focal point in flower borders and beds.

FRUIT SAGE (*S. dorisiana*) This type has large, soft, highly aromatic leaves. Some varieties mimic pineapple (*Salvia elegans*). Use fruit sage leaves and flowers raw in sauces, fruit salads, and many desserts.

GOLDEN SAGE (*S. officinalis* 'Icterina') Stunning, variegated golden-tipped leaves are used medicinally and in cooking as you would *S. officinalis*.

SCARLET SAGE (*S. coccinea*) Often called Texas Sage or Blood Sage, its flowering spikes are bright red, making it a beautiful ornamental herb.

SILVER SAGE (*S. argentea*) Low-growing, with large, soft gray-green foliage and blooms of white clusters, it acts as a focus or foil in the flowerbed.

WHITE SAGE (*S. apiana*) Native to the southwestern United States, it is often used in ceremonial smudge sticks.

Poultry Stuffing

Sage is the main ingredient in commercial dried, ground poultry seasoning; however, fresh sage from the garden is the very best form to use in this recipe. Use stale but not rock-hard dried bread and either tear it into small pieces or cut it into 1-inch cubes. Bacon, chopped oysters, or ground sausage may be cooked with the onion in step 1 if you wish. Use this fragrant and aromatic mixture to stuff one turkey (8 to 10 pounds) or bake at 325°F in a lightly oiled covered casserole dish for 40 minutes or until steamy and browned around the edges.

Makes 4 cups

¼ cup butter or extra-virgin
   coconut oil
1 onion, chopped
3 stalks celery, chopped
1 cup sliced mushrooms
4 cups stale bread cubes
   (see headnote)
1 apple, shredded
¼ cup chopped fresh parsley
1 to 2 tablespoons chopped
   fresh sage
1 teaspoon fresh thyme
1 teaspoon sea salt
2 eggs, beaten
2 to 3 tablespoons chicken
   broth, or as needed

1. In a skillet, melt butter over medium-high heat. Sauté onion and celery for 5 minutes. Add mushrooms and cook, stirring frequently, for 5 minutes or until soft. Remove from the heat and let cool in the pan.

2. In a large bowl, combine bread, apple, parsley, sage, thyme, and salt. Add vegetables and any juices from the skillet. Drizzle eggs over and toss to mix well. Add enough broth to moisten the mixture so that it clumps together. Cover and refrigerate until ready to use, or freeze for up to 3 months. Thaw in the refrigerator.

Sage Fritters

This dish was served in Volterra, Italy, during my recent trip to Tuscany with other plant lovers. This is my interpretation of that incredible dish. Use the largest sage leaves available (leave the stems on), and wash and pat them dry. Serve the fritters immediately because they are best when hot and crispy.

Makes 24 fried leaves

1 cup all-purpose flour
1 teaspoon baking soda
1 teaspoon sea salt
2 eggs, separated
5 to 6 tablespoons extra-virgin
    olive oil, divided
½ cup beer
24 large sage leaves, stems intact
Coarse sea salt

1. Line a baking sheet with a clean tea towel or double thickness of paper towels.

2. In a bowl, combine flour, baking soda, and salt. In a separate bowl, using a fork, whisk egg yolks and 1 tablespoon of the oil together. Whisk egg mixture into flour. Keep whisking constantly and slowly add beer until the mixture is the consistency of thick pancake batter.

3. In a bowl, beat egg whites until they form soft peaks. Fold whites gently into the batter. Add about 1 teaspoon of cool water to the batter to keep it the consistency of thin pancake batter.

4. In a large skillet, heat 4 tablespoons of oil over medium-high heat. Test the oil by dropping a small amount of batter into it. When the batter starts to brown, turn the heat to medium.

5. Grasp sage leaves by the stem and dip, one at a time, into the batter, coating each side. Drop coated leaves into the hot oil and fry until golden brown on both sides, turning with tongs. Using a slotted spoon, remove to the towel-lined baking sheet and continue to cook more sage leaves until all are done. Add more oil to the skillet for frying as needed. Sprinkle lightly with coarse salt and serve immediately.

Baked Winter Vegetables with Sage

¼ cup melted extra-virgin
   coconut or olive oil
1 large yellow onion,
   quartered and sliced
3 cloves garlic, finely chopped
4 small carrots, cut into chunks
2 potatoes, quartered
1 parsnip, cut into chunks
¼ green cabbage, chopped
2 sprigs dried sage
2 cups vegetable or
   chicken broth

1. Preheat oven to 350°F.

2. In a large, ovenproof skillet, heat oil over medium high heat. Add onion, reduce heat to medium, and cook, stirring occasionally, for 7 minutes or until soft and translucent. Add garlic and cook, stirring frequently, for 2 minutes.

3. Add carrots, potatoes, parsnip, and cabbage and cook, stirring constantly, for 2 to 3 minutes to coat with the oil. Rub sage over and mix in well. Add broth, increase heat to high, and bring to a boil. Cover and bake in preheated oven for 30 minutes or until vegetables are tender.

Asiago, Apple, and Sage Tarte Tatin

Makes 1 tart, 4 to 6 servings

½ cup all-purpose flour
½ cup large-flake rolled oats
1 cup packed brown sugar, divided
1 cup grated Asiago cheese
6 tablespoons butter, softened
1 tablespoon ground dried sage or 2 tablespoons chopped fresh sage
½ package (14 ounces) puff pastry, thawed
4 tart apples, cored and sliced
Juice of ½ lemon

1. Preheat oven to 375°F.

2. In a bowl, combine flour, oats, ½ cup of the brown sugar, cheese, butter, and sage. Press, using the back of a spoon, into the bottom and 1 inch up the sides of an 8-inch tart pan or ovenproof skillet.

3. Roll out one square of puff pastry to about 9 inches square.

4. In a bowl, toss apples with lemon juice. Add remaining brown sugar and stir well to mix. Arrange apple slices evenly over the mixture in the tart pan.

5. Cover the dish with pastry, tucking in the edges all the way around. Bake in preheated oven for 25 to 30 minutes or until the pastry has puffed up and is evenly browned. Set aside on a cooling rack to rest for 10 minutes.

6. Position a serving plate over the tart dish and turn plate and dish upside down so that the apples and crumb crust are on top of the pastry on the plate.

Savory

Satureja species

On the plan of the [ninth-century] Bénédictine Monastery at St. Gall . . .
the eighteen narrow rectangular beds are labeled onion, leek, celery,
coriander, dill, poppy, radish, carrot, beet, garlic, shallot, parsley, chervil,
lettuce, savory, parsnip, cabbage, corncockle.

—Rosetta Clarkson, *Magic Gardens,* 1939

The fact that savory was allocated its own bed in the hermitage garden plan for the Benedictine compound of St. Gall in Switzerland speaks to its importance and extended use in both the apothecary and the kitchen.

A native of southern Europe and North Africa, savory prospers in the poor, well-drained soil and sunny areas around the Mediterranean. Romans added it to sauces and long-cooking stews, while the Egyptians fashioned love potions from it. Its dense growth along with its stiff, glossy, dark green leaves makes winter savory an excellent edging plant in the herb garden or for knots or parterres. Harvest or clip it regularly to keep its compact shape.

FLAVOR

Savory has a hot, peppery bite with notes of thyme or marjoram. Winter savory (*S. montana*) is more pungent than summer savory (*S. hortensis*).

PARTS TO USE

The leaves and flowers are used.

CULINARY USES

Known as "the bean herb," or *Bohnenkraut,* in Germany, savory has traditionally been teamed with legumes, lentils, and fresh bean dishes, not only for the peppery and aromatic flavor it imparts, but also because it is known to relieve bloating and gas.

Both winter and summer savory are used in long-simmering dishes, but because it is stronger and woodier, winter savory is more often used in lamb, beef, and poultry stews. Winter savory also tempers strong-tasting cabbage, onions, broccoli, Brussels sprouts, cauliflower, and root vegetables.

Summer savory complements fresh fava beans and legumes as well as whole grains such as wheat berries and barley.

Savory is planted in a container (foreground), in a tiny stone courtyard behind two buildings on High Street, Totnes, Devon, England.

❤ HEALTH BENEFITS

Summer savory is the species thought to have the strongest medicinal benefit, although winter savory is also used medicinally. Rub bruised fresh leaves on bee stings to alleviate the pain. Drink savory tea before meals as an appetite stimulant, or after eating as a digestive to ease indigestion and flatulence.

GROWING SAVORY

Summer savory is an annual, which is why many herb gardens only sport the perennial winter savory. Both winter and summer savory can be grown from their tiny seeds. It's best to start them in seed trays indoors and plant in full sun after the last frost in the spring. Creeping and winter savory may be propagated from softwood cuttings or by dividing established plants in the spring. Do not fertilize savory unless growing it in a container, and then very sparsely.

Bean and Vegetable Herb Blend

A truly Mediterranean herb blend, this pungent seasoning mixture is rich with the flavors from sunny hilltops in southern France and Spain, Greece, Italy, western Turkey, Lebanon, Israel, and North Africa. Mix it with extra-virgin olive oil or softened extra-virgin coconut oil to rub on fish, chicken, pork, game, and lamb. Add it to casseroles, especially dishes that feature legumes or lentils. Toss a tablespoon of it with root vegetables and drizzle with olive oil for roasted vegetables. It is an excellent herb blend for homemade salami or preserved meats.

All of the herbs in this blend are first dried: gather herbs in late summer or early fall and dry (see page 187), crush, and blend.

Makes ¾ cup

¼ cup summer or winter savory
2 tablespoons sage
2 tablespoons thyme
2 tablespoons oregano
1 tablespoon rosemary
2 bay leaves

In a bowl, combine savory, sage, thyme, oregano, rosemary, and bay. Toss well to mix. Spoon into dark-glass containers. Label and store in a cool, dark place.

Savory Vegetable Tarte Tatin

Makes 1 vegetable pie

¼ cup butter or extra-virgin
    coconut oil

3 cups chopped green cabbage

1 onion, chopped

1 clove garlic, finely chopped

1 tablespoon Bean and Vegetable
    Herb Blend (facing page) or
    chopped fresh savory

1 cup chopped broccoli or
    cauliflower

1 cup chopped carrot

2 cups cooked or 1 can
    (19 ounces) white beans,
    rinsed and drained

2 tablespoons balsamic vinegar

2 tablespoons brown or
    coconut sugar

1 cup drained plain yogurt
    or sour cream

½ package (14 ounces) puff
    pastry, thawed

1. Preheat oven to 375°F.

2. In the bottom of a flameproof tart dish or ovenproof skillet, heat butter over medium heat. Sauté cabbage and onion for 5 minutes. Add garlic and herb blend and cook, stirring, for 3 minutes or until vegetables are soft. Add broccoli and carrot and cook, stirring frequently, for 3 to 5 minutes or until slightly softened. Remove from heat and stir in beans, vinegar, sugar, and yogurt.

3. Roll out one square of puff pastry to about 9 inches square.

4. Cover the dish with pastry, tucking in the edges all the way around. Bake in preheated oven for 25 to 30 minutes or until pastry has puffed up and is evenly browned. Set aside on a cooling rack to rest for 10 minutes.

5. Serve by cutting wedges in the pastry and spooning pastry and vegetables into a shallow bowl or onto a plate.

Savory Grilled Fish

Grilling fish in the summer is easy, and savory—along with other fresh herbs—makes it flavorful. Here's how to do it.

On a large rectangle of foil, lay thin slices of potato (I'm using sweet potato in the photo) and onion. Drizzle with olive oil and top with sprigs of fresh savory, oregano, thyme, sage, or rosemary. Grind sea salt and pepper over vegetables. Lay fillet of salmon, trout (as in photo), or whitefish over the vegetables and seal the foil around the vegetables and fish. Grill on medium flame on the barbeque for 8 minutes. Flip the fish over and grill for 7 to 8 minutes or until flesh is opaque and flakes easily with a fork. Be careful to avoid steam when opening the foil.

Classic Mediterranean Cassoulet

Makes 6 servings

1 cup dried white or
   black beans
1 can (28 ounces) diced
   tomatoes and juices
6 strips side bacon, cut into
   1-inch pieces
4 cloves garlic, chopped
2 stalks celery, chopped
1 onion, coarsely chopped
2 tablespoons dark molasses
2 tablespoons Bean and
   Vegetable Herb Blend
   (page 344) or chopped
   fresh savory
½ cup full-bodied, dry red
   wine (such as Burgundy
   or Cabernet Sauvignon)
¼ cup chopped fresh savory
6 whole chicken legs, back
   attached
2 chorizo sausages, cut into
   1-inch pieces ¼ cup
   chopped fresh parsley

1. In a large saucepan, cover beans with at least 2 inches of cold water. Bring to a boil and gently boil for 2 minutes. Remove from the heat, cover, and set aside to soak for 1 hour. Drain, rinse, and return soaked beans to the pot. Cover with at least 2 inches of fresh cold water. Bring to a boil over high heat, cover, reduce heat, and simmer for 1 hour or until al dente. Drain and rinse well with fresh water.

2. In a stone or earthenware pot, combine beans, tomatoes and their juices, bacon, garlic, celery, onion, molasses, and herb blend.

3. Place the covered pot in a cold oven, turn temperature to 400°F, and set the timer for 1 hour. Stir in wine, and if the mixture is dry, add warm water to moisten the vegetables as they cook. Reduce the oven temperature to 350°F and cook for 2 hours, stirring and adding more water if necessary.

4. Stir in savory. Add chicken and sausages, pushing them well down into the vegetables and liquid and cook for 1 to 1½ hours or until chicken registers 165°F on a meat thermometer. Add more water if the mixture is dry.

5. Stir in parsley and serve with boiled or roasted potatoes or cooked rice.

Sea Buckthorn

Hippophae rhamnoides

I love growing nutritional gold.

—Marlenea Wynnyk, owner, Healing Arc. Inc.'s Golden Orchard
near Teeswater, Ontario, Canada

Sea buckthorn plants, with their striking orange orbs for berries, were known to the ancient Greeks, who relied on the nutrient-rich leaves as fodder for their racehorses. The leaves, which are approximately 20 percent protein, promote weight gain and healthy, shiny coats in the animals, giving rise to the Latin genus name, *Hippophae*, meaning "shiny horse."

Sea buckthorn essential oil was used to treat Chernobyl burn victims. Now it is often combined with natural oils such as coconut, shea butter, and jojoba oil to make skin-care products designed to treat a wide range of skin conditions through its ability to activate the body's self-regulating functions.

The berries and seeds are attractive to the modern health-care industry as a nutritional supplement. The fact that sea buckthorn may be grown on marginal land and in northern climates and that the berries are both antioxidant and very high in vitamin C makes it an important "new" local fruit for Canadians and people living in the northern United States. According to a study that appeared in the *Journal of Food Science*, sea buckthorn contains approximately 400 mg of vitamin C per 100 grams as compared to 53.2 mg vitamin C found in the same amount of oranges.

Because of its hardy nature, and the fact that it may be used to prevent soil erosion, and for land reclamation, sea buckthorn is of interest to those individuals who are exploring permaculture and other sustainable living options with the goal to reduce their carbon footprint.

FLAVOR

The tartly citrus flavor of sea buckthorn is fresh and astringent.

PARTS TO USE

The orange berries, leaves, and seeds are edible.

CULINARY USES

Fresh sea buckthorn berries are most often juiced and the vitamin-rich pulp is collected and added to baked goods. Fresh or frozen berries are also used in recipes as you would blueberries, for jams, jellies, and other preserves; savory or sweet sauces, salsas, dips, or dressings; and cookies, scones, muffins, cakes, and can be added fresh or dried to herbal tea blends. Soap and skin-care products are also made from the berries, the dried pulp, or the essential oil.

The winter orchard at Healing Arc orchard in southwestern Ontario, Canada, where sea buckthorn not only survives but also thrives in the extreme climate.

♥ HEALTH BENEFITS

Sea buckthorn berries are exceptionally high in vitamin C; in fact, they are often called the "citrus of the north" because about eight of the pea-size berries supply the daily allotment of the vitamin. They also contain many nutraceutical properties such as protein, fatty acids, and antioxidants, including vitamin A. They are anti-inflammatory and antibacterial, and they relieve pain and promote the regeneration of tissues. Both the flesh and the seeds are distilled for the brilliant orange essential oil.

GROWING SEA BUCKTHORN

Native to northwestern Europe, northern China, and central Asia, sea buckthorn is a hardy (to Zone 5) deciduous, dioecious (requiring the male plant to pollinate the female plants to produce fruit) shrub. It survives temperatures from 104°F to –40°F and is drought resistant, nitrogen fixing, and pest resistant. The plant will reach 17 feet in height if unpruned, and the berries appear on second-year growth.

Berry, Nut, and Grain Trail Mix

This delicious trail mix packs a healthy punch and is an energizing way to add healing power to between-meal snacks. In fact, a serving consists of just 1 or 2 tablespoons, so use in moderation. Besides eating it as a snack, you can add it to yogurt, fresh fruit salads, egg dishes, puddings, cooked vegetables, and grain dishes as an ingredient or as a topping. Add 2 or 3 tablespoons to muffin or cookie batter, and use it as a base for tarts and bars to boost fiber and antioxidant value.

Makes 8 cups

3 cups large-flake rolled oats
   or spelt flakes
½ cup amaranth or quinoa
1 cup shredded or flaked
   coconut (see note)
1 cup chopped almonds
½ cup sunflower seeds
¼ cup sesame seeds
½ cup extra-virgin coconut oil
⅓ cup coconut nectar or honey
2 teaspoons ground cinnamon
½ cup dried sea buckthorn
   berries
½ cup chopped dried cherries
½ cup dried goji berries or
   cranberries
½ cup dried blueberries,
   chokeberries, or elderberries

1. Preheat oven to 375°F and lightly oil 2 rimmed baking sheets.

2. On one prepared baking sheet, spread oats and amaranth. On the remaining pan, spread coconut, almonds, sunflower seeds, and sesame seeds. Stagger the sheets in the preheated oven and toast for 8 minutes. Remove nuts and seeds from oven and set aside to cool. Stir the grains and continue toasting for another 6 to 8 minutes or until lightly browned, checking frequently to prevent burning.

3. Meanwhile, in a small saucepan, heat coconut oil, nectar, and cinnamon over medium heat for 3 to 5 minutes or until simmering. Turn off the heat and let sit on the burner to keep the mixture warm.

4. Transfer toasted grains to a large bowl. Stir in toasted seeds and nuts. Drizzle with warm nectar mixture. Add sea buckthorn berries, cherries, goji berries, and blueberries and stir lightly to mix and coat evenly. Let cool.

(continued on following page)

5. Store the mix in an airtight container in the refrigerator for up to three months, or freeze for up to six months.

NOTE: This mix is not as sweet as some you might purchase. I prefer to use unsweetened coconut, but the sea buckthorn berries, cherries, goji berries, and blueberries tend to be rather astringent, so use your own judgment and use sweetened coconut if you prefer.

Sea Buckthorn Berry Sauce

Makes 3 cups

1 cup water
⅔ cup sugar
¼ cup freshly squeezed orange
   juice
1½ cups fresh or frozen sea
   buckthorn berries
1 cup fresh or frozen cranberries

NOTE: Just as we use tart cranberries to aid in the digestion of fatty meat such as turkey, duck, pork, and ham, so too can we use tart and astringent sea buckthorn berries either along with or instead of cranberries.

1. In a saucepan, combine water, sugar, and orange juice. Bring to a boil, stirring frequently, over medium heat.

2. Add sea buckthorn berries and cranberries and bring to a boil. Reduce heat and simmer, stirring frequently, for about 15 minutes or until the sauce has thickened. Let cool and store in an airtight container in the refrigerator for up to 2 weeks.

Sea Buckthorn Stuffing

2 tablespoons extra-virgin olive oil
1 onion, chopped
8 slices stale bread, torn into pieces
1 cup Sea Buckthorn Berry Sauce
   (above)
½ teaspoon sea salt

NOTE: Use to stuff chicken, butterflied pork chops, or pork loin.

1. In a saucepan, heat oil over medium-high heat. Sauté onion for 5 minutes or until soft. Set aside to cool.

2. In a bowl, combine bread pieces and sauce. Add onion and salt and mix well.

Sweet Cicely

Myrrhis odorata

Sweet cicely is an underrated herb, a natural sweetener with a fine flavor,
and its leaves remain green and edible from early spring to late autumn.

—Jill Norman, *Herbs & Spices*, 2002

've brushed away snow in my herb garden and found delicate, delicious, fern-like sweet cicely ready for the first green harvest in early spring. It adds a fresh note of licorice flavor to Easter puddings, egg dishes, or almond tarts. It provides us with the first leaves from the garden, which may be teamed with store-bought herbs such as mint or parsley for an early season pesto.

In her book *Old Time Herbs for Northern Gardens*, Minnie Watson Kamm tells us that there are four species of native anise-scented plants called *Osmorrhiza* (Watson Kamm's spelling, correct botanical spelling is *Osmorhiza*) in parts of the northeastern United

States. The leaves of *O. longistylis* are described as being fern-like, and the seeds as "long slender blackish fruits," both similar to *M. odorata*; however, it is the roots of *O. longistylis* that are prized for their sweet smell and taste.

As Jill Norman claims, sweet cicely is continuously green, but only if you keep cutting it back, especially before it flowers. Well pruned, sweet cicely will bush out and be prolific, right up to the first hard frost.

Dry whole sprays of sweet cicely by hanging them upside-down in a dark, hot, dry place. Strip the leaves into a glass container with a lid and store in a cool, dark cupboard until ready to use. Crush the leaves just before using in tea blends, desserts, or syrups.

FLAVOR

All parts of sweet cicely are sweetly anise, with celery and vanilla notes. The fresh or dried seeds are more noticeably vanilla flavored.

PARTS TO USE

All parts are edible but the leaves and seeds are most popular. In the past, the roots were grated raw into salads or cooked as you would carrots.

The herb gardens at Ballymaloe Cookery School in County Cork, Ireland, featuring sweet cicely, are a cook's dream.

CULINARY USES

Sweet cicely adds natural sweetness and pleasing vanilla-anise flavor to desserts (puddings, baked goods, fruit pies, and other fruit dishes), tea blends, salads, and vegetables. Use the fresh or dried seeds in cakes and cookies. Grind the black dried seeds as you would allspice.

Fresh green leaves are chopped and used to flavor cake and cookie batters, icings, fruit salads, pies, puddings, egg dishes, cheesecakes, and other cheese desserts. The mild anise flavor teams well with almonds for sweet and savory dishes. It is especially useful in tea blends, adding sweetness and balancing other herbal flavors—use fresh or dried leaves with mint, bergamot, and lemon balm and other tea herbs.

Use the milder fresh tips in green salads, smoothies, fish, and poultry dishes; in sweet and savory sauces; and with mild spring vegetables such as peas and potatoes.

 HEALTH BENEFITS

Sweet cicely supports the digestive system and is used in a tea with chopped ginger to aid digestion and relieve flatulence.

This fern-like herb is hardy and easy to grow from seed, and it self-seeds, but it needs several months of cold winter temperatures to germinate. Sweet cicely prefers rich, moist soil with some shade. Cut it back after flowering to encourage new green growth all summer.

SWEET HERBS

Today, sweet-tasting herbs are popular for their ability to enliven teas, desserts, spice blends and, in the case of stevia, to act as a substitute for sugar and chemical sweeteners.

CINNAMON (*Cinnamomum*) The bark from about a dozen different species of Cinnamon trees may be used in cooking, *C. cassia* being the most widely used in North America although *C. verum* (syn. *C. zeylanicum*) is sweeter and less bitter.

CORIANDER The dried seeds are warmly citrus and add a sweet, spicy flavor to both sweet and savory spice blends for a wide variety of dishes.

SWEET CICELY Use it dried to sweeten and add anise flavor to tea blends.

STEVIA (*Stevia rebaudiana*) Native to South America, it was used to treat heartburn and hypertension and is now grown as a low-calorie sugar substitute. It has a minimal impact on blood sugar levels and can be used by diabetics.

SWEET WOODRUFF (*Galium odoratum*) Fresh flowers and leaves add sweet vanilla-anise flavor to wine and liquor. When dried, the fragrance is intense and pleasant for use in potpourri or dream pillows.

Herbed Berry Purée

Herbed fruit purées are easy to make and easy to store, and they may be used for a variety of drinks and dessert dishes. When combined with sugar and frozen, they become sorbets to serve on their own or with baked sweets, and they especially complement chocolate cookies, mousses, cakes, and brownies. Use berry purée as the flavor base in baked goods by adding ½ cup with the fat or wet ingredients. Serve a dollop with Greek-style yogurt or vanilla ice cream. Herbed fruit purées are also combined with vinegar for a delicious base for drinks.

Makes 6 cups

½ cup sugar
¼ cup water
⅓ cup lightly packed fresh
    sweet cicely
¼ cup lightly packed fresh basil
6 cups fresh berries (see note)
⅓ cup freshly squeezed
    lemon juice

NOTE: A mixture of berries is best: use any combination of raspberries, blueberries, blackberries, elderberries, sea buckthorn berries, or strawberries.

1. In a saucepan, combine sugar and water and bring to a boil over medium-high heat. Stir to dissolve sugar and add sweet cicely and basil. Reduce heat to medium-low and simmer for 2 minutes. Remove from the heat and set aside to cool completely.

2. Using a fine-mesh strainer, strain herbed syrup into a blender container, discarding herbs. Add berries and lemon juice. Secure the lid and blend on high speed for 1 minute or until puréed. Using a fine-mesh strainer over a large bowl, strain the herbed berry purée, pressing down with a wooden spoon. Discard the seeds and ladle the purée into pint or quart freezer containers or glass jars.

3. Store in the refrigerator for up to 2 weeks or in the freezer for up to 4 months and thaw or partially thaw before using.

Herbed Berry Vinegar Refresher

Makes 1 drink

¼ cup thawed or partially thawed Herbed Berry Purée (page 357)
3 tablespoons white wine vinegar
Soda water to taste
1 sprig fresh sweet cicely, for garnish, optional

Fill a glass with chipped ice. Stir in the berry purée and vinegar. Stir in soda water and garnish with sweet cicely sprig if using.

Sweet Herbed Whitefish with Zucchini

Makes 4 servings

12 ounces whitefish fillets, cut into bite-size pieces
2 cloves garlic
2 tablespoons coarsely chopped fresh sweet cicely
2 tablespoons coarsely chopped fresh marjoram
6 tablespoons extra-virgin olive oil, divided
2 tablespoons freshly squeezed lemon juice
1 onion, chopped
2 small zucchini squash, diced
1 red pepper, diced
1 can (14 ounces) diced tomatoes with juices

1. Arrange fish pieces in a shallow nonmetallic dish.

2. In a blender, combine garlic, sweet cicely, marjoram, 4 tablespoons of the oil, and the lemon juice. Secure the lid and pulse for 30 seconds or until herbs are finely chopped but not blended into a paste. Pour over fish, cover, and set aside in the refrigerator for at least 20 minutes or overnight. Return to room temperature.

3. In a large skillet, heat remaining oil over medium-high heat. Sauté onion for 5 minutes. Add zucchini and red pepper and cook, stirring frequently, for 2 minutes. Vegetables should be only slightly cooked.

4. Add fish, herb marinade, and tomatoes with their juices and bring to a boil. Reduce heat, cover, and simmer for 15 minutes or until vegetables are crisp-tender and fish is cooked. Fish is cooked when it flakes easily and turns opaque. Serve over cooked noodles, pasta, or rice.

Sweet Cicely and Almond Tart

Makes 1 tart, 4 to 6 servings

1 cup blanched, sliced almonds,
    toasted
½ cup all-purpose flour
½ teaspoon salt
⅛ teaspoon baking powder
Pinch baking soda
1 cup sugar
⅓ cup chopped fresh
    sweet cicely
4 large eggs
½ cup butter, melted and cooled
¼ teaspoon pure almond extract
Confectioners' sugar for dusting
Sweet cicely fronds, optional
    for garnish

1. Preheat oven to 300°F. Grease an 8-inch round cake pan and line with parchment paper.

2. In the bowl of a food processor, pulse almonds once or twice. Add flour, salt, baking powder, and baking soda. Pulse four or five times or until almonds are finely ground. Transfer almond mixture to a bowl.

3. In the same food processor bowl, combine sugar and sweet cicely. Pulse once or twice to mix. With the motor running, add eggs, one at a time, through the opening in the lid. Add melted butter slowly with motor running. Add almond extract and pulse once or twice to mix. Add almond mixture and pulse four or five times to combine well.

4. Transfer the mixture to the prepared pan. Bake for 55 to 65 minutes or until the center of the tart is set and bounces back when gently pressed and a toothpick inserted in the center comes out clean. Let the tart cool to the touch in the pan on a wire cooling rack. When cool, invert onto the wire rack or a serving plate. Remove the pan and let the tart cool completely, at least an hour. Dust with confectioners' sugar and serve on sweet cicely fronds if desired.

Thyme

Thymus species

Thyme is the wallflower of the herb shelf, blending inconspicuously into
the flavors of soups, stews, sauces, marinades, and meat dishes without
attracting attention to itself. It is just as modest in the herb garden, with low
growth and inconspicuous blooms. In either place, it is a joy to encounter.

—Barbara Radcliffe Rogers, *Fresh Herbs*

I think Barbara Rogers was using old dried thyme that was sapped of its pleasantly spicy, slightly lemony taste with hints of pine and fresh greens. Because, if the culinary species of thyme are shy and retiring (and I would have to differ on that opinion), their wild and robust cousin, mother-of-thyme (*T. serpyllum*), is anything but timid. It boldly roams, infusing national drinks and inspiring poets. Indeed, this spunky little shrub moved Rudyard Kipling, beloved author of *The Jungle Book*, to nostalgically describe the English downs as being covered with "the wind-bit thyme that smells of dawn in Paradise."

Even on tippy-toes, *T. serpyllum* stands only a few inches high, waves its tiny perfect leaves, nods its profusion of purple flowers, and edges over open ground from Greece to Italy, sidles up the Himalayas and Atlas mountains, and creeps around the highlands of Ethiopia.

The feisty variety, *T. vulgaris*, tenaciously clings to rocky outcrops in its native Mediterranean environs from Italy to Portugal, where it offers sweet nectar for bees and fodder for goats and sheep. In particular, Italian Hyblaean and Greek Hymettian honeys are both renowned for their unique flavor that is perhaps peppery, often fruity, sometimes resinous and herbal, but always pleasantly assertive.

I think the Roman philosopher Pliny the Elder should have the last word on the taste of thyme. In his *Naturalis Historia*, he wrote, "the honei which commeth of Thyme, is held to bee the best and most profitable: in colour like gold, in taste right pleasant."

Featured at Blue Heron Herbery, Sauvie Island, Oregon, a tiny perfect thyme wooden garden structure adds height, showcases several varieties of thyme, and keeps them separate.

FLAVOR

Each variety of thyme has its own unique essence that ranges from citrus to spice and even to caraway, but most have an underlying warm and peppery medicinal hint or punch of resinous pine and camphor from the *thymol* essential oil.

PARTS TO USE

The leaves and flowers are used.

CULINARY USES

Thyme blends well with other Mediterranean herbs and is an important ingredient in a bouquet garni herb blend. Thyme is used in soups, stews, stir-fry dishes, and slow-cooking dishes and for flavoring creams and custards and egg dishes. The lemon and spice varieties blend well in tea herbs and are used in jellies. Thyme enlivens grilled vegetables, potatoes, cheese dishes, and red meats.

♥ HEALTH BENEFITS

Thymol and *carvacrol*, key constituents of thyme essential oil, have powerful antioxidant and antimicrobial properties and can reduce bacterial resistance to common drugs. They are an effective fungicide with strong antimutagenic qualities (protecting cells from being compromised). Long used for chest and respiratory problems, including coughs (whooping cough), bronchitis, chest congestion, catarrh, and upper respiratory inflammation, thyme is effective when combined with sage and oregano or hyssop in cough syrups and teas. *CAUTION:* While the fresh and dried forms of thyme are safe to eat and use in salve, tea, and tincture, any use of thyme essential oil may have toxic effects, so avoid it.

GROWING THYME

Thyme plants grow in a range of leaf colors, fragrances, flowers, and plant forms. The majority of thyme plants are propagated using cuttings. To divide creeping or low-growing thyme plants, cut the mat into large pieces and transplant them into the garden. The culinary French thyme, *T. vulgaris*, is one of the few cultivars that grows from seed. Thyme prefers light, sandy well-drained soil and full sun.

VARIETIES

Thyme is an essential culinary and medicinal herb and, with more than sixty different varieties available, it is also an aesthetic choice for the garden or landscape. Here are a few thyme cultivars (all leaves and flowers are edible) to consider planting.

CARAWAY

Prostrate Forms of Thyme

CARAWAY (*T. herba-barona*) Caraway thyme is a small shrub with lavender flowers that grows to one foot tall. It has a distinct and strong caraway smell and taste, similar to fennel.

COMOSUS

COMOSUS (*T. comosus*) Its big, showy pink flowers make *comosus* thyme a great ornamental in herb and flower gardens.

CREEPING WOOLLY (*T. praecox* sp. *arcticus* 'Lanuginosus') This variety of thyme forms compact mats of soft, green leaves covered with tiny white hairs (called *down*) and pink flowers.

CREEPING WOOLLY

MINOR CREEPING (*T. praecox* sp. *arcticus* 'Minor') A spectacular ground cover due to its low-growing, mat-like habit, beautiful gray-green leaves, and large, deep pink flowers, it is stunning in a rock garden or between stones.

MINOR CREEPING

RED CREEPING (*T. praecox* ssp. *arcticus* 'Coccineus') The leaves are dark green and glossy and the light pink flowers form a solid mass when in bloom.

RED CREEPING

Upright Forms of Thyme

FRENCH (*T. vulgaris*) A very good culinary variety, it has narrow, gray-green, and distinctly sweet leaves. Richters (see herb suppliers, Canada, in Resources, page 395) mentions that it needs some winter protection.

FRENCH

GOLDEN LEMON (*T. ×citriodorus* 'Aureus') Most of its leaves are outlined in yellow, making the overall effect of the plant appear as yellow-green. The taste is only slightly citrus.

GOLDEN LEMON

SILVER (*T.* 'Argenteus') This plant has a variegated leaf that gives a silver tinge to it, and the lilac-colored flowers are lemon scented.

SILVER

Herbalist Tool: Za'atar

From the Arabic, the name *Za'atar* (also *Zatar* and other spelling variations) is sometimes given to one herb, Conehead thyme (*T. capitatus*). Yet there is much confusion surrounding which actual herb is meant, and according to an article by Rexford Talbert that appeared in *The Herbarist*, there is no *Thymus* species to represent za'atar in the Arab culinary and medicinal world. So, according to Talbert, the herb known as za'atar is either savory (*Satureja*), Mediterranean thyme (*Thymbra*), or an oregano (*Origanum syriacum* var. *sinaicum*).

To confuse matters even further, the word *za'atar* also refers to a blend of Middle Eastern herbs, a paste-like condiment, and a hummus-style dip or spread made with thyme and other Mediterranean herbs.

T. capitatus or Conehead thyme.

ZA'ATAR HERB BLEND

If you wish to make this blend using fresh herbs, store it in the refrigerator and use within a couple of weeks. It makes a good rub for lamb, pork, or beef and adds an exotic essence to kebabs or vegetables for the grill. Use dried herbs to make this blend.

Makes 1¾ cups

½ cup thyme
½ cup oregano
¼ cup savory
¼ cup sesame seeds
2 tablespoons crushed cumin seeds
1 tablespoon dried sumac
1 tablespoon sea salt

1. In a bowl, combine thyme, oregano, savory, sesame seeds, cumin seeds, sumac, and salt. Toss to blend well.

2. Transfer to a dark-glass jar, label, and store in a cool dark cupboard for up to 3 months.

ZA'ATAR SPICY PASTE

Add one tablespoon at a time to sauce, soup, or stew recipes. Spread over chicken or fish before cooking; use in vinaigrette or other dressings or dips; spread on bread or pita rounds and bake in a hot oven for herbed crostini.

Makes ½ cup

½ cup Za'atar Herb Blend
    (facing page)
3 to 4 tablespoons extra-virgin
    olive oil

1. In a mortar, using a pestle, pound/grind za'atar blend until the herbs are coarsely ground. Drizzle oil over and grind until a moist paste forms.

2. Cover tightly and refrigerate for up to 1 week.

ZA'ATAR SPREAD

You can make using a food processor by using the pulse button and stopping frequently to check that it is not overmixed. Serve with pita points, toasted bagels, and crackers or as a condiment for steamed or grilled vegetables.

Makes 2 cups

½ cup Za'atar Herb Blend
    (facing page)
2 cups cooked or 1 can
    (19 ounces) chickpeas,
    rinsed and drained
½ teaspoon ground cinnamon
2 to 3 tablespoons extra-virgin
    olive oil
1 tablespoon toasted sesame oil
1 tablespoon honey
Sea salt to taste

1. In a mortar, using a pestle, or using a blender, pound or process za'atar blend until the herbs are coarsely ground.

2. Add chickpeas and pound/pulse until smooth. Sprinkle with cinnamon and drizzle with 2 tablespoons of olive oil and the sesame oil. Mix oils into chickpea mixture and add more olive oil if required to make a smooth paste. Drizzle honey over, add sea salt to taste, and mix well.

Thyme and Pear Cake

Makes one 10-inch cake

Crumb Topping

1 cup large-flake oats

2 tablespoons all-purpose flour

¼ cup brown sugar

1 tablespoon fresh thyme

½ teaspoon sea salt

5 tablespoons softened extra-virgin
   coconut oil or unsalted butter

Cake

1½ cups all-purpose flour

½ cup whole wheat flour

1 teaspoon baking powder

1 teaspoon baking soda

1 teaspoon sea salt

½ cup softened extra-virgin
   coconut oil or unsalted butter

1 cup granulated sugar

2 large eggs

2 tablespoons finely grated
   lemon zest

1 teaspoon pure vanilla extract

1 cup buttermilk

2 pears, cored and coarsely
   chopped (about 2 cups)

1 tablespoon fresh thyme

1. **TO MAKE THE TOPPING:** In a bowl, combine oats, flour, sugar, thyme, and salt. Using a pastry cutter or your fingertips, cut or rub in coconut oil until it resembles pea-size lumps. The mixture will be moist with well-distributed clumps. Cover and chill for at least 1 hour or up to several days.

2. **TO MAKE THE CAKE:** Preheat oven to 325°F. Lightly grease a 10-inch springform pan.

3. In a bowl, combine all-purpose flour, whole wheat flour, baking powder, baking soda, and sea salt.

4. In the large bowl of a stand mixer, beat coconut oil until creamy. Slowly add granulated sugar and beat for 2 to 3 minutes or until well incorporated. Add eggs one at a time, beating well after each addition. Stir lemon zest and vanilla into buttermilk and gradually beat into sugar mixture.

5. Slowly and steadily add dry ingredients, beating only until combined.

6. Toss pears and thyme together and fold into the cake batter. Scrape the batter into the prepared springform pan. Spread topping evenly over the top of the cake.

7. Bake in preheated oven for about 45 minutes or until a tester comes out clean when inserted into the center of the cake. Set aside to cool in the pan for at least 20 minutes and transfer to a wire rack to cool completely. May be made one day ahead. Store in an airtight container at room temperature.

Tuscan White Bean Salad

Makes 4 servings

⅓ cup extra-virgin olive oil
1 onion, chopped
2 cloves garlic, finely chopped
1 tablespoon fresh thyme
2 cups coarsely chopped kale
3 tablespoons balsamic vinegar
½ cup chopped sun-dried
   tomatoes
½ cup ½-inch cubes feta cheese
½ cup pitted black olives
2 cups cooked or 1 can (19 ounces)
   white beans, rinsed and drained

1. In a large skillet, heat oil over medium-high heat. Add onion and sauté for 5 minutes. Add garlic and thyme and cook, stirring, for 3 to 5 minutes or until the onion is soft and the garlic is fragrant. Add kale, cover, reduce heat to low, and cook for 2 minutes or until wilted.

2. Turn heat off and stir in vinegar and tomatoes. Toss well and transfer to a salad bowl. Add cheese, olives, and white beans. Toss well to combine.

Mediterranean Chicken Pot

Makes 4 to 6 servings

2 cups medium pasta shells
5 slices bacon, cut into
    ½-inch pieces
½ cup red lentils
1 large onion, chopped
1 zucchini squash, chopped
2 cloves garlic, finely chopped
½ pound skinless, boneless
    chicken thighs
6 cremini mushrooms, sliced
3 tablespoons fresh thyme
1 can (14 ounces) diced
    tomatoes and juices

1. Preheat oven to 350° F. In a saucepan, bring 4 cups of salted water to a boil. Stir in pasta shells and boil for 7 to 10 minutes or until al dente.

2. Meanwhile, in a 9 × 13-inch stovetop and ovenproof casserole dish, cook bacon over medium-low heat for 7 minutes.

3. Using a slotted spoon, lift shells out of water into a colander and rinse under cold water. Set aside to drain. Drain all but about 2 cups of the pasta water, return to the burner, and bring back to a boil. Add lentils, reduce heat, and simmer for 15 minutes or until tender but not soft. Drain and rinse under cold water.

4. Drain all but 2 tablespoons of bacon fat from the casserole dish. Add onion and zucchini to the bacon and cook, stirring occasionally, for 15 minutes. Add garlic and cook for 2 minutes, stirring occasionally. Arrange chicken thighs in the bottom of the dish and brown each side for 2 minutes. Add mushrooms, thyme, tomatoes and their juices, pasta shells, and lentils to the dish and stir to combine. Cover with a lid and bake in the preheated oven for 25 minutes or until chicken is cooked. Chicken is done when it registers 165°F on a meat thermometer.

Turmeric

Curcuma longa

Because of its brilliant golden color, it has been most closely
identified with saffron throughout the centuries and, in medieval times,
turmeric was called "Indian saffron," or *Crocus indicus.*

—Avanelle Day and Lillie Stuckey, *The Spice Cookbook*, 1964

Quite apart from its culinary uses, turmeric has served as a dye for fabric and skin, a medicine, a cosmetic, and an amulet. In India and Egypt, among other places, where saffron was cherished and lavishly used by religious leaders and the wealthy, the less-fortunate made do with turmeric—sometimes called the "poor man's saffron"—which had the result of keeping them healthier than if they used saffron, which has few known significant health benefits.

Fresh turmeric root is smaller in diameter and not as fat and fleshy as ginger. Look for fresh turmeric when in season (spring, sometimes fall) at large, well-stocked grocery stores, some whole/health food stores, and Indian and Asian grocery stores. Choose firm rhizomes with a light-brown skin and bright orange flesh.

FLAVOR

Freshly grated turmeric root is pungent and charged with a peppery, gingery-citrus, and slightly acrid taste. Dried, powdered turmeric is warm and musky but slightly more bitter in taste than fresh. The large, fresh, and tender young leaves have a subtle, citrusy-tart flavor.

PARTS TO USE

The roots and leaves are used.

CULINARY USES

Although they may be hard to find (look for them in Asian markets), the fresh, fleshy turmeric roots are superior to dried, powdered turmeric. Grate them into curry blends and pastes, sauces, and dips. Both fresh and dried turmeric lend a bright yellow color to rice, scrambled eggs, or frittatas. Dried, grated, or powdered turmeric is used in pickle seasoning, relish, mustard, and sauces or with vegetable or meat curries. Add it to juice or smoothies and to prepared mayonnaise, relishes, or other condiments to boost their healthful quality.

Fresh turmeric on sale at the Organic Farmers' Market in Forsythe Park in Savannah, Georgia.

Use the young, tender leaves to wrap fish, vegetable, or rice mixtures for steaming or grilling. To use fresh leaves, remove from the stalk and soak in cool water for an hour or as long as overnight. Use the soaking water as you would vegetable stock.

♥ HEALTH BENEFITS

A powerful healer, turmeric root is antioxidant, anti-inflammatory, antimicrobial, antimutagen, antibacterial, antifungal, antiviral, and anticoagulant. These properties help in prohibiting colon and breast cancers and treating other conditions. Herbalists use turmeric to treat hepatitis, nausea, and digestive problems, and to help when the gallbladder has been removed. Holistic medical usage appears to reduce the risk of stroke, rheumatoid arthritis, *candida*, AIDS, Crohn's disease, and eczema.

GROWING TURMERIC

Native to Southeast Asia and a member of the ginger family, turmeric is a tender perennial, hardy in Zone 8 and higher. Like ginger, it may be grown from fresh root. It does well in large containers in moist soil and with full sun exposure.

🌿 HERBS FOR CURRY BLENDS

Traditional South Asian–style dishes (those of India, Pakistan, Bangladesh, Sri Lanka, Nepal, Bhutan, and the Maldives) feature ground spice blends known as *masalas*, and roasted, brightly colored curry spice blends. In almost all of these fragrant seasonings, turmeric is a key herb, lending its own unique flavor and color. Combinations and recipes vary from region to region even within the same country, with some recipes being handed down orally from generation to generation within families.

Try prepared curry blends (or make your own) from a range of countries: French vadouvan curry is a mild blend of savory flavors; mildly hot African curry has citrus tones; Asian curry is sweetly complex, while Indian vindaloo curry is hot and peppery.

The following chart describes the flavors of some curry herbs and indicates what kinds of curry they're typically used for to get you started on developing your own curry blends. Use the chart as a suggestion only and choose 4 to 6 herbs from all those indicated for a blend. For example, I might use allspice, cardamom, coriander, ginger, Thai basil, and turmeric to make Thai curry.

Use 1 tablespoon of each dried, whole spice and 1/2 to 1 cup of chopped fresh green herb to give equal importance to all flavors. Increase or decrease the amount of one herb to emphasize or only give a hint of its flavor. The best way to know what you like is to experiment and cook with the blend, but be sure to write down your combinations so that you can duplicate a blend that you love.

HERB	FLAVOR SPIKE	VADOUVAN mild-savory	THAI sweet-spice	MASALA complex spice	MADRAS hot
Ajowan (*Rachyspermum ammi*)	Hot, bitter, thyme	x			x
Allspice (*Pimenta dioica*)	Pleasant spice (cloves, cinnamon, nutmeg)	x	x	x	x
Cardamom (*Elettaria cardamomum*)	Flowery camphor, pine	x	x		x
Cayenne	Hot				x
Cinnamon (*Cinnamomum*)	Sweet, warm-spice			x	x
Cilantro, fresh	Sage-mint-lemon		x		
Cloves (*Syzygium aromaticum*)	Sharp, fruity, camphor	x		x	
Coriander seeds	Sweet, warm, orange	x	x	x	
Cumin (*Cuminum cyminum*)	Sharp, earthy, pungent	x		x	x
Fennel seeds	Sweetly anise	x		x	

HERB	FLAVOR SPIKE	VADOUVAN *mild-savory*	THAI *sweet-spice*	MASALA *complex spice*	MADRAS *hot*
Fenugreek (*Trigonella foenum-graecum*)	Strongly curry	x	x	x	x
Galangal (*Alpinia*)	Sour-citrus		x		
Ginger	hot, citrus	x	x	x	x
Grains of Paradise (*Aframomum melegueta*)	Fruity-hot	x			x
Mustard	Acrid, hot, earthy			x	x
Peppercorns (*Piper nigrum*)	Pungent, hot: white is strongest; green is weakest; black is usually used in curry			x	x
Star anise (*Illicium verum*)	Sweetly anise		x	x	
Thai basil, fresh	Nutmeg, citrus		x		
Turmeric	Warm, citrus-ginger	x		x	x

Curry Paste

Spice pastes are easy to make and store. Once you have them prepared, you'll find yourself reaching for them often because they add a complex taste to recipes, blending in easily and with no extra effort. I use fresh turmeric in all my curry paste recipes not only because of its taste and color, but also because of its health benefits.

The one issue with using fresh turmeric is that it stains my porous, lily-white mortar and pestle, my blender container and blade, and any other preparation surface. I have found that by rubbing my equipment with half a fresh lemon after making curry paste, the color disappears.

Try to use fresh pastes within two to three weeks of making them or consider freezing them in 1-tablespoon amounts. You can add frozen paste to dishes in the same way you would fresh paste: directly into sauces, soups, stews, tagine dishes, and other simmering recipes, or add to the oil before sautéing onions.

RED CURRY PASTE

Makes 1 cup

10 fresh red cayenne peppers

3 cloves garlic

1 piece (2 inches) fresh turmeric, grated

1 piece (1 inch) fresh ginger, grated

¼ cup chopped roasted red pepper

1 teaspoon shrimp paste or 2 anchovies, optional

4 stalks lemongrass, inner white parts, minced

6 sprigs fresh cilantro or flat-leaf parsley

1 tablespoon minced Makrut lime leaves or 1 teaspoon grated lime zest

1 teaspoon cracked black peppercorns (preferably Malabar)

1 teaspoon ground coriander

1 teaspoon ground cumin

½ teaspoon sea salt

1 to 3 teaspoons toasted sesame oil

1. In the bowl of a food processor, combine cayenne peppers, garlic, turmeric, and ginger. Process until finely chopped. Add roasted red pepper and shrimp paste if using. Process until peppers are finely chopped. Add lemongrass, cilantro, lime leaves, peppercorns, coriander, cumin, and salt. Process for 20 seconds. With the motor running, add sesame oil through the opening in the lid. Process until a smooth paste is achieved.

2. Spoon paste into a sterilized jar and cap with the lid. Store in the refrigerator for 2 to 3 weeks.

GREEN CURRY PASTE

Makes 1 cup

3 cloves garlic

1 to 3 fresh, hot green chiles,
  trimmed and seeded

1 piece (2 inches) fresh
  turmeric, grated

1 piece (1 inch) fresh ginger,
  grated

1 teaspoon shrimp paste or
  2 anchovies, optional

4 stalks lemongrass, inner
  white parts, minced

½ cup chopped fresh cilantro
  or flat-leaf parsley

½ cup chopped fresh Thai or
  regular basil

1 teaspoon ground coriander

1 teaspoon ground cumin

½ teaspoon sea salt

3 to 4 tablespoons coconut milk

1. In the bowl of a food processor combine garlic, chilies, turmeric, and ginger. Process until finely chopped. Add shrimp paste if using, lemongrass, cilantro, basil, coriander, cumin, and salt. Process for 20 seconds, and, with the motor running, add coconut milk through the opening in the lid. Process until a smooth paste is achieved.

2. Spoon into a sterilized jar and cap with the lid. Store in the refrigerator for 2 to 3 weeks.

Spicy Chilled Cantaloupe Soup

Makes 4 servings

1 ripe cantaloupe, peeled,
  seeded, and cut into chunks

½ cup freshly squeezed orange juice

⅓ cup freshly squeezed lime juice

1 to 2 tablespoons Red Curry Paste
  (page 375) or Green Curry Paste
  (above)

4 sprigs cilantro or flat-leaf
  parsley for garnish, optional

1. In a regular or high-performance blender container, combine cantaloupe, orange juice, lime juice, and curry paste. Blend on high until smooth. Chill overnight in the refrigerator or place in the freezer, stirring occasionally, for 20 minutes or until cold.

2. Pour into soup bowls and garnish with a sprig of cilantro if using.

Turmeric Curry Shrimp

Makes 4 to 6 servings

Curry Spice Blend

2 teaspoons fenugreek seeds
1 teaspoon cumin seeds
1 teaspoon coriander seeds
1 tablespoon crushed cinnamon
    stick
1 tablespoon ground turmeric

Curry Shrimp

2 tablespoons extra-virgin
    coconut oil or olive oil
1 onion, finely chopped
4 medium cloves garlic, minced
1 tablespoon finely grated fresh
    ginger
1 tablespoon Curry Spice Blend
1 teaspoon Red Curry Paste
    (page 375) or 1 dried cayenne
    pepper, crushed
½ teaspoon sea salt
1 can (14 ounces) coconut milk
¼ cup peanut butter
2 teaspoons grated lime zest
3 tablespoons freshly squeezed
    lime juice
1 tablespoon firmly packed
    brown sugar
1 red bell pepper, cut in
    ½-inch dice
1 cup sliced carrots
1 cup broccoli florets
¼ to 1 cup boiled water
20 large or jumbo shrimp, fresh
    or frozen (thawed)

1. **TO MAKE THE CURRY SPICE BLEND:** Heat a large heavy-bottomed skillet over medium-high heat. Add fenugreek, cumin, coriander, and cinnamon and dry-roast over medium-high heat, stirring constantly, for 2 minutes or until golden and lightly toasted (do not let the spices smoke). Remove to a small bowl and set aside to cool.

2. Using a mortar and pestle or electric grinder, grind the toasted spices. Transfer to a small bowl, add the turmeric, mix well, and set aside. You should have about ¼ cup of curry spice blend. When the tablespoon used for this recipe is removed, transfer unused curry spice blend to a small jar, label, and store in a dark place for up to 6 months.

3. **TO MAKE THE SHRIMP:** In the same skillet, heat oil over medium-high heat. Add onion, garlic, and ginger and cook, stirring frequently, for 5 minutes or until onions are soft and translucent. Stir in curry spice blend, red curry paste, and salt. Cook, stirring constantly, for 30 seconds. Add coconut milk and bring to a simmer, stirring constantly. Add peanut butter, lime zest, lime juice, and brown sugar. Bring back to a simmer, stirring constantly.

(continued on following page)

4. Add red pepper, carrots, and broccoli, reduce heat to medium-low, and simmer, stirring occasionally, for 15 minutes or until vegetables are crisp-tender. If the sauce appears to be too thick, stir in water, 2 tablespoons at a time, until it reaches the desired consistency.

5. Add shrimp and simmer gently, stirring frequently, for 4 to 6 minutes or just until shrimp have turned bright pink (do not continue to cook once the shrimp have turned pink or they will toughen). Serve over rice.

Roasted Moroccan Cauliflower with Walnuts

Makes 4 to 6 servings

1 head cauliflower, cut into
    1-inch florets
2 cups cooked or 1 can
    (19 ounces) chickpeas,
    rinsed and drained
3 tablespoons softened
    extra-virgin coconut oil or
    olive oil
1 tablespoon Red Curry Paste
    (page 375) or Green Curry
    Paste (page 376)
Freshly ground sea salt
    and pepper
¼ cup coarsely chopped
    walnuts

1. Preheat oven to 425°F. Line a rimmed baking sheet with parchment paper.

2. Toss together cauliflower, chickpeas, oil, and curry paste to coat well. Grind salt and pepper to taste over vegetables and spread out in one layer. Roast in preheated oven for 15 to 20 minutes or until cauliflower begins to brown

3. Stir and add walnuts and roast for 6 to 10 minutes or until nuts are toasted and cauliflower is crisp-tender.

APPENDIX

HERBS TO ATTRACT POLLINATORS

Many herbs, fruits, and vegetables (along with other plants) rely on insects—including roughly 4,000 native North American species of bees, honeybees, bumblebees, mason bees, solitary bees, wasps, butterflies, moths, flies, thrips, beetles, birds, and bats—to help them to fruit. Pollinators do this by moving the pollen from one flower to another, thereby fertilizing the flowers and enabling them to produce seeds and fruit. Without pollination, much of our food supply would be devastated. In fact, bees alone pollinate more than 70 percent of our food crops.

You can help these important pollinators by taking the following steps:

* Attract and feed them with organic nectar- and pollen-rich plants, including natives and herbs (a short list follows).

* Plant a diverse collection of native flowering plants in a range of bright colors that will bloom early, mid-season, and right up to frost. Pollinators have different tongue sizes, requiring different shapes of flowers.

* Provide shelter by letting part of your garden return to a natural, wild state and leave open areas for underground nests.

* Because birds are natural bee predators, don't place bird feeders and birdhouses near bee habitat areas.

* Never use pesticides. Pesticides are toxic to pollinators, birds, animals, and humans. They are not welcome in an herb, fruit, or vegetable garden.

* Avoid using garden or lawn-care products labeled as systemic or those that contain imidacloprid or neonicotinoids.

* Learn about mason and solitary bees and provide homemade nest boxes for them.

* If you have space, learn how to keep bees or allow a beekeeper to situate her or his bees on your property.

* Plant a wide range of flowering plants, because honeybees prefer flowers with more nectar, while mason bees tend to favor flowers with more pollen.

* The list of native plants and wildflowers that are attractive to pollinators is long—see Resources (page 396) for more reading.

Following are some flowering herbs (**indicates the cultivars that are native to North America) to plant in drifts in a garden for pollinators.

BERGAMOT The bright red, showy, and long-lasting flowers are very attractive to pollinators, especially hummingbirds.

BORAGE Often called "bee bread" because it is almost always in bloom with bright blue, star-shaped flowers that attract pollinators.

CHIVES Butterflies love the brilliant pink-purple flowers that last for up to three weeks in early summer.

CLOVER (*Trifolium*) and **THYME Both favorites of honeybees, clover and low-growing thyme make a good ground cover as a substitute for grass.

**JOE-PYE WEED (*Eupatorium maculatum*) An Eastern North American native, joe-pye weed blooms in midsummer with large pink flowers.

LAVENDER All colors of lavender are aromatic and attractive to pollinators, especially bees.

MARJORAM AND OREGANO Their sweetly scented, pink labiate flowers are magnets for bees.

**MILKWEED (*Asclepias syriaca*) An extremely important plant because it is the host plant for the monarch butterfly eggs. Monarch butterfly larvae will only eat milkweed.

**MINT Butterflies and hummingbirds love mint, with its fragrance and purple flowers.

**ROSE Fragrant and flashy, roses—especially shrub roses—are good for pollinators.

CAUTION

Many big box nurseries and hardware stores sell plants that have been pretreated with bee-killing pesticides. A 2014 study released by Friends of the Earth Canada and Friends of the Earth U.S. (see Resources, page 396) with the Pesticide Research

Institute reports that 51 percent of the total plant samples collected across eighteen cities in Canada and the United States contain bee-killing neonicotinoids.

TAKE ACTION: Always plant only organic herbs and pollinator-friendly plants, never use pesticides or other insect-killing chemicals on your soil or your plants, and consider signing petitions to ask large chain stores to stop selling plants that kill pollinators.

Buy from independent herb farms and nurseries that grow only organic plants.

HERBS TO ATTRACT BIRDS

We've always known that growing a wide variety of plants provides birds with food and shelter; but according to Matt Walker, editor of *BBC Earth News*, scientists have discovered that blue tits and a number of other bird species use medicinal plants to disinfect their nests. The birds display a habit of lining their nests with antibacterial, aromatic herbs such as mint or lavender.

Adele Mennarat, a biologist at the University of Bergen in Norway, and colleagues from France's National Centre of Scientific Research based in Montpellier and the University of Toulouse tested the effects of these plants on the bacteria living on birds and found that the aromatic herbs the birds use, including lavender (*Lavandula stoechas*), apple mint (*Mentha suaveolens*), curry plant (*Helichrysum italicum*), and Egyptian yarrow (*Achillea ligustica*) significantly change the composition of bacterial communities living on blue tit nestlings. The herbs create a more sterile environment for chicks, which in turn grow faster and have a better chance of survival. The researchers described their results in the *Journal of Oecologia*.

Following are a few of many plants to grow just for the birds. While seeds and berries are bird food, some plants attract aphids, caterpillars, and hundreds of other insects, which in turn are food for birds.

AMARANTH (*Amaranthus*) Grasses such as amaranth and millet (*Pennisetum glaucum*) produce seed heads that attract goldfinches, chickadees, and towhees.

BERGAMOT All varieties, especially those with large, showy red flowers, attract hummingbirds.

ELDERBERRIES Elder trees provide food for thirty-five different North American native birds.

GOLDENROD (*Solidago*) Goldenrod and other plants such as marigold, cosmos, coreopsis, and phlox are attractive to finches, sparrows, and nuthatches.

HAWTHORN (*Crataegus monogyna*) A fast-growing shrub that is tolerant of wet areas, sun, or partial shade, hawthorn's thorns provide protection and the berries are food for birds.

HONEYSUCKLE (*Lonicera periclymenum*) Once established, its climbers make ideal nest sites and attract insects and aphids. The red, trumpet-shaped flowers offer food for hummingbirds.

JUNIPER (*Juniperus*) These low-growing trees offer shelter and attract ground-feeders such as wrens, towhees, and juncos. Cedar waxwings love the berries.

ROSE Besides offering beauty in the garden and food for humans, roses are also food for 215 species of insects, including aphids, an important bird food. Their hips provide winter food for birds. Encouraging dog rose (*Rosa canina*) in wild areas and planting shrub and climbing roses in and around the herb garden are excellent bird-friendly planting strategies for year-round birding.

SUNFLOWER (*Helianthus*) Their large heads attract birds to feed on the seeds in the fall, but they are also food for bees and other pollinators.

Tips for Planting a Bird Garden

* Include herbs as ground covers: creeping thyme, Virginia creeper (*Parthenocissus quinquefolia*) and bunchberry (*Cornus canadensis*).
* Add taller herbs that attract insects, especially aphids.
* Include fruit-bearing shrubs, deciduous trees, and evergreens of all heights around the perimeter.
* Low and tall-growing grasses add important seed heads.
* Rambling vines such as honeysuckle and rambling roses as well as raspberries offer both shelter and food for birds.

HERBS FOR BUTTERFLIES

Butterflies are important pollinators; and while they're not as efficient as bees, they do play a role in pollinating a wide variety of flowers that open during the day. Because they are perching feeders, they prefer flowers with a landing platform; so herbs in the *Lamiaceae* family, with their pouting lower lip, are perfect for butterflies.

Butterfly caterpillars are "host-specific," meaning that they lay their eggs on one native plant, or sometimes on a limited number. Making these native host plants available in a wild area or a butterfly garden is essential to their survival. It's not enough to simply attract these important pollinators to your garden. You can help by planting a butterfly garden with the types of native plants that not only feed butterflies but also host their larvae and support them throughout their life cycle. For more information on how and why to plant a native herb garden, Susan Betz has written a beautiful book, *Neighboring with Nature*; see Bibliography for details. What follows is a short list of North American native plants and the butterfly species they host, followed by some herbs that attract feeding butterflies.

NATIVE PLANT	SPECIES OF BUTTERFLY IT SUPPORTS	
Aster (*Aster*)	Pearl crescent (*Phyciodes tharos*) (see it feeding on Echinaceain the photograph, right)	
Milkweed (*Asciepias*)	Monarch (*Danaus plexippus*)	(see sidebar on page 384)
Turtlehead (*Chelone glabra*)	Baltimore (*Euphydryas phaeton*)	
Spice bush (*Lindera benzoin*)	Spicebush Swallowtail (*Papilio troilus*)	
Blue Vervain (*Verbena hastata*)	Buckeye (*Junonia coenia*) In the photo, a Zebra butterfly (*Zebra heliconian*), the Florida state butterfly, feeds on a vervain flower spike.	
Violet (*Viola*)	Gulf fritillary (*Agraulis vanillae*)	

A MONARCH'S LIFE CYCLE

1. A wild area is reserved for milkweed at Willow Pond Herb Farm, Pennsylvania.

2. A monarch feeder is surrounded by milkweed outside the interpretive building at the State Historic Site at Cahokia Mounds, Collinsville, Illinois.

3. Monarch eggs on a milkweed leaf at the same site.

4. Monarch caterpillars feasting on a milkweed leaf at the same site.

HERBS FOR THE BUTTERFLY GARDEN

BERGAMOT (also known as Bee Balm) Its sweet nectar is very attractive to both bees and butterflies; plant the native species if you can find it at nurseries.

BERGAMOT

CHIVES In the photo, an eastern tiger swallowtail (*Papilio glaucus*) feeds on chives at the Niagara Botanical Garden, Niagara-on-the-Lake, Ontario.

CLOVE PINK It blooms in shades of pink and purple, and its spicy scent attracts butterflies and other pollinators.

CHIVES

DAYLILY (*Hemerocallis*) Large and showy, the daylily attracts a wide range of butterflies.

PURPLE CONEFLOWER (*Echinacea purpurea*) In the photo, a red admiral (*Vanessa atalanta*) feeds on an echinacea flower head.

CLOVE PINK

DAYLILY

PURPLE CONEFLOWER

SAGE Because of their variety of blossom shapes, sage plants attract many insects and hummingbirds, as well as butterflies.

YARROW (*Achillea millefolium*) Its spicy scent and large umbel flowers are long-blooming, giving butterflies a continuous food supply.

SAGE

YARROW

HERBS WITH EDIBLE, HEALTH-GIVING BERRIES

European lore gave magical powers to wild berries, being thought of as omens when they appeared in dreams. Even as late as the nineteenth century, wild berries were thought to protect against evil spirits and, when eaten, were thought to cure many common ailments. Cultivating berry plants in the garden is a relatively modern practice that reached its height around the dawn of the twentieth century.

In the hedgerows, orchards, and herb gardens, berry-producing plants are abundant in the summer months from June or July through September. Each plant offers its fruit at specific times and some plants, mainly the elder tree, produce enough flowers to allow to harvest and use them fresh or preserve them by drying or freezing for later use. Berries make healthy ingredients in desserts and in baked products such as cakes and pies; in jams, jellies, or other preserves; and in sauces, dips, salsas, and dressings; as well as in smoothies and teas.

From our cultivated blueberries, strawberries, blackberries, raspberries, and cherries, and old-garden currants, to berries from South America, the Himalayas, and beyond, berries are a vital addition to a healthful diet because they contain significant quantities of vitamin C and A as well as *anthocyanins* that are anti-inflammatory, anticancer, and heart-protective. What follows is a short list of not-so-common herbs that produce edible berries. Include these berries (except bayberry) in recipes that call for any of the cultivated berries we know and that are readily available.

AÇAI BERRY (*Euterpe oleracea*) A deep black-purple berry from the Amazon rainforest that is the fruit of the açai palm tree. Extremely high in antioxidants, fiber, and fatty acids, it may be purchased from whole or natural food stores frozen, whole, or as a juice. It helps lower LDL ("bad") cholesterol and may help prevent cancer-cell growth.

BAYBERRY (*Myrica caroliniensis*) This woody, bushy shrub grows wild in dry, sandy soil around the eastern coasts of Canada and the United States. The genus includes from thirty-five to fifty species, including *M. pensylvanica* and *M. californica*, the names indicating where they are likely to be found. The dull green leaves are used as a flavoring spice in recipes, and the root bark and berries are used for medicine. The waxy, fragrant berries were once used for making candles and have been included in hot drinks for treating head colds, diarrhea, and nausea.
CAUTION: In large doses, bayberry causes vomiting. Use only under instructions from a health-care professional.

CHOKEBERRY (*Aronia melanocarpa*) Easy to grow, this hardy, deciduous shrub belongs to the *Rosaceae* family. The black, tart, and somewhat astringent berries ripen from September onward. With a high concentration of polyphenols and anthocyanins, they are low in sugars and antioxidant. They also stimulate circulation, protect the urinary tract, and strengthen the heart.

CRANBERRY (*Vaccinium macrocarpon*) Native to North America, low-growing cranberries are harvested in October in the northern United States and Canada, making them the last fruit of the season. They grow in acidic peat bogs. Cranberries are antioxidant and are most often taken to prevent and treat urinary tract infection and to promote cardiovascular health.

ELDER The frothy white blossoms appear around early to mid-June and the berries ripen around late August. Always cook the black berries before eating. Antioxidant, anti-inflammatory, antiviral, expectorant, and laxative, elderberry is very effective in preventing and shortening the effects of viral infections (herpes and shingles, for example), especially flu and cold, and it reduces fever and strengthens the cardiovascular system.
CAUTION: Elderberries must be cooked before eating to destroy toxins present in the raw berries.

GOJI (*Lycium barbarum*) A small fruit originating in the Himalayas, also called wolfberry, goji berries are most often found in whole food stores in dried form. Extremely high in antioxidants, the small, reddish-purple berry may be substituted for raisins in recipes or rehydrated by soaking in juice or water overnight and used as you would fresh or frozen berries. Try growing your own plants from the dried seeds (see Resources, page 395).

GOOSEBERRY (*Ribes uva-crispa*) The plants require hot, humid summers and severely cold winters as are found in Canada and the northern United States. They are rich in antioxidant *polyphenols* and vitamins A and C. An old garden plant, gooseberry is still found in many northern kitchen gardens.

GROUND CHERRY (*Physalis peruviana*) Also known as Cape gooseberry or Peruvian cherry, ground cherries are native to the South American Andes region. Like their cousin the tomatillo (*Physalis philadelphica*), the berries grow inside a thin paper-like husk. High amounts of vitamins A and C and other antioxidants make them a healthy addition to sweet or savory cooked dishes, salads, smoothies, and baked products. I love the flavor—a cross between vanilla-laced mango and not-too-sweet pineapple.

MULBERRY (*Morus rubra*) Native to eastern Canada and the United States, mulberry is dioecious, and it leafs out later in the spring than the maple or walnut trees in my garden. But by June, the berries have formed and are starting to mature. Very few mulberries from my tree ripen to the rich, dark red-purple color because great gusts of grosbeak and cedar waxwing birds descend on the branches, and by August, the tree is stripped bare. High in antioxidant anthocyanins, resveratrol, and vitamin C, mulberries protect against cancer, aging, neurological diseases, heart disease, inflammation, diabetes, and bacterial infections.

SEA BUCKTHORN Hardy to Zone 5b, sea buckthorn berries are extremely important for their vitamin C content and their antioxidant properties. They also contain many nutraceutical properties such as protein, fatty acids, and phytonutrients, including vitamin A. They are anti-inflammatory and antibacterial, and they relieve pain and promote regeneration of tissues.

STREWING HERBS

In the centuries before aerosol fresheners, room deodorants, and scented candles, leaves, flowers, spices, and roots were mixed into pomanders and potpourris. These mixtures scented the air while the same sweet-smelling herbs were employed as "strewing herbs" to give off their sweet and fragrant aromas as they were trod upon and, more importantly, to discourage infestations of small vermin. The "Royal Herb Strewer" might have used any or all of the following herbs in the seventeenth-century castle of King James II.

CHAMOMILE Its slightly medicinal fragrance masks other odors.

COSTMARY (*Tanacetum balsamita*) Nutmeg and spice with camphor make costmary a fragrant strewing herb.

HYSSOP Slightly pungent spikes of mint and camphor repel insects.

LAVENDER Its pleasing floral aroma makes it a favorite potpourri and strewing herb.

LEMON BALM Citrus-fresh, it adds a clean-smelling note to blends.

MEADOWSWEET (*Filipendula ulmaria*) Naturalized in North America, the plant is sweetly anise and its fragrance is enjoyed all summer along stream and riverbanks.

POISONOUS HERBS

Probably by chance and, in some cases, ill fortune, humans learned all about the helping, healing, nutritious plants as well as the ones to which we should give a wide berth. Early herbalists discovered how to consume some deadly, mind-altering plants and actually incorporated their use into ceremonies and rites. Some parts of plants are edible while other parts can prove to be fatal; some plants in the same family are safe (for example, leeks), just as others (like lily-of-the-valley) can kill; some of the most beautiful of herbs (oleander, for one) are to be seen and not eaten; and it is wise to know as much as you can about the plants you encounter, raise, and enjoy.

The following is a short list of some poisonous herbs.

CASTOR BEAN (*Ricinus communis*) An annual shrub with deeply lobed leaves, prickly red seedpods, and mottled brown seeds, the source of castor oil. *Ricin*, a protein found in the seeds, is 6,000 times more poisonous than cyanide and 12,000 times more deadly than rattlesnake venom. Three or four seeds can kill humans.

CASTOR BEAN

ELDER Cooked elderberries are safe and often eaten in pies and other desserts; however, eating the raw berries or juice from the raw berries can cause nausea, vomiting, and cramps. The leaves, bark, young buds, and roots contain bitter constituents that can produce hydrocyanic acid and should not be eaten.

ELDER

MONKSHOOD (*Aconitum napellus*) It is a sturdy, low-growing perennial with tall spikes bearing blue-purple flowers that resemble the generous hood of a monk's robe, and it is one of the most toxic plants in the garden. All parts are poisonous. Handle with care; ingestion causes death. Other deadly *Aconitum* species include *A. vulparia* (yellow flowers), *A. cammarum* (blue and white flowers), and *A. lycoctonum*.

MONKSHOOD

NIGHTSHADE (*Atropa belladonna*) Deadly and often found in the wild, the herbaceous perennial plants grow to about 2 feet in the first year. Oval leaves are dull, dark green, and the highly poisonous oval berries ripen to black in the fall and are full of a sweet, dark juice, making them attractive to children and animals.

NIGHTSHADE

OLEANDER (*Nerium oleander*)   All parts of this tall-growing evergreen shrub with beautiful white, pink, or red flowers are toxic. Common in many subtropical and tropical areas and popular as a landscape plant as far north as Washington, DC, it causes nausea and vomiting, abdominal pain, diarrhea, a slowing below normal of the heart rate, coma, and eventually death.

OLEANDER

RHUBARB (*Rheum*) While it is safe to eat the fleshy red stalks, the large leaves contain high levels of oxalic acid, which can cause a range of symptoms from difficulty breathing, to gastrointestinal problems, to death, depending on the amount consumed.

RHUBARB

GLOSSARY

ADAPTOGEN—An herb that helps the body resist stress and restore balance.

ALTERATIVE—An herb that acts as a cleanser by efficiently removing waste and toxic products from the body; also, a stimulant for digestion.

ANALGESIC—An herb that relieves pain.

ANNUAL—A plant that lives one year or less, growing, blooming, producing seeds, and dying before the first frost. Many plants and herbs (such as basil) live several years in their natural tropical or subtropical habitat and would be considered perennials, except that they can't survive the cold or freezing temperatures in northern parts of North America.

ANODYNE—An herb or drug that relieves pain.

ANTHOCYANINS—Pigments found in dark blue, purple, and black plants that protect the plant from sunlight and act as antioxidants in the body.

ANTIOXIDANT—A phytonutrient found in plants that destroys aging- and disease-promoting free radicals.

ANTI-INFLAMMATORY—A substance that reduces swelling in the body.

ANTIMUTAGENIC—A compound that keeps cells from mutating and becoming cancerous.

ANTISPASMODIC—An herb that helps relax cramps.

ANTISEPTIC—An herb that inhibits the growth of microorganisms and thereby prevents infection.

AROMATHERAPY—Massage therapy using aromatic essential oils as part of a holistic approach to health, based on the principle that different aromas have different effects on our state of mind and body.

BIENNIAL—A plant that lives for two seasons, usually producing only leaves the first year and flowering, fruiting, and dying in the second year. Biennials need exposure to winter temperatures to trigger flowering or fruit production in the second year.

BITTERS—Herbs with bitter-tasting components in their essential oils. Bitter herbs are used in liquids called "bitters" to punch up drinks and in teas or liqueurs to help stimulate appetite and digestive juices.

BUTTERFLIED PORK LOIN—A center-cut pork loin (a boneless, skinless solid roast in the shape of a log) is cut into one flat piece of meat. Your butcher will be happy to butterfly a pork loin but once you have learned how, it isn't difficult. Using a sharp 6-inch boning knife, make a slit about ½ inch from the top of the loin from one side to the other across the length of the loin. Continue to make cuts so that you slice down one side, across the bottom and up the other side of the loin resulting in a ½ inch thick piece of meat. See how to butterfly a pork loin here, https://www.youtube.com/watch?v=2eCpL6cj7Rw .

CARMINATIVE—An herb that helps to dispel gas from the body.

CATARRH—Inflammation of the mucous membranes in the nose, sinuses, and the throat. Herbs that act as expectorants help in coping with this condition.

COMPANION PLANT—One that benefits growth or discourages pests for other plants in a garden.

COUNTERIRRITANT—Herbs that produce heat (such as chiles and mustard seeds) that are used topically to relieve underlying pain or discomfort.

CULTIVAR—A plant variety that originated under human cultivation.

DECOCTION—A method of extracting active, medicinal ingredients from the woody parts of herbs by boiling them with water in a covered container for 5 to 20 minutes. The decoction is sometimes steeped with the plant material in a covered container for 10 minutes to 48 hours after boiling.

DEMULCENT—An herb that soothes, coats, and lubricates smooth muscle tissue, such as the stomach lining.

DIOECIOUS—A term applied to plants that only fruit when male and female plants can pollinate each other. Ginkgo, sea buckthorn, and junipers are examples of plants with this trait.

DIURETIC—A food or compound in herbs that flushes excess water from the body, thus helping to relieve swelling due to liquids (edema).

DYSPEPSIA—A general term indicating discomfort in the upper abdomen (upset stomach, cramps, indigestion).

EMETIC—A substance that causes vomiting.

EMMENAGOGUE—An herb that can bring on menstruation.

ESSENTIAL OIL—The oil found in aerial parts of herbs that is extracted by distillation; active constituents are concentrated in these oils, which are usually blended with almond or other plant oils before being applied topically. Use caution before taking internally.

EXPECTORANT—Also called an antitussive agent, it is an herb or herbal preparation that helps the body discharge mucus from the respiratory tract. Coltsfoot (*Tussilago farfara*) is a very good expectorant.

FREE RADICALS—Dangerous oxygen molecules released by stress, secondhand smoke, smog, trans fatty acids, and rancid fats. Free radicals float through the body and attach to the cells of organs and other tissues, causing them to deteriorate and age faster than normal. Aging is the process of oxidation from the effects of free radicals. Antioxidants in plants neutralize free radicals, rendering them harmless.

GHEE—Butter that has been clarified by simmering. The milk solids sink to the bottom of the fats and can be strained out, leaving pure, bright-yellow fatty acids.

GHRITA—Ghee that has been infused with medicinal Ayurvedic herbs and/or spices.

GROUNDING HERBS—Herbalists use "grounding" herbs to stabilize a person's mental outlook or to refocus and reestablish them to a state where they feel centered and rooted in the physical world.

HEIRLOOM SEEDS—Mostly open-pollinated seeds that have been planted and passed down for generations.

HERBACEOUS—A term applied to plants that are fleshy, with little or no woody tissue, and that tend to die back to the roots in winter. An herbaceous border is one that is made up of non-woody herbs.

HYDROSOL—A by-product of steam distillation of essential oils from herbs, it is water with tiny amounts of essential oil held in suspension.

IMMUNOSTIMULANT—Promotes healing by stimulating production of collagen at the site of wounds and minimizes scars.

INFUSION—Active ingredients from herbs drawn out into water, oil (fat), alcohol, vinegar, salt, or sugar.

JAUNDICE—A condition in which the eyes and skin turn yellow due to the malfunction of the liver.

MACERATE—A culinary technique to soften food by soaking it in a liquid. Sometimes the food is mashed before or after macerating to extract aroma and flavor.

MASLIN PAN—A heavy pan with a narrow base (to fit home burners) that is wider at the top, used for boiling down preserves.

MENSTRUUM—A liquid used to extract, dissolve, and hold or "carry" the active ingredients in plant material. Organic plant oils (coconut, olive, avocado, etc.), alcohol (vodka, rum, gin, brandy), water, or apple cider vinegar may be used as the menstruum or carrier of the medicinal components in herbs.

MUDDLE—When herbs are pressed and beaten with sugar for a drink, that process is called "muddling."

NECTAR—The sweet juice that flowers exude to attract insects. It is loaded with complex sugars that give pollinators the energy they need.

NONREACTIVE COOKING UTENSILS—Glass, porcelain, stainless steel, and ceramic cooking utensils and pots do not pit or break down when in contact with cooking acids and other corrosive components. Do not use tin, aluminum, plastic, or cast iron for herbal preparations.

ORAC (OXYGEN RADICAL ABSORBANCE CAPACITY)—The antioxidant, antiaging capacity of a food is measured and given a score relative to other plants. The higher the ORAC score, the better the food is at providing antioxidant phytonutrients that specifically neutralize dangerous free radicals.

PERENNIAL—A plant that lives for two or more seasons, its green parts dying after the first frost and reappearing in the spring.

PHYSIC GARDEN—Gardens containing medicinal plants, generally formal in layout and often with beds dedicated to specific areas of the body. For example, respiratory herbs or those that help the heart might be grouped together in a physic garden. The oldest physic garden in Britain is the University of Oxford Botanic Garden, founded in 1621, followed by the Apothecaries' Garden, established in London in 1673, now called the Chelsea Physic Garden.

PITH—The bitter, spongy white part of citrus rind that lies between the zest and the flesh; it is too bitter to use in recipes but may be included with the flesh when juicing citrus fruit.

POLLEN—The fine powder produced by a flower's stamens (male reproductive parts). It contains proteins and fats, essential food for pollinators' young. It rubs off all over the body of a pollinator and is carried to the female parts of flowers, providing the missing link for the flower to produce fruit.

POLYUNSATURATED OILS—Olive, corn, canola, hemp, grapeseed, and nut oils, among other oils. Depending on the oil, they are unstable at medium to high temperatures, at which point they break down into damaging free radicals, so store in the refrigerator and use raw or at very low temperatures.

POLYPHENOLS—A term applied to a broad group of chemicals with antioxidant properties found naturally in plant foods. Carotenoids and flavonoids are two of the many categories of polyphenols.

PREGNANCY—Many herbs, when taken in concentrated doses (tea or tincture) or even when eaten raw or cooked, can have an abortive effect on pregnant women. For this reason, we recommend that you refrain from eating most herbs in large amounts and follow the advice and guidance of your health-care provider during pregnancy.

REMORDANT—A term applied to roses when they are repeat bloomers, meaning that they bloom, and the flowers die and bloom again sometime later within the same season.

RIND—Surrounds the flesh of citrus fruits; it is made up of two parts: zest and pith.

SCOVILLE HEAT INDEX—A standard measurement of the heat in chile peppers, it measures the amount of *capsaicin*, which is the constituent that causes the skin and mouth to tingle with heat.

STILLROOM—From the early eighteenth century until as late as the turn of the twentieth century, large estate houses had a room for distilling floral or herbal essences: oils, waters, and alcohol. Although the term *stillroom* comes from the word *distill*, this room was also used for drying herbs and for making herbal vinegars, jellies, preserves, cosmetics, and other herbal preparations even if a still was not part of the equipment.

TINCTURE—A concentrated medicinal preparation of fresh herb and alcohol, usually in a 1:2 ratio. This means that for every 1 gram of herb, 2 milliliters of alcohol are used. Apple cider vinegar may be used for an alcohol-free tincture. Drops are taken directly under the tongue or in water, herbal tea, or fruit/vegetable juice.

TISANE—An herbal tea made by pouring boiled water over fresh or dried herbs and steeping for 3 to 5 minutes. Tea made with black or green tea leaves (*Camellia sinensis*) is not a tisane, it is a "tea," and it gets a bit confusing because a tisane (made with herbs) may be called a tea, but the word *herbal* should always precede the word "tea."

WARMING HERBS—Herbs that bring blood to the surface of the skin, which heats it. Examples of warming herbs are ginger, cinnamon, cayenne, and garlic, along with some green herbs such as rosemary.

WILDCRAFT/WILDCRAFTING—A term for the collection of wild herbs. It can be used as an adjective to describe wild herbs (e.g., wildcrafted ginseng). It usually applies to medicinal herbs and implies that they may be rare, more potent, or more valuable because they are handpicked— a concept that may or may not be true. There is concern that some wild plants are being taken indiscriminately and without care for their sustainability.

WORT (OR WORTE)—A general term meaning "leafy and green" from as far back as the Middle Ages, it was applied to most leafy green vegetables and herbs. Many common plant names still end in -*wort*: for example, Hogwort (*Croton capitatus*), the namesake for J. K. Rowling's Hogwarts School of Witchcraft and Wizardry.

ZEST—The colored part of the citrus rind, it contains the volatile oils that give concentrated citrus (lemon, lime, orange, grapefruit) flavor to recipes.

RESOURCES

GARLIC INFORMATION

Bhumgara, Khurshed, ed. *The Garlic Farmers' Cookbook*. The Garlic Seed Foundation, Rose, NY, 2014. garlicseedfoundation.info/

GINGER/TURMERIC

Old Friends Farm, Amherst, Massachusetts, oldfriendsfarm.com

GOJI BERRIES

BC Goji Plant Growers, bc-goji-berry-nursery-plants.blogspot.ca

Sask Goji Power Nursery, saskgojipower.ca/gpage1.html

HERB SUPPLIERS, CANADA

Organic Connections (dried herbs/spices), orgcon.ca

Richters Herbs (plants shipped worldwide), richtersherbs.com

HERB SUPPLIERS, U.S.

Allstar Organics (organic herbs/sugar/salt/hydrosols), allstarorganics.com

Frontier Co-op (organic herbs and spices), frontiercoop.com

Growers Exchange (non-GMO plants), thegrowers-exchange.com

Healing Spirits Herb Farm (mushrooms, herbal products), healingspiritsherbfarm.com

Mountain Rose Herbs (organic herbs/spices), mountainroseherbs.com

Mountain Valley Growers (organic plants), mountainvalleygrowers.com

Strictly Medicinal (medicinal plants and seeds), strictlymedicinalseeds.com

HERBS FOR BIRDS' NESTS INFORMATION

Matt Walker, "Blue Tits Embrace 'Aromatherapy,'" BBC Earth News, August 14, 2009, http://news.bbc.co.uk/earth/hi/earth_news/newsid_8199000/8199726.stm.

HISTORICAL RECIPES

The Forme of Cury: A Roll of Ancient English Cookery by Samuel Pegge (*ca.* 1390; Project Gutenberg, 2003), http://www.gutenberg.org/cache/epub/8102/pg8102-images.html

The Complete Herbal by Nicholas Culpepper, M.D. (*ca.* 1600; Project Gutenberg, 2015), http://www.gutenberg.org/files/49513/49513-h/49513-h.htm

Acetaria by John Evelyn (1699; Project Gutenberg, 2005), http://www.gutenberg.org/files/15517/15517-h/15517-h.htm

HONEY

Swarmbustin' Honey by Walt Broughton, 911honey.com

HYDROSOL

Allstar Organics (organic herbs/sugar/salt/hydrosols), allstarorganics.com

Mountain Rose Herbs, Eugene, Oregon, mountainroseherbs.com

Organic Infusions, Inc., organicinfusionswholesale.com

POLLINATOR INFORMATION

Friends of the Earth, Canada, foecanada.org

Friends of the Earth, U.S., foe.org

Monarch Butterfly, monarch-butterfly.com/monarch-conservation.html

North American Pollinator Protection Campaign, pollinator.org/guides.htm; reliable information on pollinators, how to become involved in pollinator well-being, including the "Beesmart School Garden Kit," "Ecoregional Planting Guides," and more.

Royal Horticultural Society (Great Britain) rhs.org.uk/science/conservation-biodiversity/wildlife/perfect-for-pollinators

PURSLANE

Purslane Restaurant, purslane-restaurant.co.uk

ROSES

Associations and Sites

The American Rose Society, founded in 1899, has more than 20,000 members in local affiliates throughout the United States. rose.org

The Heritage Roses Group, shares information on old garden roses. theheritagerosesgroup.org

The Canadian Rose Society, canadianrosesociety.org

The Royal National Rose Society, rnrs.org.uk

Books

Himmelman, Duncan. *500 Popular Roses for Canadian Gardeners*. Vancouver, BC: Raincoast Books, 2000.

Jekyll, Gertrude, and Edward Mawley. *Roses for English Gardens*. London: Country Life, 1902.

Krussmann, Gerd. *The Complete Book of Roses*. Portland, OR: Timber Press, 1981.

Reddell, Rayford Clayton. *The Rose Bible*. New York: Harmony Books, 1994.

Walheim, Lance. *Roses for Dummies*. Foster City, CA: IDG Books, 1997. An excellent reference for gardens, nurseries, and equipment.

Nurseries

The following is a short list of nurseries specializing in old garden roses:

Amity Rose Garden & Nursery—heritage roses and mail-order roses from Hydesville, California, amityheritageroses.com

Antique Rose Emporium in Brenham, Texas, (800) 441-0002 or antiqueroseemporium.com

Blossoms & Bloomers in Spokane, Washington, (509) 922-1344

Heirloom Old Garden Roses in Saint Paul, Oregon, (503) 538-1576 or heirloomroses.com

High Country Rosarium in Denver, Colorado, (800) 552-2082 or highcountryroses.com

SAFFRON INFORMATION

Saffron.com/cons_guide.html

Official site of the Spanish regulatory council, showing the growing, drying, and processing of Spanish saffron, doazafrandelamancha.com/en≠description

SEA BUCKTHORN INFORMATION AND PRODUCTS

The Healing Arc Inc. (plants and products), thehealingarc.com

SEEDS

Baker Creek Heirloom Seed Company, Mansfield, Missouri, rareseeds.com

Seed Savers Exchange, seedsavers.org

United Plant Savers, unitedplantsavers.org

BIBLIOGRAPHY

Alfs, Matthew. *Edible & Medicinal Wild Plants of Minnesota & Wisconsin*. New Brighton, MN: Old Theology Book House, 2001.

Bardswell, Frances A. *The Herb Garden*. New York: Macmillan, 1930.

Beebe, Ruth Anne. *Sallets, Humbles & Shrewsbery Cakes: A Collection of Elizabethan Recipes Adapted for the Modern Kitchen*. Boston: David R. Godine, 1976.

Belsinger, Susan, ed. *Dill: Herb of the Year 2010*. Jacksonville, FL: International Herb Association, 2009.

———. *Horseradish: Herb of the Year 2011*. Jacksonville, FL: International Herb Association, 2010.

Betz, Susan. *Neighboring with Nature*. Jonesville, MI: Susan Betz, 2017.

Buchanan, Rita. *The Dyer's Garden*. Ft. Collins, CO: Interweave Press, 1995.

Clarkson, Rosetta E. *Magic Gardens*. Toronto: Macmillan, 1939.

Correvon, Henry. *Rock Garden and Alpine Plants*. New York: Macmillan, 1930.

Crocker, Pat. *Oregano: 2005 Herb of the Year*. Neustadt, ON: Riversong Studios, 2005.

Crocker, Pat, Caroline Amidon, and Joyce Brobst. *Pelargonium: 2006 Herb of the Year*. Neustadt, ON: Riversong Studios, 2006.

Culpeper, Nicholas. *Culpeper's Complete Herbal & English Physician*. London: Parkgate Books, 1997. First published in 1652 by King's English Bookprinters Limited.

Day, Avanelle S., and Lillie M. Stuckey. *The Spice Cookbook*. New York: David White, 1964.

DeWitt, Dave, and Nancy Gerlach. *The Whole Chile Pepper Book*. Toronto: Little, Brown, 1990.

Diamond, Denise. *The Complete Book of Flowers*. Berkeley, CA: North Atlantic Books, 1982.

Duerr, Sasha. *The Handbook of Natural Plant Dyes*. Portland, OR: Timber Press, 2010.

Duke, James A., PhD. *The Green Pharmacy*. Emmaus, PA: Rodale Press, 1997.

Forsell, Mary. *Herbs: The Complete Guide to Growing, Cooking, Healing, and Pot-pourri*. London: Anaya Publishers, 1990.

Foster, Steven, and Rebecca L. Johnson. *National Geographic Desk Reference to Nature's Medicine*. Washington, DC: National Geographic Society, 2006.

Fox, Helen Morgenthau. *Gardening with Herbs for Flavor & Fragrance*. New York: Macmillan, 1938.

Gibbons, Euell. *Stalking the Blue-Eyed Scallop*. New York: David McKay, 1964.

———. *Stalking the Healthful Herbs*. New York: David McKay, 1966.

———. *Stalking the Wild Asparagus*. New York: David McKay, 1962.

Grieve, Maud. *A Modern Herbal*. 1931. Unabridged and unaltered reproduction of the original. New York: Dover Publications, 1971.

Hageneder, Fred. *The Meaning of Trees*. Berkeley, CA: Ten Speed Press, 1996.

Harvey, John H. *Garden Plants of around 15:25: The Fromond List*, article in The Garden History Society, Vol. 17, No. 2, Autumn, 1989, pages 122 to 134.

Hieatt, Constance B., and Sharon Butler. *Curye on Inglysch: English Culinary manuscripts of the Fourteenth Century (Including the "Forme of Cury")*. London: For the Early English Text Society by the Oxford University Press, 1985, http://www.godecookery.com/goderec/grec49.htm.

Hollis, Sarah. *The Country Diary Herbal*. Chicago: University of Chicago Press, 2014.

Holmes, Caroline. *Herbs for the Gourmet Gardener*. Markham, Canada: Penguin Books Canada Ltd., 1990.

Holy Bible. King James Version. Toronto: William Collins, Sons and Company, Ltd., 1939.

Humphries, John. *The Essential Saffron Companion*. Emmaus, PA: Rodale Press, 1997.

Leyel, Mrs. C. F. *Green Medicine*. London: Faber and Faber, 1952.

Lis-Balchin, Maria, ed. *Geranium and Pelargonium, the Genera Geranium and Pelargonium*. New York: Taylor and Francis, 2002.

Maril, Lee. *Savor & Flavor: Berries in Fact and Fancy*. New York: Coward–McCann Publishers, 1944.

McVicar, Jekka. *Jekka's Herb Cookbook*. Richmond Hill, Canada: Firefly Books, 2011.

Moldenke, Harold N., PhD, and Alma L., BA. *Plants of the Bible*. New York: Ronald Press Company, 1952.

Norman, Jill. *Herbs & Spices: The Cook's Reference*. New York: DK Publishing, 2002.

Ody, Penelope. *The Complete Medicinal Herbal*. Canada: Key Porter Books, 1993.

Rogers, Barbara Radcliffe. *Fresh Herbs: Over 100 Uses for Growing, Cooking, Cosmetics, and Garden Design*. New York: Michael Friedman Publishing Group Inc., n.d.

Sinclair Rohde, Eleanour. *A Garden of Herbs*. London: Philip Lee Warner Publisher to the Medici Society Limited, n.d.

———. *The Scented Garden*. London: Medici Society, 1936.

Stewart, Amy. *The Drunken Botanist*. New York: Workman, 2013.

Talbert, Rexford. "Za'atar," *The Herbarist*, a publication of the Herb Society of America, no. 60, 1994.

Talbot, Rob, and Robin Whiteman. *Brother Cadfael's Herb Garden*. New York: Little, Brown, 1997.

Tillona, Francesca, and Cynthia Strowbridge. *A Feast of Flowers*. New York: Gramercy Publishing Company, 1969.

Tucker, Arthur O., and Thomas DeBaddio. *The Encyclopedia of Herbs*. Portland, OR: Timber Press, 2009.

Verey, Rosemary. *Classic Garden Design*. New York: Congdon & Weed, 1984.

Voigt, Charles, and Susan Belsinger, eds. *Lemon Balm: Herb of the Year 2007*. Jacksonville, FL: International Herb Association, 2007.

Watson Kamm, Minnie. *Old Time Herbs for Northern Gardens*. New York: Dover/Little, Brown, 1938.

Willard, Pat. *Secrets of Saffron*. Boston: Beacon Press, 2001.

ACKNOWLEDGMENTS

For most of my adult life, not only have I raised herbs in my own gardens, but I've also been fortunate to explore the gardens—both private and public—of others. Much of my knowledge of the plants in this book comes firsthand from growing them and working with them in the kitchen, spa, and stillroom. At the same time, I've learned from gardeners, medical herbalists, from chefs, and herbal practitioners of all kinds. To those who freely share their knowledge of the miracle and magic of herbs, thank you.

Some of my most pleasurable experiences have been with members and plant teachers of the International Herb Association, the Herb Society of America, and the Ontario Herbalists' Association, among other plant groups. It would take a separate chapter to list the kind plant lovers I'm blessed to have met on the garden path, but I remember them and thank them all.

In particular, Matthias and Andrea Reisen, Rosemary Gladstar, Caroline Holmes, Conrad Richter, Susan Belsinger, Christine Hume, Sharon Lovejoy, Art and Sherry Tucker, Marion Bardman, Mary Wohlleb, Lori and Dave Schaeffer, Rex Talbert, Tina Marie Wilcox, Gloria and John Hunter, Sharon (and the late Gerry) Channer, Shantree Kacera and Lorenna Bousquet-Kacera, Pat Kenny, Chuck Voigt, Joyce Brobst, Ruth and Doug MacDonald, Jane Hawley Stevens, Betsy and Ned Williams, Ann Bridgeman, Pam Montgomery, Theresa and Jim Mieseler, Gert Coleman, Carolee Snyder, Rita Salman, Steven Foster, Caroline Amidon, Annie McIntyre, Susan and Dave Betz, Lucia Bettler, Kathy Schlosser, Davina Verney, the late Linda Lain, Jim Long, Donna Frawley, Lois Sutton, Ann Lamb, Tarrah Young and Nathan Carey, PJ Kitchen, Don Haynie, Jane Taylor, Marge Powell, Pat Reppert, Dava Stravinsly, . . . you have inspired me in ways as diverse as your gardens.

Many thanks, of course, go to my garden creator and keeper, my husband Gary McLaughlin, who is at the center of my life in and out of the garden.

Several people helped with the technical herbal information and kept the botanical terms accurate. I owe much to Theresa Mieseler, who proofread for the botanical terms. Those who also freely lent their expertise are: Rex Talbert (cilantro), Ann Sprayregan (Jewish use of horseradish on Passover), Art Tucker (mint), Lori Schaeffer (photo ID), Chuck Voigt (garlic), and both Marlene Wynnyk and Sandra Rae (sea buckthorn), and Rita Salmon (za'atar).

In the herb world, life is often accented by random acts of kindness, for which I am truly grateful. One day in August, Terry McFarlane and his wife, Alma, arrived at my door with four huge pots of basil, from which I made gallons of pesto . . . that then became gifts to others. Simon de Boer always drops by in early summer with fresh garlic scapes and again in the fall with bags of organic garlic—mostly Music, but other varieties as well. And one day Tarrah Young, my enthusiastic winter CSA (Community Supported Agriculture) farmer shared a dozen stunningly beautiful colored eggs from her heritage hens.

Charmian Christie, author and baker extraordinaire (themessybaker.com) contributed her delightful Frangipane Tart recipe (page 64) with such grace and goodwill. Kathy Kinghorn shared her soft Sage Cheese recipe, which I adapted for the chamomile chapter (page 54), and Chuck Voigt contributed his Horseradish Sauce, page 178.

I'm grateful to Whitecap Books, Nick Rundall for believing in the value of a modern kitchen herbal, Linda Konner for working to find a home for it, and to Jennifer Williams at Sterling for keeping the green dream alive. Heather Rodino is a rare and intuitive editor and Shannon Nicole Plunkett brought my words alive in her beautiful design. A lot of work goes into building a book from a manuscript, and I am most thankful to have had the steady hand of Hannah Reich shepherding the work through every detail of production.

Like the passionate growers of organic food, some enlightened companies helped in no small way with the testing and photography for *The Herbalist's Kitchen*. Fiskars® has been making excellent garden tools for over 365 years. I use their Micro-Tip Blades to harvest tender herbs almost every summer day. The Cuisipro® Herb Keeper stores fresh herbs in the refrigerator for up to two weeks, and I keep mine filled all year long. Maxwell and Williams and Emile Henri products grace many of the photographs throughout the book.

Conrad Richter (see Resources) is instrumental in providing herb seeds, plants, and information to Canadian and International gardeners. Thanks to him, my garden prospers with herbs from Richters.

Thanks to the team at Organic Connections (see Resources), who source and distribute high-quality organic dried herbs and herbal products. Many of my recipes and photographs feature their products.

ABOUT THE AUTHOR

Teacher, photographer, and author of 22 cookbooks, **PAT CROCKER** is first and foremost a culinary herbalist, with more than 1.25 million books in print. She was honored twice by the International Herb Association's Professional Award for outstanding contributions to the Herb Industry, and also received the 2009 Gertrude H. Foster award from the Herb Society of America for Excellence in Herbal Literature. Her books, *The Juicing Bible* and *The Vegan Cook's Bible* have won "Best in the World" awards from the International Gourmand Culinary Guild. A professional home economist (BAA, BEd), specializing in herbs and healthy foods, Crocker has been growing, photographing, teaching, and writing about herbs, herb gardens, food, and healthy diets for over two decades. Pat's articles have appeared in national magazines and newspapers in Canada and the U.S. The past president of both the Ontario Herbalists' Association and Home Economics Associations, Pat actively participates in the Herb Society of America, the International Herb Association, the International Association of Culinary Professionals, Cuisine Canada, and the Culinary Historians of Canada. She lives in Neustadt, Ontario, Canada. To learn more about Pat Crocker, visit www.patcrocker.com.

INDEX OF RECIPES, TECHNIQUES, AND TOOLS

INDEX

Buttered Advieh Chicken Tagine, 317

Butterflies, herbs for, 382–385

Butters

Ayurvedic Ghee (*Ghrita*), 332
Garlic Butter Spread, 160
Green Herb Butter, 332
Herb or Flower Butter, 332
Saffron Butter, 332

C

Cabbage

about: as potherb, 232–233
Root Slaw, 46
Smoked Chicken and Cabbage Salad, 271

Calendula, 36–46

about, 36–37; African/French marigolds and, 36; culinary uses, 37; drying flowers, 41; flavor, 36; growing, 37; health benefits, 37, 38; name origins, 36; parts to use, 37; as spa herb, 275
Aching Muscle Bath Blend, 275
Calendula-Infused Oil (coconut and vegetable), 41–43
Herbal Body Lotion, 276
Medicinal Herb Salves (coconut and vegetable oil), 44
Root Slaw, 46
Summer Flower Frittata, 45
Summer Flower Vinaigrette, 46

Candied Angelica or Ginger, 6–7

Canning jars, sterilizing, 243

Cantaloupe, in Fruit in Spiced Bergamot Tea Syrup, 29

Cantaloupe soup, spicy chilled, 376

Caraway and caraway seeds, 114, 233

Cardamom, 372

Carminatives, 133–134

Carrots, clove-glazed, 96

Carrots, in Baked Winter Vegetables with Sage, 340

Castor bean, 388

Categories of herbs. *See* Herb categories/primers

Catnip, 274

Cauliflower

Baked Cauliflower and Garlic, 160
Roasted Moroccan Cauliflower with Walnuts, 378
Savory Vegetable Tarte Tatin, 345

Cayenne pepper, 71, 176, 372

Chamomile, 47–57

about, 47–49; bathing with, 274; culinary uses, 48; flavor, 48; German vs. Roman, 47, 49; growing, 49; health benefits, 38, 47, 49, 134; for herb tea, 50; in landscaping, 47; parts to use, 48; for skin/hair care, 47, 49; as stewing herb, 388
Chamomile Beurre Blanc, 56
Chamomile Cooler, 57
Chamomile Syrup, 55
Herbed Soft Cheese, 54–55
Raisin and Chamomile Scones, 56–57

Cheese

Asiago, Apple, and Sage Tarte Tatin, 341
Dilled Cream Cheese Dates, 120
Herbed Soft Cheese, 54–55
Three-Cheese Gratin of Root Vegetables, 237

Cherries

Baked Cherries and Plums with Rose Cream, 318
Broccoli Sauté with Dried Cherries and Horseradish, 180
Pork Chops with Angelica-

Spiked Dried Cherry Sauce, 9

Chervil, 58–65

about, 58–60; anise flavor in, 5; culinary uses, 5, 59, 61, 326; flavor, 58; growing, 59–60; health benefits, 59; historical perspective, 58; parts to use, 59; as potherb, 232–233
Apricot and Anise Frangipane Tart, 64
Chervil Lemon Cream Sauce, 65
Fines Herbes, 62
Fines Herbes Pesto, 63

Chicken. *See* Poultry

Chickweed, 212

Chicory, 212, 262

Chiffonade, 16

Chile peppers, 66–77

about, 66–68; appeal and virtues of, 66–67; chile vs. chili, 73; culinary uses, 67–68, 70–72, 100; flavor, 67; growing, 68; health benefits and caution, 66–67, 68, 109; hot chile varieties, 70–71; paprika, 72; parts to use, 67; sweet chile varieties, 71–72; varieties, 70–72
Chimichurri, 282
Grilled Vegetables with Peppers, 75
Harissa, 69
Pulled Chicken and Beans, 74
Roasted Corn Salsa, 77
Roasted Peppers, 76

Chimichurri, 282

Chives, 78–87

about, 78–80; attracting pollinators, 380; for butterfly garden, 384; culinary uses, 79, 80, 100, 326; flavor, 78; growing, 79; health benefits, 79; historical perspective, 78;

Salads (*cont.*)
  Smoked Chicken and
    Cabbage Salad, 271
  Spring Flower and Seafood
    Cocktail, 259–260
  Tabbouleh, 244
  Three Grain Tabbouleh,
    283
  Tuscan White Bean Salad,
    367
Salmagundi, 255–256
Salts
  Citrus Salt, 206
  Herbes Salée, 203–205
  Perfumed Finishing Salts
    (green; yellow/orange;
    red; purple/blue; brown),
    204–205
  Roasted Pears with Citrus
    Salt, 211
  Tuscan Salt, 207
Salves, medicinal herb, 44
Sauces/salsas. *See* Condiments,
  sauces, and dressings
Savory, 342–347
  about, 342–343; culinary
    uses, 61, 144, 177, 327, 343;
    flavor, 177, 342; growing,
    343; health benefits, 343;
    herbs to blend with, 144;
    historical perspective, 342;
    parts to use, 342
  Bean and Vegetable Herb
    Blend, 344
  Classic Mediterranean
    Cassoulet, 347
  Savory Grilled Fish, 346
  Savory Vegetable Tarte Tatin,
    345
Savory Rose Soufflés, 316
Scones, raisin and chamomile,
  56–57
Sea buckthorn, 348–353
  about, 348–350; for butterfly
    garden, 387; culinary uses,
    349; flavor, 349; growing,
    350; health benefits,

348–349, 350; historical
  perspective, 348; parts to
  use, 349
Berry, Nut, and Grain Trail
  Mix, 351–352
Sea Buckthorn Berry Sauce,
  353
Sea Buckthorn Stuffing, 353
Seasonings
  about: herbs for curry blends,
    371–373. *See also* Curry
  Advieh Seasoning, 313
  Bean and Vegetable Herb
    Blend, 344
  Bouquet Garni, 21–22
  Chowder Soup Herb Blend,
    234
  Citrus Red Curry Paste,
    218–219
  Citrus Salt, 206
  Culinary Citrus Rub, 206
  Culinary Herbalist Tool:
    Mediterranean Herb Paste,
    322
  Culinary Herb/Spice Rubs,
    207
  Curry Paste, 374–376
  Curry Spice Blend, 104
  Fines Herbes, 62
  Green Curry Paste, 376
  Gremolata, 281
  Harissa, 69
  Herbalist Simple: Rose-
    Scented Leaf Water, 295
  Herbalist Tool: Za'atar,
    364–365
  Herbes de Provence Spice
    Blend, 199
  Herbes Salée, 203–205
  Lavender Garlic Paste, 199
  Lemon Seasoning, 222
  Perfumed Finishing Salts
    (green; yellow/orange;
    red; purple/blue; brown),
    204–205
  Pickling Spice Blend, 116–117
  Red Curry Paste, 375

Roasted Garlic, 155
Soup Herb Blends, 234–235
Tomato Soup Herb Blend,
  234
Tuscan Salt, 207
Za'atar Herb Blend, 364
Za'atar Spicy Paste, 365
Seeds. *See* Nuts and seeds
Shallot, Onion, and Chive Tart,
  86–87
Shrimp. *See* Fish and seafood
Side dishes
  Broccoli Sauté with Dried
    Cherries and Horseradish,
    180
  Chicken Paella, 333
  Clove-Glazed Carrots, 96
  Couscous Leek and Pepper
    Loaf, 84–85
  Grilled Vegetables with
    Peppers, 75
  Minted New Peas, 244
  Mixed Rice and Cranberries,
    188
  Peppery Zucchini Gratin, 188
  Poultry Stuffing, 338
  Quinoa and Sweet Potato
    Terrines, 304
  Roasted Moroccan
    Cauliflower with Walnuts,
    378
  Roasted Peppers, 76
  Roasted Vegetables with
    Angelica Fig Glaze, 7–8
  Sage Fritters, 339
  Savory Vegetable Tarte Tatin,
    345
  Scape Pesto Potatoes, 158
  Sea Buckthorn Stuffing,
    353
  Shallot, Onion, and Chive
    Tart, 86–87
  Three-Cheese Gratin of Root
    Vegetables, 237
  Tomato and Purslane Tarte
    Tatin, 305
  Vegetable Fritters, 269

Roasted Moroccan
  Cauliflower with Walnuts,
  378
Spicy Chilled Cantaloupe
  Soup, 376
Turmeric Curry Shrimp,
  377–378
Turtlehead, 383
Tuscan Salt, 207
Tuscan White Bean Salad, 367

V
Valerian, 39, 274, 308
Varieties of herbs. *See specific
  herbs*
Vegetable oil, calendula-infused,
  40
Vegetable Oil Herb Salve, 44
Vegetables
  Bean and Vegetable Herb
    Blend, 344

Bouquet Garni for, 21–22
Grilled Vegetables with
  Peppers, 75
Roasted Vegetables with
  Angelica Fig Glaze, 7–8
Rosemary-Roasted Vegetable
  Spaghetti, 324
Three-Cheese Gratin of Root
  Vegetables, 237
Vegetable Fritters, 269
Vervain, 223, 274, 383
Vinegar refresher, herbed berry,
  358
Vinegars/Vinaigrettes. *See*
  Condiments, sauces, and
  dressings
Violet, 125, 263, 274, 383

W
Warm and peppery herbs primer,
  176–177

Warm/hot herbs, 176
Wasabi, 177
Watercress, 144, 177, 185, 213,
  255–256
Whitefish Chowder, 236
Wildcrafting guidelines, 308
Wild Fresh Spring Tonic, 289
Wild herbs, forager's primer to,
  306–308
Winter vegetables, baked with
  sage, 340
Wormwood, 5, 125, 185

Y
Yarrow, 133, 385

Z
Za'atar Herb Blend, 364
Za'atar Spicy Paste, 365
Za'atar Spread, 365
Zucchini. *See* Squash

PHOTO, ILLUSTRATION, AND OTHER CREDITS

All photographs on the cover and in the interior © Pat Crocker except for the following with permission:

Susan Belsinger: 97, Coriander plant; 109, Milk Thistle; 213, Perilla; 354 and 355, Sweet Cicely

iStock Photo: © alxpin: 193, Provence; © AntiMatina: 114, Caraway; © ElenaMedvedeva: all illustrations of leaves, hearts, and circles throughout, along with the illustrations on pages v, 1, 9, 10, 18, 36, 47, 74, 78, 86, 88 (with © EKaterina Skorik), 94, 97, 103, 112, 129, 138, 146, 157, 172, 180, 189, 197, 211, 221, 222, 228, 235, 238, 244, 251, 260, 264, 270, 277, 287, 297, 303, 317, 319, 324, 328, 335, 341, 346, 353, 357, 360, 378; © LazingBee: 193, Hidcote Giant; © Mantonature: 241, pennyroyal; © sebastianosecondi: 193, Ballerina; © simona flamigni: 193, Fringed Lavendar

Pat Kenny: 50, Costmary; 163, Ginger; 328 and 329, Saffron; 369, Turmeric; 388, Monkshood

Debra Knapke: 107, Dandelion lawn

Gary McLaughlin: 403 and back cover, author photo

Theresa Mieseler: 182, Hyssop; 241, Mint, Kentucky Colonel; 363, Minor Creeping Thyme and French Thyme

Lori Schaeffer: 58 and 59, Chervil; page 213, Salad Burnet

Illustrations by Alexis Seabrook: iii, v, vii, 2, 25, 32, 34, 58, 66, 106, 121, 131, 139, 148, 161, 173, 182, 223, 229, 235, 245, 290, 298, 309, 342, 348, 354, 369, and cover spine

Shutterstock: © artdig: 285, Devil's Claw

Stocksy United: © Pixel Stories: ii-iii and bottom front cover image

Marlenea Wynnyk: 349, Sea Buckthorn in winter

Botanical proofreading by Theresa Mieseler